COGNITIVE DEVELOPMENT AND
THE ACQUISITION OF LANGUAGE

CONTRIBUTORS

Melissa Bowerman

Eve V. Clark

Herbert H. Clark

Susan Ervin-Tripp

Olga K. Garnica

Jean Berko Gleason

John Limber

Timothy E. Moore

Breyne Arlene Moskowitz

Gary M. Olson

Thomas Roeper

Eleanor H. Rosch

H. Sinclair-de Zwart

COGNITIVE DEVELOPMENT AND
THE ACQUISITION OF LANGUAGE

Edited by
Timothy E. Moore
Department of Psychology
Glendon College
York University
Toronto, Canada

ACADEMIC PRESS New York and London   1973
A Subsidiary of Harcourt Brace Jovanovich, Publishers

ACADEMIC PRESS, INC.
111 Fifth Avenue, New York, New York 10003

United Kingdom Edition published by
ACADEMIC PRESS, INC. (LONDON) LTD.
24/28 Oval Road, London NW1

LIBRARY OF CONGRESS CATALOG CARD NUMBER: 72-7690

PRINTED IN THE UNITED STATES OF AMERICA

CONTENTS

LIST OF CONTRIBUTORS

Numbers in parentheses indicate the pages on which the authors' contributions begin.

MELISSA BOWERMAN (197), Bureau of Child Research and Department of Linguistics, University of Kansas, Lawrence, Kansas

EVE V. CLARK (65), Committee on Linguistics, Stanford University, Stanford, California

HERBERT H. CLARK (27), Department of Psychology, Stanford University, Stanford, California

SUSAN ERVIN-TRIPP (261), Department of Rhetoric, University of California, Berkeley, Berkeley, California

OLGA K. GARNICA (215), Committee on Linguistics, Stanford University, Stanford, California

JEAN BERKO GLEASON (159), Department of Psychology, Boston University, Boston, Massachusetts

JOHN LIMBER (169), Department of Psychology, University of New Hampshire, Durham, New Hampshire

TIMOTHY E. MOORE (1), Department of Psychology, Glendon College, York University, Toronto, Canada

BREYNE ARLENE MOSKOWITZ (223), Department of Linguistics University of California, Los Angeles, Los Angeles, California

GARY M. OLSON (145), Department of Psychology, Michigan State University, East Lansing, Michigan

THOMAS ROEPER (187), Department of Psychology, University of Chicago, Chicago, Illinois

ELEANOR H. ROSCH (111), Department of Psychology, University of California, Berkeley, Berkeley, California

H. SINCLAIR-DEZWART (9), Ecole de Psychologie et des sciences de l'éducation, Université de Genève, Geneva, Switzerland

PREFACE

The relationship between cognitive development and language acquisition has intrigued and puzzled psychologists for several decades. In the past, language has been treated as a product or consequence of cognitive development—with relatively little attention directed toward the question of *how* language emerged from the concurrently developing cognitive structures of the child. Lately, however, language development has been recognized as a phenomenon worthy of investigation in its own right; and discovering the nature of the connection between linguistic and cognitive ability appears to be crucial to the understanding of language acquisition.

This book is the product of a conference on developmental psycholinguistics, sponsored by the National Science Foundation, and held at the State University of New York at Buffalo, August 2–5, 1971. The conference was planned and organized by Dr. David G. Hays, grant director, and Dr. Timothy E. Moore, associate director. The purpose of the conference was to review current work, identify new directions, facilitate reconceptualization, and orient and stimulate newcomers to this rapidly expanding field. This is an essential book for any linguist, psychologist, or anthropologist interested in cognition and linguistic development.

The original papers in this volume attempt to describe some of the ways in which cognitive growth is reflected in, and interacts with, the development of language. Language learning is examined in light of a number of cognitive capacities, including the acquisition of semantic categories, memory processes, and speaking styles. In addition, three papers discuss possible strategies through which syntactic structures are perceived and used by the child. A chapter relating Piaget's theory of intellectual development to modern grammatical theory, and two experimental studies on phonology acquisition make this volume unusual among its kind.

The introduction provides a brief overview of generative transformational grammar, and presents some of the methodological problems inherent in the study of language acquisition. The last chapter contains an integrative review of the latest research on language development and suggests some ways in which cognitive development and language acquisition are interdependent.

Most of the original papers presented at the conference were subsequently modified and expanded as a result of the interactions and discussions among participants. Preparation of this volume was assisted by a grant from the National Science Foundation (GS 28589). I am grateful to the authors, their colleagues, and the students who helped make this venture a success. I am also indebted to David Hays for making the conference, and this book, possible, and to John Lyons for helpful advice before and during the conference.

INTRODUCTION

TIMOTHY E. MOORE
York University

During the last decade and a half there has been a dramatic increase in psychological studies of grammar and language acquisition. Developments within the fields of information theory (Shannon, 1948), computer simulation (Reitman, 1965), and linguistics (Chomsky, 1957; 1965) have resulted in new approaches and new modes of thought, which are supplanting neo-behavioristic S–R attempts to explain cognitive processes—including those of language. Each field has provided a formalism for operating upon symbolic entities—lending fresh conceptual properties, as well as rigor, to psychological hypotheses about language behavior. Undoubtedly, the most influential and dynamic position is that of Chomsky. The proposed system is fundamentally different from the structural or descriptive linguistics popular 20 or 30 years ago. A detailed rationale of the new approach will not be given here (but see Katz, 1964; Chomsky, 1965, 1966; Bever, 1968; McNeill, 1968). Suffice it to say that a transformational grammar (TG) of the type suggested by Chomsky concerns itself with and at least *attempts* to account for aspects of natural language which, heretofore, have been either inadequately explained or completely ignored. A TG attempts to: (1) assign to each sentence it generates a deep and a surface structure, and (2) provide a systematic description of the relations between the two. "Generative" here, refers to a system of rules which can explicitly assign structural descriptions to sentences. The term comes from formal logic where it is typically used to indicate the elaboration of a set or series from a single base. When we consider that any speaker of English is capable of uttering an infinite variety of sentences, the applicability of the term becomes obvious. If the generative rules are valid, only grammatical sentences will be derived, and no un-grammatical ones. Chomsky (1965) takes some pains to point out that a generative grammar is not a model of how a person might actually produce or understand a sentence. "When we say that a sentence has a certain deriva-tion with respect to a particular generative grammar, we say nothing about how the speaker or hearer might proceed, in some practical or efficient way to construct such a derivation. These questions belong to the theory of language use—the theory of performance [pp. 8–9]."

The introduction of deep and surface structures constitutes one of the most important contributions of TGs. The deep structure determines the semantic interpretation of a sentence, while the surface structure is phono-logically interpreted. Such a distinction is necessitated by the fact that there is a considerable amount of information about a sentence which is abstract, and not contained directly in the superficial string of words composing the sentence. For example, in

They are drinking glasses.

They are drinking companions.

the two sentences do not differ on the basis of their surface structure; thus syntactic theory must do more than describe surface groupings.

The syntactic component of Chomsky's system contains two different sets of rules: phrase structure rules, and transformational rules. The latter permit changes only in the structural description of a sentence, while leaving the meaning unchanged. Transforming an active sentence to a passive would be an example. While transformational rules take into account the derivational history of the elements involved, phrase structure rules operate blindly upon fixed strings of symbols, by rewriting a single symbol as a new string. For example:

$$S \longrightarrow NP + VP$$
$$VP \longrightarrow Verb + NP$$
$$NP \longrightarrow T + N$$

It is these two syntactic components which allow us to make the distinction between the deep and surface structures of a sentence. Transformational rules operate upon the output of the phrase structure rules, and map the abstract deep structures onto actual phonetically interpretable sequences. Thus, many different actual sequences have a common underlying structure. In:

John hit the ball.

The ball was hit by John.

It was John who hit the ball.

the deep structure descriptions differ only in minor ways, if at all. That is, the relationship between the actor (John), the action (hit), and the recipient of the action (ball), is the same in each sentence, and it is the deep structure which reflects this identity. Linguistic theories of the past have usually assigned less importance to the role played by deep structures in linguistic description, than do contemporary TGs. Chomsky's system clearly differs from a taxonomic approach which views syntactic structure as being determined solely by segmentation and classification techniques.

In 1959 Chomsky provided a devastating critique of Skinner's (1957) *Verbal Behavior*. Fodor (1965) later extended the argument to encompass mediational models. Still more recently an attempted formal refutation of any associationistic account of language has been advanced by Bever, Fodor, and Garrett (1968). While these investigators were demonstrating the insufficiencies in traditional empiricist accounts of language behavior, others were attempting to apply Chomsky's new system to psychological studies of language comprehension. Experimenters were hopefully seeking psychological relations between sentences which would reflect the number of rules required by the grammar to generate those sentences. They wanted evidence that people process or evaluate sentences by going through the steps in their grammatical derivations. Such an approach assumed that performance mirrored in some relatively straightforward way, the underlying competence described by the grammar (Miller, 1962; Miller & McKean, 1964; Savin & Perchonock, 1965). It now appears that this assumption was unwarranted; in fact Chomsky (1964) cautioned that "the attempt to develop a reasonable account of the speaker has been hampered by the prevalent and utterly mistaken view that a generative grammar in itself provides or is related in some obvious way to a model for the speaker." Many of the earlier studies have proved irreplicable, and the derivational theory of complexity is no longer adhered to.[1] Garrett and Fodor (1968) and Hayes (1970) provide critical reviews of this literature.

Even though a variety of syntactic manipulations have been shown to have an effect upon the cognitive processing of sentences (Wales & Marshall, 1966), any direct, one-to-one correspondence between grammatical rules and sentence processing has yet to be discovered. Chomsky (1961) reflects that "... the important question is to what extent significant aspects of the use and understanding of utterances can be illuminated by refining and generalizing the notions of grammar [p. 385]." Six years later, Fodor and Garrett (1967) suggest that "... the most profound problem in psycho-

---

[1] Brown and Hanlon (1970) have rejuvenated this concept within a developmental context— asking whether derivational complexity can be related to the order of acquisition of various grammatical constructions.

linguistics is perhaps to specify the nature of the relation between the grammar and the recognition routine [p. 296]."

Not surprisingly, this relatively recent recharacterization of the nature and goals of linguistic science has had considerable impact upon the study of language acquisition. Men have always had language, and their offspring have always learned it. That this phenomenon has been occurring for thousands of years, may sometimes cause us to forget what a fantastic accomplishment language learning is. Children all over the world learn to speak their native tongues at approximately the same time—3 to 4 years of age. The complexity and difficulty of this task have led some to postulate the existence of innate capacities for language learning. Language certainly appears to be species-specific. Although there are no agreed upon formal criteria, to the best of our knowledge no other animal has a true language. Lenneberg's (1967) work on recovery from aphasia suggests that children who for some reason have not been exposed to a linguistic environment will be unable to learn their language once they are past the age of 15 or so. This seems to be equally true for the learning of a second language. After the early teens, foreign languages are not acquired spontaneously, but must be taught and learned through conscious and deliberate effort. Additional evidence suggesting that there is a genetically determined critical stage for language learning comes from observations on deaf children who learn sign language from their parents. Such children begin to learn the sign language at approximately the same time that normal children begin speaking (Braine, 1971b). The precise nature of whatever a priori knowledge, or predispositions the child may bring to the task of acquiring language, is a controversial and complex issue. Some of the papers in this volume address themselves specifically to this problem.

The rankest nativist would not claim that the child is genetically endowed with a complete grammatical system. Even if we acknowledge a few language universals, different languages contain different rule systems. Since the young child can acquire any language to which he is exposed, the rule systems per se cannot be innate. Within a relatively brief period, the child appears to learn a complicated and abstract network of rules—a system which enables him to produce and understand an infinite variety of unique utterances. These rules are only indirectly represented in the corpus of utterances to which the child is exposed. The task becomes more difficult when we consider that the corpus does not typically consist of only well-formed, grammatical utterances. In the face of these obstacles children everywhere, without teaching or training, readily acquire their native language at about the same time—regardless of just about any variable one cares to look at, short of deafness or severe retardation.

Since neither differential reinforcement contingencies, nor traditional psychological principles of associationism can account for language development, how does the child succeed in constructing a grammar for his language? The problem is a difficult one, and the psycholinguist's chore of discovering how the child accomplishes it, is fraught with its own headaches. In the first place, the child's grammar, for any period of time between birth and 5 years, is in a state of flux. Language learning is a discovery procedure; in a sense it is a series of successive approximations to the adult system. This succession need not be, however (and probably is not), an orderly one. A set of rules, once perceived, may be overgeneralized, and the child seems to regress. Moreover, depending upon what language is being learned, different aspects of that language will be more readily apparent to the child than others, at any one acquisition period. Thus speed of learning, and interlanguage differences require that the psycholinguist be very quick with his tape recorder. Once a corpus has been collected, analysis may be arduous. What could the child have said, but did not say, due to sampling limitations? What did the child not say, because he could not? The investigator's analysis of the corpus will not be independent of his knowledge of his own grammar. He must be careful with his assumptions and inferences, so as to not unjustly attribute too much (or too little) to the child's developing grammar.

Rather than study a collected corpus, some researchers perform experiments, in an attempt to discover directly what aspects of a language the child can comprehend or produce. The danger here is that some of the experimental instructions may call for a depth of understanding beyond that for which the child is being tested. Also, although many ingenious techniques have been developed, they tend to yield knowledge of specific language competencies, rather than a general overall picture of the child's system. It is one thing to know what the child has or has not got with respect to an adult grammar—it is quite another to characterize his linguistic world. Excellent, detailed analyses of these and other methodological problems can be found in McNeill (1970c) and Braine (1971b). Clearly, there is no well-defined paradigm for the study of language acquisition. To quote Braine (1971b): "There is no general method of analysis which can be mechanically applied to a corpus of text materials from a child in such a way as to guarantee discovery of the grammatical rules commanded by the child [p. 20]."

Until quite recently, investigators of children's language have concentrated mainly upon analyses of utterances collected in experimental situations, or obtained through recordings of spontaneous speech in the home. Relatively little attention was directed at either the physical and social characteristics of the environment in which the utterances occurred, or to the general cognitive capacities of the child at that particular time. Researchers were attempting to discover the syntactic structure of children's language, with an emphasis upon the content of the child's grammar, rather than the mechanisms of its acquisition. While the study of *what* is acquired must to some extent precede the study of the acquisition process, we now think we know enough about children's language to devote some effort to the latter question. Many of the contributors to this volume have done so. The papers contained here reflect a field in mild turmoil. Although the investigation of children's syntactic competencies has not been abandoned, various other aspects of language development—including the acquisition of meaning, developmental changes in memory, differences in speaking styles, concurrent cognitive development, and phonology acquisition—are herein examined.

Sinclair-de Zwart's chapter provides a timely integration of Piaget's theory of intellectual development with contemporary notions about language acquisition. Cognitive development, according to Piaget, involves a restructuring or modification of a previously acquired network of concepts, which itself is established as a result of the child's interaction with objects and people in his environment. While Piaget has captured the interest of child psychologists and educators, his latest views on language development are too recent to have had much impact in the United States. Sinclair-de Zwart's study may be a glimpse of things to come. She shows how the child's growing awareness of himself as only one agent among many who act upon the environment, is related to his gradual use of grammatical functions expressing agent–action, and action–object. If a theory of cognitive development (such as Piaget's) can ultimately connect linguistic structures to a general cognitive framework, it would indeed, to quote McNeill (1970c) "contribute a fundamental insight, for it would explain some aspect of the universal form of human language on the basis of general psychological principles [p. 1063]." H. H. Clark's chapter also investigates the interaction of cognitive developments with certain aspects of language learning—specifically the acquisition of expressions denoting space and time. He argues that the child must obtain a knowledge of the concepts before the terms can be used in his language. Not only, proposes Clark, should the properties of the child's *perceptual space* be reflected in his emerging linguistic abilities, but the order of acquisition of spatial terms may be predictable on the basis of the conditions necessary fot the appropriate use of the term.

E. V. Clark outlines a possible strategy by which children learn to use words as a means of representing external objects and events. Children initially use words whose full meaning is unknown. Since many of the semantic features belonging to a word are as yet unlearned, the child will misuse and overextend it. Gradually, however, as additional features are perceived by the child, he learns to refine the too-general meaning until it corresponds to the adult usage. E. V. Clark presents research and suggests in some detail how this refinement process might operate.

The provocative studies described by Rosch support her thesis that psychological categories have internal structure. Category instances differ with respect to how well they reflect the ideal of that category. Certain perceptual categories, such as color and form, are shown to develop according to perceptually salient features of "natural prototypes." Semantic categories are also shown to contain a psychologically meaningful internal structure, which affects the processing of the categories. Rosch discusses the possible application of her findings to the development of categories in children, and to cross-cultural studies of category formation.

Olson's chapter discusses the role of a specific cognitive capacity—that of memory—upon early language performance. The child's developing memory system is seen to interact in a complex way with such production variables as sentence length and sentence complexity. Berko Gleason gives a fascinating account of how children make use of different styles of speech, depending upon whom they are addressing. As the author points out, we do not communicate with a policeman in the same manner in which we address children or old friends. This preliminary study describes the different styles of speech used by the same child in a variety of different situations. Future research will attempt to outline details of the acquisition and utilization of these different speech codes.

The chapters by Roeper and Limber are both concerned with describing, in some detail, the syntactic competencies of young children. Both present some proposals concerning how observed syntactic regularities emerge and develop in the order in which they do. Similarly, Bowerman is interested in the child's syntactic system, but she suggests that the linguistic characterization of what the child knows may be more complex and abstract than is necessary. Structural relationships observed in child language have typically been described in syntactic terms within the framework of a transformational grammar. On the basis of her study of Finnish and American child speech, Bowerman concludes that the evidence used to attribute to the child an understanding of basic grammatical relations, is inconclusive. She proposes an alternative view—that children's initial word combinations are based primarily on semantic considerations.

The chapters by Garnica and Moskowitz investigate aspects of phonology development—a relatively neglected area of the language acquisition process. As we saw earlier, the syntactic component of a grammar contains a finite number of rules from which an infinite number of syntactic descriptions can be generated. The syntactic description of any sentence consists of a "deep" and a "surface" structure; the deep structure is basic to the semantic interpretation of the sentence, while the surface structure is phonetically interpreted. The phonological component of the grammar attempts to specify the rules by which a phonetic representation can be assigned to each surface structure. Before a child can acquire or learn an abstract system of rules which governs the use of his speech sounds. he must first acquire the speech units necessary for that language. Children seem to be aware of fairly subtle differences in speech sounds at a remarkably early age. Infants as young as 1 month can distinguish human speech from other noises in the environment. Some phonemic discriminations are present at this age, as well as an ability to recognize differences in intonation. Two variables which could conceivably determine the order of acquisition of phonemes are the difficulty of production, and the frequency of occurrence in the language. Roman Jakobson (1941) has proposed a distinctive feature theory of phonological development. According to Jakobson, it is not phonemes per se which are learned, but rather distinctive features or contrasts which permit the child to reliably differentiate phonemic units. There are a finite number of distinctive features occurring in all languages, and any one particular language uses a subset of these universal features. Jakobson further proposed that the order of acquisition of distinctive features is fixed and invariant (Jakobson & Halle, 1956). Garnica's chapter describes an empirical test of the notion that the learning of phonemic speech perception follows an invariant order. The results are not consistent with some earlier findings of Shvachkin (1948), but reliable trends are present, which may help suggest how the task of acquiring phonology proceeds. Moskowitz has performed an extensive and in-depth analysis of the relationship between the phonological system and English orthography, as they pertain to the Great Vowel Shift. Her experiments demonstrate that the English spelling system contains phonological information which is not a direct reflection of the "facts" in the underlying phonology. If, as Moskowitz proposes, knowledge of the symbolic system significantly effects performance aspects of phonological development, then this interaction must become an integral part of any grammar of English phonology. Lastly, Ervin-Tripp provides a comprehensive and integrative review of much of the latest literature—suggesting some possible prerequisites, and strategies for language learning during its early stages.

The contributors to this volume do not presume to have found the key to the elusive nature of the relationship between linguistic and cognitive development. Rather, the chapters here reflect a variety of orientations and conceptualizations which may raise more questions than they answer. Such is the state of the art—however, much work is in progress. It is hoped that this volume will contribute to, and accelerate the growth of research in this area by generating new experimental hypotheses and opening up additional areas of investigation.

LANGUAGE ACQUISITION
AND COGNITIVE DEVELOPMENT

H. SINCLAIR-de ZWART
University of Geneva

Lately, much has been written about the relationship between linguists' grammars and interiorized or mental grammars; what used to be called the problem of the psychological reality of linguistic theory is now usually re-phrased in terms of relations or links between different models. Generative grammar can certainly qualify as a model—but what should we compare it with? Nothing resembling a psychological language model has as yet been constructed, and though the heuristic value of generative grammar has been amply demonstrated, its use for the discovery of the constructive mechanisms through which humans learn and use their language appears more doubtful.

The Genevan position as regards the relationship between linguistic theory and the study of the way the (epistemic) speaker–listener understands and produces utterances is parallel to the position Piaget has adopted on logic and cognitive psychology. Logic is an axiomatization of reasoning and is a purely formal discipline. Starting from axioms, theorems are derived in a mechanical, deductive manner. There is, however, a corresponding experi-mental science, which should not be confused with the formal discipline, and that is the psychology of thinking. The two have indeed often been confused —Aristotle intended to describe thought as the reflection of logical laws, with the proviso that this only concerned true thought, by contrast with everyday thought, which is subject to many social, emotional, and other error-inducing influences.

According to Piaget, the relationship between logic and the corresponding experimental science, cognitive psychology, has to be seen in the following manner, to quote Piaget (1967):

> Formal logic does not have to appeal to psychology, since factual questions have no place in a hypothetico–deductive theory; inversely, it would be just as absurd to invoke formal logic for the purpose of deciding an experimental question—as for instance the question of the mechanisms of intelligence. However, in so far as psychology aims at analyzing the final states of equilibrium attained by thought, there is, not a parallelism, but a correspondence between experimental knowledge and logic, as there is a correspondence between a schema and the reality it represents. Each question which arises in one of the two disciplines corresponds to a question in the other, though neither their methods nor their solutions are interchangeable [p. 37].

Since mathematics and logic have become tools in linguistics, and especially since linguists have tried to axiomatize their procedures, a similar confusion to the one Piaget noticed in the case of German *Denkpsychologie* has arisen in linguistics and psycholinguistics. It is probably no coincidence that the distinction between true thought which was considered to be a direct reflection of logic, and thought in general reminds us of the distinction between competence and performance in its first formulation, when performance was regarded as the debased expression of competence. The necessity pointed out by Piaget, to distinguish clearly axiomatization and experimental science, has since then also been felt in psycholinguistics. A second necessity, also pointed out by Piaget, and, in fact, taken by him as a prerequisite for our understanding of cognitive functioning, especially from an epistemological point of view, is the following: Different axiomatizations can be evaluated as to their resemblance to what he calls dynamic or living thought; and most importantly, certain axiomatizations will show greater resemblance to the way cognitive structures are elaborated in development than others. To understand structures at their various levels of equilibrium it is necessary to know how they have been formed.

Chomsky (1965) distinguishes two levels of adequacy for grammars: The first level, that of descriptive adequacy, is reached when the grammar correctly describes its object, namely the linguistic intuition—the tacit competence—of the native, adult speaker.

> The much deeper and hence much more rarely attainable level of explanatory adequacy is reached when the grammar is justified on internal grounds. The problem of internal justification—of explanatory adequacy—is essentially the problem of constructing a theory of language acquisition, an account of the specific innate abilities that make this achievement possible [pp. 26–27].

Except for the word *innate*, there is nothing here with which Piaget would not agree. I think that too much rather vacuous discussion has been devoted to this innate issue. *Pace* Washoe, only human babies learn to talk, only human babies become mathematicians, bakers, and candlestick makers. In that sense, obviously, language and many other abilities as well are innate.

In the case of intelligence, Piaget has shown conclusively that it is possible to follow the slow construction of cognitive structures from birth to formal logic, and that no sudden emergence of preformed logical concepts takes place. This view does not mean that therefore learning takes place in a passive, associative sense, according to what the environment imposes upon a child. Quite the contrary, this development obeys internal laws, and though interaction with people and things is a necessary condition, concepts are formed in the same way by children all over the world, despite very different environmental influences. It has been said that the strict nativist position is a philosophical lazy Susan—that may be so, but as regards linguistic theory it makes matters more difficult, not easier. Chomsky (1965) says:

> A theory of linguistic structure that aims for explanatory adequacy incorporates an account of linguistic universals, and it attributes tacit knowledge of these universals to the child. . . . The important question is: what are the initial assumptions concerning the nature of language that the child brings to language learning and how detailed and specific is the innate schema that gradually becomes more explicit and differentiated as the child learns the language [p. 27]?

It would seem to be an impossibly difficult task to make hypotheses about *innate* schemata; also, until neurology provides precise data, the nativist idea seems to put the burden of finding explanatory hypotheses of the nature of human language on linguistics rather than on psychology—and one may well ask if this is an efficient division of labor. Since the child has to be taken into account, developmental psychology seems to be better suited for this purpose. Moreover, it seems easier, and much more hopeful, to suppose that the child brings to the task of acquiring his mother tongue a set of universal cognitive structures which have been built up during the first year of life and which provide enough assumptions about the nature of human language to enable the child to begin to join the talking community at about the age of $1\frac{1}{2}$. In this sense one could indeed, to quote Slobin (1971), take Piaget as a handbook for psycholinguistic development. Hopefully, such a point of view would also make it possible to explain *how* the child's initial assumptions become more and more explicit and differentiated, while agreeing that, up to the end of the period when children everywhere seem to produce utterances that are remarkably alike in structure, there is little question of learning taking place on the basis of presented linguistic data through some kind of inductive generalization. Up to this point, then, we may assume that we are dealing with utterances which are made possible through the assumptions children everywhere make about the nature of human language. These universal linguistic assumptions and the acquisitions they make possible would be reflections of the universal cognitive structures acquired by that age, just as what Piaget calls the structure of sensorimotor intelligence is a reflection of these same general cognitive structures. McNeill (1970b) supposes the existence of basic, language-definitional universals—strong linguistic universals—which reflect a specific linguistic ability and may not be a reflection of a cognitive ability at all. I find it impossible to admit that language might not be a cognitive ability; and I find it equally difficult to admit another interpretation of the same statement, that is, the idea (also proposed by Vygotsky) that language stems from totally different roots from those of sensorimotor intelligence, and that preverbal intelligence and preintelligent speech only join at the period of the first utterances which are comprehensible for the adult speaker. This view introduces a dichotomy which is not backed up by any facts, and which leaves the beginnings of language shrouded in mystery. Quite to the contrary, I suppose that the closest link between language and intelligent activity dealing with reality is to be found during the earliest period of language learning, and that therefore Piaget's analyses of cognitive structures will be of the greatest use when one deals with the question of the basic hypotheses about the nature of human language.

As soon as children start producing utterances of more than three elements, matters become immensely more complex, and at that point some kind of inductive procedure has to be supposed to account for the appearance of forms and structures belonging to the grammar of one specific language. Clearly, inductive ability is also something that develops; and therefore Piaget can once again give some indications as to the interpretation to be given to the progressive acquisitions children make in the grammar of their mother tongue. But equally clearly, this will depend on many other factors as well, perhaps mainly on the complexity of the language in question as regards the expression of certain grammatical relations. Piaget sees the construction of cognitive operations as following structurally defined stages and as a universal phenomenon. Their progression toward a state of equilibrium is functionally determined by the necessary character of these operations, in the sense that to be internally consistent they cannot be different from what they are. No such necessary and universal character is attached to the morpho-syntactical rules of specific languages, and therefore we cannot expect either universality or clearly defined structural stages; in fact we expect them less and less as language learning proceeds. For the same reason we expect less and less correspondence with the development of intellectual operations, and the occasions to use Piaget for explanatory hypotheses will be correspondingly fewer. However, even in this later period, say from 3 or 4 to 10 and beyond, it is sometimes possible to find in Piaget's theory an interpretation of the difficulties children have with a certain sentence pattern, whereas a pattern that to the adult seems identical or very similar is easily understood and correctly used much earlier. An example from Geneva is the slow elaboration of time relationships studied by Ferreiro (1971), and studied for English by E. Clark (1971a), with remarkably similar results in both languages. It seems important that evidence of such relatively late and laborious constructions is accumulating; other examples are to be found in C. Chomsky (1969). It is conceivable that the corresponding phenomenon (i.e., the early correct appearance of certain patterns), can be interpreted by features of the cognitive apprehension young children have of certain situations which give rise to what can be called natural patterns. It should be emphasized that this remark does not refer to so-called iconic characteristics of the situation but to the child's cognitive interpretation which can be quite different from the adult's.

Piaget's theory of cognitive development could therefore be used: first, to help us attain explanatory adequacy by trying to define the child's initial set of linguistic universals, and second, to study from a cognitive point of view the unexpected difficulties which arise later in development.

It is, of course, quite impossible to sketch Piaget's theory in a few paragraphs. However, as regards our first problem, the initial set of linguistic universals, a few remarks will suffice; after discussion of one of our experiments, some further elaboration will follow. The second problem has been dealt with at some length by Ferreiro (1971).

Piaget qualifies his epistemological theory as interactionist and biological. Knowledge is acquired through the subject's action upon, and interaction with, people and things. Action patterns become established, extended, combined with others, and differentiated under the influence of internal regulatory mechanisms; later, they become interiorized (i.e., mentally representable), and organized into grouplike structures. Acting upon environment, rather than copying it or talking about it, is the source of knowledge. Language is only one way among others to represent knowledge. Representation in general does not appear until the end of the sensorimotor period (around the age of 1½) when direct-acting-on-objects has become organized in a first grouplike structure: A move from a to b (e.g., when the child goes from one point to another himself, or when he moves objects, or when he observes other people moving) can be retraced to find the starting point a; it can also be composed of two different moves: from a to x, and x to b. Simultaneously and in close connection with this action structure, objects acquire what Piaget calls permanence; that is to say, no longer does the child act as if they have ceased to exist when they disappear from his field of action, but he knows that he can find them again, even if they are successively hidden in different places (as long as he has seen the moves) by using the action structure described above. This achievement is the result of a long development about which we will have more to say later on; it is the culmination of sensorimotor, practical intelligence and at the same time the beginning of representational intelligence. Representation has several forms—symbolic play, mental images, imitation, drawing—and in some of them objects and events are symbolized by something else; it is likely that this is only possible when objects have acquired a certain identity of their own, and no longer exist only when the child acts upon them. To be able to symbolize in play a car by a pebble, one has to know, to a certain extent, both cars and pebbles. To progress, intelligence now has to go beyond the *hic et nunc*; to do this, representation is necessary for recapitulation and anticipation.

Between 2 and 6 years of age Piaget analyzes what is in many respects a reconstruction of sensorimotor intelligence on a different, i.e., representational, level. Slowly, action patterns become interiorized, leading to the system of concrete operations and their invariants. The interiorization leads to reversibility—the capacity to undo mentally what has been done, and therefore to be able to conserve quantities; or the capacity to understand that if one finds out that one stick is shorter than another, the latter is inevitably longer than the former. This development of the preoperational period is subject to certain laws which determine what Piaget calls its semilogical character, comparable to the one-way mappings of set theory.

Similarly, knowledge of objects, their properties, and their behavior develops—moving toward more and more specificity. In a way, the development of logic and that of knowledge of the physical world are contrastive and complementary: A logical structure is more powerful when it becomes more general and less linked to a particular content, whereas understanding of object properties is more powerful when it becomes more specific and differentiated. We are tempted to think that syntactic structures and lexicon follow similar opposite and complementary directions, with here, too, a close link between the two so that new acquisitions in either lead to new acquisitions in the other. However, in the rest of this paper the emphasis will be mainly on syntactic structures.

Among the many questions that can be asked about basic linguistic capacity, the following has recently been discussed in several papers: What is the status of the basic grammatical relations subject-of, main-verb-of, object-of, etc., which in many languages are expressed by the order of the words in surface structure, and presumably, also in base structure (cf. Hayes, 1970). Greenberg (1961) has shown that in most languages the subject precedes the object, and that of the three possible orders where this is so (SVO; SOV; VSO), SVO and SOV are the most frequent. The fact that in some languages the order is relatively free does not seem highly relevant, since even in those languages a basic SVO or SOV order is always preferred whenever a sentence would be ambiguous (as for instance in the case of neuters in Latin, for which nominative and accusative have the same form). It has been supposed by Jackobson (1961) and N. Chomsky (1965, p. 225) that the explanation for the quasi-universality of this order of the elements in the base is to be sought in iconic factors. As Watt (1970) puts it: "Here of course the presumption is that our attention tends to be seized first by the "subject" of an action being perceived and being put into language—and only secondarily by the "object," if any or perhaps only secondarily by what (in the VP) is to be predicated [p. 65]." Though I cannot agree that the explanation lies in any iconic factors or in a supposedly fundamental characteristic of perception, it does seem plausible that some universal psychological factor is involved. I will come back to this question later on, but for the moment, I suppose that the order of the elements in the base as an expression of grammatical relationships, is one of the structures that, for very young children, belongs to their expectancies about the nature of language; or at least, that this hypothesis gets instilled very early in language learning.

It has often been said that in the very first two- and three-word utterances, children already use word order consistently to express relations. However, many counterexamples can be found in French publications (Bloch, 1924). We find just as often *maman partie* as *partie maman*; or *cassée poupée* as *poupée cassée*. What is more, we find children apparently trying out different kinds of word order, saying, e.g., *couper cheveux papa*; *cheveux couper papa*; *papa couper cheveux*. We also noticed such unusual word order when we asked 3-year-olds to describe some simple events (acted out in front of them with toys). For instance when a monkey knocked a teddy bear down, a 3;2 child said first: "*Il fait tomber le nounours*" ("He makes the bear fall"); but when the experimenter asked "Yes, that's right, who did it?" the child answered: "*Il a tombé le singe le nounours*" ("He made fall the monkey the bear"): VSO. During the same session this child said, when the cat caressed the pig: "*Il a caressé le cochon le chat*": VOS. Another child said, when the girl doll caressed the dog: "*le chien a caressé la fille*": OVS. From 3½ onward, the only departure from the SVO order seems to be *il* + VOS: "*Il a poussé les oiseaux le cochon*." This pattern persists in French in colloquial adult language, but is avoided when ambiguity would result. "He's mowing the lawn, John" is frequent; "He met Peter, John" is not.

The problem of linguistic universals has to do with competence, and competence, of course, has to do with our intuitions about language. Since adults' utterances do not necessarily correspond to their intuitions about language, there is no reason to suppose that children's utterances correspond to their intuitions. However, the existence of word order that deviates from SVO or SOV, both in three-word utterances without any grammatical markers, and in the utterances of 3-year-olds which already incorporate pronouns and some inflections, made us wonder about the universality and about the fundamental nature of the SVO order.

We decided on an experiment of the type "let's see what happens"— and we presented children from 2;6 to 7 with childlike utterances of the type: *cheveux couper papa.* We simply pronounced either two nouns and a verb in the infinitive,[1] or two verbs and a noun (in different orders and with different types of verbs and nouns), and asked the children to guess, and to show us with toys, what we could mean; adding, for the older children, that we were not speaking good French, that what we said was not quite right, but that we want them to guess. We hoped that in this way the children might use their set of basic assumptions about language to guess the meaning. We wondered whether they would use word order, and if so, in what way; or whether they would act randomly.

We chose five different three-word combinations, and presented each one in the six possible orders (30 items in all, presented in random succession). A first group consisted of the permutations of girl-push-boy: two animate nouns (N) and a verb (V), where no pragmatic considerations suggest one particular SVO construction. These six permutations are:

NVN: boy-push-girl; girl-push-boy

NNV: boy-girl-push; girl-boy-push

VNN: push-boy-girl; push-girl-boy

The second series consists of the permutations of boy-open-box, where pragmatic considerations suggest one particular solution. A third series is car-roll-truck; the verb *rouler* or *avancer* was chosen because it can be both transitive and intransitive. A fourth series is: pig-horse-leave, two animate nouns and an intransitive verb, and the last group: bear-shout-jump, one noun and two intransitive verbs (we had a toy bear who made a noise when pressed). Our subjects are divided into four age groups: 2;10–4; 4–5; 5–6; and 6–7. For the moment we have 15 to 20 subjects per group (Sinclair & Bronckart, 1972).

Before discussing the results, I would like to point out that the six possible orders of patient, agent and action can be obtained through transformations in surface structure in the following manner, where P = patient, A = Agent, V = action.

---

[1] For verbs in -er, the infinitive has the same spoken forms as the past participle and the polite or plural imperative. This is not the case with verbs in -ir, which we also used.

AVP: *Le garçon pousse la fille.*
   The boy pushes the girl.

VAP: *Poussée par le garçon, la fille . . .*
   Pushed by the boy, the girl . . .

APV: *C'est par le garçon que la fille est poussée.*
   It's by the boy the girl is pushed.

PAV: *C'est la fille que le garçon pousse.*
   It's the girl the boy pushes.

VPA: *Poussant la fille, le garçon . . .*
   Pushing the girl, the boy . . .

PVA: *La fille est poussée par le garçon.*
   The girl is pushed by the boy.

We are starting to study these surface structures as well, and we hope to be able to use the results of the first experiment to interpret the way children of different age-groups understand these sentences.

The main results of the first experiment, the only one to be discussed here, may be described as follows. The actions for the two series with verbs that are intransitive from the adult point of view (pig-horse-leave, and bear-cry-jump) and the series with "roll" (which was almost always taken in its intransitive sense) differ from the series boy-push-girl and boy-open-box in three ways:

(*a*) Though in general we had little difficulty in making the children understand what we wanted them to do, these intransitive items were the easiest, especially for the youngest subjects. They did not hesitate, they did not stop and think as they did for the others. One of them expressed this clearly: when boy-box-open followed horse-pig-leave he said, "The other one was easier."

(*b*) The solutions given to the two transitive-verb series changed from age-group to age-group, whereas no change in behavior with age was noticed for the intransitive items, apart from a tendency on the part of the youngest group to use only one of the animals or to act out only one of the verbs mentioned.

(*c*) For the intransitive series, the subjects almost always gave the same solution in all six items, whatever the order in which the words were presented; whereas in the transitive series, and especially in boy-push-girl, solutions were consistently different according to the order of the words.

The most interesting series were therefore boy-push-girl and boy-open-box, and these are the only items I will discuss. To start with boy-push-girl, we had foreseen only two solutions: Either the boy pushing the girl or the girl pushing the boy, and we supposed that at least the younger subjects would choose one of these solutions randomly. Our first surprise was that this was not true at all; and an analysis per subject of solutions for all items shows astonishing consistency, so that we have to suppose that the children used quite specific strategies. These strategies changed with age, and the following pattern emerges.

In Group 1 (2;10–4) two types of action account for about two thirds of all solutions: (a) the verb *push* is understood in an intransitive sense, and the child makes the boy and the girl walk on the table and says *They are walking, they go ahead*—something like *they push on*. One child thought for a long time, chose this solution and then said: *You should have said: "They walk!"* (b) the child himself performs the action of pushing on the boy and the girl and says, *I push them down*. Evidently, it was sometimes difficult to distinguish these two types, but most of the time the children's remarks and behavior made the distinction clear.

These two strategies disappear in the older age-groups, but not at the same time for the different word order patterns. For NVN and VNN the intransitive solution (SSV_{intr}) has disappeared in Group 2, and the solution in which the child (C) acts upon both nouns—(C)VOO—disappears in

Table 1   *Percentage of (C) VOO[a] and SSV_{intr}[b] Solutions as a Function of Age[c]*

		Solution	
Presentation order	Age group	(C)VOO	SSV_{intr}
VNN	1	18	41
	2	23	3.5
	3	0	7
	4	12.5	0
NVN	1	18	50
	2	20	4
	3	3.5	3.5
	4	4	0
NNV	1	16	59
	2	31	21
	3	23.5	3.5
	4	8.5	0

[a]Child himself acts on both nouns.
[b]The two nouns are made to perform an "intransitive" action.
[c]See text for explanation.

Group 3; but for NNV, the intransitive solution only disappears in Group 3, and the solution in which the child acts on both nouns only in Group 4.

Two other strategies appear when the children start decoding this series as either "the boy pushes the girl" or "the girl pushes the boy." One of these is the establishment of a link between the verb and the noun which is nearest to it as an agent–action relationship; and the other is the establishment of a link between the verb and the noun nearest to it as an action–patient relationship. In the case of VNN the first strategy (for push-boy-girl) results in the boy pushing the girl (and, results correspondingly, for push-girl-boy, in the girl pushing the boy). The second strategy gives the opposite solution, that is to say: push-boy-girl = "the girl pushes the boy." VNN is either decoded as VSO or as VOS. In the NNV series the two strategies again give different solutions: SOV or OSV. The establishment of the verb–object link may be a little later than the verb–subject link; it is mainly for subjects of Group 3 that the two strategies seem to be in conflict. It is to be noted that in the case of VNN, the strategy of taking the noun immediately following the verb as its object runs counter to a later strategy, which seems preponderant in Group 4, namely that of considering the relative position of the two Ns and choosing the first as the subject, whereas in the case of NNV the verb–object link concurs with that of choosing the first of the two Ns as the subject.

For the NVN series the developmental trend is quite clear: This is of course the only series that corresponds to the normal SVO order in French. As soon as the two primitive strategies have been eliminated NVN = SVO becomes the preponderant solution, already at 65% in Group 2 and at 92% in Group 4. However, for the youngest group this solution represents only 37% of answers, the others belonging to one of the two primitive strategies. Solutions whereby NVN is decoded as OVS are extremely rare. In this series it is impossible to distinguish between the subject–verb link, the verb–object link, and the N_1 = subject, N_2 = object solution; all three result in NVN = SVO.

It is noticeable that in all three combinations the developmental tendency is clearly directed towards the solution: first noun is subject, second noun is object, whatever the place of the verb (cf. Bever, 1970).

Before giving some tentative interpretations of the results, a few points have to be made about the series boy-open-box. We expected that almost all children would decode all six permutations (boy-open-box, boy-box-open, open-boy-box, etc.) as "the boy opens the box." This expectation was not at all confirmed. In the first place, these items, especially if box preceded boy gave rise to between 10 and 20% refusals—which never happened with the other items. Second, here, too, we saw the primitive solution of the child himself acting; that is to say, leaving the doll out and opening the box

Table 2 *Types and Percentages of Solutions*[a] *as a Function of Age*

Presentation order	Age group	Solution	
		VSO	VOS
VNN	1	23	18
	2	60	13
	3	52	41
	4	66	21
		SVO	OSV
NVN	1	37	0
	2	65	11
	3	80	13
	4	92	4
		SOV	OSV
NNV	1	4	21
	2	31	17
	3	46	26
	4	52	39

[a]Solutions other than those reported in Table 1.

himself (or herself). Partly, this may just be due to a manipulatory difficulty. More interestingly, in all cases where box preceded boy, and
especially in box-open-boy, some children took the box, poked at the boy,
lifted up his jacket and said something like: *The box can't really do it, it
pricks him.* Percentages of the "box opens the boy" solution for Groups 1–
4 were: 11, 12.5, 20, and 36, respectively. The 6-year-olds seem to be
particularly convinced formalists and choose this remarkably antipragmatic
solution to our riddle; at that age the SVO pattern seems to be so firmly
established that a good proportion of our subjects prefer the most im-
probable solution.

Our tentative conclusion regarding the building up of the subject-object-
verb relationship runs somewhat as follows. We suppose that by our technique the children are put into a position of listening to a language of which
they know certain words but not the syntactical rules. We suppose that their
initial set of hypotheses about the structure of human language is again set in
motion and leads them to choose certain solutions.

At first there are two possibilities: Either the child considers all three-word
combinations as describing an event in which he himself takes no part, in
which case he supposes names of animals or persons to be the agent to whom
is ascribed an action expressed by the verb. Alternatively, he supposes the
utterance to describe an action in which he himself takes part, and in that
case it is he himself who performs the action on the persons or objects

mentioned. His initial pattern for the understanding of an utterance would thus be either subject–predicate and predicate–subject, with no preference for a fixed order, or verb–object and object–verb, again without a fixed order; and in the latter case the subject is not mentioned and is taken to be himself.

Subsequently, these two patterns get combined to form the trilogy SVO; the subject–verb link becoming an orderd pair first, and whatever is left is taken to be the object, as a sort of extension of the subject–predicate construction. A little later, the verb–object link becomes firmly established to form the verb phrase which can be combined with the noun phrase. This results either in SVO, or in SOV, Greenberg's two most likely candidates for the universal base. In both, the subject precedes the object, and the VP node, i.e., the link between object and verb, remains unbroken. In arboreal presentation:

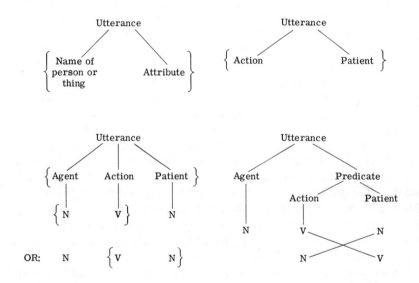

The developmental phase presented here is preceded by the holophrastic period, during which, as I have argued elsewhere, there is no differentiation between subject and predicate or between topic and comment. The above diagrams can be taken to represent either the analysis the child makes of a heard utterance or the child's own production, i.e., the way he combines the elements at his disposal into a surface structure.

To continue speculating, we can now ask how far this supposed construction of the basic grammatical relations corresponds to Piaget's structural analysis of the basic patterns of intelligence. During the sensorimotor period, and starting from reflex activity, the baby extends his action patterns to an ever greater number of objects (sucking his fingers, his toys, etc.) and acquires new action patterns on the basis of already existing ones (e.g., when he tries to grasp an object hanging from his cot, he may accidentally set it in motion so that it swings; this spectacle being interesting, he will then repeat the action of making objects swing). At the same time his actions become differentiated because the properties of the objects acted upon demand certain adjustments and modifications (e.g., he cannot grasp a corner of his blanket in the same way as he grasps his mother's finger). Though all things and persons are only seen in relation to his own actions and desires, the coordination of several patterns and their differentiation will bring knowledge about the objects themselves. The child discovers, for example, that certain things when shaken produce a noise, and links this action both to listening and to looking. New objects, looked at, listened to, and acted upon, can then be put into two categories: those that make a noise and those that do not. New discoveries will be made when the baby intentionally starts shaking objects to see whether they make a noise.

The establishment of ever more complex action patterns leads to a bipolar construction of knowledge: On the one hand coordinations are established between the action patterns themselves, and on the other hand between the action patterns and objects. The child introduces some organization into reality by assembling, separating, putting on top of, putting into, etc.; at the same time he discovers properties of the objects themselves. However, the properties of things and persons are discovered through the child's activity, and not through his submission to them. At first, objects are not heavy or sharp in the adult sense, but they are "hard to lift," "hurting," etc.; and they have these properties mainly at the moment the child is in contact with them. Only gradually will the child change his view of reality so that he himself is not the only agent or the only person concerned; he realizes that he is only one agent among many (first, other persons and later, objects, are understood as acting on other objects).

The earliest spontaneous utterances can be interpreted in this conceptual framework. As Piaget (1949) has remarked, the first holophrastic utterances can be seen as an expression of actual or possible action patterns, partly desubjectivized, but mainly referring to the subject himself. For example, when a 1;6-year-old girl says *vaou* when she sees a dog from the balcony, this *vaou* will be extended to animals that resemble dogs, but also to everything she can see from the same viewpoint: a horse, a baby in a pram, when seen from the balcony are called *vaou*. *Panana* (from grandpapa) is said whenever she wants somebody, not necessarily her grandfather, to do something her grandfather used to do with her. In general one can say that these holophrases accompany in the present an action done by the child or interesting to the child; or they express a desire for an action the child wants to perform or to have performed immediately by someone else. It is only a little later that these *judgments d'action* get supplemented by *jugements de constatation*; that is, descriptions of past events or of properties of objects or persons (again, obviously, properties important to the child). *Fille méchant, poupée cassée, papa parti* belong in this category. It is probably no coincidence that among the very first universal utterances the indication of disappearance and apparition is so frequent; one of the first permanent properties of objects is their very existence.

Following this analysis, we might interpret the linguistic patterns as follows: At first the child expresses a (possible) action pattern related to himself, in which agent, action and eventual patient are inextricably entwined. Second, he either expresses the result of an action done by somebody else (but not the action–object link in that case), or an action he performs or is going to perform himself. In this way, the capacity for representing reality follows at a later stage the same evolution which took place when the child was still dealing directly with reality without representation. The first direct-action differentiations—i.e., between the subject's own action and the object acted upon on the one hand, and the child himself as an agent and some other person or object as agent—give rise to the first grammatical functions of subject–predicate and object–action. It is to be emphasized that in this analysis the SVO structure is established through and around the verb. That there is no question of the rule $N_1 = S$ becoming established on its own, as it were, is further confirmed by the fact that when we present only two nouns, and nothing else, no action follows—either the child does nothing at all and asks, *et puis quoi?* or he takes the two objects named. The order in which we present these nouns makes no difference. Some spontaneous utterances are apparent contradictions to this hypothesis. Utterances such as *maman café* look like a concatenation of subject-object in certain circumstances. But since we suppose that at this level word-classes have not yet been established *café* may very well represent an action-pattern: coffee-drinking. In other cases such utterances are no more than a juxtaposition of two holophrases; and in more advanced examples the same combination is a noun–modifier pattern: *mommy's coffee*. Just as action-patterns lead to first groupings of objects (pushable, suckable, shakeable, etc.) the first patterns of grammatical relations lead to categorizations: nounlike words, verblike words, modifiers, etc.

From this point of view, during the second year of life the child's fundamental assumptions about the nature of human language would become established and would develop in the following manner. To leave aside many important points that need clarification, and to attempt no more than a first approximative sketch: Once the child has made the link between a series of sounds pronounced by the adult and an event, and singles out a short combination (how and why is a mystery), he assumes that these sounds express the action-pattern aspect of the event, and he will use the same series (in better and better phonetic approximation) whenever there is, in his view, a recurrence of the action pattern. Just as he has made differentiations in his own former direct dealings with reality, he will then notice that the utterances he hears are composed of different parts—for instance, having singled out *aplu* (all gone) from utterances such as *il n'y a plus de gateau* and having used it in the manner described, he will now assume that the part of the utterance which until now was left out of account has a certain relation to the other part—a relation of subject to predicate (that is, a description of an interesting state or property of an object or a person) or a relation of action–patient (that is, the expression of an action being, or to be performed by or in the interest of the child himself). Both assumptions then get combined into the expectation of a three-constituent structure, without as yet any established order, and with only the beginnings of word-categorization. At this point the child can express the distinction (which has already been well-established in his direct dealings with reality) between himself as an acting and desiring person and other actors or desirers. Finally, this combination gives rise to the coordination of Agent + Action (+ Patient), and again, the new structural pattern goes together with more refined categorizations; at this point we might suppose that the pattern NP + VP (with the VP composed of either only a predicate, or a verb and a noun) is established concurrently with the functional relationship SV_{intr}, SVO, or SOV.

This long piece of speculation is based on two important Piagetian postulates. (1) Very general cognitive structures composed of systems of actions are established during the first 2 years of life; these systems constitute the basis for many different types of cognitive structures, as much for the construction of logico-mathematical knowledge as for knowledge of the physical world and for the understanding and use of linguistic structures. (2) Higher-level knowledge involves a reconstruction of already acquired concepts and patterns, and thus shows a formation process isomorphic to that by which earlier knowledge was acquired.

Clearly, this explanatory interpretation of the universal base is very different from the justification by some sort of iconic factor quoted above. In the first place, our interpretation supposes this universal base to be constructed, and not to be innate; in the second place, it supposes this construction to be based on the way the child acts on reality, and changes it by his action, instead of basing it upon a perceptive constant, which implies a more passive, copylike apprehension of reality. The universal base is a result of universal cognitive activity, not of a tendency whereby our attention tends to be seized first by the subject of an action. Moreover, our adult experience, cognitive and perceptive as well as linguistic, surely contradicts this hypothesis; in particular, linguistic transformations allow us to topicalize or to emphasize any one of the three components, (Action, Agent, or Patient) according to our apprehension of the event to be described. Young children do this too, first by using a rather free order of the three elements, and later by using substitutions, deletions and permutations which result in grammatically not-quite-acceptable sentences such as quoted earlier.

It would seem that to take Piaget as a handbook for developmental psycholinguistics is not a simple task. It implies rather involved, and (to many, maybe) rather devious, reasoning. A direct transposition of his theory of cognitive development is impossible. Moreover, until recently, Piaget concentrated on logico-mathematical knowledge, and his studies of the development of physical concepts such as force, movement, etc. are as yet little known outside Geneva. These recent studies show that there are close links between knowledge in one field and that in another, but they also show that what were initially described as universal cognitive structures are more properly considered as symptoms (in the field of logical thinking) of even more general structures which also underlie concepts of causality, time, etc., where they may acquire rather different forms. Piaget (Ferreiro, 1971, Preface) himself has suggested the possible application of these ideas to language acquisition: Linguistic structures may well be yet another symptom of the very general, universal cognitive structures.

SPACE, TIME, SEMANTICS, AND THE CHILD[1]

HERBERT H. CLARK
Stanford University

In the last decade psychology has witnessed a resurgence of interest in the mechanisms and processes by which the child learns his first language, and a primary issue in the recent literature has been the question, What is innate? The main proponent of the innateness hypothesis is N. Chomsky (1965, 1968), who has argued roughly as follows. The child must acquire his first language from the speech he hears around him. But this speech is simply too meager and too full of errors to enable him to induce the correct structure as quickly as he does. Therefore, he must have some a priori knowledge about that structure—some innate knowledge of language—that he brings to bear in acquiring language. Chomsky has also argued that the innate knowledge must be capable of accounting for those aspects of language that are truly inherent to language, i.e., to all possible human languages. So far, however, the innateness hypothesis has had a certain air of mystery about it, for most of the talk has been about disembodied ideas affecting the acquisition process in unspecified ways. Clearly, however, if a priori knowledge is to enter into the acquisition process, it must be transported by particular vehicles which can be followed through their course of development. Instead of appearing out of thin air, a priori knowledge must be seen as arising out of specific learning mechanisms, memory constraints, perceptual abilities, motor abilities, and the like.

[1] The preparation of this paper was supported in part by Public Health Service Grant MH-20021 from the National Institute of Mental Health. I wish to thank Eve V. Clark for her suggestions and comments in the writing of this paper.

The thesis of the present chapter is that the child acquires English expressions for space and time by learning how to apply these expressions to the a priori knowledge he has about space and time. This a priori knowledge is separate from language itself and is not so mysterious. The knowledge, it will be argued, is simply what the child knows about space given that he lives on this planet, has a particular perceptual apparatus, and moves around in a characteristic manner. The exact form of this knowledge, then, is dependent on man's biological endowment—that he has two eyes, ears, etc., that he stands upright, and so on—and in this sense it is innate. For the present, however, it is more constructive to consider the present paper within a cognitive framework. The thesis is simply that the child knows much about space and time before he learns the English terms for space and time, and his acquisition of these terms is built onto his prior cognitive development.

The structure of the present argument is roughly as follows. The child is born into a flat world with gravity, and he himself is endowed with eyes, ears, an upright posture, and other biological structure. These structures alone lead him to develop a perceptual space, a P-space, with very specific properties. Later on, the child must learn how to apply English spatial terms to this perceptual space, and so the structure of P-space determines in large part what he learns and how quickly he learns it. The notion is that the child cannot apply some term correctly if he does not already have the appropriate concept in his P-space. Since this is so, the concept of space underlying the English spatial terms, to be called L-space, should coincide with P-space: any property found in L-space should be also found in P-space. This line of argument leads to two hypotheses about language and language acquisition, the correlation hypothesis and the complexity hypothesis.

The correlation hypothesis simply claims that the structure of P-space will be preserved in L-space—that is, there will always be a close correlation between P-space and L-space. In the following section, for example, it will be argued that verticality is a fundamental direction of P-space and that up is positive and down negative. The correlation hypothesis implies that verticality should therefore also be a fundamental dimension in spatial expressions, and that there, too, up should be positive and down negative. The correlation hypothesis, however, does not spell out the mechanisms by which this correlation comes about. The central thesis of the chapter will be supported even if we find evidence for the correlation hypothesis without being able to specify the acquisition mechanism.

This hypothesis is not a new one. In his important discussion of spatial adjectives in German, for example, Bierwisch (1967) has argued for much the same hypothesis:

> There are good reasons to believe that the semantic markers in an adequate descrip-
> tion of a natural language do not represent properties of the surrounding world in the
> broadest sense, but rather certain deep seated, innate properties of the human orga-
> nism and the perceptual apparatus, properties which determine the way in which the
> world is conceived, adapted, and worked on [p. 3].

Relying on this premise, Bierwisch laid out a number of properties in German adjectives which he characterized as "semantic universals." He did not, however, try to specify the "innate properties of the human organism" any further, nor did he try to set down the process by which the child would acquire the spatial terms and thereby manifest the semantic universals. In the language of the present paper, Bierwisch has supplied some of the properties of *L*-space, but none of the properties of *P*-space.

The complexity hypothesis is perhaps of more direct interest to developmental psycholinguists. It posits that the order of acquisition of English spatial terms is constrained by their rules of application. A rule of application is a condition that must be met before a word can be applied to a perceptual event. *Tall*, for instance, can be applied to a dimension only if that dimension is vertical (or canonically vertical, cf. below). More specifically, the complexity hypothesis claims that given two terms *A* and *B*, where *B* requires all the rules of application of *A* plus one or more in addition, *A* will normally be acquired before *B*. One aim of the present paper is to suggest rules of application for some of the English spatial terms and thus to allow the hypothesis to be tested on the pertinent acquisition data.

The complexity hypothesis is obviously a close cousin of Brown and Hanlon's (1970) "cumulative complexity hypothesis." The latter was proposed to account for the order of acquisition of certain complex sentence constructions. Their hypothesis was that given two constructions *A* and *B*, where *B* requires all the syntactic transformations required for *A* and then some, *A* will be acquired before *B*. There are two main differences between the Brown and Hanlon hypothesis and the present one. First, the Brown and Hanlon hypothesis pertains to syntactic forms whereas the present one pertains mainly to particular lexical items. Second, and more important, the Brown and Hanlon hypothesis makes use of transformations and other constructs internal to linguistic theory itself; in contrast, the present hypothesis refers only to the correspondence between lexical items—specifically, spatial or temporal terms—and perceptual events. The rules of application in the latter theory are not simply rules concerning structure internal to the language; they are rules about extension, about meaning. This complete reliance on meaning alone, in fact, might well be a critical defect of the complexity hypothesis, but such a hypothesis is worth pursuing to see just how far it can go in accounting for order of acquisition.

The complexity hypothesis is also not unique. In this volume, E. Clark presents an equivalent hypothesis—the semantic feature hypothesis—which posits that children learn to apply words to perceptual and cognitive events one semantic feature at a time. Because of this, E. Clark's chapter is an important companion piece to the present one. The chapters, in fact, are more complementary to each other than they would first appear. Besides positing a compatible hypothesis, E. Clark lays out an impressive array of data on the child's first words showing that their overextended meanings are based almost exclusively on perceptual features. Although many of these perceptual features are different from and less specific than those to be discussed here, they constitute further evidence for the first correlation hypothesis: The perceptual features in the child's early cognitive development (his *P*-space) are reflected directly in the semantics of his language (his *L*-space).

The present chapter therefore consists of four sections. The first lays out the properties of *P*-space based as completely as possible on physical and biological criteria. The second explores the comparable properties of *L*-space, those properties that underlie English spatial expressions and that can be derived wholly from linguistic considerations. The third section presents some properties of English time expressions; these terms, it is argued, are based on a spatial metaphor, and they therefore contain some of the same properties as the spatial expressions. The final section examines the correlation and complexity hypothesis in more detail, and discusses some of the available evidence for them.

PROPERTIES OF *P*-SPACE

Man is an inhabitant of a world consisting of objects, people, space, and time. And because of his biological makeup, he perceives these objects, people, space and time, and their interrelations in a particular way. These are the conditions under which all speakers of any language have learned to speak and to describe the location of objects. But clearly man's physical and biological environment itself places a large number of constraints—a priori constraints—on how he can describe the location of objects. It is these constraints—the properties of *P*-space—that I want to delve into first, for as we will see, the properties of *P*-space are strikingly close to the properties of the linguistic system (or *L*-space) the speaker of English actually uses in describing the locations of objects in space.

There are a number of ways we could describe the physical location with respect to man. If we were physicists or geometers, we would be inclined to see how physical location might be specified in general. Or, if we were geologists, then we might be more interested in specifying man's location and environment with respect to certain terrestial characteristics—e.g., gravity and the perceived flatness of the earth. Or, if we were biologists, we might want to emphasize that fact that man has the predictable biological characteristics of a human, and these could enter into how we describe man's P-space. And finally, if we were social psychologists, we might be more interested in how man talks and interacts with other people, and in what role these other people might have in specifying his P-space. That is, there are many ways of viewing man, and as we will see, each of them adds to our understanding, eventually, of why at least the English speaker talks about space and time the way he does.

Reference Points, Lines, Planes and Directions

The physicist or geometer would ask, first, about what it means to locate an object in space. In answer, he would probably point out that one object must always be located with respect to other positions in the space, and normally that means with respect to other objects in space. For instance, an object's location can be uniquely defined in three-dimensional space by specifying its distance from each of four other (noncoplanar) locations in space. But this abstract way of specifying location is too clumsy for most purposes, and this has led to the development of reference systems or co-ordinate systems. The advantage of these coordinate systems—for example, the familiar Cartesian coordinate system with its x-, y-, and z-axis—is that they make distances easier to define and, once defined, easier to use. Let us examine the Cartesian coordinate system in more detail and see what its properties are.

Consider how a physicist would specify the location of a point on a straight line, say, the x-axis in a Cartesian coordinate system. By one method, he could set up two points on this line, say zero and one, and then locate the point of interest as five units from zero and four units from one (where the unit is defined as the distance from zero to one). In this instance, he has to specify four things—two reference points and two distances—to locate the point of interest. But in a second and more convenient method, the physicist would first define the x-axis as having a single reference point at the origin, or zero, and as having positive values in one direction from that reference point and negative values in the other. Now he can specify his point of interest simply as five units in the positive direction from zero. Although the two methods are exactly equivalent—in fact, one can be translated directly into the other—the second is more convenient, especially in more than one dimension. The point to be gained here is that in one dimension, location is best defined as a directed distance from a zero reference point.

In two or three dimensions, this type of specification generalizes in a convenient way. In two dimensions, i.e., on the Cartesian x- and y-axes, location is specified by two directed distances, one distance from the reference line designated as the x-axis and the distance from the other reference line designated as the y-axis. In three dimensions, location is specified by directed distances away from the three possible reference planes, the x,y-plane, the x,z-plane, and y,z-plane. To illustrate, we can locate a fly near the corner of a room as being 6 inches (a distance) up (a direction) from the floor (the x,y-plane), 10 inches into the room from the front wall (the x,z-plane), and as 13 inches into the room from the left side wall (the y,z-plane).

The most basic notions in the physicist's specification of location are: (1) reference points, reference lines, and reference planes; and (2) reference directions. Objects are located with respect to other things in space, and these other things can be other (reference) points in the one-dimensional case, reference lines in two dimensions, and reference planes in three dimensions. These reference points, lines, and planes, by simple geometry, define directions. Consider the reference plane. One can always draw a line perpendicular to the reference plane and call it a direction. Furthermore, it will be a signed direction, for distance away from the reference plane on one side will be positive, and on the opposite side, negative. We will see that the notions of reference points, lines, and planes, and their associated signed directions, are basic to our conception of man's P-space.

Gravity and Ground Level

Given the physicist's constraints on how we must specify P-space, the geologist would immediately point out that our planet affords us at least one natural reference plane and associated direction. Consider gravity. It defines a natural direction—verticality—which can be specified locally anywhere on the earth. Furthermore, there is a natural, terrestrial plane of reference—ground level. This reference plane is also found everywhere on the earth, and in any local area, it is normally flat and roughly perpendicular to the vertical, at least enough so that it can be used quite easily as a reference plane. As invariant aspects of man's environment, ground level and gravity can serve as a natural reference plane and reference direction in P-space.

For verticality to be useful, however, it should have a natural positive and negative direction from ground level. The x-axis in the Cartesian coordinate system, for example, has a positive and negative direction from the reference point at zero. Fortunately, gravity helps us to define a natural positive and negative direction, for gravity is asymmetrical, pulling objects in one direction and not the other. At this point, it would be arbitrary to call upward or downward positive, although we will later examine biological

SPACE, TIME, SEMANTICS, AND THE CHILD

reasons why it would be more natural to consider upward positive and downward negative.

Asymmetries of Perceptual Space

When the biologist considers man, he might first note that the human body has bilateral symmetry. The external organs of the body are approximately symmetrical left and right of a vertical plane running through the center of the body. The left eye is matched by the right one, the left ear by the right one, the left arm by the right one, and so on. And there are no other lines or planes of symmetry in the body. So man's *P* space contains only one natural plane of symmetry, the vertical plane separating left and right.

In particular, man has a bilaterally symmetrical perceptual apparatus, including, most prominently, eyes for seeing, ears for hearing, nose for smelling, mouth for tasting, and lips, hands, fingers, and face for sensitive touching. This apparatus makes perception itself bilaterally symmetrical, further helping to define a plane of symmetry through the length of the body separating left and right. Another property of all these senses is that they are most sensitive to stimulation in front of the body, and least sensitive to stimulation in back of the body. The ears, even, have pinnae that are directed forward and not backward. The perceptual apparatus therefore defines a clear plane of *asymmetry*, the vertical plane running through the body separating front from back. Notice that by similar criteria, there is another plane of asymmetry at the base of the feet: Objects above ground level are characteristically visible, audible, smellable, tasteable, and touchable, whereas objects below ground level are not. In short, man's perceptual apparatus alone quite naturally defines three reference planes: one plane of perceptual symmetry (the vertical plane separating left and right) and two planes perpendicular to this plane and to each other about which perception is asymmetrical (the vertical plane separating front from back, and the horizontal plane at ground level).

These facts of perception also suggest how we could assign positive and negative values to the directions away from the two planes of asymmetry. First, since everything in front of the vertical plane is easily perceptible and everything behind it is not, the forward direction can be considered the positive perceptual direction, and backward the negative one, where *positive* is taken in its natural sense to mean the presence of something, and *negative*, the absence. Similarly, since everything above ground level is perceptible and nothing below it is, upward is naturally positive and downward is naturally negative. On the other hand, the reference plane separating left from right is symmetrical, and therefore, there appears to be no reason, at least perceptually, to choose either leftward or rightward as being the positive direction.

Another biological characteristic of man is his bipedal stance. When man is talking or walking, or in general when he is alert and in the optimal position to perceive other objects visually, auditorily, tactually, etc., he will normally be upright. This is what I will call man's canonical position, since it is the position from which he carries out most important activities. Note that when man is in canonical position, the biological vertical coincides with geological vertical (where the biological vertical is simply the intersection of the two vertical reference planes, i.e., the line running from head to feet through the middle of the body). So although it is logically possible for there to be two different verticals in *P*-space—a biological and a geological one—when man is in canonical position, these two verticals reduce to one, thereby simplifying *P*-space considerably. We will see later where the notion of canonical position has several important consequences for language.

The final biological fact to be discussed is that man characteristically moves in a forward direction. That is, he walks in the direction he faces, not to the side or backward. Needless to say, this fact fits in well with man's perceptual apparatus, for he moves in the direction over which he has optimal perceptual regard. So we can also define a front–back dimension in man's biological makeup simply from the characteristic direction in which he moves. And from these considerations forward is again the positive value on the dimension, and backward negative, since movement is normal in the forward direction, and abnormal in the backward direction.

To summarize briefly, the biologist would assert that man's *P*-space contains three natural reference planes. The vertical plane separating left and right is symmetrical biologically so that positive and negative values cannot be attached to the left and right directions in any appropriate way. The vertical plane separating front and back, in contrast, is biologically asymmetrical, with frontward positive and backward negative. And ground level, the third reference plane, is asymmetric with upward positive and downward negative. Biological vertical and ground level are even more convenient as reference planes in *P*-space since when man is in canonical position, they coincide exactly with the geological vertical and ground level.

The Canonical Encounter

From the social psychologist's viewpoint, man is a social animal, who enjoys, perhaps even needs, to interact socially with other people. What are the characteristics of the most usual interaction between two people, John and Mary? For our purposes, the most important property is that they will be facing each other a short distance apart. It is in this position that John and Mary are situated for the optimal perception of messages—both verbal and nonverbal—from the other person. John is in Mary's positive perceptual field, and Mary is in John's. If John and Mary were side by side, or back to back, or back to front, or in any other position, these conditions would no longer be optimal. It is no accident that normal conversations are carried out face-to-face. This face-to-face situation is what I would like to refer to, for convenience, as the canonical encounter. As we will see, the canonical encounter, as another basic property of man's P-space, has some very important consequences in language.

It is also of interest to note how movement occurs in man's social surroundings. First, other people and objects can move into John's field of view. In doing so, they must first be out of view, then come from the distance, and finally approach his position. Characteristically, if the approaching object is another person (say, Mary), she will approach in his forward (positive) field of vision, walking forward, facing him. The final position will be the canonical encounter. Second, John could move and approach other people and objects which are standing still. These objects will at first be out of his sight, and then they would come into view in his positive field of vision—he is walking forward—and finally he would be in a canonical encounter with that object or person. The point to be made from these observations is simply that potential objects to be described come in and out of John's field of vision in a characteristic manner: They enter the field toward John and leave the field away from him.

Summary

We are now in a position to summarize at least the main characteristics of man's P-space. When man is in canonical position, P-space consists of three reference planes and three associated directions: (1) ground level is a reference plane and upward is positive; (2) the vertical left-to-right plane through the body is another reference plane and forward from the body is positive; and (3) the vertical front-to-back plane is the third reference plane and leftward and rightward are both positive directions. Only when man is not in canonical position can we define a geological vertical that is separate from the biological vertical. Finally, there is the notion of canonical encounter, which consists of one man confronted face to face by another man a short distance away.

THE PROPERTIES OF ENGLISH L-SPACE

Having surveyed the properties of man's P-space, we turn to the structure of the L-space of English, the tightly organized semantic structure of English spatial terms. The main concern here will be with adjectives (like *long* and *short*) and prepositions (like *above* and *below*), but we will also have occasion to refer to the many nouns that must be considered spatial too (e.g., *top*, *side*, *front*, etc.). Fortunately, there have been a number of excellent studies recently on English (and related) spatial terms, including Bierwisch's (1967) studies of German spatial adjectives, Teller's (1969) related study of English spatial terms, several chapters in Leech's (1970) book on semantics, and a series of papers and lectures on spatial, temporal, and deictic terms by Fillmore (1967, 1971, and unpublished). Although in this and the following sections I have borrowed freely from these sources, these investigators should not be held responsible for the use to which I have put their evidence, nor for the linguistic evidence and proposals that I have added myself.

General Properties of *L*-Space

Probably the most obvious property of English adjectives and prepositions is that they require the notion "point of reference," following exactly on the definitions of point of reference from the previous discussion of *P*-space. Consider the prepositions *above* and *below*. The sentence *John is above Mary* is a statement of John's position with respect to Mary's position. Her location is taken as the point of reference, and John is being located with respect to her. The same holds for all prepositions in English. In each case, the object of the preposition serves as a reference location—either a point, line, or plane—for locating other objects.

What is less obvious is that the spatial adjectives also require the notion "point of reference": in fact, each adjective has two points of reference. Consider the adjectives *high* and *low*. To say *The balloon is high* (or *low*) is really to say *The balloon is high* (or *low*) *off the ground*. Implicit in such simple statements is a zero point, an origin, the point of reference from which all measurement is taken. *High* and *low* happen to have a particular reference plane—ground level—unless some other reference plane is mentioned explicitly. This origin or zero point could be called the primary point of reference. Adjectives also have a secondary point of reference. *High* and *low*, to continue the example, both refer to height off the ground, but *high* indicates a distance that surpasses some implied standard, and *low* indicates a distance that fails to meet that standard. This standard depends very strongly on what exactly is being measured, as many linguists have pointed out, for one would describe a balloon as high in a room when it was perhaps 6 feet high, but in a large auditorium perhaps only when it was 10 to 20 feet high. The main point here is that *high* has two implicit reference points: ground level (the primary one) and some standard height (the secondary one). *The balloon is high* may therefore be paraphrased as "The balloon is above some standard height from the ground level." Because of these double points of reference, adjectives are more complex than they first appear.

Another basic property of English spatial terms is the notion of direction. Certain adjectives and prepositions in English apply only to certain directions. *High* and *low*, for example, apply only to verticality, and this is derived from the fact that their primary plane of reference is ground level. *Above* and *below* also apply only to verticality. What will be of interest is whether there is any intrinsic positivity or negativity on the directions defined by these adjectival and propositional scales, as there was in *P*-space. As we will see, there is.

To be able to discuss the structure of *L*-space in detail, we will have to refer often to the notion of markedness. In linguistics there are many structural indications that show that one particular form is less complex than another. The general cover term for these differences is markedness: The more complex term is said to be marked with respect to the less complex term. The structural indications of markedness are quite varied. One of the most general is the use of an extra linguistic element in specifying the marked form. For example, *unhappy* would be said to be marked with respect to *happy* since *unhappy* contains the extra prefix *un-*. Another indication is given by Bierwisch: "A sentence is the less normal [is marked] the more conditions outside of it have to be met for it to be acceptable." To give an example, *How tall is Harry?* is a neutral question about Harry's height, whereas *How short is Harry?* asks about Harry's height, but in addition it presupposes that Harry is relatively short. This presupposition is an additional condition outside of the sentence that has to be met, and therefore *short* can be said to be marked with respect to *tall*. In the sections that follow, I will refer to a number of different criteria, mostly taken from Greenberg (1966), all specifying which of two forms is marked. Since not all of these criteria are as transparent as the two I have listed here, one should consult Greenberg (1966) for further justification of the criteria.

The Structure of Nonegocentric *L*-Space

The uses of the spatial terms in English can be divided generally into two categories: those that demand reference to the ego as either a primary or secondary point of reference, and those that do not. In this section, I will consider the second category of uses, what Fillmore has called the non-deictic use of the spatial terms. We will examine the information presupposed in adjectives more carefully and determine some of the points of reference and directions implicit in English *L*-space.

Adjectives

English has only a small number of basic spatial adjectives, but they reveal a number of very important properties about English *L*-space. The adjectives to be examined are: *long–short, far–near, tall–short, high–low, deep–*

shallow, *wide–narrow*, *broad–narrow*, and *thick–thin*. These adjective pairs
define the dimensions length, distance, tallness, height, depth, width,
breadth, and thickness, respectively. Furthermore, the first member of each
pair is unmarked and the second is marked (cf. H. Clark 1969). Note that it
is the first member of each pair that is used as the basis for each scale name.
Thus, one can define a positive direction for the *long–short* scale as extending infinitely in one direction from the primary point of reference, the zero
point of no length. This dimension is called length in English, whereas shortness is defined only with respect to the secondary point of reference. Shortness is a defective scale extending only from that secondary standard in a
negative direction to the zero point, the primary point of reference. Each of
the other scales works in the same way, with the unmarked member of the
pair used as the name of the scale defining the positive direction and as the
term labeling an excess in that direction.

These adjective pairs differ, however, in their conditions of application.
High–low, for example, requires that the object to which the adjectives are
applied be three-dimensional and have a vertical dimension. To say *The
glip is tall* is to presuppose these two conditions about glips. In this sense,
the adjective pairs can be classified into three categories: (1) those that
presuppose objects of at least one dimension; (2) those that presuppose
objects of at least two dimensions; and (3) those that presuppose objects of
at least three dimensions. They can also be classified as to whether they
specify the extent of an object or the position of an object.

Far–near and *long–short* are the two most elementary pairs of adjectives
in that they presuppose only that the object described is at least one-dimensional. The extent of any one-dimensional object—like a line in geometry—
is called its *length*; and one speaks of the *distance* from one point to another.
The difference between *length* and *distance* is that *length* is extensional—it
specifies the extent of an object—whereas *distance* is positional—it specifies
the position of one point with respect to another. As the two most neutral
terms among the spatial adjectives, *length* and *distance* can be used in the
definitions of all the rest.

Tall–short and *high–low* are more complex since they presuppose three-
dimensional objects and require that the dimension they are applied to be
vertical. (Though slightly wrong, this statement will be corrected later.)
Normally, tallness and height cannot be defined unless there is some ground
level usable as a plane or line of reference, and this condition automatically
rules out applications of these terms to objects in only one dimension.
Furthermore, tallness and height show the same extensional–positional split
as do length and distance. Note that *tallness* can be glossed as "vertical
length" and *height*, as "vertical distance," and *high*, for example, means "far
off the ground." As already pointed out, height is always taken with respect

to ground level unless some other reference plane is specified, as in *The balloon is high off the table*. Tallness, too, is always measured from some ground level up, although the base of the object specifies what is to be taken as ground level, as in *The flagpole on top of that building is very tall*. As for the properties of *L*-space, *height* and *tallness* are the first terms to show that *L*-space contains: (1) ground level as a plane of reference, and (2) verticality, the direction perpendicular to ground-level, as a reference direction.

Deep–shallow is the next pair that presupposes a three-dimensional application, and it means, roughly, "distance into something from its surface." That is, an object to which *depth* is applied must be thought of as a container, having a definable surface and an inside dimension. Thus, we can speak of a deep mine, a deep cupboard, a trail deep into the forest, but not of a deep flagpole (meaning "a long flagpole"), a deep window, or a deep tree. Frequently, the earth is taken to be the container, and ground level as the surface, and then *depth* is taken to be the vertical distance downward from ground level. The facts about this vertical *depth*, in fact, show that upward from ground level is unmarked, or positive, and downward is marked, or negative. Note that whereas the extensional and positional terms are separate for dimensions above ground level—*tallness* and *height*, respectively—these two functions are carried by the same term *depth* for dimensions below ground-level. *The mine is fifty feet deep* speaks of the extent of the mine, while *John is fifty feet deep in the mine* specifies John's position. This is a case of syncretism, to use Greenberg's term, indicating that the two senses of *depth* are marked with respect to *tallness* and *height*, respectively. Furthermore, the positional use of *depth* is defective. Whereas the unmarked term *deep* can be used positionally (as in *the deepest level in the mine*), *shallow* cannot (*the shallowest level in the mine*); this should be compared with *high* (*the highest level in the mine*) and *low* (*the lowest level*), both of which can be used positionally. This, by Greenberg's criteria, would be another indication of *depth*'s markedness with respect to *tallness* and *height*. This evidence shows that distance up from ground level is positive, and distance down is negative. This property of *L*-space coincides exactly with the corresponding property of *P*-space.

Not much will be said about the last two pairs, *wide–narrow* (and its close relative *broad–narrow*) and *thick–thin*. Width can generally be applied to objects with two or more dimensions, and *thickness* (in its linear sense), to those with three dimensions. *Width* is a term applied to objects once *tallness* or *length* has applied to the maximal dimension. *Thickness* is generally applied to objects once *tallness*, or *length*, and *width* have been applied to their two maximal dimensions; we speak of a door 6 feet tall, 2 feet wide, and 2 inches thick. Both *width* and *thickness* are normally extensional terms, although *wide*, but not *narrow*, can be used in a positional sense, as in *The arrow*

Table 1 *A Summary of Some Properties of English Spatial Adjectives*

Adjective pair	Extent or position	Number of dimensions	Unmarked point of reference	Dimen-sion
long–short	+ extent	1	ego	length
far–near	+ position	1	ego	distance
tall–short	+ extent	3	ground level	tallness
high–low	+ position	3	ground level	height
deep–shallow	+ extent	3	any surface	depth
deep	+ position	3	any surface	depth
wide–narrow	+ extent	2	a secondary edge	width
wide	+ position	2	a secondary edge	width
broad–narrow	+ extent	2	a secondary edge	breadth
thick–thin	+ extent	3	a tertiary edge	thickness

went wide of the mark. The main point here is that both *width* and *thickness* are marked with respect to *length* and *tallness*, since the former require more conditions to be met before they can be used. The main properties of all these adjectives are summarized in Table 1.

Prepositions

The adjectives of English share many of their properties with prepositions. For example, prepositions contain certain presuppositions about their point of reference—e.g., whether it is one-, two-, or three-dimensional, what types of inherent properties it has, and so on. The prepositions we will be interested in consist of *at, on, in,* and related terms, the pairs *ahead–behind, in front–in back, above–below, over–under, on top of–underneath, up–down,* and certain other pairs.

The most neutral prepositions in English are *at, on,* and *in.* Consider the frame *A is at/on/in B.* All three prepositions assert that *A* is in the same location as *B,* but *at, on,* and *in* presuppose that the location of *B* is a one-, two-, and three-dimensional space, respectively. So, as Fillmore has pointed out, *John is on the grass* treats the grass as a two-dimensional surface, whereas *John is in the grass* treats the grass as a three-dimensional space where John is inside the space with grass all around him. Furthermore, these three positional terms—*at, on,* and *in*—are closely related to the three positive direction terms *to, onto,* and *into,* to the three negative directional terms *from, off (of),* and *out of,* and, as Fillmore has also pointed out, to the three path terms, *via, across,* and *through,* which I have listed in Table 2. It is clear from this table that the following markedness relations hold: First, positionals are unmarked with respect to positive directionals, since the latter are generally formed by adding *to* to the former. Second, the one-dimensional prepositions are unmarked with respect to the two- and three-dimensional prepositions, since the latter are often formed from the former plus an additional morpheme. (This is particularly the case when one considers *of* simply to be a neutralized variant of *from*.) Third, negative directions can be shown to be the negatives of their positive counterparts (cf. Gruber, 1965), and in this sense, positive directionals are unmarked with respect to negative directionals. Thus, *at* appears to be the least complex preposition, and the farther the word is from *at* in this table, generally, the more complex (or marked) it is.

What should we conclude from these facts? The main point, perhaps, is that the most primitive notion in the use of prepositions is punctual location—the positioning of something at a point. This coincides with the physicist's most basic definition of location. The markedness of two- and three-dimensional terms shows that they presuppose more complex properties of the location—that the location is on a surface (for *on*), or within a space (for *in*). Thus the point of reference is simple in one dimension and more complex in more than one dimension, a fact coinciding with the relative simplicity of one-dimensional *distance* and *length* compared to the more-than-one-dimensional *tallness*, *height*, *depth*, and the other adjective scales. Furthermore, the specification of motion, or directionality, with respect to these locations is more complex than the simple locative specification. This also coincides with the physicists definition of motion, which requires the concept of position plus direction.

The directional prepositions have several other revealing properties. Note that a *from*-phrase indicates the beginning of movement and a *to*-phrase indicates a positive direction for the end of movement. Using this information, one can see that the spatial dimensions that were said to have a certain positive direction are consistent with these prepositional uses. One says *height off the ground*, but not **height to the ground*, indicating that groundward is the negative direction for the height dimension. The analogous statements hold for *John is a great distance from (*to) here* and *John is at a great depth from (*to) the surface of the ocean*. Also, it is more natural to specify a location as from *three to six feet up the tree* rather than as *from six to three feet up the tree*. The metaphor here is one of a journey. *Distance,*

Table 2 *Prepositions of Location and of Location + Direction*

Number of dimensions	Location	Positive direction	Negative direction	Path
1	at	to	from	via
2	on	onto	off	across
3	in	into	out of	through

height, and *depth* have their positive directions defined by a metaphorical movement in the positive direction. This fact, too, coincides with the properties of *P*-space: the direction of movement in *P*-space is towards the positive perceptual field.

I next consider what I will call relational prepositions, words like *above–below*, *ahead–behind*, *over–under*, and so on. These indicate location, just like *at*, *on*, and *in*, but they do so by specifying a direction from the point of reference in which the object is located. *Above B*, for example, could be glossed as "at a position in an upward direction from *B*." What is important for our purposes is the direction indicated in these prepositions. Clearly, *above–below*, *over–under*, *on top of–beneath*, etc. presuppose a vertical direction, but this vertical could be defined (1) by direct reference to gravitational vertical; or (2) with reference to the top and bottom sides of the reference object, which are in turn defined (canonically) with respect to gravitational vertical. Even though it is more complex, the second specification appears to be preferable because it will be required for uses of *above–below*, etc., with dimensions not coincident with gravitational vertical, and because it accounts for the explicit reference to top and bottom sides in such terms as *on top of*, *underneath*, *at the bottom of*, etc., which are used as simple prepositions. Furthermore, the second specification fits nicely with the front–back terms—e.g., *in front of–in back of*, *ahead–behind*, *before–after*—which also have to refer to intrinsic properties of the referent objects. To use these terms, one must define the front and back of the point of reference—say, the front and back of a car—and then refer to the space adjacent to the front and back sides as *in front of* and *in back of*, respectively. Unlike the top and bottom, however, the front and back of something can be defined in a number of sometimes conflicting ways. As Fillmore has pointed out, the front is normally the end of the object containing the perceptual apparatus (e.g., dogs, fish, crabs, etc.), or the end that leads when the object is in typical motion (e.g., *in front of the rocket in outer space*), but in some cases these two criteria conflict and one must be chosen as primary (as in *crabs move sideways*).

The relational prepositions vary in the number of dimensions they presuppose of the space their point of reference defines. *In front of–in back of*, *ahead–behind*, and the like presuppose simply a one-dimensional space. One can define the front and back of a point in a single dimension simply by referring to the direction in which the point is moving, although, of course, *front* and *back* can also be defined for three-dimensional objects. These terms, then, are close relatives to *length* and *distance*, which can also be defined in one dimension alone. In contrast, the top and bottom of an object can only be defined in a three-dimensional space, where a ground level and a corresponding vertical are well-defined. Thus, *above–below*, *over–under*, *on top of–underneath*, and the like presuppose a three-dimensional space, just like their close relatives *tallness* and *height*. Furthermore, *beside* presupposes at least two dimensions, since the *side* in *beside* refers to a facet of an object not defined as the front or back, or top or bottom; in this sense, *beside* is like *width* and is applied to a secondary dimension once the primary dimension has been designated. But as we will see later, the use of these prepositions is complicated by the introduction of ego as primary point of reference. The relative simplicity of these terms, therefore, is not exactly comparable to the relative simplicity of the spatial adjectives.

Another point can be made about certain relational prepositions. Consider the definitions of *front* and *back*, and consequently the definitions of *in front of–in back of*, *ahead–behind*, *before–after*, and similar pairs of prepositions. It is *front* that is always defined in a positive way. The front of an object is the facet that contains the perceptual apparatus, as in animals, whereas the back is that facet which does not. The front is the direction towards which an animal moves, and the back is the direction from which an animal moves; front is the positive direction, and back is the negative direction, as discussed above for *to* and *from*. Furthermore, *ahead of* metaphorically indicates positive direction on any scale to which it can be applied, as in *John is ahead of Pete in height* (which means "John is taller than Pete"), *in competence* (which means "John is more competent than Pete"), *in size*, *in weight*, *in intelligence*, and so on. *Back*, on the other hand, is found in many negative constructions, as in *Pete is backward in school*, *John is behind in his work*, etc. In short, *front* and all its prepositional offspring are positive, and *back* and its offspring negative, indicating that *L*-space has a *front–back* dimension that coincides exactly in its asymmetry properties with *P*-space.

Notion of Canonical Position in *L*-Space

The previous discussion of adjectives and prepositions that presuppose a vertical dimension was complicated by the fact that English recognizes two kinds of verticality—geological (or gravitational) and intrinsic. Certain objects are considered to have intrinsic tops and bottoms, just as some objects have intrinsic fronts and backs. Among these objects are bottles, chairs, tables, people, some boxes, doors, desks, and buildings. The tops and bottoms are not defined relative to gravity, for, even if a bottle, for instance, were on its side, we could speak of a fly on the top of the bottle, meaning "on the side with the opening." Indeed, tops and bottoms in these cases appear to be defined relative to a canonical position, the upright position. Bottles, chairs, tables, people, and so on are normally found in a particular position, and tops and bottoms are defined by gravitation relative to this position. One striking example of this phenomenon is the convention for measuring the head-to-toe length of people in English. One speaks of very young babies, whose canonical position is *not* upright, as "18 inches *long*," yet of adults whose canonical position *is* upright, as "72 inches *tall*." Also, one does not speak of a girl lying on a beach as "5 feet long," even though she is not in an upright position: We automatically speak of her height *as if* she were in canonical position. In yet another example, Herb Caen (*San Francisco Chronicle*, November 18, 1969) reported a story about a Bank of America vice-president who was asked what would happen to the Bank of America Building in an earthquake three times as strong as the strongest quake ever recorded. The vice-president is said to have replied, "Then, instead of having the tallest building in town, we'll have the longest."

The distinction between gravitational top–bottom (the top and bottom sides defined by an object's present position) and intrinsic top–bottom (the top and bottom defined by canonical position) often leads to ambiguities. If a chair is on its side, then one can say, "There is a fly on top of the chair," no matter whether the fly is on the gravitional top or the intrinsic top. The sentence "There is a fly on *the* top of the chair," however, seems to refer only to the intrinsic top. Furthermore, to the girl lying on the beach, one could say, "There is a fly three inches above your knee," and this could be taken to mean either "There is a fly flying three inches vertically from your knee" or "There is a fly on your leg three inches headward from your knee." In short, canonical position plays an important role in the application of English prepositions to certain types of objects.

The Structure of Egocentric Space

When the speaker and/or addressee is included in the specification of English spatial terms, their structure becomes more complicated. Yet, significantly enough, the structure becomes complicated in a direction quite compatible with the properties of *P*-space, for it is at this point that the canonical encounter and other *P*-space properties also appear in *L*-space.

The introduction of the speaker or ego into these specifications means that the ego is now able to serve as a point of reference, and English makes considerable use of this factor. As I pointed out above, the positional adjectives *high*, *low*, and *deep* have a naturally defined plane of reference (ground level) which is inferable whenever no other plane of reference is specified explicitly or by context. As for *distance*, it is the ego that serves as the point of reference in unmarked cases. Consider the sentence *San Francisco is far*. This implies that San Francisco is far from here or from me. The same point of reference is found in variants of this sentence, e.g., *It is far to San Francisco, San Francisco is far away, San Francisco is 30 miles away*, and so on.

The ego is also often taken as the primary point of reference for *length*, the extensional counterpart of *distance*. Recall that *length* is applied to the primary dimension of an object, while *width* is applied to the secondary dimension. When ego is involved, the question is, what is the primary dimension? Evidence shows that the primary dimension is taken as the one running forward from ego, with ego as the primary point of reference. Consider objects toward which ego has a conventional orientation. People normally face desks, sit on couches and in chairs, face stoves, and so on. The *width* of each of these objects in considered to be the dimension running from side-to-side while ego is in this conventional position. The side-to-side dimension must have been considered secondary, then, to the front–back dimension. Unfortunately, in many objects, the front–back dimension is shorter than the side-to-side dimension, and since there is another rule that states that *length* should be applied to the nonegocentrically longer dimension, we tend not to call this dimension *length*; in couches, for example, it would be confused with the width, the longer dimension. Instead, we use a term like *depth* which is also acceptable. Notice that nonegocentrically, a couch would be described as 10 feet long and 3 feet wide, but when the egocentric viewpoint is taken it is described as 10 feet wide and 3 feet deep. (As we will see, this difference between egocentric and nonegocentric points of view will cause ambiguities again and again in English spatial descriptions.) The main point, nevertheless, is that the ego enters into the specification of length and width, serving as the point of reference for length and thereby defining width as the secondary side-to-side dimension.

In prepositions, the introduction of the speaker and the addressee has even more significant consequences. Note, first, that ego could only have an effect on the relational prepositions, since the others make no reference to directions. And the most important consequences occur in the words referring to *front* and *back*. Again, these prepositions, when used without specific points of reference, implicitly refer to ego as the point of reference, unless context indicates otherwise. *San Francisco is ahead* means "San Francisco is ahead of me" (or of here); and this is also true of *San Francisco is ten miles ahead*, *San Francisco is ten miles behind*, etc.

The use of *front* and *back* to refer to objects without specifiable fronts and backs, however, requires the notion of the canonical encounter. If the speaker is looking at a ball and a fly across the room, he can say: *The fly is in front of the ball.* By this he means, "The fly is between the ball and me." Since the ball has no front or back, we are forced to the following conclusion on the application of these words: the speaker treats such an object *as if* it were the other person in a canonical encounter, a person facing directly towards the speaker. Once we assume this principle of application, all sentences like *The fly is in front of the ball*, *The ball is in back of the tree*, etc., become explicable. It should be noted that, in general, the nearer side of such a point of reference is the positive side, since that is the side that will always remain unobscured by the point of reference. In this sense, the application of the positive *in front of* is quite consistent with its other applications. Finally, it is important to note that *this side* and *the other side* (of, say, a tree) have the same properties: *the other side* specifies that side negatively by saying that it is the side that is *not* assumed to be primary.

In English, therefore, there are two fronts and backs: (1) an inherent front and back, as of a car, person, rocket, or whatever; and (2) an egocentric front and back, that defined by the canonical encounter. Unfortunately, these two uses do not always coincide, and when they do not, they can cause considerable problems in communication. Consider a speaker standing not far from the side of a car who announces: *There is a ball in front of the car*. This statement is ambiguous between an inherent meaning of *front* ("the ball is near the front bumper of the car") and an egocentric reading ("the ball is between the car and me"). Someone else looking for the ball would search two quite different areas depending on how he interpreted the description.

Two other egocentric prepositions are *beside* and *beyond*. When used egocentrically, *beside* requires the notion of canonical encounter. One can say, *The ball is beside the tree*, and this would mean that the ball is to the left or right of the tree from the speaker's point of view. The side of the tree is defined in this instance as a facet of the tree not covered by the terms *front* and *back*. If the tree is viewed as an object in canonical encounter, then this definition of *side* can be seen as the one transferred from the nonegocentric definition of *side*.

Beyond is one of the most complex prepositions in English, for it always demands the specification of two points of reference, not just one. Consider *A is beyond B*. Implicit in this sentence is a more primary reference point *C*, such that the sentence means "*A* is on the far side of *B* from the point of view of *C*." Normally, *C* is taken to be the speaker, so that *The ball is beyond the fence* means that it is on the other side of the fence from the speaker. In other cases, however, *C* can be made explicit, as in *The ball is beyond the fence from you*.

Finally, it should be noted that *to the left of* and *to the right of*, when used egocentrically, do *not* follow the proper rules of canonical encounter. If one says, *Mary is to the right of the tree*, one would mean "Mary is on the right with respect to me." One does not take the view of the tree, decide what is left and right in that position, and then reverse the application of *left* and *right* as one should. The reason for this failure to reverse is not clear. Perhaps it is because the left and right directions in space are symmetrical, so the terms are difficult to apply to objects in a canonical encounter. We have no trouble with the asymmetrical pairs *top–bottom* and *front–back* in this situa-

Table 3 *Some Prepositions of Location + Relation*

Nonegocentric, nonintrinsic prepositions
  three-dimensional:
    above–below
    on top of–underneath
    over–under

Nonegocentric, intrinsic prepositions
  one-dimensional:
    in front of–in back of
    ahead of–behind
  three-dimensional (requires canonical position):
    above–below
    on top of–underneath
    over–under
  two-dimensional:
    beside
    at the left of–at the right of

Egocentric, nonintrinsic prepositions (requires canonical encounter)
  one-dimensional:
    in front of–in back of
    ahead–behind
    beyond
  two-dimensional:
    beside

---

tion, because their criteria for application are intrinsic to the asymmetries in the situation. But *left* and *right*, even in their normal use, are applied under fairly arbitrary criteria; the reversal of this application in a canonical encounter would seem unnecessarily complex.

The properties of English prepositions are summarized in rough form in Table 3.

Deixis

The asymmetries of *L*-space are also seen in the deictic words *here* and *there*, and *this* and *that*. Note first that *there* and *here* can be paraphrased, approximately, as "the far place" and "the near place," respectively. Of course, *far* and *near* here are being used egocentrically, for *far place* means, more specifically, "the place far from me," and *near place* means "the place near to me." Since *far* and *near* are the positive and negative terms on the dimension of distance, one should expect, likewise, for *there* to be unmarked and *here* to be marked. And this is the case. The difference between *there* and *here* can be seen in *There are three men there in the room* and *There are three men here in the room*. The first *there* is used in English exclusively for existential statements and is a neutral specification of location. To say that something exists is to say that it is to be found at some location, *there*. The other *there* and the *here*, on the other hand, specify locations with respect to the speaker of the sentence. In other words, *there* is the only term that can be used neutrally for location, and this indicates that it is the unmarked or positive term. Similar arguments have been made (cf. Kuroda, 1968) for the markedness of *this* with respect to *that*. In brief, the deictic terms follow the same pattern as do the other adjectives in English: the term specifying distal location with respect to the speaker is considered unmarked vis-à-vis the proximal term.

Summary of *L*-Space

English spatial terms, therefore, reveal that *L*-space has properties that are identical with those of *P*-space. First, *L*-space shows the universal use of points, lines, and planes of reference, both in prepositions, where there is one or two, and in adjectives, where there are two. Second, there are three specific primary planes of reference: (1) ground level, with upward positive and downward negative; (2) the vertical left–right plane through the body, with forward positive and backward negative; and (3) the vertical front–back plane of symmetry through the body, with right and left both equally positive.[2] Third, *L*-space requires the use of canonical position to define uses of vertical expressions for dimensions that do not coincide with gravitational vertical. And fourth, *L*-space requires the notion of canonical encounter to account for the egocentric uses of terms like *front* and *back*. The coincidence of these properties with those of *P*-space is obvious.

TIME AS A SPATIAL METAPHOR

For a long time, linguists have noted that the spatial and temporal terms in English and other related languages overlap considerably. On this evidence, furthermore, it can be argued that the description of time in English is based on quite a specific spatial metaphor. That is, it is possible to describe a second level of *L*-space that is found in time expressions and to show that this level is identical to, and therefore derived from, the first level of *L*-space that we have just examined. In this section, therefore, I will sketch out at least some of the main properties of this important metaphor.

---

[2] In this paper, I ignore the secondary asymmetries of *left* and *right* that appear to be the result of the fact that man is normally right-handed. This symmetry appears to be of quite a different character, since it does not have reflexes in the adjectives as do the other asymmetries. Nevertheless, the asymmetry is compatible with the main thesis of this paper, since the positive connotation of *right* is derived ultimately from an innate biological asymmetry.

The physicist views time in his theories as a one-dimensional continuum with asymmetrical properties. In this sense, the time axis is like the x-, y-, or z-axes in that it is linear, can be given an arbitrary zero point, and is asymmetrical about this zero point. The asymmetry of time is obvious in such phenomena as chemical reactions, which work in one direction only, in entropy, which always increases with time, and in memory, which contains the past but not the future. Furthermore, the physicist does not require time to enter into his equations unless he is describing something with a history, with dynamic properties, with motion. These properties need not be belabored, for they have been discussed by physicists and philosophers for centuries.

What kind of a spatial metaphor would be appropriate for time, given that it has these properties? First, because time is one-dimensional, it ought to be described using one-dimensional spatial terms—that is, terms that do not presuppose two or three dimensions for their application. The appropriate adjectives are *long–short* and *far–near*, and these are certainly used in temporal expressions—e.g., *Time was short, The day has been long, The end of the world is near,* and *Monday seems so far away.* The inappropriate adjectives include *wide–narrow, tall–short, high–low, deep–shallow,* etc., and these apparently do not occur in productive time expressions in English. The same one-dimensional constraint is satisfied in the spatial prepositions. Note that all the positional and most of the directional prepositions can be used on one spatial dimension, as in *at a point, on a line, in an interval on the line, to or from a point, between two points, through an interval,* etc., and the same expressions apply to time, as in *at noon, on Monday, in the afternoon on Monday, up to noon, from Monday, between noon and six, through Thursday,* etc.

Second, because time is asymmetrical or directed, it ought to be described with one-dimensional relational prepositions which are, in addition, asymmetrical. As we noted above, the *front–back* prepositions are the only ones in English that do not presuppose more than one dimension in the space they describe; futhermore, they have the happy property that they are asymmetrical, with front positive and back negative. Significantly, the only relational prepositions used for time in English are those derived from *front* and *back*, i.e., *before, after, ahead, behind, in front, in back,* etc. English does not use relational terms derived from *top–bottom,* except in very specialized terms like *over the weekend,* where *over* is probably derived from its use in spatial expressions like *over the line segment,* a linear expression without vertical properties. Nor does English use *left of* and *right of* in temporal expressions. The generalization here seems significant: the asymmetry of time is expressed in English in the simplest possible way with *front–back* terms that presuppose only one dimension.

Third, because time is required only for events with dynamic properties, time ought also to be described by expressions that involve motion through space. This, too, is the case in English, as in such expressions as *Noon has come, Thursday has gone by, through Tuesday into Tuesday night, five o'clock came up on us before we knew it*, etc.

What Is the Metaphor?

Given this introduction into the spatial metaphor of time, let us consider its exact form. Time can be viewed as a highway consisting of a succession of discrete events. We humans are seen in one of two ways with respect to this highway: either (1) we are moving along it, with future time ahead of us and the past behind us; or (2) the highway is moving past us from front to back. These two metaphors might be called the *moving ego* and *moving time* metaphors, respectively.

First, consider the moving time metaphor. As this highway moves from front to back, we describe events appropriate to this metaphor: future events are *coming* events; past events have *come* and *gone by*, are *past* events (= events that have passed), are *bygone* events, are things that happened a while *ago* (ago = gone). Although these particular expressions are relatively frozen, the metaphor is nonetheless productive, as can be seen in *Noon crept up on us, Friday arrived before we knew it, Thursday rushed by, Time flew by*, and so on.

Perhaps the most interesting terms that derive from the moving time metaphor are those used to describe priority in time. Consider *before* and *after*, two spatial prepositions that have now come to be almost exclusively used in a temporal sense. In their use as prepositions, *before* (= in front of) means "pastward of" and *after* (= in back of) means "futureward of," as in *John left before noon, Mary left after midnight*, etc. Their use as conjunctions is derived from this prepositional usage. It can be shown (E. Clark, 1969; McKay, 1968) that *John left before Mary arrived* is derived from *John left before the time at which Mary arrived*, in which *before* is explicitly used as a temporal preposition. The same meanings are found in *ahead* and *behind*, as in *Mary arrived ahead of time, John left behind schedule*, etc. The moving time metaphor gives a nice account for the meanings of these expressions. Expressions like *ahead of noon* or *before noon* attribute to noon a front and a back. If time is viewed as moving pastward, then the front face of noon is the one that leads and is directed pastward, and the back face is the one that follows and is directed futureward. Thus, *ahead of noon* and *before noon* take on just the right interpretation, namely, "pastward of noon." *Ahead of*, furthermore, is an expression which, when used spatially, generally implies that the object of the preposition can move or is moving in a forward direction; one can say, *John was standing ahead of my car*, but not *John was standing ahead of my house*. That *ahead of* can also be used temporally, then, is further indication that time is viewed as moving pastward.

There are other expressions for temporal priority that derive from the equations *frontward* = "pastward" and *backward* = "futureward." As spatial terms, *precede* and *follow* mean "go in front of" and "go in back of," respectively, *Pre-*, the Latin prefix meaning "in front of," appears in all sorts of expressions in the sense of "pastward of," e.g., *previous, prediction, precursor, preheat, preprint*, etc. Similarly, *post-* means literally "in back of," but figuratively, "futureward of," as in *postpone, postwar, postelection*, etc. The Anglo-Saxon terms *fore* and *after* have similar meanings, as in *forethought, afterthought, foreknowledge, forecast, aftertaste*, etc. More such examples are easy to find.

The moving ego metaphor has quite different consequences. If the ego is seen as moving along a sequence of events, then words like *ahead, behind, in front*, and *in back* should refer to the ego's, not the event's, front and back, since ego is moving now and not the events. That this is so can be seen in such expressions as *Trouble lies ahead, The worst of it is behind us, We are just coming into troubled times, I look forward to Monday, John will be here from Monday on(ward)*, etc.

The moving ego and moving time metaphors, it should be noted, have exactly contradictory equations: for moving ego, the equations are *front* = "future" and *back* = "past", whereas for moving time, the equations are *front* = "past" and *back* = "future." In certain instances, this contrast can be seen quite clearly. Compare *We will be in Paris in the days ahead (of now)*, that is, "in the days future to today," and *We will be in Paris in the days ahead of Christmas*, that is, "in the days pastward to Christmas." The difference between these two expressions is that the first takes the ego as its reference point, so it requires application of the moving ego equations, whereas the second takes Christmas as its reference point, so it requires the moving time equations. It appears that every use of the moving ego and moving time equations is correlated with just such a difference in point of view, although this is still a speculation that remains to be verified in full.

Time descriptions do make use of terms that are not locative, yet these terms evince properties that are in harmony with the locative-based terms. First, consider the trio of adjectives *soon, early*, and *late*. Just as *high* and *low*, for example, are closely related to *above* and *below, early* and *late* are akin to *before* and *after* (cf. Geis, 1970) in the moving time metaphor. *Early* means something like "before the standard moment" and *late* means "after the standard moment," where the standard moment is a point of reference taken as the dividing point between *early* and *late*. *Soon* also contrasts with *late* in certain contexts and, like *early*, it means "before the standard moment"; for *soon*, however, the standard moment and the event described must be future to the speaker's point of reference. Following Greenberg's criteria for marking, then, *early* and *soon* are unmarked (or positive) with respect to *late*, since the *early–soon* distinction is syncretized in *late*. The positive nature of temporal priority in *early–soon* parallels the positive nature of *before, ahead of, in front of*, etc., in the spatial prepositions. The parallels here are striking, although it is mysterious why there are no spatial adjectives corresponding to *early, soon*, and *late*.

Next consider *old–young* (or equivalently *old–new*). *Old* has two senses, one extensional and one positional. Extensional *old* is seen in *That man is old*, and positional *old*, in *I long for the old times we had*. In this sense, positional *old* is analogous to *long–short*, and extensional *old*, to *far–near*. Furthermore, *old* is unmarked with respect to *new* and *young*, and so even the marking relations coincide with those locative terms.

Finally, time, like space, also has its ego-centered deictic expressions. Just as *there* and *here* mean "at that place" and "at this place," *then* and *now* mean "at that time" and "at this time." Of course, the expressions *at that time* and *at this time* must be accounted for, too. Imagine the time line (the highway of events) with a point on it labeled "the present moment." Spatially, one would speak of events occurring proximally and distally with respect to that point using *that* and *this*, respectively. The same relations hold temporally. *Then* normally refers to events temporally distal from the speaker's present time, and *now* refers to events that are temporally proximal. Previously, we noted that *there* is unmarked with respect to *here* in that *there* neutralizes in certain contexts. *Then* appears to have the same property, for it also neutralizes in various timeless expressions (e.g., *If x is 6, then the equation is false*), whereas *now* does not. As an expression meaning "at that time," *then* can refer to either the future (*I will do it then*) or the past (*I did it then*), but in either case, it is distal and contrasts with *now*.

To summarize briefly, English descriptions of time appear to be based on a spatial metaphor in which time is viewed as a single dimensional, asymmetric continuum, running horizontally from front to back through the speaker. Furthermore, there appear to be two (not incompatible) movement metaphors: (1) the moving time metaphor views events as moving forward (pastward) past a stationary ego, and (2) the moving ego metaphor views the speaker as moving forward (futureward) past stationary events. These two metaphors give rise to two quite different uses of the relational prepositions derived from *front* and *back*. The spatial terms, as we have observed before, exhibit certain asymmetries of usage—as shown in the marking relations— and these asymmetries appear to transfer to the spatial metaphor of time. This is seen particularly in the terms used exclusively for time (e.g., *early, late, soon, old, new, then, now*, etc.), whose marking relationships are consistent with the spatial metaphor.

PSYCHOLOGICAL IMPLICATIONS

After first examining the properties of P-space, L-space, and English time expressions, we return to a consideration of the two main hypotheses considered at the beginning, the *correlation hypothesis* and the *complexity hypothesis*.

The Correlation Hypothesis

In the previous sections, evidence was brought forward to demonstrate that P-space and L-space had virtually the same properties: both required points, lines, and planes of reference; both revealed the same three specific planes of reference with the same positive and negative directions from them; both exhibited the notions of canonical position and canonical encounter; and so on. This evidence alone constitutes strong support for the correlation hypothesis, namely that there should be a strong correlation between P-space and L-space. The correlation hypothesis itself, however, remains somewhat mysterious, for little has been said about what might mediate this correlation. Recall that the main thesis of the paper is that the child is forced to make use of the P-space in learning the semantics of spatial terms in English. But how exactly does it follow from this thesis that P-space should be directly reflected in L-space?

The easiest way to answer this question is to imagine what would happen if the child attempted to learn a language that did not conform nicely to P-space. A term with rules of application that referred to natural dimensions of P-space will be learned easily, and therefore early, by children, but a term whose rules of application did not refer to any concept the child knew would, according to the thesis of the paper, be impossible to learn. But consider several intermediate cases. First, let us define the preposition *vig*, as in *vig the ball*, to mean "in an upward, leftward, and egoward diagonal direction from." *Vig*'s rules of application are complex in that they do not refer to natural directions in P-space. It should therefore be very difficult for children to learn and difficult too for adults to apply correctly. It should become rarer over generations of speakers (unless it has some especially important function to fill) and could well become extinct. As a second instance, let us examine a case more aptly described as an exception. Imagine that *deep* and *shallow* referred to objects in the reverse of English—*deep* referring to shallow things and *shallow* referring to deep things—but yet the name for their superordinate dimension was still *depth*. The child learning the triplet *deep-shallow-depth* would find this exception difficult to learn, since the positive term—*shallow*—would not double as the dimension name —*depth*—as in all other such English triplets. Because this triplet constitutes an exception, the child might mistakenly but consistently use the term *shallowness* for the dimensional name, and this would tend to make the term *depth* drop out and the system come to equilibrium. Or the child might switch around the terms *deep* and *shallow* to bring about the same equilibrium. In either case, the child's difficulties would have the effect of bringing the semantic system in closer conformity to *P*-space.

The internal structure of *L*-space must be consistent not only with *P*-space, but also with the semantics of the remainder of English. As English is constructed now, for example, the name of each adjective dimension is taken from the positive member of the adjective pair defining the dimension; *length* comes from *long*, *depth* from *deep*, *height* from *high*, and so on. Consider altering this rule so that the dimension name is derived from the negative member instead. The scale names would thereby become *nearness*, *shortness*, *lowness*, etc. The argument is that the child would have great difficulty learning such a system, consistent and thorough as it is, for it is incompatible with the rest of English. Note that for other nonspatial adjectives the *neutral* dimensional names are always derived from the unmarked or positive adjective, as can be seen in the triplets *efficiency–efficient–inefficient*, *happiness--happy–unhappy*, *ability–able–unable*, etc. Given that *P*-space indicates that extent is positive and lack of extent is negative, *long*, *deep*, *far*, and so on will be taken to be positive. If the child generalizes from other English dimension names, then he will take *length* to be the proper name for *long–short*, not *shortness* as our example would have it. If a case like this ever arose, it would certainly evolve into a more regular pattern, with the spatial adjectives coming into line with the rest of English. This example shows that the child is subject to constraints both from *P*-space and the rest of English, all of which conspire to bring *L*-space into conformity with *P*-space.

Finally, the correlation hypothesis implies that since *P*-space is a human universal, it should condition *L*-space in every language. The *L*-space of each language should therefore exhibit properties that are consistent with the *P*-space as briefly described in this paper. This hypothesis does not imply that each language should have the same spatial terms (except for translation) or terms drawn from the same small inventory of spatial terms. Rather, the hypothesis implies that the possible rules of application—those spatial conditions presupposed by the spatial terms—should be universal. Since these rules of application can be combined in a number of different ways, many systems will be consistent with *P*-space. Significantly, the few spatial systems of other languages that I am at all acquainted with appear to be very similar to the English *L*-space (cf. Greenberg, 1966; Bierwisch, 1967).

The Complexity Hypothesis

This hypothesis is that given two terms *A* and *B*, where *B* requires all the rules of application of *A* plus one or more in addition, *A* will normally be

SPACE, TIME, SEMANTICS, AND THE CHILD

acquired before *B*. To see how this hypothesis would be applied, consider *in*, *into*, and *out of*, and a very preliminary specification of their rules of application. The correct spatial use of *in* presupposes simply (1) that its object denote an enclosed three-dimensional space. *Into* presupposes (1) too, but in addition, it presupposes (2) that the subject of the preposition is moving in one diréction and (3) that that direction is positive—i.e., in the direction of the space denoted by the object. *Out of* presupposes (1), (2), and (3), but as an implicit negative it specifies (4) that the direction of motion is not positive. These rules are given in Table 4. If these rules are the correct ones for *in*, *into*, and *out of*, then the complexity hypothesis predicts that these terms will be acquired in their correct use in this order.

From this introduction, we can determine some of the specific predictions this hypothesis would make.

(1) In antonymous pairs, the positive member should be acquired before the negative member. This has just been illustrated in the *into–out of* example. The notion is that the positive member specifies the assumed normal direction or relation, and the negative member specifies its direction or relation by negating the assumed one. With *into* and *out of*, the normal direction is toward the space denoted by the object, and *out of*, the negative, specifies its direction of motion by negating that assumed direction. For another case, consider *A above B* and *B below A*. Both presuppose a vertical relation, and as we have seen, the assumed relation is with the point of reference below the object being located, since upward from a point of reference is positive. Thus *A above B* need not specify the relation, other than to say it is the assumed relation; *B below A* must negate the assumed relation, and this requires an extra rule of application. The prediction of asymmetry in antonymous pairs, then, should apply to the adjectives *far–near, long–short, high–low, tall–short, deep–shallow, wide–narrow, thick–thin*, and others, to the directional prepositions *to–from, into–out of, onto–off*, and to the relational

Table 4 *Illustrative Rules of Application for* in, into, *and* out of

Preposition	Rules of application
A in B	(1) B denotes a three-dimensional enclosed space.
A into B	(1) B denotes a three-dimensional enclosed space. (2) A is moving in one direction. (3) The direction is positive.
A out of B	(1) B denotes a three-dimensional enclosed space. (2) A is moving in one direction. (3) The direction is positive. (4) Rule (3) is not the case.

prepositions *above–below, on top of–underneath, up–down, over–under, ahead–behind, in front of–in back of, before–after,* and so on. As we will see, this prediction has much support.

(2) If the above characterization of *in, into,* and *out of* is correct, then the location prepositions *at, on,* and *in,* should be acquired earlier than their correlative location plus direction prepositions *to, onto,* and *into.*

(3) The relational prepositions *above, below, in front of,* etc. all require two notions: the notion of location, as expressed by *at, on,* or *in*; and the notion of relation, where the location is related to something else, as being *above it,* or *beside it,* etc. Thus, these relational prepositions should enter the child's vocabulary after the simpler locational prepositions *at, in,* and *on.*

(4) The application of spatial terms to a secondary dimension requires that the primary dimension (like *height* or *length*) be already specified. Therefore, those terms that refer to a secondary dimension—*wide–narrow, broad–narrow,* and *beside*—should be acquired after those terms that refer to primary dimensions—*long–short, tall–short, above–below,* etc. Those requiring both primary and secondary dimensions (e.g., *thick–thin*) should be acquired still later.

(5) It was noted earlier that as adjectives referring to vertical position or extent, *high–low* and *tall–short,* are unmarked or positive with respect to *deep–shallow.* Therefore, the former should be acquired before the latter.

There are certain predictions that the complexity hypothesis seems to make which nevertheless do not hold up on closer examination. Consider the question of whether the prepositions presupposing verticality (e.g., *above–below, on top of–underneath,* etc.) are acquired before or after those presupposing only one dimension (e.g., *ahead of–behind, in front of–in back of,* etc.). At first, one might predict that the one-dimensional prepositions should be acquired before the three-dimensional ones. After all, one is less than three. But the one-dimensional prepositions require knowledge about the direction of motion of objects, whereas the three-dimensional ones require knowledge about geologial verticality. These two types of knowledge are not comparable, and a prediction about the priority of one over the other would seem unwarranted without other information about what the child knows.

Time

In English, time expressions are based directly on a spatial metaphor, and they therefore also fall into the jurisdiction of the correlation and complexity hypotheses. The correlation hypothesis is immediately confirmed if each temporal term can be shown to be based on a spatial term, and each spatial term in turn, on *P*-space. Insofar as evidence has been presented for these two conditions, the correlation hypothesis is upheld for the time expressions. The complexity hypothesis makes the same predictions for the temporal terms as for the corresponding spatial terms; for example, positive adjectives and prepositions in the time realm should come in before negative ones, just as they should in the space realm. But the complexity hypothesis makes one additional prediction. Since time is a spatial metaphor, the use of a term to denote time must have been preceded by the use of the comparable term to denote space. In general, therefore, spatial expressions should appear before time expressions, and in particular, each term that can be used both spatially and temporally should be acquired in its spatial sense first.

It is interesting to speculate about how the time–space correlation might be learned by the child. Consider the moving time metaphor. It could begin by the child noting that certain spatial and temporal relations are correlated. If John is walking *in front of* Mary toward ego, then John will arrive *before* Mary arrives; the event of John's arrival will occur before the event of Mary's arrival. Note that this analysis depends only on the fact that events are usually defined by movement and that events come upon the ego by their moving into his perceptual field. The definitions of *in front of, ahead of, before*, and so on then immediately specify the correlation. The moving ego metaphor works analogously. The ego can come upon events by moving in a forward direction, and in that case, the ego can say, "John's dancing is in front of me," which would change from the *place* of John's dancing to the *event* of John's dancing. At present, although these accounts are merely speculations, their plausibility makes it seem worthwhile to pursue them further.

Evidence for the Complexity Hypothesis

Evidence from Adults

Although the complexity hypothesis does not apply to adults, a closely related hypothesis, not specified so far, does. This *comprehension hypothesis* might be stated as follows: the less complex of two expressions, as defined by the complexity hypothesis, should be comprehended more quickly than the other. This thesis, essentially a generalization of the "principle of lexical marking" in H. Clark (1969), has a considerable amount of support.

First, positive terms are comprehended more easily than negative terms. In studies on comparative adjectives, this has been shown for the spatial pairs *far–near, long–short, tall–short, high–low, deep–shallow* and *thick–thin*, for *big–little* and *much–little*, if these are considered spatial, and the temporal pairs *early–late* and *old–young* (cf. H. Clark, 1969; in press, for the specifics). The advantage of positive over negative has also been noted for the directional prepositions *to–from* and *into–out of* and for the relational prepositions *above–below, on top of–underneath, ahead–behind, in front of–in back of,* and *before–after*; the last two terms were used as temporal prepositions (cf. H. Clark, in press, for details). The consistency of this finding across such a range of adjective and preposition pairs is impressive and adds considerable weight to the hypothesis.

Second, in two other studies, it was found that *higher* and *lower* are comprehended more quickly than *deeper* and *shallower*. In one study (Troyer, 1971), people were given sentences like *If John is deeper/lower in the well than Mary, then who is farther from the top?*, which they were to answer as quickly as possible. And in the second study (H. Clark & Peterson, unpublished), people were asked to verify sentences like *Star is deeper/lower than plus* against a picture of a star and plus at different heights. *Height* was easier to cope with than *depth* in both studies, and this is consistent with the finding both in *P*-space and *L*-space that *height* is positive with respect to *depth.*

Evidence from Children

Children, it is well known, show different facilities in producing and comprehending sentences, since they are often able to comprehend something they cannot produce. Furthermore, there is no guarantee that what should be acquired first in comprehension should also be acquired first in production. So there is a fundamental problem with the application of the complexity hypothesis to the child: does it apply to comprehension or production? The hypothesis itself was stated neutrally with respect to this question, but before it can be tested, some decision must be made. For reasons to be elaborated, I will take the hypothesis as applying mainly to comprehension.

Although there has been relatively little work on the comprehension of particular lexical items, especially spatial expressions, what there is supports the complexity hypothesis. First, the correct comprehension of antonymous adjectives and prepositions has been found to occur earlier for the positive members of each pair than for the negative members. Donaldson and Wales (1970), using a simple comprehension task, found this to be true for the comparative pairs *more–less, bigger–wee-er, longer–shorter, thicker–thinner, higher–lower,* and *taller–shorter,* as well as for the superlatives of these same forms. In a similar study, Tashiro (1971) supported this generalization even for adjectives in their uninflected noncomparative form: *tall–short, long–short, wide–narrow, thick–thin, big–little,* and *large–small.* In most cases, when the child misunderstood the negative form, he did not simply refuse to carry out the comprehension task set before him; rather, he usually indicated, with considerable confidence, the response that was appropriate to the positive term. In this sense, the child could be said to know all the rules for the positive term, but not the extra rule for the correct application of the negative term. These data support the notion that the child acquires the rules of application one at a time; the same point is argued in this volume by E. Clark in support of her semantic hypothesis. (For more detailed discussion of the Donaldson and Wales data, see H. Clark, 1970a.)

The same positive–negative generalization holds for spatial and temporal prepositions as well. Bem (1970) asked children to place objects into arrays of items, and in doing so, she used the prepositions *on top of* and *underneath*. She found (personal communication) that the positive preposition (*on top of*) was comprehended correctly by more children than the negative (*underneath*). E. Clark (1971a), in a study on the comprehension and production of the temporal prepositions *before* and *after*, found the comparable result: *before* was understood correctly at an earlier age than *after*. She also noted that some children appeared to take *after* to mean the same thing as *before*, and from this evidence, she concluded that for these children *before* and *after* had the same semantic features, or the same rules of application; later, a feature was added to *after* to give it the appropriate meaning. This evidence again is consistent with the complexity hypothesis.

The complexity hypothesis also predicts that the primary adjectives *tall–short* and *long–short* will be understood correctly before the secondary adjectives *wide–narrow* and the tertiary adjectives *thick–thin*. Tashiro (1971), in her comprehension study, noted that the primary adjectives elicited fewer errors than the secondary and tertiary adjectives, at least for the 3- to 5-year-old children she studied.

Finally, E. Clark (1971a) reports that two of the youngest children she tested interpreted *when* questions incorrectly as *where* questions. When asked questions like "When did the boy jump the fence?" these children answered "there" or "right there." These locative answers to temporal questions are consistent with the notion that time expressions are based on a spatial metaphor acquired after spatial terms are acquired, and therefore, time expressions will at first be misinterpreted as spatial expressions.

Before considering the evidence from production, we must look at several qualifications, or cautions, to be observed in relying on such data. First, as E. Clark points out in this volume, children do not always mean what adults mean when they use a word, and so the child's use of a word cannot be taken as indicating the acquisition of the adult rules of application for that word. Second, the child's first utterances are full of omissions and deletions of adult prepositions, and it is difficult to know how to treat such utterances. For instance, one of Brown and Bellugi's (1964) children said "Baby high-chair," which his mother interpreted immediately as "Baby is in the high-chair," Should this child be credited with production of a sentence appropriate to *in*? This seems too strong, for the child might not understand, or have knowledge about, the distinction between *at*, *in*, and *on*. Perhaps then he should be credited with knowing the notion of location common to *at*, *in*, and *on*, but this seems problematic too, although less so.

Third, one must use caution in interpreting the child's first explicit use of a locative term, even given the first qualification. The problem is that the child might produce a more complex term first simply to mark the sentence with respect to a less complex, but deleted term. For example, the child might contrast *Baby highchair*—meaning "Baby is in the highchair"—with *Baby in (or into) highchair* to indicate that the latter is marked for directional movement, i.e., "Baby is going into the highchair." That is, the child would not need to mark the sentence expressing location alone, but he would need to mark the sentence as expressing location plus direction. Therefore, it seems quite consonant with the complexity hypothesis to expect the child to produce the marked term explicitly before the unmarked term, at least at the earliest stages when terms like prepositions are often omitted. Of course, the complexity hypothesis also appears to predict the opposite, but the contradiction is more apparent than real. The complexity hypothesis is based on the order of acquisition of the rules of application, and so data such as the *into* example are consistent with the more basic hypothesis. Nevertheless, this qualification points out the caution required for application of this hypothesis to the earliest production data.

The fourth qualification is that production is also affected by surface complexity which results in perceptual and production difficulties that interact with semantic complexity. In languages in which different spatial components are expressed by different surface features, the production (and comprehension too, probably) of these components will also vary with their surface complexity. Slobin (in press) discusses just such instances in Hungarian and Serbo-Croatian. So the complexity hypothesis is uncontaminated only when the *A* and *B* terms are of the same syntactic form; when they are of different syntactic forms, the predictions break down. In English, this has not been a problem, for the prepositions and adjectives both form relatively homogeneous classes with respect to syntactic complexity. But applications across classes even in English—say, across prepositions and adjectives—should be complicated by the surface complexity factor.

Now let us consider a few examples of spatial and temporal terms in the child's spontaneous speech. Two of the first spatial terms to be noted are the simple deictic expressions *there* and *here*, which have been reported in most children with two-word utterances (cf. e.g., Braine, 1963b; Brown & Fraser, 1963; Miller & Ervin, 1964), with perhaps the positive term *there* predominating. *There* and *here* are location terms that neutralize the *at/on/ in* distinction and, in this sense, have very simple rules of application. *That*, *this* and a deictic *it* also appear early, with *that* perhaps predominating. Unfortunately, little is known about whether the use of *there–here* and *that–this* implies that the child has a primitive distal–proximal distinction, using the ego as point of reference. If this were true, it would show the very early use, perhaps necessarily earlier than other spatial uses, of the ego as a reference system, and this would clearly be consonant with the centrality of ego in the *P*-space.

The first prepositions to appear consistently seem to be *on* and *in*. According to Brown (in press), they came into his subjects' speech in obligatory contexts at about the same time and apparently before any other prepositions. According to the complexity hypothesis and the discussion of *L*-space, however, *at* should appear before either of these, since it appears to be less marked. One problem could be that *at* does not need to be explicitly marked, whereas *in* and *on* do, and so the latter appear first. (Note that *there* and *here* implicitly contain the neutral notion of *at*, and they do appear earlier.) Other early prepositions include *out*, *over*, *under*, and *away*, according to Miller and Ervin (1964). Though relatively sparse, these data at least suggest that, in agreement with the complexity hypothesis, the location prepositions (e.g., *in*) appear before location plus direction (e.g., *into*) and before location plus relation (*over, under*).

With respect to time, the general impression of the acquisition literature is that spatial terms are used spontaneously before temporal terms, as the complexity hypothesis predicts. In Brown's data (in press), the listing of the uses of *in* includes only three temporal uses (*in a week*, *in a while*, and *in a minute*) compared to a large number of locative uses. These temporal uses might also be nonproductive, with phrases like *in a week* being holophrastic. Also, E. Clark (1969), Ervin-Tripp (1970), and D. Ingram (unpublished data) all report the use of *where* questions before *when* questions. *There* and *here*, of course, appear before *then* and *now*, their temporal counterparts. The examples could be multiplied. In addition, E. Clark (1969) noted that the positive *before* appeared spontaneously before the negative *after* in the $3\frac{1}{2}$-year-olds she studied, and that the previous literature has reported similar findings for other temporal expressions like *first–last*, *early–late*, etc.

In applying the complexity hypothesis to children, it has been assumed that the child knows all about space before he even begins to learn language. Although this assumption seems plausible, it is in no sense necessary. It could be, for example, that the child comes to know *P*-space—at least the intricacies of *P*-space—very slowly, and so the learning of specific spatial terms must wait until the child knows the appropriate properties of *P*-space so that he can learn the correct rules of application. This alternative assumption, which implies a closer relation between the learning of *P*-space and *L*-

space, predicts that the order in which the child learns spatial terms should be affected by the order in which the child learns the properties of *P*-space, not just by the complexity of the rules of application. The evidence for either assumption is slight, although Slobin (in press) does present evidence for the first assumption. He discusses the case of Hungarian–Serbo-Croatian bilingual children, who learn the locative terms in Hungarian long before they learn the locative terms in Serbo-Croatian. The child would have had to know *P*-space to learn Hungarian; therefore, the lack of knowledge of *P*-space could *not* have been the cause of the late development of spatial terms in Serbo-Croatian. Rather, Slobin suggests, the later development of Serbo-Croatian appears to result from the complexity of the surface features required for expressing the spatial notions in Serbo-Croatian.

CONCLUDING REMARKS

In this chapter, I have presented the thesis that the child acquires English spatial expressions by learning how to apply them to his prior knowledge about space, and that he acquires English temporal expressions in turn by extending the spatial terms in a metaphor about time. The main evidence for this thesis is the strong correspondence between the properties of the spatial terms and the properties of man's innate perceptual apparatus, and between English spatial and temporal expressions. The correspondence is so strong, I would argue, that it simply could not be coincidental and it therefore needs explanation. Time, for example, is not just expressed with an occasional spatial simile, but rather it is based on a thoroughly systematic spatial metaphor, suggesting a complete cognitive system that space and time expressions have in common. In this paper, my purpose has only been to outline the thesis, its evidence, and what it could mean for the acquisition of English. Admittedly, the discussion is preliminary, and there will have to be much more thought about how to specify the rules of application more accurately, how to describe the mediating mechanisms for the correlations between *P*-space, *L*-space, and temporal expressions, how to specify the complexity hypothesis more satisfactorily, and so on. Laying all details aside, however, the present discussion does attest to the plausibility of the thesis and suggests that further work along these lines will be profitable.

Although I have argued only that knowledge of *P*-space is a prerequisite for the acquisition of spatial and temporal terms, this knowledge might well turn out to be prerequisite for far more of language than that. It would be very exciting, for example, if *P*-space could be implicated even in such fundamental properties of language as the syntactic notions *subject of a sentence*, *agent of an action*, *object of the verb*, and so on. In fact, Anderson

(1971) has recently made just such an argument in reviving the traditional so-called "localist theory of case." This theory argues that grammatical relations are fundamentally locative in nature, and they are therefore derived ultimately from notions of location. Anderson demonstrates that there is a wealth of evidence to support such a view and suggests himself that the localist theory has significant "ontological and chronological" implications. Indeed, with this type of evidence, it is not far-fetched to believe that knowledge of P-space is the basis for much more of the universality of language than I have argued in this paper. In any case, these theories concerning space and location present intriguing possibilities for future work in language acquisition, and it is the student of language acquisition who will ultimately be called on to solve the important puzzles about the relation between language and prior knowledge.

WHAT'S IN A WORD? ON THE CHILD'S ACQUISITION OF SEMANTICS IN HIS FIRST LANGUAGE[1]

EVE V. CLARK
Stanford University

INTRODUCTION[2]

Any hypothesis about the development of semantic knowledge in first language acquisition has to deal eventually with many different issues, but the central question is: what meaning has the child attached to a particular phonological sequence, and how does the child's meaning for this word develop into the adult meaning? Because the answer to this general question is crucial to any theory about the acquisition of semantic knowledge, the present chapter will explore the following topics: What sort of lexicon does the child have in the very early stages of language acquisition? What form does the child's semantic knowledge take, and does it differ from the adult's? How is the child's knowledge structured and how does its structure change over time to resemble more closely the adult model?

Although there has been a considerable resurgence of interest in the topic of language acquisition over the last decade, most recent research has

[1] This research was supported in part by NSF Grant GS-1880 to the Language Universals Project, Stanford University, and in part by NSF Grant GS-30040 to the author.

[2] I should like to thank H. Clark for drawing my attention to some of the data used to support the arguments in this chapter, as well as for making comments on earlier versions of the manuscript.

centered on the acquisition of the syntactic structure of language. Little attention, by comparison, has been paid to the acquisition of semantics.

The work that has been done on semantics has been concerned principally with the semantic functions of words within the context of an utterance. Slobin (1970), for instance, classified early two-word utterances on the basis of the semantic function of the utterance, e.g., whether it expressed need, possession, location, etc. He found singular resemblances in the types of two-word utterances used by children speaking a number of different languages; his examples were drawn from data on the acquisition of English, Finnish, German, Luo, Russian, and Samoan. Brown (in press) has also done some very detailed functional semantic analysis, concentrating mainly on the acquisition of morphology in the early stages of acquiring English. In his analysis, he pointed out that semantic distinctions that are already known to the child must underlie the introduction of new morphological markers.

The approach to semantics considered by Slobin and Brown is quite different from the one to be pursued in the present chapter. Their approach is essentially concerned with the *semantic functions* of words in utterances, while the present one will be concerned with a different issue, one basic to language acquisition as a whole. That is the issue of how words are used to *refer to* or represent external objects and events appropriately, from the earliest stages in acquisition on.

In the present chapter, I shall propose a general hypothesis about the acquisition of semantic knowledge by the child and shall present linguistic data on the referential use of language from various stages of language acquisition in support of the hypothesis. In the first part, I shall consider three hypothesis that have recently been entertained by some psychologists and linguists. I shall then present the Semantic Feature Hypothesis on acquisition and relate it to the earlier proposals. In the next section, I shall consider evidence from the early referential use of words by children from a number of different linguistic backgrounds, as well as some data on the later acquisition of word meanings. For these data as a whole, I shall show how the phenomenon of *overextension* provides strong support for the Semantic Feature Hypothesis. In the third section, I will relate semantic features or components of meaning to other developmental phenomena such as perception in discussing the possible sources for semantic features. I shall conclude by stressing the importance of semantics for language acquisition as a whole.

THEORIES OF SEMANTIC DEVELOPMENT

Three previous proposals about semantic development will be described in this section. The first is McNeill's (1970b) hypothesis about the nature of the child's lexicon in the earliest stages (implicit grammatical relations) as well as the later possibilities for the reorganization of the lexicon as it goes from a sententially based store to a word-based store. This hypothesis will be referred to as the Grammatical Relations Hypothesis. The second proposal to be considered is Anglin's (1970) Generalization Hypothesis about the growth of word meaning as judged from evidence of children's overt knowledge of form class for words in isolation rather than in sentential contexts. The third proposal is in a sense more speculative but some of its assumptions will, I suspect, eventually prove to be essential to a unified theory of first-language acquisition. This hypothesis, proposed by Postal (1966) and Bierwisch (1967, 1970a) will be referred to as the Universal Primitives Hypothesis. Following the discussion of these three proposals, I shall describe the hypothesis of the present chapter, the Semantic Feature Hypothesis.

The Grammatical Relations Hypothesis

McNeill (1970b) proposed that when the child begins learning his language, he has some form of sentence-meaning dictionary in which each lexical entry is tagged with all the grammatical relations that are used (implicitly) at the one-word stage. Because of the need to store information about the underlying (innate) grammatical relations, McNeill claims that the child does not have semantic features at this stage since they would be too great a burden on memory. However, in stating his assumptions about the primacy of grammatical relations in the earliest stages of language acquisition, McNeill seems to have ignored the issue of what the child knows about the referential use of words, and how or where this knowledge about reference is stored. Notice that such knowledge of the referential properties has logically to precede knowledge of any grammatical constraints on word use (i.e., what are grammatical relations and what are not). In other words, the child has to know at least something of what a word *means* before he can use it grammatically (cf. further Bloom, in press; Bowerman, 1970, this volume).

Later on, as soon as the child begins to use rules for sentence construction (presumably, then, as soon as the first two-word utterances appear in the child's speech), he begins to reorganize his dictionary, according to McNeill, on a word-meaning basis rather than on a sentence-meaning one. This is because it is now more economical given the number of items to be stored. At this point, McNeill considers two possibilities for the growth of the child's reorganized lexicon (1970b, pp. 116f.). His first proposal is that the child's lexicon develops "horizontally." This means that only some of the semantic features associated with a word need enter the dictionary when the word itself does. As a result, the child could have words in his vocabulary that had different overall semantic properties to the *same* words in the speech of older children or adults. The child could then proceed to complete the dictionary entries for words horizontally, by the gradual addition of features to each entry. While this seems to be an inherently reasonable proposal, McNeill does not go on at this point to discuss which features might appear first in the lexical items entering the dictionary, nor whether there might be any order of acquisition for semantic features in general. Another omission is any discussion of the nature of the semantic features: Where do they come from? Do they suddenly appear just when the child is about to reorganize his lexicon to accommodate word entries? McNeill appears simply to assume that the features are the same somehow as the adult's features.

The alternative to the horizontal model of dictionary organization is what McNeill calls "vertical" development of the lexicon (he does not choose between the two in his book). By vertical development, he appears to mean that all the semantic features of a word enter the child's dictionary at the same time (when the word itself does), but at first the dictionary entries are "separated" from each other. In other words, the same semantic features are not necessarily recognized as being the same in different entries within the lexicon. This form of organization, though, would seem for one thing to entail that words would then have to have the same semantic properties for young children as for adults. (It will be shown, however, that such an assumption is not supported by the data.) Under this proposal, semantic development would seem to consist simply of collecting separate occurrences of the same features into some sort of unified group or schema. It is unclear what form the organization of such a lexicon would take developmentally, beyond one's being able to list a gradual increase in the number of vocabulary items used by the child.

Although McNeill cites some data in support of each of the above proposals, the weakness of both lies in the fact that all of the evidence discussed in their favor comes from children older than 6 or 7 years of age. Nonetheless, it is obvious that children much younger than this, indeed from the age of 2 or $2\frac{1}{2}$ upward, must already know a great deal about the semantics of their language in order to (a) communicate with others with considerable success, and (b) use many of the syntactic rules of their language appropriately.

The Generalization Hypothesis

Anglin (1970) proposed that semantic development follows a generalization process in which the child's ability to see semantic relations between the names of objects (words), for example, goes from the concrete to the abstract, where the abstract relations are also the more general ones (i.e., they include larger categories). Anglin (1970, p. 53) attaches this generalization process directly to the lexical level of language and appears to equate the acquisition of more general, superordinate, lexical items with the acquisition of general (abstract) superordinate concepts. At the earlier stages of acquisition, then, he claims that the young child is only aware of the specific, concrete relations between words; as the child's semantic knowledge increases with age, he comes to make generalizations over larger and larger (more abstract) categories. These generalizations are expressed through the use of superordinate lexical items. For example, at an early stage a child might learn the words *rose, tulip, oak*, and *elm*; at the next stage he will group these words into pairs, each with a superordinate lexical item: *flowers* and *trees*. These words in turn could eventually be grouped as *plants*, then ultimately as *living entities*.

In support of his generalization hypothesis, Anglin presented data from a variety of tasks, most of which asked about explicit knowledge of form-class membership (a syntactic rather than a semantic property). He was concerned with the relations among some twenty words in the context of sorting tasks, free recall, structured recall, and a sentence-frame completion task. The words he used were arbitrarily selected from the semantic point of view in that he chose them largely on the basis of whether one could in any way group words sharing the same form-class membership on at least one superordinate dimension. For example, the six nouns used were *boy*, *girl* (children), *horse* (all three are animate or all are mammals), *flower* (all four are living), *chair* (all five are material objects), and *idea* (all six are entities, or all six are nouns).

The superordinate, more abstract or more general, relations between such words, then, are ones which can be named by use of a word (usually a superordinate) or phrase in English. Anglin was much more concerned with the lexical items as wholes, though, than with any potential components of meaning. Thus, his final definition of a feature (which he equates with a word) is fairly far removed both from the term used in perception (Gibson, 1969) and from any recent linguistic definition, viz., "... a feature is a complex verbal concept rich in properties just as a word is [Anglin, 1970, p. 95]." Overall, his data simply showed that children learn explicit notions of form class (that is, for words divorced from their sentential contexts) fairly late, up to two or three years after such notions are first broached in school. Anglin claimed that such knowledge of form class is semantic development. However, his theory, which runs counter to much of the data in the literature, is quite unable to account for the fact that children can use words appropriately in sentential contexts at an age when they are unable to say anything about form class.

As in the case of the supporting evidence cited by McNeill for his two proposals vis-à-vis the structure of the child's lexicon, Anglin's data too were all collected from children aged 9;0 years and older. He practically ignores the fact that younger children must have some semantic knowledge in order to use their language.

In formulating the Generalization Hypothesis, Anglin said nothing about the nature of lexical entries in the child's dictionary at any stage. It is therefore difficult to compare this hypothesis with McNeill's, beyond pointing out that both McNeill and Anglin, probably because of their concentration on syntactic notions and grammatical relations in language acquisition, assumed that semantic structure develops both later and more slowly than syntactic knowledge of the language. They both presented data from children of 6 years and older, yet the fact remains that younger children can and do use language in a meaningful way. Even if certain aspects of semantic knowledge were not acquired until the age of 6 or 7, much of it—including some knowledge about reference—must be acquired earlier on.

The Universal Primitives Hypothesis

Beginning from a rather different standpoint, Postal (1966) has recently suggested that underlying all languages is a set of universal semantic primitives, together with rules for the combination of primitives into lexical items. Languages differ from each other principally in the rules of combination used to go from the semantic primitives to the lexical items. These primitives would be equivalent or even identical to the semantic components of componential analysis, to Hjelmslev's minimum units of content or to Katz and Fodor's (1963) semantic markers. Furthermore, Postal (1966) pointed out that:

> . . . each of these primitives bears a fixed relation to the universe which is determined by the biological structure of the organism. Thus the relation between the semantic primitives and their combinations which are part of the combinatorial structure of language and the world is not learned but innate. What must be learned is only the relations between fixed sets of semantic primitives and sets of phonological and syntactic properties [p. 179, fn. 10].

This view of universal semantics has been spelled out in more detail by Bierwisch, who pointed out (1967) that "the idea of innate basic elements of semantic structure does not entail a biological determination of concepts or meanings in a given language, but only of their ultimate components [1967, p. 4]." In other words, the child would not have to learn the components themselves since they would be innate in the sense that they are biologically given through the structure of the human organism (cf., e.g., H. Clark, this volume). Postal, however, oversimplified somewhat in claiming that *all* that had to be learned was "the relations between fixed sets of semantic primitives and sets of phonological and syntactic properties." The child acquiring his first language has undoubtedly got to do this, but he has to learn first which combinations of primitives have lexical exponents in his language, and which do not.

Bierwisch (1970a) has put the Universal Primitives Hypothesis position most clearly and succinctly in a recent article on semantics. He further elaborates the idea of innate semantic primitives or components of meaning, and their relation to external physical attributes of objects and events:

> It seems natural to assume that these [semantic] components represent categories or principles according to which real and fictitious, perceived and imagined situations and objects are structured and classified. The semantic features do not represent, however, external physical properties, but rather the psychological conditions according to which human beings process their physical and social environment. Thus they are not symbols for physical properties and relations outside the human organism, but rather for the internal mechanisms by means of which such phenomena are perceived and conceptualized. This then leads to the extremely far-reaching, though plausible, hypothesis that all semantic structures might finally be reduced to components representing the basic dispositions of the cognitive and perceptual structure of the human organism. According to this hypothesis, semantic features cannot be different from language to language, but are rather part of the general human capacity for language, forming a universal inventory used in particular ways by individual languages [pp. 181–182].

This suggests that Bierwisch would have to claim that there is a common interpretive format into which all percepts are translated, where the components used in interpreting any sort of input to the human organism, whether linguistic or no, *are* the semantic primitives, or at least are isomorphic in some significant way with these semantic primitives. The extension of the Universal Primitives Hypothesis to account for first-language acquisition would then ultimately have to relate the development of semantic knowledge to general perceptual and cognitive development. That there is a close relation between language and cognitive development has often been assumed, but few attempts have been made so far to investigate the nature of this relationship (cf., e.g., Sinclair-de Zwart, 1967; Slobin, 1971).

The Universal Primitives Hypothesis is, as Bierwisch points out, a very plausible one and it has important implications for a developmental theory; at the same time it is extremely difficult either to verify or to disprove, since we still have little idea how to identify the primitives, much less any notion of what form the rules for their combination into the appropriate lexical items would take within a particular language. It is possible that some of the work being done within generative semantics (e.g., Lakoff, 1970a,b, 1971; McCawley, 1968; Postal, 1970) may eventually provide solutions to such problems.

THE PRESENT HYPOTHESIS: SEMANTIC FEATURE ACQUISITION

The hypothesis to be presented and tested here is concerned with what the child learns about the meanings of words as he goes through the process of acquiring his first language. Since the child's knowledge, in general, is greatly restricted in comparison to the adult's, this will affect his language development as well as his other behaviors. The Semantic Feature Hypothesis states that when the child first begins to use identifiable words, he does not know their full (adult) meaning: He only has partial entries for them in his lexicon, such that these partial entries correspond in some way to some of the features or components of meaning that would be present in the entries for the same words in the adult's lexicon. Thus, the child will begin by identifying the meaning of a word with only one or two features rather than with the whole combination of meaning components or features (qua Postal) that are used criterially by the adult. The acquisition of semantic knowledge, then, will consist of adding more features of meaning to the lexical entry of the word until the child's combination of features in the entry for that word corresponds to the adult's. The hypothesis therefore assumes that the child's use and interpretation of words may differ considerably from the adult's in the early stages of the language-acquisition process, but, over time, will come to correspond to the adult model.

Although the child does not know the full meaning of some word, there is nothing to tell him this fact and he will, therefore, use the word. As soon as he has attached some feature(s) of meaning to it, it simply has that meaning for him. The child will use those one or two features criterially in deciding when to apply the word and when not. Since he has only a partial characterization of the word's meaning set up, his referential categories may often differ considerably from the adult's for the same words. The child will make referential errors because he does not yet know the combinations of features that will allow him to delimit his categories differently. The principal difference between child and adult categories at this stage will be that the child's are generally larger since he will use only one or two features criterially instead of a whole combination of features.

For example, let us suppose that the child has learned the word *dog* (or *doggie*); however, he only uses one feature to characterize the meaning of this word, so the set of objects that he will put into the category named *dog* will be larger than the set in the adult category. For instance, he might have characterized the word *dog* as meaning *four-legged*; the sets of objects referred to as *dog*, therefore, might include cows, sheep, zebras, llamas, dogs and anything else that is four-legged. This feature, four-leggedness, is clearly inadequate to specify the meaning of the word *dog* in such a way that the child's category will coincide with the adult's (unless the only four-legged creatures the child sees are dogs). However, with the addition of other features, the child will gradually narrow down this initially very general meaning of *dog* until it means what the adult means. This narrowing-down process will presumably run concurrently with the introduction of new words into the child's vocabulary that take over parts of the overextended semantic domain. To continue with the same example as an illustration, if the child next acquires the word *zebra*, he must add something to the feature *four-legged* to keep the meaning of this word distinct from that of *dog*; he might add any of the following features: *hoofs*, *mane*, *striped*. For the word *cow*, further specifications might include the sound made (*mooing*), or other features of shape like *horns* or *udders*. At the same time, the child will probably add to the lexical entry for *dog* things like *sound: barking, size: relatively small* (in comparison to cows, zebras and llamas), etc. These combinations of features are then used criterially, and eventually come to delimit the adult categories.

Let us now consider the child who has arrived at a more advanced stage: many of his dictionary entries are practically complete. However, there are other words or word pairs in his language that are very closely related in meaning, and therefore have a large number of semantic features in common. For example, the pair of words *more* and *less* both refer to quantity but *more* is unmarked (Greenberg, 1966) and positive: It refers to an amount that is positive with respect to some standard on a scale, whereas *less* refers to an amount that is negative with respect to some standard. The dimensional adjectives in English are similarly related: Both *high* and *low*, for example, refer to a single dimension, both specify that the dimension is a vertical one, but *high* refers to a positive distance along the dimension while *low* is negative in the same way as *less*. Thus, if the child learned a feature like + Amount first in learning the meanings of *more* and *less*, the meanings of these two words could well be confused. It would not be until the child learned the contrasting values of polarity—that *more* was positive and *less* negative—that this pair of antonyms would be interpreted correctly. Similarly, there might be a stage in acquisition at which the meanings of *high* and *low* would be confused by the child, for the same reason.

Another area in which words share a number of semantic features in common is where there is an overlap in meaning: One word may refer to a subset of objects that may be included within a category covered by another word. An example of this sort of relationship is the overlap between the words *brother* and *boy*. All brothers are boys, but not all boys are brothers. The word *brother*, in fact, singles out a subset of the category named by the word *boy*. It is predicted in this instance that the child will confuse the more specific term (*brother*) with the more general one (*boy*) until he learns the other semantic features needed in the entry for *brother*.

Thus, if two words are opposites and their meanings differ simply by one feature (or by the value on a feature within a binary system), or if they share a number of features in common, but one word has some additional, more specific, features in its entry as well, then they are likely to be regarded at some point as having the same meaning. Later, of course, the child will learn the contrasting values on a feature or the more specific features that differentiate between the meanings of such closely related words.

So far, in outlining the present hypothesis, no real attempt has been made to define what is meant by *feature* or *component of meaning*. One of the basic assumptions of the theory clearly is that the meanings of words can be broken down into some combination of units of meaning smaller than that represented by the word. These units may be talked about in many ways, and have been variously called features, components, minimal units of content, semantic markers, etc. These units have generally reflected some of the notational constraints imposed on the form and scope of the semantic theory being proposed (cf., e.g., Bierwisch, 1969, 1970b). No theoretical issues will be raised here, although I will use a binary type of notation to represent the child's semantic knowledge about particular sets of words. This notation does not imply any theoretical commitment to binary features, and will simply be used for clarity's sake in presenting the data.

The main question, though, remains: What is a feature? And its corollary: Does the child use the same features as the adult? In an ideal world where we knew what the universal semantic primitives were, we could assume these would be used by both child and adult. However, we are not in a position at present, theoretically or empirically, to (a) identify the set of universal semantic primitives postulated by Postal and Bierwisch, or (b) claim that these primitives are what the child uses when he first attaches some meaning to a word. The present theory will simply make the following, testable, assumptions: (a) the first semantic features that the child uses are liable to be derived from the encoding of his percepts, and (b) at a later stage, as the child learns more about the structure of his language as a whole, he will learn which percept-derived features play a particular linguistic role (e.g., *animacy*) and which are relatively redundant within a set or combination of features. Since the adult also uses perceptually derived information, many of the semantic features used by the adult are also used by the child. The main differences will lie in the fact that the child has to learn the rules of combination for each lexical item.

One further point to be stressed in the present discussion of semantic features is the relation between the child's perception of objects and events and his learning to use words to encode a particular meaning. The fact that the child may begin by simply attaching the feature or component of meaning *four-legged* to the word *dog* says nothing about the child's perception of different objects or of the differences between objects. A child can clearly see the differences between dogs, cows, and horses, but there is no a priori reason for the child to respect either adult or biological taxonomies when he first begins to learn the meaning of a word. In the example of *dog* being taken to mean something like *four-legged*, the child simply sees that all these animals (cows, dogs, and horses) have the appropriate perceived characteristic for this word to be applied. He will therefore include all three adult categories under *dog* (= *four-legged*) until he adds further specifications or features of meaning to the word that will lead him to reduce the size of his category to something nearer the adult one. The growth of lexical entries for word meanings, therefore, makes no claims about what the child actually perceives, only about the sorts of meaning that he will attach to a word in the very early stages of language acquisition.

Besides considering the source of the child's earliest semantic features (perceptual attributes and their encoding), the present hypothesis is also concerned with whether some kinds of semantic features are learned before others: Does the child learn features that are general or specific to the meaning of a word first? The Semantic Feature Hypothesis would predict that it is the more general semantic features that will be acquired earliest. This claim is concomitant with the predictions made earlier about the confusion of antonyms and of words that overlap in meaning. It also follows from the prediction that children will overextend (by adult standards) many words in such a way that their categories will be delimited differently from the adult's. Furthermore, on the basis of some recent experimental work, it would appear that if the features which, combined, make up the meaning of a word are related to each other hierarchically, then the order of acquisition is top-down, i.e., the top feature, being the most general in the definition of the word, is acquired first with the other features being acquired in the order of their hierarchical dependence. For example, in the acquisition of the meanings of *before* and *after*, children first learn that both words have to do with time: + Time; next they learn that these words refer to sequence rather than to simultaneity of some sort: − Simultaneous. The feature − Simultaneous carries with it a specification of ordering in the sequence: + Prior. This combination of features (+ Time, − Simultaneous, + Prior) characterizes the meaning of *before* but not that of *after*. The last feature that children learn is − Prior, i.e., that *after* is in fact the opposite of *before* (E. Clark, 1971a).

Finally, it is essential to point out that the features for each word separately have to be learned in the acquisition of the word itself. Therefore, the acquisition of a feature or even of a combination of features in one context (one word) does not imply, for example, that the child will immediately recognize synonyms. He has to find out first that the new word does, in fact, contain the same combination of semantic features (though it may have different syntactic properties). For example, in acquiring the meanings of various time-related words, children learn what *first* means before they learn what *before* means; and, in learning the meaning of *before*, children add the features in turn to this new lexical item. However, the combination of features (+ Time, − Simultaneous, + Prior) is one they already know because they know what the word *first* means.

How is the present theory related to those discussed earlier? First, it is clear that a number of the assumptions in the present theory are related to the Postal and Bierwisch formulations. For instance, that there is a universal set of semantic primitives, although we do not yet have a good way of identifying them; and that semantic knowledge is closely related to the human organism's interpretation of perceptual inputs.

Superficially, the present hypothesis also appears to draw on one of McNeill's proposals about the structure of the child's lexicon—that lexical entries are completed horizontally. However, McNeill said nothing about the nature of the semantic features used by the child after the purported reorganization from a sentential store with grammatical relations to a lexical store with semantic features of words. In contrast, the present theory makes specific proposals about the earliest semantic features used, and assumes that the child stores semantic information about the words he has from the earliest stages on. McNeill also does not say anything about the order of acquisition of semantic features with respect to individual words, whereas the present theory claims that there is an order of acquisition in which the more general features are acquired first. The later addition of more specific features is what eventually distinguishes between several words which share the same general feature(s). This form of semantic development will automatically result in what McNeill called horizontal completion of the dictionary entries in the child's lexicon.

Lastly, how is the present theory related to Anglin's Generalization Hypothesis? The direction for the development of semantic knowledge proposed by Anglin was specific to general. Anglin took words as his units rather than anything smaller, but even at the word level the Generalization Hypothesis cannot adequately account for the vocabulary data (cf. Brown, 1958) since children do not invariably acquire subordinate terms, e.g., *oak*, *elm*, before they acquire superordinate ones, e.g., *tree*. The present hypothesis, in considering features of meaning below the level of the word, predicts that general features will be acquired first, and only later (as the child learns more about the meaning of the word) does the child gradually add the specific features that differentiate the meaning of one word from another.

From the description of the Semantic Feature Hypothesis, it is clear that the areas most likely to yield information about the child's semantic structures in the earliest stages of language acquisition are the referential use of words, the use of opposites and the use of overlapping terms. Since the theory predicts that the meanings of many (and maybe all) words are not equivalent for the young child and the adult, how can we detect this lack of

correspondence? First of all, if the child uses only one or two features criterially in the application of a word, then there should be evidence of overextension in his speech—the establishment of categories that do not correspond to adult ones. The term extension will be used to refer to the child's
use of a word once it has entered his vocabulary. Some uses will appear to be
appropriate and others not. It is the inappropriate ones that will be referred
to as overextensions. By considering the actual categories that result from an
overextension, one should be able to infer which features the child has used
criterially. The domain of each set of overextensions can be treated as a
semantic field, and the changes in its structure (either because of more overextensions or because of the later narrowing-down of the word's meaning)
can be studied over time. One should, then, be able to work back from the
structure at a particular stage to the criterial features that would have to have
been used in order to produce such a structure within the semantic field.

The phenomenon of overextension and its subsequent elimination (with
the narrowing-down of categories) as the child learns more about the word's
meaning will allow (a) the investigation of criterial features used by the child,
and (b) more detailed proposals about which semantic features are known
to the child. In the next section, I shall present data on several kinds of overextension in the child's use and comprehension of words in various naturalistic and experimental settings. These data provide a preliminary test of the
present hypothesis.

THE EVIDENCE

In this section, I shall discuss data from the following sources: first, the use
of words by very young children as reported in the many nineteenth and
twentieth century diary studies; secondly, some work on various relational
terms carried out more recently by Donaldson and Balfour (1968), Donaldson and Wales (1970), and E. Clark (1971a), with 3- to 5-year-old children;
and lastly, some work with school-age children on verbs by C. Chomsky
(1969), and on complex relational nouns by Piaget (1928).

Overextension in Early Speech

The first form of overextension to be described is one that is widely reported in the diaries kept on the early speech of children from a number of
different language backgrounds. The accounts of this phenomenon are remarkably alike and consistently report similar findings. As a result, overextension appears to be language-independent (at least at this early stage in
acquisition), and is probably universal in the language acquisition process.
Among the sources for the present data, for example, are: Ament (1899):

German; Chamberlain and Chamberlain (1904): English; Guillaume (1927b): French; Idelberger (1903): German; Kenyereš (1926): Hungarian; Imedadze (1960): Georgian, Russian; Leopold (1939, 1949a): English, German; Luria and Yudovich (1959): Russian; Moore (1896): English; Pavlovitch (1920): French, Serbian; Rasmussen (1922): Danish; Shvachkin (1948): Russian; Taine (1877): French; Taube (cited by Preyer, 1889): Estonian; etc.

The general characteristics of the diary data are the following:

(1) The studies consulted all reported overextension within approximately the same age-range, generally between 1;1 and 2;6 years. The period in which this phenomenon is noticed lasts for up to a year for each child, but the overextension of a particular word rarely lasts much more than 8 months, and may take place only very briefly.

(2) The more detailed studies relate overextensions in the child's speech to vocabulary growth. They point out that there seems to be a sudden increase in the child's vocabulary, usually combined with intensive questioning activity of the *what('s) that?* variety, which often marks the end of this early form of overextension.

(3) The reports suggest that generally only some words in the child's vocabulary are noticeably overextended. Others appear to be used in a manner consistent with adult criteria from the moment of their introduction into the child's speech.[3] I use the word *appear* advisedly, since there are un-

[3] A number of studies in the literature have pointed out that proper names tend to be extremely stable even in the earliest stages of language acquisition. They are among the first words to have specific, identifiable referents and, according to several reports, are among the first words learned by the child (Perez, 1892, p. 299; Sully, 1896, p. 161). The stability of such words in the child's repertoire is further attested by Bloch (1921), Decroly (n.d.), Guillaume (1927b), and more recently by Leopold (1949a). Guillaume (1927b) makes the further claim that proper names are among the first words the child seems to segment out and recognize in the flow of adult conversations.

Both Bloch (1921) and Leopold (1949a), though, specifically exclude the terms *mama* and *papa* from the category of proper names since they exhibit none of the stable usage noted for proper names elsewhere in the child's early speech. In the earliest uses, *mama* (and often *papa* and *baba* too, cf. Jakobson, 1962) is simply a general expression of need based on hunger, discomfort or fright. This is reported, for instance, by Bloch (1921, p. 706), Grégoire (1937), Guillaume (1927b), Leopold (1949a), Lindner (1882), Moore (1896, p. 122), Nice (1925, p. 107), Preyer (1889), Scupin and Scupin (1907), and Smoczynski (1955). At the next stage, *papa* seems to become more specialized as the male parent, but *mama* continues to refer to needs in general. Leopold (1948) reports that shortly after this, his daughter used *papa* for all men for a period lasting about a month, and then narrowed the range of application to a single referent. The *mama–papa* forms and the confusions in their use are cited in most studies (cf. references above). *Mama* continues to be used for needs and for the provider of food (male or female) for some time (cf. Grégoire, 1937, pp. 86f.). On the other hand, a few reports claim proper name status for *mama* and *papa* also, e.g., Pavlovitch, 1920. In the few instances where a proper name is extended by the child, he appears to have assumed that the word was in fact a class name (Leopold, 1949a).

doubtedly many occasions on which an adult simply does not notice whether the child used an overextension or not. The adult's report will depend very heavily upon the context in which the child uses a word: an overextension has to be noticeable and therefore has to occur in contexts in which it cannot be put down as a reference to some other appropriate object that is in the same vicinity, and so on.

(4) Finally, the features that are used criterially in the overextensions of words appear to be derived predominantly from the perceptual input to the child—whether the percepts come from visual, tactile, olfactory, or auditory sources. Thus, the majority of overextensions reported in these data appear to be based on the perceived similarities between the objects or events that are included referentially within a single category. The principal criterial characteristics can be classified into several categories such as *movement, shape, size, sound, taste,* and *texture.* The categories are clearly derived from the child's perception of the properties of the objects around him.

Examples of these early overextensions are given in Tables 1–7. The examples have been grouped according to the type of feature that appears to underlie the overextension. Table 1, for instance, contains examples in which the child appears to have attached the meaning *movement* to the vocabulary items in question. The main kinds of feature (shape, size, sound, etc.) used in the overextensions are illustrated in Tables 1–6, in which the perceptual source of the criterial feature(s) is generally quite clear. In Table 2, for example, one can infer immediately from most of the overextensions which shape is being used criterially: For many small children, the category of *small round objects* crops up very frequently (cf. the examples cited from

Table 1 *Some Overextensions Related to Movement[a]*

Source	Lexical item	First referent	Extensions and overextensions in order of occurrence
Kenyeres̀ (1926)	titi	animals	> (pictures of animals) > (things that move)
Leopold (1949a)	sch	sound of train	> (all moving machines)
Moore (1896)	bird	sparrows	> (cows) > (dogs) > (cats) > (any animal moving)
Pavlovitch (1920)	dzin-dzin	moving train	> (train itself) > (journey by train)
Pavlovitch (1920)	tutu	train	> (engine) > (moving train) > (journey)
Schulte (cited in Preyer, 1889)	ass	goat with rough hide on wheels	> (things that move, e.g., animals, sister, wagon) > (all moving things) > (all things with a rough surface)

[a]Overextensions will be indicated by > where the following object—in parentheses—was given the same name. The probable source of the child's phonological form in the parents' speech is indicated by < .

Table 2 *Some Overextensions Related to Shape*

Source	Lexical item	First referent	Extensions and overextensions in order of occurrence
Chamberlain & Chamberlain (1904)	mooi	moon	> (cakes) > (round marks on window) > (writing on window and in books) > (round shapes in books) > (tooling on leather book covers) > (round postmarks) > (letter O)
Grégoire (1937)	wawa	dog	> (small white sheep)
Guillaume (1927b)	nénin "breast"	breast, food	> (button on garment) > (point of bare elbow) > (eye in portrait) > (face of person in photograph)
Idelberger (1903)	bow-wow	dog	> (fur piece with glass eyes) > (father's cuff links) > (pearl buttons on dress) > (bath thermometer)
Imedadze (1960)	buti [< burti] "ball"	ball	> (toy) > (radish) > (stone spheres at park entrance)
Leopold (1949a)	tick-tock	watch	> (clocks) > (all clocks and watches) > (gas-meter) > (fire hose wound on spool) > (bath scale with round dial)
Lewis (1951)	kotibaiz	bars of cot	> (large toy abacus) > (toast rack with parallel bars) > (picture of building with columns)
Lewis (1951)	tee [< Timmy]	cat	> (dogs) > (cows and sheep) > (horse)
Pavlovitch (1920)	wau-wau	picture of hunting dog	> (small black dog) > (all dogs) > (cat) > (woolen toy dog)
Pavlovitch (1920)	deda	grandfather	> (picture of Vul Karadžić in post-card) > (photos of grandfather and King Peter of Serbia)
Pavlovitch (1920)	kutija "box"	cardboard box	> (match box) > (drawer) > (bedside table)
Pavlovitch (1920)	gumene [< dugme] "button"	coat button	> (collar-stud) > (door-handle) > (light-switch) > (anything small and round)
Pavlovitch (1920)	bébé	reflection of child (self) in mirror	> (photograph of self) > (all photo-graphs) > (all pictures) > (all books with pictures) > (all books)
Pavlovitch (1920)	vata [< vrata] "door"	door	> (shutters in window)
Rasmussen (1922)	vov-vov	dog	> (kitten) > (hens) > (all animals at zoo) > (picture of pigs dancing)
Taube (cited in Preyer, 1889)	ball	rubber ball	> (apples)

Table 3 *Some Overextensions Related to Size*

Source	Lexical item	First referent	Extensions and overextensions in order of occurrence
Kenyeres (1926)	baba	baby	> (adults in pictures) > (pictures in books)
Moore (1896)	fly	fly	> (specks of dirt) > (dust) > (all small insects) > (his own toes) > (crumbs of bread) > (a toad)
Rasmussen (1922)	Born	children	> (all pictures of people)
Rasmussen (1922)	Dina [< name of 9-year-old girl]	young girl	> (all little girls)
Romanes (1888)	quack	duck on water	> (all birds and insects) > (all coins, after seeing an eagle on coin face) > (flies)
Sully (1896)	pin	pin	> (crumb) > (caterpillars)
Taine (1877)	bébé	baby	> (other babies) > (all small statues) > (figures in small pictures and prints)

Table 4 *Some Overextensions Related to Sound*

Source	Lexical item	First referent	Extensions and overextensions in order of occurrence
Leopold (1949a)	sch	noise of train	> (music) > (noise of any movement) > (wheels) > (balls)
Pavlovitch (1920)	koko	cockerel's crowing	> (tunes played on the violin) > (tunes played on the piano) > (tunes on an accordion) > (tunes on a phonograph) > (all music) > (merry-go-round)
Preyer (1889)	rollu	noise of rolling	> (wheels) > (balls)
Shvachkin (1948)	dany	sound of bell	> (clock) > (telephone) > (door bells)
Taine (1877)	fafer [< chemin de fer] "railway"	sound of trains	> (steaming coffee pot) > (anything that hissed or made a noise)

Chamberlain and Chamberlain, 1904; Guillaume, 1927b; Imedadze, 1960; and Leopold, 1949a). Another category based on shape that appears quite often is *square container* as in the example from Pavlovitch; Lewis reports a rather different category for which the criterial feature was a set of parallel,

Table 5 *Some Overextensions Related to Taste*

Source	Lexical item	First referent	Extensions and overextensions in order of occurrence
Leopold (1949a)	cake	candy	> (cakes)
Leopold (1949a)	candy	candy	> (cherries) > (anything sweet)
Taine (1877)	cola [< choco-lat]	chocolate	> (sugar) > (tarts) > (grapes, figs, peaches)

Table 6 *Some Overextensions Related to Texture*

Source	Lexical item	First referent	Extensions and overextensions in order of occurrence
Grégoire (1949)	sizo [< sciseaux]	scissors	> (all metal objects)
Idelberger (1903)	bow-wow	dog	> (toy dog) > (fur piece with animal head) > (other fur pieces without heads)
Leopold (1949a)	wau-wau	dogs	> (all animals) > (toy dog) > (soft home-slippers) > (picture of old man dressed in furs)
Pavlovitch (1920)	p'ašak∂ [<prašak] "powder"	powder	> (dust) > (ashes)
Shvachkin (1948)	kiki	cat	> (cotton) > (any soft material)
Shvachkin (1948)	va	white plush dog	> (muffler) > (cat) > (father's fur coat)
Stern & Stern (1928)	puppe	doll	> (toy rabbit) > (other playthings [excluded toy bell; only noncuddly object])

upright bars—a category which resulted from the child's overextension of the word used for the bars of his cot.

While the large majority of overextensions fit into the categories illustrated in Tables 1–6, there is a residual group of overextensions in which the words used usually seem to refer to actions rather than to objects. A few examples are listed in Table 7. The perceptual basis for these overextensions with verbal force cannot be as readily identified with one or two perceived attributes of the situation. Nevertheless, there are obvious similarities between the contexts in which these overextensions occurred.

Table 7 *A Few Early Overextensions Involving Actions Rather Than Objects*

Source	Lexical item	First referent	Extensions and overextensions in order of occurrence
Guillaume (1927b)	our [< ouvrir] "open"	in relation to father's door	> (in relation to piece of fruit-peel) > (in relation to box) > (in relation to pea pod) > (in relation to shoes that needed to be unlaced)
Preyer (1889)	atta [= all gone]	departures	> (opening or closing of doors) > (raising box lid) > (any disappearance of object from sight)

The headings for Table 1–6 give a somewhat oversimplified picture of the perceptual categories that the child appears to use in overextensions. In fact, in many of the instances cited, more than one kind of feature may be involved in a series of overextensions: For example, shape and size are not always separable, and sound often accompanies movement. Furthermore, inspection of the data in the tables will reveal several examples in which two features may be playing a criterial role, but it is unclear whether one is dominant or whether they are being used as a criterial combination. In a few instances, two features seems to alternate in dominance, giving rise to some overextensions on the basis of shape, for example, and then, after a switch, giving rise to others on the basis of sound or texture, etc.[4] Most of the examples presented, though, are reasonably unambiguous with respect to the type of criterial feature used, even if the actual feature itself cannot always be identified in these data with absolute certainty.

The six classes of overextensions in Tables 1–6 cover all the kinds of overextension found in relation to objects. Although the overextensions are clearly based on perceived features of different objects, there is one surprising omission among these features: the attribute of *color* does not appear criterially at all. Its insignificance in comparison to other physical attributes has been pointed out, for instance, by Pavlovitch (1920): "Toutefois il faut indiquer que la couleur comme élément constituitif ne joue qu'un rôle minime [p. 116]." Pavlovitch also found that taste was less used than the other classes of perceptual attributes as a basis for overextension. This accords with the literature as a whole which contains comparatively fewer overextensions in this class (Table 5). The most important perceptually

[4] This switching of features is reminiscent of Vygotsky's (1962) discussion of the phenomenon he called *chaining*, in which young children would move from the use of one attribute to another when asked to group different objects.

derived criteria for overextensions are based on movement, shape, size, and sound (cf. Tables 1–4).[5]

Once the child gets past this main period of overextensions, how does he begin to narrow down the meaning of overextended terms? The present hypothesis claims that the child will gradually add more specific features to the word as new words are introduced to take over subparts of a semantic domain. The addition of other features to the word combined with the introduction of new words will require the further differentiation of quasi-synonyms, and a considerable restructuring of the semantic domains of overextensions. This, unfortunately, is where a major weakness of the diary literature becomes apparent. Although so many observers duly reported the first appearance and the types of overextensions used, only a few provide any form of systematic documentation on their disappearance. In many studies, one has to rely on the reports of new vocabulary acquisitions in order to infer that the domain of a particular overextension has been restricted to something nearer the domain of the adult lexical item. Only two diaries give fairly clear accounts of some of the restructuring due to the narrowing-down of meanings: Pavlovitch (1920) and Leopold (1949a).

The narrowing-down or restructuring process that goes on provides data that can be used to find out which (criterial) features are being added by the child as the meaning of a word becomes more specific. One way of analyzing both the overextensions and the narrowing-down processes is to treat the domain of any one word as a semantic field (Lyons, 1968; Öhman, 1953). As an example, I have taken data from several studies and presented it in composite form in Table 8 to illustrate some of the possible changes in a semantic field.

Notice that at Stage I the child acquires *bow-wow* which is used to refer to dogs (the semantic field or domain). No records give enough detail for us to know whether this is a distinct stage or whether, given the opportunity, overextensions begin immediately a word has been acquired. At the second

[5]In classifying the overextensions as examples of the use of certain classes of criterial features, I have emphasized the perceptual source of the phenomenon of overextension. This emphasis contrasts with the so-called functional viewpoint, first put forward by Dewey (1894), and more recently taken up by Lewis (1957), which posits that the extension of any term to an inappropriate referent occurs only because the child sees their potential equivalence of function. The sort of examples cited are the postulated extension of the word *ball* to the moon because the child knows that if the moon were within reach, it could be thrown like a ball! However, the perceptually based explanation of such an extension is rather more satisfactory for the earliest stages since it has simply to assume that the child has the ability to use his eyes to match objects on the basis of something like shape; he does not have to know anything about the uses of objects in order to overextend items of vocabulary. The diary literature as a whole supports a perceptual basis rather than a functional one for such early overextensions.

Table 8 *A Sample Instance of Overextension and Restructuring*[a]

	Word	Semantic domain	Possible criterial feature(s)
Stage I	bow-wow	dog(s)	shape
Stage II	bow-wow	dogs, cows, horses, sheep, cats	shape
Stage III	(a) bow-wow[b]	dogs, cats, horses, sheep	
	(b) moo	cows	sound, (horns?)[c]
Stage IV	(a) bow-bow	dogs, cats, sheep	
	(b) moo	cows	sound
	(c) gee-gee	horses	size, (tail/mane?)
Stage V	(a) bow-wow/doggie	cats, dogs	size
	(b) moo	cows	
	(c) gee-gee/horsie	horses	
	(d) baa	sheep	sound
Stage VI	(a) doggie	dogs	
	(b) moo	cows	
	(c) gee-gee/horsie	horses	
	(d) baa lamb	sheep	
	(e) kitty	cats	shape, sound

[a] Cf., e.g., data in Ament (1899), Grégoire (1937), Leopold (1948), Lewis (1957), Perez (1892) and Shvachkin (1948).

[b] There may be some overlap in the use of the two words if *new* animals are seen at this point.

[c] Size may be an important factor: e.g. Shvachkin (1948) found that *vava* was used for dogs and *mu* for cows and big dogs.

stage, *bow-wow* has been overextended to cover a domain comprising dogs, cats, cows, horses, and sheep. As soon as the child adds other words to his vocabulary, though—words that also apply to subparts of this domain—he will have to add other features of meaning to the entry for the new word so as to keep their meanings apart. Thus, at Stage III, the addition of the word *moo*, which then takes over only the subset of cows from the domain of *bow-wow*, suggests that the entry for *moo* must contain something like a feature denoting the particular sound made by this subclass or else additional features of shape such as *horns* or *udders* besides the original feature of shape, *four-legged*. At the next stage when *gee-gee* is introduced and takes over the subclass of horses from *bow-wow*, one could infer that either the entry for *gee-gee*, like that for *moo*, has added to it additional features based on shape or sound, or else that the entry for *bow-wow* has had added to it a feature of size restricting its application to relatively small members of the category (i.e., cats, dogs, and sheep) leaving horses to be covered by the new term *gee-gee*. Or, alternatively, both entries (*bow-wow* and *gee-gee*) have such features added to them at the same time. With the introduction of *baa* (Stage V) for sheep, the entries for the lexical items have to be restricted or specified still further: besides shape and size, the entry for *baa* might contain a feature coding the sound this type of animal makes or the texture of its coat. Finally, at the last stage in narrowing down the original (overextended) domain of the word *bow-wow* (or *doggie* which replaces the baby word), the child adds the lexical item *kitty* which results in a subdivision of the dogs–cats class into two separate categories. Since overextensions are rarely reported once a domain has been restricted, one might propose that by this stage, the child has analyzed and coded particular configurations of perceptual features, and it is now the configurations of features that are used criterially in deciding on appropriate instances. However, the use of a configuration rather than isolated features does not necessarily mean that the lexical entry for a particular word is complete, but simply that the child has by now coded what appear to be the relevant set of attributes used to identify a certain set of objects or events. These perceptually based configurations are often represented in a shorthand form of notation as something like + Canine or + Bovine in the adult lexicon.

This example of overextension followed by narrowing-down is to some small degree fictitious although sequences of many of the stages are actually reported for the children in the diaries referenced. However, the details of the criterial features are largely speculative, and new detailed studies of the phenomenon of overextension are needed for a more careful investigation of the exact criterial features used at this stage by the young child.

What form has the restructuring been reported to take in those diaries that do discuss this phenomenon as well as overextension? Pavlovitch (1920) refers to this restructuring as "restriction du sens," and suggests that it occurs because of the acquisition of new words by the child. It must also occur as a result of parental prompting: *That's not a dog; it's a cow*, and so on. Pavlovitch gives a number of quite detailed examples of the narrowing-down process, describing how new words take over parts of a domain resulting from overextension, just as in the partly hypothetical example presented above. One of the domains he described in detail is that of word *bébé* which was first widely extended and then gradually narrowed down. The narrowing-down process is schematized in Table 9. The different stages that Pavlovitch describes are very similar in kind to those in the example given in Table 8. He also lists the changes in a number of other domains in which he had previously observed overextensions.

Leopold (1949a) also reports on a number of restructured domains that resulted from the breaking-down of a large domain into several smaller ones. One example which he presented in some detail (p. 134) is that involving the

Table 9 *The Restructuring of a Semantic Domain*[a]

	Word(s)	Semantic domain
Stage I	bébé	reflection of self in mirror; photo of self; all photos; all pictures; books with pictures; all books
Stage II	(a) bébé	reflection to self in mirror; photo of self; all pictures; books with pictures.
	(b) deda [grandfather]	all photos
Stage III	(a) bébé	reflection of self in mirror; photo of self; books with pictures; all books.
	(b) deda	all photos
	(c) ka′ta [karta = card]	all pictures of landscapes, views
Stage IV	(a) bébé	reflection of self in mirror; photo of self.
	(b) deda	all photos
	(c) ka′ta	all pictures (not of people)
	(d) kiga [book]	all books
Stage V	(a) bébé	self; small children in pictures
	(b) deda	photos
	(c) ka′ta	pictures
	(d) kiga	books
	(e) slika [reflection]	reflections in mirror
	(f) duda [Douchau, own name]	photo of self

[a]Data from Pavlovitch (1920).

words *sch* and *auto*, which for a short time were used as synonyms in some contexts. *Sch* was the first of the two words to appear in the child's speech (1;0) and was used initially to refer to the sound of trains, extended to music, and then extended (1;4) to any moving object (e.g., cars, trains, a chair pushed across the floor). After this, *sch* was extended to anything that could move but it was not necessary for the objects to be in motion, e.g., pictures of cars and carriages, a toy wheelbarrow. At 1;8, *sch* was replaced by *auto* which had been synonymous with *sch* in referring to cars and pictures of cars since 1;5. At the same time, the word *ride* was introduced and seemed to take over the idea of moving, while *choo-choo* began to share part of the domain of *sch* with *auto*. *Auto* by 1;8 was simply used to refer to cars, and *choo-choo* took over the rest of the domain of *sch*, being applied to all complicated instruments, then to trains, then to machinery (1;9), to airplanes and a wheelbarrow (1;10), and to a streetcar (1;11). At this point, the three words *train*, *wheelbarrow*, and *airplane* were acquired, and each took over the appropriate part of the domain of *choo-choo*. The latter word was then abandoned, except for occasional use in *choo-choo train*.

It is clear from these examples in Pavlovitch (1920) and in Leopold (1949a) that we can tentatively identify some of the features that the child uses in overextending and then narrowing down the domain referred to by a particular word. It is also clear from the numerous examples summarized in Tables 1–7 that the initial overextensions are based on some of the perceived characteristics of the objects around the child. Equally, the child uses a complex of such characteristics or features when he narrows down the referential application of a word to the appropriate (adult) domain. Among the questions that these data raise are: How many "correct" instances of an object does the child have to see, and hear named, before he picks out a criterial feature to use in applying the word in other contexts? And, is there any way of finding out whether each new word in the child's vocabulary goes through a brief period of referring only to "correct" instances before being overextended? The lack of detail in many of the diaries prevents us from answering these questions at the moment. New studies, paying far more attention to the context of each utterance will have to be undertaken before we can identify the exact features used, for example, or any order in the use of perceptually derived features.

Relational Terms

The second type of overextension to be discussed is much less obvious to the observer, and is possibly never noticed in the context of spontaneous utterances by the child. The phenomenon only comes to light when one begins to study the child's comprehension of certain word pairs, such as *more–less*, *big–wee* (small), *tall–short*, *before–after*, and so on, which are closely related in meaning. In each instance, the meaning of one of the pair is extended to cover both words. Without specific contexts which will distinguish between understanding and misunderstanding of an instruction that contains a particular word, this form of overextension will not be noticed. The studies to be described, therefore, have dealt mainly with comprehension rather than production.

The children who took part in these studies were slightly older than those using the first form of overextension that was discussed. Several of the comprehension studies were done with fifteen children whose ages ranged from 3;5 to 4;1 years; the same children were also given some follow-up tasks six months after the first experiments (cf. Donaldson & Balfour, 1968; Donaldson & Wales, 1970; Wales & Campbell, 1970). Another experiment studied forty children between the ages of 3;0 and 5;0 years in an cross-sectional study of meaning acquisition (E. Clark, 1971a). The data from each of these studies will be described in turn.

Less Is More

The first research that found evidence of this second form of overextension was done by Donaldson and Balfour (1968). In their study, they
looked at how 3-year-old children interpreted the relational terms *more*
and *less*. The stimuli used were two cardboard apple trees on which one
could hang up to six apples. Beginning from situations in which the trees
either had the same or different numbers of apples on them, the experimenter asked various questions about the state of the trees ("Does one
tree have more/less apples on it than the other?") and also asked the children
to alter certain states ("Make this tree so that it has more/less apples...,"
etc.). The most consistent and surprising finding was that the majority of
the children gave no indication that they could differentiate the word *less*
from the word *more*. Questions that contained the word *less* were answered
in exactly the same way as those with the word *more*.

The general pattern of the children's responses is shown in Table 10.
When asked whether one tree had more or one had less apples on it than
the other, the children nearly always responded affirmatively. Then, when
asked to point out which tree had more on it, 91% of the responses were
correct. However, when asked to point out which tree had less on it, 72.7%
of the responses were wrong. Thus, on 40 of the trials in which children had
previously judged that one tree had less on it, they subsequently chose as the
one with less the one that actually had more. All the questions asked by the
experimenter produced the same results: *less* was treated as if it were synonymous with the word *more*. In addition, the children showed no signs of hesitation over giving the word *less* the interpretation of *more*. Donaldson and
Balfour (1968) point out that the children responded to *less* as if they knew

Table 10 *More and Less* [a]

A.	Question	Yes	No[b]	Same	Total
	Does one have more?	65	3	1	69
	Does one have less?	55	0	0	55

[a] Based on Donaldson and Balfour (1968, p 464).
[b] Subsequently changed to "Yes."

B.	Question	Correct choice	Incorrect choice	No choice	Total
	Which one has more?	63	5	1	69
	Which one has less?	15	40	0	55

that it referred to quantity: "What seems to occur is that 'less' is understood to refer to quantity but ... it remains largely undifferentiated from 'more' as the consistently dominant interpretation for the undifferentiated pair [p. 468]."

Another way of stating their conclusion is to say that the meaning of *more* has been overextended to cover the word *less* as well, and this results in *less* being interpreted as the synonym rather than as the antonym of the word *more*.

What relations are there between these acquisition data and the semantic components that make up the meanings of these relational terms? In his discussion of the Donaldson and Wales (1970) paper, H. Clark (1970a) related some of their data to the relevant linguistic analyses. He pointed out that many of the words that Donaldson and Wales had studied were what are called unmarked–marked pairs. The unmarked member of the pair can be used nominally (i.e., naming a dimension, as in *The man is six feet tall*) and contrastively (where it means "taller than average," as in *The man is tall*). The marked term, on the other hand, can only be used contrastively (*The man is short*) and cannot be used simply to refer to height (**The man is six feet short*). The nominal *tall* has to precede contrastive *tall* and contrastive *short* since the dimension itself has to be there before one can talk about greater or lesser extent along that dimension. For the set of dimensional adjective pairs in English (and in many other languages), it is always the unmarked term that denotes physical extent along the dimension.

These linguistic facts were then used in positing a particular developmental sequence in the acquisition of the terms *more* and *less*: First, the child uses *more* and *less* in the nominal noncomparative sense only. Next, since the nominal term refers to extension rather than to lack of extension, the child will use both *more* and *less* to refer to the extended end of the scale, and finally, he will distinguish *less* from *more* and use it contrastively to apply to the less extended end of the scale.

At the first stage, therefore, *more* is simply taken to mean "amount" or "a quantity of," and its comparative nature is not understood. (This interpretation of *more* accords very well with many of the diary accounts of the early use of this word.) While this nominal interpretation of both words would explain why *more* and *less* were treated as synonyms, it does not account for why *more* and *less* both mean "more." As H. Clark points out, one has to make one assumption at this point: that the notion "having extent" is always best exemplified by the object with the *most* extent. Thus, the child asked to point out which tree has *more* or *less* apples on it will indicate the one with more, because it best exemplifies a tree with *some* [quantity, amount] apples on it. At the last stage, *more* and *less* will be used comparatively in their contrastive sense, and *less* is then differentiated from *more*.

These stages can be summarized using a feature notation where first of all the meaning attached to the words *more* and *less* can be represented as + Amount. Next, where extent is the best exemplar of amount, the child's entry for *more* has added to it the feature + Polar; but since the child knows that *less* also "means" + Amount, he will assume it too contains the feature + Polar. Finally, in the last stage of the acquisition of these meanings, the child learns that *less* refers to the other end of the scale, and thus contrasts in meaning with *more*: *less* is − Polar.

Same and Different

In another study carried out with the same group of children, Donaldson and Wales (1970) looked at instructions which used the words *same* and *different* in a sorting task. The task involved either everyday objects such as toothbrushes, eggcups, etc. (I and II) or else formal geometric shapes (III and IV). Within each of these classes, form and color were either coincident (I and III) or not (II and IV). The experimenter in the task asked children to give him an object that was either "the same in some way" or "different in some way" from the item he picked. The results of this task are equally striking: The children nearly all picked objects that were the same both when asked to choose one that was the same and when asked to choose one that was different (see Table 11).

In effect, the word *different* was interpreted as though it meant *same*. Here, then, is another example of the meaning of one of a pair of antonyms being overextended to cover the other term. Both *same* and *different* meant "same" to these children.

Dimensional Adjectives

Besides the pairs *more–less* and *same–different*, Donaldson and Wales (1970) also reported some preliminary studies of children's comprehension and use of several pairs of dimensional adjectives. The comprehension task involved the use of comparative and superlative forms. The adjective pairs were *big–wee* (small), *long–short*, *thick–thin*, *high–low*, *tall–short*, and *fat–thin*. (Except for the last pair—*fat–thin*—these dimensional adjectives consist of unmarked–marked pairs.)

In the comprehension task, the children had to point first to the biggest and to the wee-est of the objects, and then to one that was bigger or wee-er than a standard among the stimuli. They responded correctly more often when the adjective belonged to the positive-pole set (i.e., the unmarked adjectives together with *fat* according to the Donaldson and Wales defini-

Table 11   *Same and Different*[a]

Instruction	Choice same	Choice different	"There isn't one"	No response	Total
Tasks I and III					
One that's the same	28	0	2	0	30
One that's different	25	5	0	0	30
Tasks II and IV					
One that's the same	28	0	2	0	30
One that's different	24	2	3	1	30

[a] Based on Donaldson and Wales (1970, p. 244).

tion) than when it belonged to the negative-pole set. This difference was much larger in the case of the superlative forms than in that of the comparative forms used in the instructions. Furthermore, from the data presented in Wales and Campbell (1970), it is clear that the children did much better overall when the superlative forms were derived from the pair *big–wee* (100% correct) than on any other pair of adjectives in the instructions (cf. Wales & Campbell, 1970, p. 379).

Although Wales and Campbell discuss the quasi-superordinate status of the pair *big–wee* in relation to the other pairs of dimensional adjectives (e.g., *big* can be substituted in most contexts for the positive-pole terms, and *wee* for the negative-pole ones), they do not explicitly relate these facts to the data they present. However, that there is a close relation between the pair *big–small* and the other dimensional adjectives can be seen both from their data and from some data I recently collected from 4-year-olds on opposites (E. Clark, 1972). In this study, I found that *big* was treated as a synonym for many of the unmarked adjectives, while *small* or *little* was substituted in the same way for the corresponding marked members of each adjective pair. For example, *big* was given as the opposite of *small*, *short*, *thin*, *low*, *young*, and *shallow* (ranked by frequency) while *small* or *little* were given as the opposite to *big*, *high*, *tall*, *long*, *wide*, *thick*, and *old* (ranked by frequency). These data support the interpretation that the meaning of *big* at first extends over the meanings of the unmarked dimensional terms like *long*, *high*, *tall*, *wide*, and only later does the child learn to apply the other dimensional adjectives to more specific areas of the semantic domain. *Small* (*little*, *wee*) likewise, for a time, acts as the cover term for the marked members of the dimensional adjective pairs.

In a production task used to elicit the same dimensional terms, Wales and Campbell (1970) found that the adjective *big* was the most frequently used by the children (aged 3;5 to 4;1); this finding was repeated in the posttests on the same children (mean age of 4;8) where 46.2% of all the positive-pole adjective responses used the word *big*, versus an average of 25.2% for all the other positive-pole adjectives combined (see Wales & Campbell, 1970, p. 393). Combining the pretest and posttest data on the unmarked versus the marked adjectives used by these children (i.e., omitting the data on pairs like *fat-thin*), unmarked adjectives were used an average of 68.5 times, while marked adjectives were used only an average of 29.5 times. These data show that children have a strong preference for using unmarked rather than marked dimensional terms in their descriptions. One reason for this (that will require further research) could be that they do not yet understand many of the marked terms.

Another experiment designed to explore the child's knowledge of unmarked–marked pairs somewhat further was recently carried out by Tashiro (1971). Tashiro used a picture-identification task to look at the child's interpretations of the noncomparative forms of some pairs of dimensional adjectives. Overall, she found that the pair *big–little* was significantly better understood by the children (average age 3;4) than the other pairs of dimensional terms. Furthermore, the unmarked members of the pairs were significantly better understood than their marked counterparts. Tashiro argues that these results support an order of acquisition going from the more general concept to the more specific ones, i.e., from *big* to the more specific *tall*, *long*, *wide*, etc. The children in this study also appeared to comprehend *tall* better than *high*, and found *thick* and *wide* the most difficult of the unmarked dimensional adjectives used (see also E. Clark, 1972).

The data on dimensional terms can also be represented in terms of components of meaning known by the child at different stages in the acquisition process. *Big* is substituted for other unmarked dimensional terms because it is specified (like them) as + Dimension(3) and + Polar, but the child at this stage has not yet worked out how many dimensions are necessarily presupposed by the other terms such as *long* and *tall*. He has yet to differentiate between the dimensional properties of linearity, surface, and volume. While *big* simply applies to three dimensions, *tall* is more complex since it supposes that all three dimensions are present, and then talks about one specific dimension: + Vertical. The child appears to learn first the feature of dimensionality, then, later on, he specifies further what kind of dimensionality he is talking about; for instance, whether the dimension is + Vertical as in *tall* or *high*, or – Vertical as in *long*, *deep*, *far*, etc. (cf. further discussion of the properties of different dimensional terms in H. Clark, this volume). In addition to this, the child also has to learn that these pairs contrast in meaning: One member of the pair is unmarked and can be used nominally as well as contrastively, while the other, marked, adjective is only used contrastively. Where the children did much better on the unmarked terms than the marked, it looks as though they are still at the second stage, or else in transition to the third stage, where H. Clark (1970a) posited that both members of an adjective pair will be treated as if they refer simply to the "most extent." In other words, both are treated as if they contain the feature + Polar; they have not quite reached the stage where the unmarked adjective + Polar is in contrast with its opposite, which is eventually specified as − Polar.

To summarize, these data provide considerable evidence that the pair *big–small* is overextended to cover the domain of the other more specialized dimensional terms such as *tall–short, high–low, wide–narrow, long–short,* etc. Moreover, within each of these subordinate pairs of terms, there is a certain amount of evidence that the unmarked member of each pair is at first easier to understand than the marked member. It seems more than probable that further investigation with younger children might reveal an overextension phenomenon among these pairs of adjectives also that would be comparable to the data on *more–less* and *same–different.*

Before and After

Lastly I shall present some of the data from E. Clark (1971a) on the acquisition of the meanings of the relational conjunctions *before* and *after*. Unlike many of the terms studied by Donaldson and Wales (1970), the pair *before* and *after* are not unmarked and marked, respectively, by linguistic criteria, but can be characterized as positive and negative (cf. E. Clark, 1971a). In this study, I used both an elicitation task designed to find out when children would spontaneously use the words *before* and *after* to encode temporal relations, and a comprehension task to find out what they understood of the meaning of the two words at different stages in the acquisition process.

After an analysis by age of the results, the children were sorted into groups representing different stages on the basis of the error pattern in their data (see Table 12). At the first stage in the comprehension task, children did

Table 12 *Percentage Errors by Comprehension Stage for Each Construction (E. Clark, 1971a)*

Compre- hension stage	N^a	Before$_1$	Before$_2$	After$_1$	After$_2$
I	21	80	4	10	83
IIa	7	4	4	0	89
IIb	3	25	8	75	92
III	8	9	0	0	6

[a] One *S* from the youngest age-group was unclassifiable.

not understand either word and simply used a strategy based on order of mention: The event mentioned first was treated as the first event in the sequence. Therefore instructions with a *before*-clause in initial position (*before*₁) and with an after-clause in second position (*after*₂) were consistently wrong. At Stage II, *before* was generally correct; *after* in IIa was still dealt with by using an order-of-mention strategy, but in IIb, the word *after* produced a completely different error pattern. Both *after*₂ and *after*₁ produced errors significantly above chance showing that *before* had been overextended to cover *after* as well.

Further evidence that Stage IIb involved overextension of the meaning of *before* comes from the production task used in the same study. Children were asked either (a) "When did [Event 1] happen?" or (b) "When did [Event 2] happen?" For adults, appropriate answers would be "Before [Event 2]" and "After [Event 1]," respectively. Several of the children in the transitional answer stage used the word *before* quite appropriately in answer to *when-1* questions, but evinced a lot of hesitation and even used the word *before* when they tried to answer *when-2* questions. The transitional answer stage in the production task was highly correlated with Stage II of the comprehension task.

The interpretation of these data given in E. Clark (1971a) was that at this stage, the meaning of *before* was in fact extended to cover *after*. In other words, children interpreted *before* correctly, and treated *after* as if it meant the same thing as *before*. At Stage III, the two words have been correctly recognized as being opposite, rather than synonymous, in meaning.

The order of acquisition can be represented in terms of the semantic features added to the entries of temporal words, as follows: First of all, the child learns whether or not a word refers to time: + Time.[6] The first temporal words used spontaneously by the child have, in addition, the characteristic of referring to events that are cotemporaneous with the speech act or with the event being described, and can therefore be specified as + Time, + Simultaneous. Only after this stage does the child learn that there are words that refer to nonsimultaneous events, i.e., to events in sequence: These words can be described as − Simultaneous. However, when two or more events occur in sequence, the order (which came first?) has to be specified. To begin with, − Simultaneous is always interpreted as + Prior. Thus the child at this stage

---

[6] In an analysis that takes account of the close relation between spatial and temporal terms in English, the feature represented as + Time would probably be better characterized as + Location, − Place. The corresponding spatial terms would belong to the hierarchy dominated by + Location, + Place. The validity of this characterization is borne out by some of the responses to *when* questions given by children aged about 3;0 years. They treated *when* as if it meant *where*, i.e., as a question about + Location, + Place rather than as about + Location, − Place, giving answers like "just here" or "here" (E. Clark, 1971a).

will interpret *before* correctly, but if he has realized that *after* is also + Time and − Simultaneous, he will misinterpret it since − Simultaneous is further specified simply as + Prior. It is only later on that the feature − Prior is acquired (E. Clark, 1971a). The same sequence of acquisition for *before* and *after* (*avant que, après que*) was observed by Ferreiro (1971) in her research with French-speaking Swiss children.

The data on *before* and *after* look very similar to the *more–less* data and the *same–different* data reported in Donaldson and Wales (1970). This kind of overextension, then, appears to be a fairly widespread phenomenon in the acquisition of several different kinds of relational terms. What all these terms have in common is (a) they occur in pairs that are closely related in meaning, and (b) the term that is overextended always appears to be the unmarked member of the pair in the case of dimensional adjectives or else the one that is positive in some sense. Furthermore, (c) it is the meaning of the term that is overextended that is acquired first by the child.

Verbs and Complex Nouns

The third type of overextension that will be presented is also less notice-able than the first type, and is generally observed only in contexts similar to those discussed in connection with relational terms: where the child makes a mistake in carrying out instructions that use certain verbs, or else where he fails to give adequate definitions of certain complex relational nouns.

The data come mainly from two studies, the first, by C. Chomsky (1969), concerned with the acquisition of knowledge about the complements taken by certain verbs—this work has since been replicated by Kessel (1970); and the second, by Piaget (1928), concerned with the child's ability to give definitions of complex relational nouns. The children studied by C. Chomsky ranged in age from 5;0 to 10;0, while Piaget's subjects were between 5;0 and 12;0 years old. The children in these studies, then, are considerably older than those who used the first two types of overextension.

Ask and Tell

C. Chomsky (1969) studied children's comprehension of the English verbs *promise, ask* and *tell*, used with various complement structures. Mis-understandings among the younger children (who usually assigned the wrong NP as the subject of the complement verb) were attributed to a lack of syntactic knowledge on the children's part. However, in the present paper, an interpretation of the *ask* and *tell* data will be offered that takes a semantic point of view rather than a syntactic one (cf. also E. Clark, 1971b).

It was C. Chomsky's general finding that children under the age of 8;0

years consistently interpreted the verb *ask* as if it meant *tell*. For example, in response to an instruction like:

(a) *Tell X what to feed the doll.*

the child will answer quite correctly with:

(a') *A banana.*

However, when given instead the instruction:

(b) *Ask X what to feed the doll.*

the child does *not* ask a question of the other child present, but instead simply *tells* him:

(b') *A banana.*

A rather more extended dialogue from the many protocols that C. Chomsky quotes took the following form:

E:	Ask Linda what time it is.
BARBARA:	*I don't know.*
E:	Ask Linda her last name.
BARBARA:	*La Croix.*
E:	Ask Linda her teacher's name.
BARBARA:	*Miss Turner.*
E:	Now I want you to tell Linda some things. Tell Linda how many pencils there are.
BARBARA:	*Three.*
E:	And tell Linda what color this crayon is.
BARBARA:	*Yellow.*
E:	And ask Linda what's in this box.
BARBARA:	*I don't know.*
E:	Could you ask Linda? Maybe Linda knows.
BARBARA:	*Do you, Linda?*
LINDA:	No.

[From the protocol for Barbara, aged 5;3, Chomsky, 1969, p. 63f.]

C. Chomsky used several different forms of complement with both *ask* and *tell*. These are shown under the heading "Sentence form" in Table 13, which summarizes the interpretations made of *ask* in the different constructions. The children fell into five different groups (Stages I–V) on the basis of their interpretations of *ask*. Their interpretations of all the instructions containing *tell* were always correct at all age-levels. Furthermore, the

Table 13   *Ask and Tell* [a]

Sentence form	Interpretation Stage				
	I	II	III	IV	V
(1) *Ask x what time it is*	tell	ask	ask	ask	ask
(2) *Ask x his last name*	tell	tell	ask	ask	ask
(3) *Ask x what to feed the doll*	tell	tell	tell	ask[b]	ask
(1′) *Tell x what time it is*	tell	tell	tell	tell	tell
(2′) *Tell x your last name*	tell	tell	tell	tell	tell
(3′) *Tell x what to feed the doll*	tell	tell	tell	tell	tell

[a] Based on C. Chomsky (1969).

[b] *Ask* is interpreted as a question, but the wrong subject is assigned to the complement verb.

> *What are **you** going to feed the doll?*

instead of:

> *What should **I** feed the doll?*

errors on *ask* [except for (3) in Stage IV] were all the result of interpreting *ask* as though it meant the same thing as *tell*. This can be seen very clearly in the protocol quoted above in which the 5-year-old persistently treated *ask* as *tell*, responding to all the experimenter's instructions accordingly.

If *tell* is interpreted in the imperative contexts given in Table 13 as meaning roughly something like "I order you—you say to *x*—complement sentence," we can contrast it with the related analysis of *ask*: "I order you—you say to *x*–you request *x*—*x* say to you—complement sentence." This analysis contains the added information that this is a question that will need an answer, and not simply an assertion. From this rough performative analysis, it is clear that *ask* and *tell* overlap in meaning, but *ask* has some additional properties that are not found in *tell*. The meaning of *ask* involves learning the request feature and also the allocation of roles: The third person (*x*) and not the initial addressee is to supply the answer. One possible semantic interpretation of C. Chomsky's results, therefore, is that the meaning of *tell* is used for *ask* until the child learns the rest of the semantic information about the verb *ask* which will differentiate it in meaning from *tell*. This, then, is an instance of the synonymy form of overextension.

Brother and Sister

In *Judgment and Reasoning in the Child* (1928), Piaget describes a series of investigations that he undertook on the child's conceptions of various complex relational nouns like *brother* (or *sister*), *family*, *friend*, and *country*. His work on *brother* and *sister* has since been replicated with English-speaking children (Danziger, 1957; Elkind, 1962), and one of the replications found the same kind of results with three other kinship terms, viz., *daughter*, *uncle*, and *cousin*. The technique used in all these studies was to ask the children for definitions (e.g., "What is a brother?"), and then to examine the difference between the definitions given at the various stages of conceptual development.

Piaget found that the definitions could be divided into three main classes: first, those that simply defined a brother as a boy (and a sister as a girl); at the second stage, the child would recognize that there had to be more than one child in the family, but he still did not realize that each sibling was a brother (or sister, according to sex) and would insist that only one of two siblings was a brother. At the third stage (rarely achieved before the age of 9;0), the child would recognize that terms like *brother* and *sister* are in fact reciprocal, so that if one has a brother, one is either a brother or a sister.

At the earliest stage, Piaget (1928) found that the words *brother* and *boy*, *sister* and *girl* are treated as synonyms:

(1)   Lo [aged 5;0]
        —What is a sister?
        —*A sister is a girl you know.*
        —Are all the girls you know sisters?
        —*Yes, and all the boys are brothers.*

(2)   KAN [aged 7;6]
        —What's a brother?
        —*It's a boy.*
        —Are all boys brothers?
        —*Yes.*
        —Is your father a brother?
        —*No, because he's a man.*

(3)   SOB [aged 7;0]
        —Is your father a brother?
        —*Yes, when he was little.*
        —Why was your father a brother?
        —*Because he was a boy.*   [pp. 104f.]

From the examples in (2) and (3), it can be seen that the first definitions of *brother* may also exclude adults. Some of the children, though simply defined *brother* on the basis of sex with no age constraints.

At the next stage, the children recognize that there have to be other children in the family:

(4)   So [aged 8;0—an only child, not sure if he himself is a brother]
        —*A brother is when someone has a child, well the child who comes next is a brother.*

(5)   HAL [aged 9;0]
           —What's a brother?
           —*When there's a boy and another boy, when there are two of them.*
           —Has your father got a brother?
           —*Yes.*
           —Why?
           —*Because he was born second.*
           —Then what is a brother?
           —*It is the second brother that comes.*
           —Then the first one is not a brother?
           —*Oh no, the second one that comes is called brother.*   [p. 105]

Despite the recognition of the need for two children, the term *brother* is still restricted in that there is no reciprocal sense attached to it: It appears to apply only to the second child (or occasionally only to the first if the child being questioned had an older brother), not to both of them.

Finally, children realize that *brother*, besides involving sex and other siblings, defines a reciprocal relationship among siblings:

(6)   BERN [aged 10;0]
           —*A brother is a relation, one brother to another.*   [p. 106]

At the first stage, then, *brother* and *boy* (like *ask* and *tell*) are treated as synonyms. The lexical entries for *brother* and *boy*, then, could both be represented as:

(7) $$\begin{bmatrix} + \text{Male} \\ - \text{Adult} \end{bmatrix}$$

As the child gets older, he adds to the lexical entry more specific features which begin to differentiate the meaning of *brother* from that of *boy*. One of the first signs of this separation is the recognition that adults may also be brothers. The next feature of meaning that is added to *brother* can be characterized as *requires sibling*. In a feature notation, the entry for *brother* is now the following:

(8) $$\begin{bmatrix} + \text{Male} \\ \pm \text{Adult} \\ + \text{Sibling} \end{bmatrix}$$

The word *brother* still does not, for the child, designate a reciprocal relationship. It is at this stage that he will claim that only one of two boys in a family is a brother, or only the smallest child is a brother, and so on. Then, at the last stage, the child adds to the meaning of the word *brother* the idea of reciprocity:

(9)
$$\begin{bmatrix} + \text{ Male} \\ \pm \text{ Adult} \\ + \text{ Sibling} \\ + \text{ Reciprocal} \end{bmatrix}$$

Piaget described this process as the development of the "concept" of *brother*. I have argued, though, from a different point of view that it is the addition of the specific semantic features to the meaning of the word *brother* that eventually allows the child to differentiate between *boy* and *brother*.

Summary

In presenting the data from three different areas of research in language acquisition, I have shown that what the data have in common is that they are the result of some form of overextension, where overextension entails that the lexical entry for the meaning of a word in the child's vocabulary is incomplete. After the first stages of language acquisition, the overextensions that are made are fairly inconspicuous, and usually go by unnoticed.

The child's early referential overextensions show, first, that children use certain kinds of features criterially; second, these criterial features are derived from the child's percepts of objects and events; thirdly, the domain of the overextension of a word can be used to infer which features are being used. Last, the narrowing-down process toward the end of this period also provides some information about the features that the child is using by the constraints that are placed on the use of the new words that help break up a semantic domain. The more restricted use of new words suggests that the child has more detailed entries for these lexical items. As a result, more criteria have to be met before a word can be applied to an object or situation.

In the second kind of overextension discussed, the children were far more advanced linguistically. They no longer used noticeable overextensions, but where two words were very closely related, they confused their meanings. Of the relational terms that have been studied, the tendency was to use the meaning of the unmarked term (or where marking criteria did not apply, the term that was positive) to cover both words in the pair, e.g., *more–less*, *same–different*, *before–after*. The marked term, moreover, was wrongly interpreted, as if it meant the same thing as its unmarked counterpart. It was not until the children learned the more specific semantic feature(s) that closely related words became differentiated. Again, the children's errors (this time in interpretation rather than in spontaneous production of speech) are a good guide to which features they did know, and which they did not.

In the data from the pairs of dimensional terms, there was also evidence that the child knew that they were all related to each other as a set; the proof of this comes from his use of *big* and *small* as cover terms for unmarked and marked dimensional adjectives respectively. This usage also suggests that the meanings of the other adjectives had not yet been sufficiently fully specified for the child to differentiate in any detail between, for example, *big* and *tall*. The meaning of *big* is simply extended to cover the other terms because the child's lexical entries for them do not yet contain all the features needed to differentiate them from *big* (cf. further E. Clark, 1972).

The third kind of overextension described is somewhat similar to the second. The child is again in the position of having some incomplete lexical entries that lead him to treat some words synonymously (*tell–ask*, *boy–brother*) until he learns some of the other features that have to be added to the lexical entry for one of the words in order to differentiate their meanings. Again, the child's errors of interpretation or his inability to give adequate definitions allow one to infer what he does know about the meaning of a word and what remains for him to learn.

SOURCES OF SEMANTIC FEATURES

In this section, I shall consider what we know about the kinds of semantic features that could be said to have been acquired and used by the child on the basis of the data presented. First, the features used in the early stages of semantic acquisition, as well as some used later, will be related to features in perceptual development. Then I shall touch on the part played later on by non-percept-based features, features that are derived from the social or cultural conventions of the group using a particular language.

Early Features—A Perceptual Basis?

One assumption of the present hypothesis is that the earliest semantic features probably belong to the universal set of semantic primitives. However, there is no way yet of knowing which features are primitive and which are not. Can the problem be approached from another direction? The primitives are assumed to be universal precisely because they derive from the human organism's interpretation of his perceptions and cognitions. Therefore, it is possible that the development of perception in infants might provide some clues about the kinds of features that might underlie early semantic features.

Since learning to attach meanings to words involves the interpretation and encoding of perceptual data, we might expect to find an analogous sequence of development in perception: the use of single criterial features followed later by the use of configurations of features. Gibson (1969) points out that the young infant at first singles out individual areas (single features) for attention when looking at objects: He focuses on high contrast edges, vertices, spots and moving parts. This initial attention to single features then develops into the use of what Gibson (1969) calls "bundles of features": "Distinctive features develop later out of these properties as contrasts are discovered ... the specificity of discrimination is thereby increased. *Gestalten* or higher order structured units develop still later, as bundles of features are processed with greater simultaneity and relations between features are registered as units of structure [p. 345]."

In illustration of this progression within perceptual development, one can consider the infant's stages in coming to recognize human faces. At the earliest stage, one can elicit from the infant a smiling response to dots or lines; later he will require the dots to appear within some contour: Thus, eyes will have to appear within a given setting (the top half of the face). Soon after this, he begins to require there to be a mouth present, preferably in movement, and this has to be combined with eyes and facial contour. By the age of 5 months, the infant can distinguish between realistic heads and un-realistic ones. Gibson states further: "Development seems to proceed from simple contours to differentiated features to structured relations or patterns to unique patterns of individual faces [p. 347]." This account of the develop-ment of perception going from attention to individual features to attention to configurations or structured relations between features is remarkably similar to what appears to go on in the use of early semantic features that are attached to a word. It is possible that the use of perceptual features that are then interpreted as the meaning of a word thus follow a developmental pattern for perception. To begin with, only single features are interpreted and put down as the meaning for a word, but later on, configurations of perceptual features are used as a structured whole to code (some of) the word's meaning.

In using perceptual information about objects, there also seem to be certain preferences among children: Some perceptual attributes are domi-nant. Ricciuti (1963), for example, found that contour dominated details of objects in a similarity judgment task. He asked children between the ages of 3;0 and 8;0 years to tell him which object was most similar to a standard where the set of objects offered to the child differed in contour (shape) or in detail (the squares and circles had ears or dots added to them). At all age-levels, the children most often chose the item that was similar in contour rather than in any detail. As second choices made clear, however, they did perceive the detail, but the contour was given priority in classifying objects as similar. This tendency to rely on contour or shape may account for shape being the most frequent basis for overextensions.

Since the different classes of overextensions are most easily classified on the basis of certain perceptual features (movement, shape, sound, size, taste, and texture), it should hardly be surprising that the use of perceptually derived features should display some of the characteristics found in the development of perception itself. While the studies reported in Gibson on the use of single (global) features prior to the use of bundles of features or combinations of features were of infants less than a year old, it is quite possible that this progression is recapitulated when the child has to begin interpreting his perceptual input in order to use it in attaching a meaning to a word. The child therefore begins by using a single general feature, such as shape or contour, and considers that to be the meaning of some term. As he becomes compelled to differentiate more meanings, he can no longer simply use a single perceptual feature: He must begin to use more than one and eventually will encode the information from a bundle or combination of features (whose relations to each other are structured) and use this in attaching meaning to lexical items.

In conclusion, the data on the child's first use of components of meaning in the referential uses of words suggest very strongly that the earliest semantic features could be derived directly from the interpreted bundles or combinations of perceptual features. Thus, the perceptual features themselves may well belong to the set of universal semantic primitives postulated by Bierwisch (1967, 1970a). While a great deal of research is obviously needed before we can make such claims conclusive, what data we have clearly point in that direction.

Features Used in Relational Terms I

The earliest semantic features used by the child appear to be derived mainly from the perceptual information that he has about his surroundings. While most of the instances reported in the literature (cf. Tables 1–6) involved the learning of words used to name things, I shall argue in this section that the meanings of relational terms may also be derived from their perceptual features. The child has to learn which properties of objects such terms describe, and what the conditions are for the use of particular relational words. In the case of the dimensional adjectives studied by Donaldson and Wales (1970), the conditions for use include, at the very least, learning which adjectives name the properties of objects and which name the relations between objects in space. The set of dimensional adjectives, in fact, belongs to a larger set of terms that is used to describe spatial relations in English. Learning the meanings of these terms involves learning which words talk about reference points, which about lines, and which about planes, i.e. one-, two-, and three-dimensional spaces, respectively; and furthermore which words deal with extent, with position, and with directionality. The child has also to make the further distinction between the properties of space and the intrinsic properties of objects used as reference points, e.g., the front and back of a tree (Fillmore, 1971) versus the front and back of a house (Leech, 1970; Teller, 1969).

Of the pairs of adjectives examined, *big–wee/small* has very few constraints on its application: it can be used in the description of any three-dimensional object. The pairs *tall–short* and *high–low* (extension and position), on the other hand, refer to one particular dimension (verticality). At the same time, one of the conditions for using these two adjective pairs is that the objects be three-dimensional. With the exception of *big–wee*, each pair of unmarked–marked terms applies to one specific dimension, e.g., *long–short, high–low*, etc. Measurement in the positive direction along the dimension is named by the unmarked term which also serves as the name of the dimension, e.g., *long–length, high–height*, etc. The marked terms, such as *short* or *low*, though, measure in a negative direction along the dimension. Each dimension is measured from a zero point (or primary reference point) so the positive direction goes away from the zero point.[7] In addition, each dimension may have several secondary reference points or standards against which an object is compared. The marked terms necessarily involve such a standard, and measure from this standard back to the zero point, in the negative direction along the dimension (for a more detailed discussion of these properties, cf. H. Clark, this volume).

In the acquisition of these terms, the data show that the pair *big–wee/small* is the best understood and the most used by children aged about $3\frac{1}{2}$ years old. *Big–small* is the pair of terms that is the most general in meaning, referring simply to overall size, and it has the fewest conditions to fulfill for its use. It also appears to act as a cover term for the more specific pairs of dimensional adjectives that refer to particular dimensions.

Within the pairs of adjectives, there were decided asymmetries in their acquisition by children: The unmarked, positive terms such as *long* or *high* were understood better and used more than the corresponding marked, negative terms such as *short* or *low*. Is there any perceptual basis for these asymmetries (unmarked/positive adjectives versus marked/negative ones) found in the acquisition of dimensional adjectives? In fact, the structure of the human organism's perceptual apparatus does possess certain asymmetries in terms of the perceptual fields available. If the earth's surface is taken as a natural (horizontal) plane with gravity as a reference direction (vertical), then the human being standing upright has a symmetrical left–right field of vision (the body is symmetrical about its left–right axis), but has an asymmetrical front–back perceptual field: Those things in front are visible, those behind are not; and he also has an up–down asymmetry: Those

[7]The analysis and the terms "primary and secondary reference points" are borrowed from H. Clark (q.v.).

things on or above the earth's surface are visible, but those below are (normally) out of sight. Thus, as H. Clark has argued (this volume), the asymmetries among the pairs of terms used to describe spatial relations in English appear to reflect the asymmetries present in the perceptual capacities of the human organism (cf. also Bierwisch, 1967; Teller, 1969), e.g., *up* is positive, *down* negative; *in front* is positive, *behind* negative, etc., where *positive* is roughly equivalent to "within the field of vision" and *negative* to "not within the field of vision." However, what have been called negative terms here may simply involve reversal of direction, e.g., among dimensional adjectives such as *tall–short*, or among prepositional pairs such as *in–out* or *on–off.*

These asymmetries in the description of space apply also to the description of time in English where many temporal relations have a spatial model underlying them. This is the reason why *before* (parallel to *in front of*) may be called positive and *after* (parallel to *behind* or *in back of*) negative. Moreover, the same asymmetry, positive before negative, was found in the acquisition of the meanings of *before* and *after* as was found in the acquisition of dimensional adjective pairs in which the unmarked, positive members of the pairs were acquired before the marked, negative members.

One might argue, therefore, on the basis of the early data and of these data on relational terms that perceptual information is all that need be available in order for the child to be able to set up appropriate lexical entries for the vocabulary of his language. This view, though, would be an oversimplification for it ignores what have variously been called the functional, social, or cultural factors in the determination of word meanings. In addition to encoding perceived characteristics of an object, the meaning of the word used to name it may require some further specification of its function or culturally determined role. For example, on the basis of perceptual information, a child would see no reason to distinguish between a *chair* and a *throne*. The difference between them is simply a functional or cultural one within some societies that is defined by how the object is used in the social context, i.e., who sits there. This kind of culturally derived information will be called knowledge about roles. While the child begins by using perceptual information in attaching meanings to words, he eventually has to add to his perceptual information details about the roles that certain words name or assign to participants in particular contexts.

Features Used in Relational Terms II

For the data on certain verbs (C. Chomsky, 1969) and on some kinship terms (Piaget, 1928), both perceptually based information and information about roles have to be taken into account in studying the acquisition of their meanings by children. One of the things that the child has to learn about these more complex relational terms is which roles are implied and assigned by their use. As an example, let us take another verb that was studied by C. Chomsky (1969), the verb *promise*. At first, the child appears to treat *promise* as if it belongs to the class that includes *tell*, *say*, *assert*, *state*, etc., but in addition the word *promise* involves some notion of obligation.[8] In Chomsky's experiment, this knowledge alone would be enough to give the appearance of being able to define what a promise was, without actually knowing which roles it assigned; i.e., without yet understanding that the person who does the promising—whether in a first-person context (*I promise you that x*), or in a second- or third-person context—is always the one who is meant to carry out the promised action (E. Clark, 1971b). The roles assigned by *promise* are not understood correctly until about age 8;0 or 9;0. Learning what a verb like *promise* means necessitates learning which roles the verb assigns to the speaker and/or addressee, and which roles the speaker may expect to see carried out by a third person.

In the same way, the child has to learn which roles are assigned to the addressee by the verbs *ask* and *tell*. Within the imperative context of the experiments, the child (who was always the addressee) had to know whether he was to take the role of asserting something to a third person present in the room (*tell*), or whether he was to put a question to that third person (*ask*). These roles cannot be easily derived from the interpretation of the perceptual characteristics of the situation in which the child observes the use of such words. The child has to observe not only the contexts but further to infer from the consequences (reactions to the use of these words) exactly what kinds of roles exist and which roles are assigned to speaker and/or addressee by the use of a particular word. The exact interpretation of these roles is often dependent on the social structure and conventions of the speech community in which the child grows up.

The other data for which the acquisition of knowledge about roles is essential come from the work on the acquisition of the meanings of some kinship terms. Societies vary widely on the definitions given to different terms and on the number of terms used. The legal definitions depend in turn on the social organization, while biological factors are not always obvious and are not necessarily integrated into the social and legal systems. The child, therefore, has to learn many new social facts about the roles played by different people before he can find out what a particular kinship relation

[8] D. I. Slobin (personal communication) reports that a child of 4;6 years used *promise* in the following context: Early on in the day she had told her friend to come over to her house. Then later, when the friend did not come, she said: "I promised that Amy would come over but she didn't." This example (which is supported by others from the same source) clearly shows that knowledge of the role assigned by the word *promise* has not yet been acquired.

means. If we take the term studied in most detail by Piaget, we find that the child's first meaning for the word *brother* could very easily be said to be based on perceptually derived information, e.g., "Brothers are boys," "Brothers are little boys," and so on. However, the child also makes incorrect inferences from these facts, for example that the converse holds: "All boys are brothers" or "Only small boys are brothers." At a later stage, the child adds further components to the meaning of the word, principally that there have to be at least two children in order for there to be a *brother* (although only one of them is a brother, even where the children are both male). This too, it can be claimed, is an observable fact from which the child could make appropriate inferences about the meaning of *brother*. About this time, some children begin to give social or functional definitions too: "He's someone who lives with you." Soon after this, the child learns that *brother* involves a reciprocal relationship. However, it is not clear whether he knows exactly what the role named *brother* consists of within the family structure, since he does not give adult definitions yet of the word *family* (Piaget, 1928). At this stage, his definitions are functional and perceptually derived: A *family* is "people who live together in the same house." The child has still to learn what all the different roles are, and how they are related to each other within the kinship system. Although Piaget's study was limited to the study of the terms *brother* and *sister*, with a little work on the definition of *family*, Danziger's (1957) study was somewhat more extensive. In his work also, the first meanings for kinship terms were those things that are perceptually derived (e.g., sex- and age-based characteristics), followed later by the addition of social or functional factors (living in the same house, eating together, etc.). Thus, acquiring the full (adult) meaning of the set of kinship terms within a language necessarily involves knowledge of the social structure as well as of the perceived attributes of the people who can appropriately be called *brother* or *sister*.

To summarize, the first semantic features used by the child appear to be based on his perceptions of the world. To this kind of semantic feature are later added those features of meaning that are contributed by social or functional factors within the cultural context. These social factors have been described in terms of the different roles that may be named or assigned to participants in some situation. While some roles are assigned on a temporary basis (e.g., by verbs like *promise* or *ask*), others are more permanent in character (e.g., *brother, father*).

The analysis of the kinds of meaning component or feature that knowledge of roles adds to the lexical entry for individual words has necessarily been less detailed than the discussion of semantic features derived from perceptual information. In mitigation, I can only report that very little is yet known about what I have called roles, either in terms of their semantic structure or in terms of the acquisition of knowledge about them by children learning their first language.

CONCLUSIONS

The present chapter has attempted to characterize some of the knowledge that one has to have about a word in order to use it appropriately. In considering such knowledge from the developmental point of view, I have shown that one has to begin by finding out what it is that the child knows about the meaning of a word, and how this knowledge changes during the language acquisition process. The Semantic Feature Hypothesis assumed that the meanings of words are made up of features or components of meaning, and proposed that children learn word meanings gradually by adding more and more features to their lexical entries. This hypothesis was derived originally from a consideration of some of the diary data (E. Clark, 1971c). In the present paper, the general predictions made by this theory have been shown to be remarkably consistent with data from several different sources in the literature on children's language.

Nonetheless, the theory contains a number of lacunae that future work will have to fill. For example, there is no account of the internal structure (or lack of it) in the child's earliest lexical entries. Is the child's choice of the first semantic feature(s) attached to a word, over and above the perceptual basis, an arbitrary one or not? Another issue that has not been dealt with is the structuring or restructuring of the child's lexical entries as a result of language-particular constraints. For example, there are a number of selectional restrictions which in many languages are governed by the presence of features such as $\pm$ Animate or $\pm$ Human: At what point does the child pull these features out from among the other percept-based features and accord them special status? Furthermore, data on the internal organization of entries in the adult lexicon suggest that the features are arranged in much the same way for all speakers of a language (cf. the discussion of word-association data in H. Clark, 1970b): When does the child adopt this adult form of lexical organization? Yet another issue that will require further elucidation is the order of acquisition of semantic features. Where the entries appear to be hierarchically structured, children learn the most general features first and then the more specific ones (e.g., E. Clark, 1971a; Piaget, 1928). But what is the order of acquisition for those lexical entries that do not contain hierarchically related features?

These constitute only a few of the questions that remain to be answered within the framework of the present theory, and indeed within the framework of any developmental theory about the acquisition of semantic knowledge. Thus, although the data discussed in this paper do support the Semantic Feature Hypothesis, I want to point out that the hypothesis itself still needs further elaboration and testing.

In conclusion, I have tried to show that we cannot take for granted what children say. If we are to study language acquisition properly, then we cannot ignore semantics, for it is essential to know what the child means by what he says, and to know how he understands what he hears. One of the most basic steps the child has to take in acquiring his first language is to attach meaning to words, and therefore semantics is central to the study of language development. Furthermore, the acquisition of semantic knowledge needs to be better studied in relation to the development of the child's perceptual and cognitive abilities. Language, after all, is what provides the child with a means of encoding and communicating his percepts and thoughts about the world around him.

ON THE INTERNAL STRUCTURE OF PERCEPTUAL AND SEMANTIC CATEGORIES[1]

ELEANOR H. ROSCH
University of California, Berkeley

Some colors to which English speakers apply the word "red" are "redder" than others. Some breeds of "dog" (such as retriever) are more representative of the "meaning" of "dog" than others (such as Pekinese). There are colors which subjects do not know whether to classify as "red" or "brown," and dogs whose breed is uncertain. However, psychological and linguistic research has tended to treat categories (whether perceptual or semantic) as though they were internally unstructured—that is, as though they were composed of undifferentiated, equivalent instances—and as though category boundaries were always "well defined" (Neisser, 1967). For the artificial categories used in concept formation research, all members of the positive subset are, in fact, rendered equivalent by definition of the task. The semantic categories of natural languages are made to appear quite similar to such artificial concepts when they are treated as bundles of discrete

[1] This research was supported in part by a grant to the author (under her former name, Eleanor Rosch Heider) from the Foundations Fund for Research in Psychiatry # G67-392, in part by funds made available to the Child Study Center of Brown University from the Grant Foundation and from the National Institute of Neurological Diseases and Blindness, National Collaborative Project (Ph-43-68-13), and in part by research funds made available by the University of California at Berkeley (220 Grant #K9PF-429). I wish to thank Karl G. Heider for his help in the field in West Irian (Indonesian New Guinea), Dr. Robert Olton for assistance in carrying out Experiment 3, and Keith Burton, Randy Street, and Peter Lewitt who assisted with Experiment 4. Experiment 4 was performed with Dr. Richard Millward while the author was a research associate at Brown University.

features which clearly differentiate the category from all others and which determine the selection restrictions of category labels used in sentences (cf. Katz & Postal, 1964). It is the contention of the present paper that most "real" categories are highly structured internally and do not have well defined boundaries; thus, we may presently have a quite distorted view of how real categories are learned and how they function in cognitive processes.

By "internal structure" the following is meant: categories are composed of a "core meaning" which consists of the "clearest cases" (best examples) of the category, "surrounded" by other category members of decreasing similarity to that core meaning. The first part of the paper deals with semantic categories in the perceptual domains of color and form. For such categories, "internal structure" can be given a relatively concrete meaning. It will be argued that, in these perceptual domains, the core meaning of categories is not arbitrary but is "given" by the human perceptual system; thus, the basic content as well as structure of such categories is universal across languages. (Color, in particular, seems to provide an interesting case in which a linguistic-behavioral fact, the nature of color categories, can be tentatively related to the physiology of color vision.) A second part of the paper describes initial attempts to apply the idea of "internal structure" to "nonperceptual" semantic categories—that is, to the type of common noun categories (e.g., "bird," "vehicle," "crime") which have been used extensively in measures of clustering in recall (Tulving, 1968) and in studies of semantic memory retrieval (Collins & Quillian, 1969; Meyer, 1970; Schaeffer & Wallace, 1970).

PART I: PERCEPTUAL CATEGORIES

Let us look in more detail at what is artificial about the structure of the categories learned in concept formation research. In the typical concept formation experiment (cf. Bourne, 1968), the stimuli consist of discrete attributes (such as red versus green, square versus circle, one versus two borders); the categories to which those attributes themselves belong are generally already well-known to the subject (e.g., American college sophomores have long since learned the concepts "red" and "square"); and the subset of attribute combinations which comprise the to-be-learned concepts can be formed, at the will of the experimenter, out of any logically possible combination of the attributes (e.g., the experimenter can call "red and square" the positive subset or "two borders or circle" the positive subset). For such concepts, once the subject has learned the rule(s) defining the positive subset, any one stimulus which fits the rule is as good an exemplar of the concept as any other—it makes no sense to ask the subject whether the red square on one of the experimenter's cards is a better example of the concept "red square" than one on another card. Concept formation tasks were designed to test questions about problem solving which could only be approached with limited and controlled stimuli like these; such tasks do not, however, represent the full range of actual human concepts.

In contrast, many "real" categories (concepts designable by words in "natural languages") partition domains whose stimuli are not discrete but composed of continuous physical variations; natural language categories are not necessarily composed of combinations of simpler, already-learned attributes; and, in most, if not all, natural language concepts, some stimuli are clearly better exemplars of the concept than others. The domain of color serves as an example of all three points: physical properties of light, such as wavelength, intensity or reflectance, are continuous variables; perceived colors are not "analyzable" into combinations of discrete dimensions (Shepard, 1964); and, as is apparent from natural language terminology, there are colors which are considered "better" members of particular color categories than other colors (a "good" red versus an "off" red).

Concepts somewhat more like those in natural languages have been employed in a series of studies of the "process of abstraction," reviewed by Posner (1969). In this work, categories were typically composed of distributions of attributes, and some instances of categories were designed to be more "typical" members of the category than others. However, the categories themselves were invariably artificial; for example, Posner and Keele's (1968) categories were sets of distortions of random dot patterns; Reed's (1970) were combinations of Brunswik schematic faces. With such stimuli, subjects appear to operate inductively by abstracting a "prototype" (a central tendency) of the distribution (e.g., of dot patterns, schematic face features), a "prototype" which then appears to "operate" in classification and recognition of instances.

It is the contention of the research to be reported that there are categories in perceptual domains such as color and form which are not arbitrary. Neither a "concept-formation model" of category formation in terms of learning the "correct" (defined either by an experimenter or a culture) combination of discrete attributes nor an "abstraction-process model" of category formation in terms of abstraction of the central tendency of an (experimentally or culturally determined) arbitrary grouping of distributions of attributes is adequate to account for the nature and development of categories in these perceptual domains. The following alternative account of the development of color and form categories is proposed: there are colors and forms which are more perceptually salient than other stimuli in their domains. A working hypothesis is that salient colors are those areas of the color space previously found to be most exemplary of basic color names in many different languages (Berlin & Kay, 1969) and that salient forms are the "good forms" of Gestalt psychology (circle, square, etc.). Such colors and forms more readily attract attention than other stimuli (E. R. Heider, 1971) and are more easily remembered than less salient stimuli (E. R. Heider, 1972). When category names are learned, they tend to become attached first to the salient stimuli (only later generalizing to other instances), and by this means "natural prototypes" become foci of organization for categories.

From this account it can be predicted that learning natural perceptual categories differs from the abstraction process found in previous studies of artificial category learning in the following specific ways: (*a*) It is easier to learn categories in which the natural prototype is central to a set of variations than it is to learn categories in which a distortion of a prototype is central and the natural prototype occurs as a peripheral member. (*b*) The natural prototype will tend to be learned first, whether or not it is central to the category. (*c*) Subjects will tend to "define" the category as a set of variations on the natural prototype (operationally, they will identify the natural prototype as the "most typical" example of the category) even when the natural prototype is not central to the category.

Colors

The color space was long considered a domain of uniform, physical variation which languages could partition arbitrarily into color name categories (cf. Lenneberg, 1967). Thus, colors were considered an ideal domain in which "language-cognition" research could demonstrate the effects of linguistic categories on nonverbal cognitive processes such as memory (Brown & Lenneberg, 1954; Lantz & Stefflre, 1964; Stefflre, Castillo Vales, & Morley, 1966). Such a view of the nature of the color space has been challenged recently from several sources.

Berlin and Kay (1969) argued that there were a limited number of "basic" color terms (defined by linguistic criteria) in any language—three achromatic and eight chromatic terms. When informants from diverse languages were asked to choose the best examples of their language's basic color terms from an array of Munsell chips, they tended to choose the same areas of the color space. Berlin and Kay called these clusters of best examples of color terms "focal points," and argued that the previous anthropological emphasis on cross-cultural differences in color names was derived from looking only at the boundaries of color names—a more variable aspect of categorization than the focal points. Although Berlin and Kay's data do not constitute unequivocal support for their claims (cf. Hickerson, 1971), the claims are arresting and clearly warrant further research.

E. R. Heider (1971, 1972) provided evidence that the focal points of basic color terms represented areas of the color space which possessed a particular perceptual-cognitive salience "prior" to color naming. "Prior to naming" can be taken in two senses: developmentally, E. R. Heider (1971) showed that 3-year-old American children oriented toward focal colors in preference to nonfocal colors and that 4-year-old American children matched focal colors more accurately than nonfocal colors. Cross-culturally, E. R. Heider (1972) demonstrated that the Dani of New Guinea, speakers of a language which lacks all of the basic chromatic color terms (K. G. Heider, 1970), remembered focal colors more accurately than nonfocal colors—both in a short-term recognition task similar to that used by Brown and Lenneberg (1954) and in a long-term memory task.

The research to be reported here was designed to explore the manner in which color categories are learned. The basic research design involved comparison of the learning of color categories structured according to the supposed natural organization of the color space (focal colors the physically central members of categories) with the learning of color categories structured in other "unnatural" ways. Such a study obviously could not be adequately performed with subjects who already knew a set of basic chromatic color terms provided by their language. Even young children of a culture whose language contained basic color terms were not appropriate subjects since, among other problems, their prior history of exposure to the color terms of their language could not be controlled.

Ideally, subjects were required whose language did not contain basic color terms; for such subjects, the input stimuli for learning color categories could be precisely specified and controlled within the context of the experiment. Such a language is spoken by the Dani of Indonesian New Guinea, a stone-age people previously described by K. G. Heider (1970) as possessing only two color terms, which divide the color space on the basis of brightness rather than hue. Color systems of that character have been reported for other cultures as well; they are classified by Berlin and Kay (1969) as Stage I, the first and simplest stage of a proposed evolutionary ordering of color systems. A description of a study verifying the nature of Dani color terminology and tables showing the distribution of the two basic Dani color terms over arrays of Munsell chips are available in Heider and Olivier (1972).

If the color space were undifferentiated or if the saliency of focal color areas were irrelevant to the learning of color categories, then any set of color categories should be as easy for subjects to learn as any other set of equal discriminability. On the other hand, if the basic hypothesis of this study is correct, categories with a "natural" organization should be learned more easily than other categories. The present experiment contrasted the learning of three types of category sets: sets in which focal colors were physically central to categories; sets in which colors from the "internominal" areas of the color space were central to categories (focal colors did not necessarily occur in such sets); and sets in which the central members of categories were "adjacent" to the focal areas, focal colors occurring as peripheral members of the categories. The specific basic hypotheses were: (a) Sets in which the focal colors are central are learned faster than other sets. (b) Focal colors are learned faster than nonfocal even when they are peripheral. (c) Subjects will tend to "define" the category as composed of a central focal color (by identifying the focal color as the "most typical" example of the category) even in sets where focal colors are peripheral.

Experiment 1: Color Learning
METHODS

Subjects. A total of 68 male Dani, prescreened for color blindness, served as subjects. Only Dani whose color term usage was restricted to the two basic Dani color terms "mili" (roughly "dark") and "mola" (roughly "light") were used. Because the learning task required a number of days of consecutive attendance, it was necessary to use subjects who were physically present at a local school; however, care was taken to use only subjects who were still monolingual in their own language (that is, subjects who, essentially, had not yet learned anything verbal in the school, which was conducted in Indonesian). Dani do not measure age, but, from their size and general physical maturity, subjects were judged to be 12–15 years of age or older. Because the number of volunteers was limited, subjects who learned the three different types of color-category sets were matched in threes according to height (as a rough estimate of age), and according to their ability to interpret the logic of their own kinship structure (as a rough estimate of "intelligence"—see K. G. Heider, 1971). Subjects were volunteers and were paid after they had learned the set assigned them to criterion.

Stimuli. Munsell color chips of glossy finish were used, and are referred to in Munsell notation. The Commission International de l'Eclairage (CIE)-tristimulus values and chromaticity coordinates are obtainable from Nickerson, Tomaszewski, and Boyd (1953).

Six different category sets were used: two sets in which focal colors were central; two sets in which internominal colors were central; and two sets in which focal colors were peripheral. In three of the six sets (one set of each type), categories were composed of chips of the same brightness, varying only in hue; in the other three sets (one set of each type), categories were composed of chips of the same hue, varying only in brightness. The three brightness-varying sets were considered a replication, with different stimuli, of the design of the three hue-varying sets.

Each set consisted of eight categories (consistent with the eight basic chromatic color terms claimed by Berlin and Kay, 1969). Categories were

Table 1 *Sets of Stimuli Used in Color Learning Experiment*[a]

Category	Stimuli					

Hue-varying sets

	Set 1[b]		Set 2		Set 3	
	Central color	Peripheral colors	Central color	Peripheral colors	Central color	Peripheral colors
1	5R 8/6	10RP 8/6 10R 8/6	7.5YR 8/8	2.5YR 8/6 2.5Y 8/10	10RP 8/6	5R 8/6 5RP 8/6
2	5R 4/14	10RP 4/14 10R 4/12	10R 4/10	5R 4/14 5YR 4/10	10RP 4/14	5R 4/14 5RP 4/12
3	2.5Y 8/16	10YR 8/14 5Y 8/12	2.5GY 8/12	10Y 8.5/12 5GY 8/10	10YR 8/14	2.5Y 8/16 5YR 8/16
4	2.5 YR 6/16	10R 6/14 5YR 6/12	5YR 6/12	2.5YR 6/16 7.5YR 6/14	10R 6/14	2.5YR 6/16 5R 6/12
5	5YR 3/6	2.5YR 3/8 10YR 3/4	5Y 3/4	2.5Y 3/2 7.5Y 3/6	2.5YR 3/8	5YR 3/6 10R 3/10
6	2.5G 5/12	7.5GY 5/10 7.5G 5/10	5BG 5/8	10G 5/10 10BG 5/8	7.5BG 5/10	2.5G 5/12 2.5GY 5/10
7	2.5PB 4/10	10B 4/10 5PB 4/12	7.5PB 4/12	2.5PB 4/10 2.5P 4/10	10B 4/10	2.5PB 4/10 2.5B 4/Max
8	5P 3/10	10PB 3/8 10P 3/10	5RP 3/10	10P 3/8 10RP 3/10	10PB 3/8	5P 3/10 5PB 3/10

Brightness-varying sets

	Set 4[b]		Set 5		Set 6	
	Central color	Peripheral colors	Central color	Peripheral colors	Central color	Peripheral colors
1	5R 8/6	5R 9/2 5R 7/6	7.5YR 8/8	7.5YR 9/2 7.5YR 7/10	5R 7/6	5R 8/6 5R 6/12
2	5R 4/14	5R 5/14 5R 3/12	10R 4/10	10R 5/16 10R 3/10	5R 3/12	5R 4/14 5R 2/8
3	2.5Y 8/16	2.5Y 9/4 2.5Y 7/12	2.5GY 8/12	2.5GY 9/6 2.5GY 7/10	2.5Y 7/12	2.5Y 8/16 2.5Y 6/10
4	2.5YR 6/16	2.5YR 7/10 2.5YR 5/12	5YR 6/12	5YR 7/Max 5YR 5/12	2.5YR 5/12	2.5YR 6/16 2.5YR 4/8
5	5YR 3/6	5YR 4/10 5YR 2/4	5Y 3/4	5Y 4/6 5Y 2/2	5YR 2/4	5YR 3/6 5YR 1/2
6	2.5G 5/12	2.5G 7/10 2.5G 3/10	5BG 5/8	5BG 7/8 5BG 3/6	2.5G 3/10	2.5G 5/12 2.5G 1/6
7	2.5PB 4/10	2.5PB 6/10 2.5 PB 2/8	7.5PB 4/12	7.5PB 6/10 7.5PB 2/10	2.5PB 3/10	2.5PB 4/10 2.5PB 2/8
8	5P 3/10	5P 4/Max 5P 2/8	5RP 3/10	5RP 4/12 5RP 2/8	5P 2/8	5P 3/10 5P 1/6

[a]Munsell steps between stimuli sometimes uneven to balance discriminability (measured by technique described in Brown & Lenneberg, 1954) between categories.

[b]Categories of these sets correspond to "basic" color terms: 1=pink, 2=red, 3=yellow, 4=orange, 5=brown, 6=green, 7=blue, 8=purple.

composed of three chips because a pilot study showed this the optimum number for Dani learning in this task. Each subject learned one, and only one, of the sets.

The stimuli used in all categories for all sets are shown in Munsell notation in Table 1. Sets 1, 2, and 3 were composed of hue-varying categories. The presumed "natural prototypes" of color categories were represented by eight focal color chips, that is, by one chip from the center of each of the areas where best examples of the eight basic chromatic color names clustered in Berlin and Kay's (1969) study. (A more complete description of the method of selection of these chips is available in E. R. Heider, 1972.) In Set 1, each category was composed of one central natural prototype (a "focal" chip) and chips of the same brightness two Munsell steps to either "side" (roughly longer and shorter wavelength) in hue. For example, for an English speaker, the "blue" category might be described as a "pure" blue chip, a blue chip (two Munsell steps) toward green and a blue chip (two Munsell steps) toward purple. Set 1 was, thus, constructed to coincide with the proposed natural structure of the color space.

In contrast, Set 2 was constructed to violate that proposed natural structure. Artificial (nonnatural) prototypes for categories were represented by eight chips from the "internominal" areas of the color space; that is, from the centers of those areas in which no chips had been designated as the best example of a basic color name by any language in the Berlin and Kay (1969) study. For the present study, eight internominal chips were chosen which, in addition to being central to internominal areas, fell "between" two basic color-name areas. Set 2 categories were composed in a manner analogous to those of Set 1; each category consisted of the central internominal chip and the chip of same brightness two Munsell steps to the longer and two Munsell steps to the shorter wavelength of the central chips. However, because internominal chips had been chosen that fell between two different basic name areas, Set 2 categories tended to "violate natural hue concepts." That is, the two peripheral chips in each Set 2 category consisted of chips from areas that speakers of languages containing basic hue terms would label with two *different* basic color names—e.g., an English speaker might label Set 2 categories "red *and* brown," "yellow *and* green."

Set 3 differed from Set 1 only in that the focal color was a peripheral rather than the central member of each three-chip category. Each category of Set 3 contained a focal chip and the two chips of the same Munsell brightness but two and four Munsell steps of longer wavelength than the focal chips (for purposes of defining the "red" category in this set, the color space was considered circular with red adjacent to purple).

Sets 4, 5, and 6 were constructed in a manner analogous to Sets 1, 2, and 3 with the exception that categories were composed of chips of the same

Munsell hue, varying in brightness. In Set 4, the same focal colors were central to categories as in Set 1; however, the other two chips in each category were the chips one Munsell step lighter in brightness and one Munsell step darker in brightness than the focal chip. For example, the "blue" category in this set contained the same central chip as in Set 1 but with it were now a lighter blue and a darker blue. In Set 5, categories were composed of the same central internominal chips as in Set 2, however, combined with the Munsell chips one step lighter and one step darker in brightness. Because of this change in construction, the chips of a Set 5 category, instead of cross-cutting basic name areas as those of the Set 2 categories had done, tended to fall into the same internominal area. That is, whereas a Set 3 category might be labeled "yellow *and* green," by an English speaker, the equivalent Set 5 category would probably be considered three brightnesses of "yellow-green." The categories of Set 6 (analogous to Set 3) consisted of the focal color and the two chips of the same hue but one and two steps darker in brightness (special chips of 1/brightness were obtained for the brown, green, and purple categories).

For purposes of the present study, the comparison between hue-varying and brightness-varying sets was not of particular concern; the comparison of primary interest was between sets composed of categories in which focal colors were central, internominal colors central, or focal colors peripheral (i.e., the comparison between Sets 1 versus 2 versus 3, and between Sets 4 versus 5 versus 6). Before sets were completed, discriminability between chips within and between categories for each set were computed by the formulas (omitting the correction for "edges") in Brown and Lenneberg (1954). Neither the mean discriminability within nor between categories differed between Sets 1, 2, and 3 nor Sets 4, 5, and 6. However, all three of the latter (the sets composed of brightness-varying categories) had lower mean discriminability within categories and greater mean discriminability between categories than the former (the sets composed of hue-varying categories). Triads of subjects matched in height and understanding of the logic of their own kinship system were taught Sets 1, 2, and 3; other matched triads were taught 4, 5, and 6.

Procedure.   Twelve subjects learned Set 1; 12 subjects learned Set 2, and 11 subjects learned each of the other sets. A subject learned one set only.

Subjects learned a set as a paired associate task; colors as stimuli, the same Dani word as correct response for the three colors in a category. Finding suitable response words at first seemed a serious obstacle to the study; however, it proved possible to use as responses names of Dani sibs (a sib is a nonterritorial, unilineal descent group, somewhat like a clan). Sib names were all well known to Dani and, as nearly as could be determined in pretesting, all approximately equally frequent, familiar, and meaningful.

Furthermore, measures of association between sib names were easily obtained (Dani readily listed sib names), and it was possible to use names with approximately equal interassociation value. In order to randomize effects of any uncontrolled memorability differences in sib names, each subject received a different set of pairings of colors and names. A subject's own sib name was never used as one of his responses.

The task was described to each subject as learning a new language which the experimenter would teach him and for which he would be paid when learning was completed. He was warned that the learning could take several days. At the start of the first testing session, the colors (mounted on 3 × 5-inch white cards) were laid in random order in front of the subject; and he was told the "name" of each which he repeated after the experimenter. Thereafter, the cards were gathered into a pack, shuffled, and presented one at a time to the subject who was required to say the name of the color. The subject received feedback after each response; he was praised if correct and told the correct response if incorrect. After each run, the cards were reshuffled. Subjects received five runs a day on successive days until the criterion of one perfect run had been achieved. A record was kept of the stimulus color and the subject's response on each trial.

Immediately after reaching criterion, subjects performed two additional tasks: the first intended to ascertain whether the three-chip category had been learned as a transferable concept, the second designed to measure the subject's ideas of the central (most typical) member of each of the categories in the set he had learned. As a transfer task, subjects were asked to "name" eight colors which had not been in the training categories. For the hue-varying sets, each transfer color was the chip one Munsell step darker than the central chip of each category; for the brightness-varying sets, each transfer color was the chip two Munsell steps of shorter wavelength than the central chip. To measure the second variable, the subject was shown, successively, all three chips of each category of his learning set and asked to point to the best (most typical) example. There is a Dani verb form used specifically for usual or typical activities which served to make such questions readily understood, at least in regard to some stimuli.

RESULTS

Of the 68 Dani who undertook the learning task, 63 completed learning to criterion. That categories within a set were learned as transferable concepts was shown by the results of the transfer task. By chance, subjects would have been correct in the transfer task 1/8 of the time; the obtained overall ratio of correct transfers was 7.2/8.

The first basic hypothesis of the study concerned differences in the relative ease with which the different sets were learned. Figure 1 shows the learning curves for all six sets. Each point in Fig. 1 represents an average over subjects and over the five runs for that day. The mean number of errors per stimulus chip per subject learning each of the sets to criterion was, for hue-varying sets: Set 1, 8.54; Set 2, 18.96; Set 3, 12.91; for brightness-varying sets: Set 4, 6.67; Set 5, 8.77; Set 6, 9.58. A two-way analysis of variance, Treatments × Levels (Lindquist, 1953) was performed on number of errors to criterion. Classification of sets by the type of color categories in the set (focal colors central, internominal colors central, focal colors peripheral) constituted the treatments variable; whether the sets were hue-varying or brightness-varying constituted the levels variable.

Both main effects were significant: treatments, $F(2, 61) = 7.02, p < .01$; levels, $F(1, 61) = 8.29, p < .01$. The interaction was not significant, $F(2, 61) = 1.63$. The significant effect of treatment is directly relevant to the main hypothesis of the study. The t tests between all pairs of sets confirmed that the following differences between sets were statistically significant; $p < .05$ or better: within hue-varying sets: Set 1 < Set 3 < Set 2; within brightness-varying sets—Set 4 < Set 5, Set 6. These results show that, in both the hue- and brightness-varying sets, sets in which the presumed natural prototype

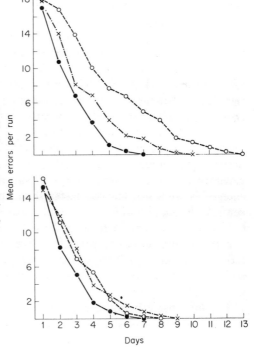

FIG. 1. Mean errors per run per day for the six color-category learning sets. Top: Hue varying sets. (●) Set 1, Focal colors central; (○) Set 2, Internominal colors central; (×) Set 3, Focal colors peripheral. Bottom: Brightness varying sets. (●) Set 4, Focal colors central; (○) Set 5, Internominal colors central; (×) Set 6, Focal colors peripheral.

were central (Sets 1 and 4) were learned with significantly fewer errors than either of the other sets. Set 2, composed of "hue-violating" categories, was more difficult to learn than any of the other sets. (There is additional anecdotal evidence for the difficulty of Set 2; not only were three of the five subjects who failed to reach criterion assigned to Set 2, but an additional four Set 2 subjects could only be pursuaded to continue to criterion with great effort on the part of the experimenter, a difficulty not encountered with the subjects who had been assigned to other sets.) The significant main effect of level was of less interest to the purpose of the study. It was not surprising that the brightness-varying sets (4, 5, and 6) should be learned with fewer errors than the hue-varying sets (1, 2, and 3); such an effect was predictable on the basis of discriminability differences between the hue- and brightness-varying categories.

The second basic hypothesis of the study concerned the relative ease with which names were learned for colors as individual stimuli within categories; the prediction was that focal colors would be learned faster than non-focal even when the focal colors were peripheral members of categories. In light of the abstraction research findings concerning the central tendencies of artificial categories (Posner, 1969), it was also reasonable to expect that central members of categories would be learned more rapidly than peripheral members. The data from Sets 1, 3, 4, and 6 could be grouped into a row by column table: focal versus nonfocal, and central versus peripheral. A two-way analysis of variance for the variable number-of-errors-per-stimulus was performed on this data. The main effect for the focal dimension was significant, $F (1, 26) = 8.72, p < .01$; however, neither the main effect for centrality, $F (1, 26) = 1.94$, nor the interaction, $F (1, 26) = 1.13$, reached significance. Such results indicated that focal colors were learned with fewer errors than nonfocal, an effect which was independent of the centrality of the colors. That names for focal colors were learned faster than for nonfocal colors is consistent with E. R. Heider's (1972) finding that focal chips were better remembered than nonfocal in memory tasks which did not involve category learning. It was, however, surprising that central members of categories were not learned faster than peripheral. The ease of learning central and peripheral colors could also be compared for Sets 2 and 5 (which did not contain focal colors). Errors per stimulus for central and peripheral chips were compared by t tests for each of these two sets. The difference was not significant in Set 2, but the hypothesis that central would be learned more rapidly than peripheral was weakly supported in Set 5, t (10) $= 2.01, p < .10$.

The final basic hypothesis concerned subjects' judgments of the "most typical" examples of categories—this hypothesis could not be tested for Dani color learning. Dani subjects, although they readily transfered color category names to new instances, were unwilling to designate one of the color chips as the most typical member of the three-chip category. Since Dani easily made such a judgment for form categories, discussion of the color task will be deferred until the form data have been presented.

In summary, the major findings of the color learning task were: (a) The presumed natural prototypes of color categories were learned more rapidly than other colors even when they were peripheral members of categories, and (b) it was easier for Dani subjects to learn sets of color categories organized around the presumed natural prototype colors than to learn categories organized around other areas of the color space.

Forms

Learning of form categories was studied for two reasons: (a) to demonstrate the role of natural prototypes in category formation in more than one perceptual domain, and (b) to replicate the logic of the color research with stimuli in which "natural" and "unnatural" category sets could be constructed in a more controlled manner than had been possible with colors. That is, because of the nature of the color space, it had not been possible for focal colors to occur as peripheral members of sets in which internominal colors were central, nor, using both focal and internominal colors, had it been possible to construct a group of sets in which all stimuli occurred both as central and as peripheral members. Such manipulations were possible with forms.

The Dani language does not possess readily accessible monolexemic codes for geometric forms (K. G. Heider, 1970), not surprising in light of the fact that Dani live in an "uncarpentered world" (Segall, Campbell, & Herskovitz, 1966) in which three-dimensional shapes are irregular and in which two-dimensional geometric line drawings do not occur. Even so, it was possible that Dani had nonverbal concepts which would lead them to group the experimental forms in a particular way prior to the category learning of the experiment itself and/or that Dani had readily available verbal circumlocutions which could designate the experimental form categories. Three pilot studies were therefore performed, designed to determine whether Dani showed evidence of preexperimental biases in categorizing the experimental stimuli.

Pilot Studies

The stimuli used in the pilot studies were 21 two-dimensional line drawings, 3 "basic" forms (circle, square, and triangle), and 6 transformations of each of the basic forms. These were the forms of Set 1, described in detail later. The object of the pilot research was to determine whether Dani showed tendencies to group these stimuli into circle, square, and triangle categories prior to the experimental name learning.

The possibility of nonverbal grouping of the stimuli was tested in two tasks: free sorting of the 21 figures, and a series of oddity problems in which the subject was required to point to the two figures most alike when his choice was two variants of one basic form and one variant of one of the other forms. Seven subjects performed the sorting task; nine performed the oddity problems. The results were uniform and unequivocal. Both in the sorting and in the oddity problems, grouping of variants of the same form was at chance.

The possibility of verbal circumlocutions to designate the form categories was tested in a two-person communication task. Two subjects were seated on either side of a screen; each had before him (arranged in different orders) the 21 figures of Set 1. One subject, designated as speaker, was required to describe each form so that the listener could pick the correct form from among the others. When the listener thought he had found the form, he held up the card so the speaker could see his choice. If incorrect, the speaker was required to give a new description and the listener to choose a second time. Twenty pairs of subjects performed the task. This communication task is one in which American subjects tend to verbalize both the basic form category and the variation (e.g., "It's the square with a hole in it."); Dani codings, however, were almost all the names of specific objects ("It's a pig"; "It's a broken fence."). If the form class of the figure had affected Dani verbalizations, listener errors should have been greater within the form class of the encoded stimulus; for example, if the intended stimulus were a variant of the circle, and the listener's choice were incorrect, he should be more likely to choose a different variant of the circle than some other form. The actual result was that errors were randomly distributed over the three form classes—even on the second guess where the speaker had been given a chance to correct an initially erroneous choice.

It appeared safe to conclude from the pilot research, that the two-dimensional figures used in the form learning study were not already classified into form classes by Dani subjects.

Experiment 2: Form Learning

METHOD

Subjects.   A total of 94 Dani were subjects in the form learning experiment. None had participated either in the color research or in the pilot studies. Because form learning required fewer days to reach criterion than color learning, it was possible to use subjects from the surrounding villages who had no contact with the local school. As in the previous experiment, subjects were paid after they reached criterion on the learning task. Approximately 14 subjects learned each form set.

Stimuli. The "good forms" of Gestalt psychology were presumed the natural prototypes of form categories. Two-dimensional line drawings of a "perfect" square, circle, and equilateral triangle, approximately 1 in.^{2} in area, served as prototype (focal) forms.

Seven sets of stimuli were constructed. In Set 1, the presumed natural set, a "perfect" basic circle, square, and equilateral triangle were "central" to a group of transformations. By "central" it is meant that the transformations were performed on the "perfect" basic forms. As an aid to visualization, Fig. 2 shows the square and its transformations. There were six transformations: (*a*) Gap—a ¼-inch gap was placed in one side of the figure. (*b*) Line-to-curve—for the square and triangle, one line was changed to a curve the midpoint of which was ¼ inch to the inner side of the figure; for the circle, an arc was changed to a line which cut off an equivalent amount of the area of the circle. (*c*) One-line-extended—for the square and triangle, one line was extended ¼ inch with the adjoining line extended to meet it; for the circle, an equivalent extension of the arc was produced. (*d*) Two-lines-extended—two opposite lines (or, for circle, arcs) were extended as in *c*; thus, the square became a rhombus, the triangle a scalene triangle, and the circle a regular elipse. (*e*) Irregular figure—all four sides of the square and the three sides of the triangle were of different length; the circle was changed to an ameboid form. (*f*) Freehand—all three forms were changed to freehand drawings of the prototype forms, modeled after actual copies made by Dani of the original forms.

Each of the other sets of stimuli were derived by using the three figures produced by one of the transformations as prototype and performing the listed transformations upon the new prototypes. The perfect figures occurred peripherally in these sets (Sets 2–7) in the place which the prototype of the new set had occupied in Set 1. For example, in Set 2, gapped figures were the prototypes; the line-to-curve, one-line-extended, etc. transformations were all performed upon the gapped figures. The perfect (nongapped) figures were produced by a "gap closing" transformation which took the place of the gap producing transformation which had yielded the gapped figures as peripheral members of Set 1. In Set 3, the line-to-curve (arc-to-line) figures were the prototypes; in Set 4, the one-line-(arc)-extended figures the prototypes; in Set 5, the two-line-(arc)-extended figures; in Set 6, the irregular figures; and in Set 7, the freehand figures.

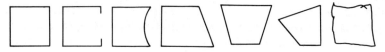

FIG. 2. Basic square and six transformations.

Figures were printed on 2 × 3-inch white cards. During learning and test-ing, they could appear randomly in any orientation.

Procedures. Each learning set consisted of 21 figures, 7 in each of the 3 categories. Each subject learned one, and only one, set. As in the color learning task, subjects learned a set as a paired associate task: figures as stimuli, a Dani word (sib name) as correct response for the seven figures in a category. Figures were shown in a different random order each run, five runs a day, with feedback after each response. When the criterion of one perfect run was achieved, subjects performed two additional tasks: a transfer task and a task designed to elicit the subject's conception of the most typical member of each of the categories in the set he had learned. As a transfer task, each subject was asked to name three irregular figures (four-sided, three-sided, and ameboid) constructed as variants of the central form (actual prototype) of the set he had learned but differing from the irregular figures of his own set. To measure the second variable, the seven figures in a cate-gory were placed before the subject and he was asked to pick the "most typical" example of the category name. The figure which he chose was then removed and he was asked to pick the most typical of those that remained. This technique was applied successively until the subject had rank ordered each member of each category.

Results

Of the 94 subjects who participated in the form learning, only 2 failed to complete learning to criterion. Scores on the transfer task were almost perfect—of 92 subjects, each making three transfer choices (one per cate-gory), there were only six errors. Dani subjects clearly could learn two-dimensional form categories as transferable concepts.

The logic of the form learning experiment was essentially the same as that of color learning. The first basic hypothesis concerned the relative ease of learning the different sets. The mean number of errors to criterion per stim-ulus per person for each set was: Set 1 (basic figures prototypes), 2.62; Set 2 (gap prototypes), 4.07; Set 3 (line-to-curve), 4.32; Set 4 (one-line-extended), 3.91; Set 5 (two-lines-extended), 3.78; Set 6 (irregular), 5.88; Set 7 (free-hand), 7.47. A one-way analysis of variance showed that there was significant variation between sets, $F (6, 12) = 4.19, p < .05$. The t tests between all pairs of sets indicated the following order of difficulty among the seven sets (the differences which are indicated were significant at least $p < .05$): Set 1 < [Set 2, Set 3, Set 4, Set 5] < Set 6 < Set 7. The first hypothesis of the study was confirmed; a set composed of categories to which the presumed natural prototypes were central to a group of distortions was learned with fewer errors than sets in which the distorted forms were central and the presumed natural prototypes peripheral.

The second basic hypothesis was that natural prototypes would be learned faster than other stimuli even when they were peripheral members of categories. In the seven form sets, each stimulus type (basic, gap, line-to-curve, etc.) occurred once as the prototype of a set and six times as peripheral members of other sets. It was, thus, possible to test this hypothesis by comparing the mean number of errors made in learning each stimulus type across all sets. The means for the three categories (square, circle, and triangle) combined are shown in the first line of Table 2. A one-way analysis of variance indicated that there was significant variation between stimuli, $F(6, 12) = 3.82, p < .05$. The t tests between all pairs of stimuli showed the following significant order of difficulty among the seven types of stimulus: basic < gap, line-to-curve, one-line-extended, two-lines-extended < irregular, freehand. It was, thus, confirmed that the presumed natural prototypes were easier stimuli to learn to pair with names than were the distortions of the basic figures.

The third hypothesis was that subjects would attempt to define categories as though the natural prototype were central even when it was peripheral—operationally, that subjects would tend to identify the natural prototype as the most typical example of the category even when it was peripheral. Although Dani subjects had been unable to pick a most typical example of the color categories, they easily made this judgment in the case of the forms.

Table 2 *Errors and Best-Example Rank for Each Form Type*

Category	Form type						
	Basic	Gap	Line-to-curve	One-line-extended	Two-lines-extended	Irregular	Freehand
Mean errors per stimulus per person (all sets combined)							
All categories combined	1.97	3.87	3.86	3.11	2.92	6.07	7.29
Circle	.57	1.71	1.40	1.79	1.67	6.02	6.24
Square	2.06	6.29	4.30	4.47	4.24	8.57	9.21
Triangle	3.27	3.58	5.86	3.09	2.84	3.62	6.43
Mean rank[a] as best example (all sets combined)							
All categories combined	1.81	3.82	4.37	3.77	3.32	4.99	5.94
Circle	1.18	4.00	3.63	4.09	3.22	5.54	6.72
Square	1.54	3.91	4.28	4.11	3.56	6.27	4.90
Triangle	2.69	3.54	5.17	3.07	3.18	3.16	6.19

[a]Rank of 1 meant first choice as best example.

Table 2, line 5, shows the means of the rankings of best example for each stimulus type combined across categories. A one-way analysis of variance was significant, $F(6, 12) = 5.73$, $p < .01$. The t tests between the mean rank orders of all pairs of stimuli showed the following differences: basic < gap, line-to-curve, one-line-extended, two-lines-extended < irregular < freehand. These results confirm that Dani were more likely to identify the presumed natural prototype as the most typical member of a category than they were to identify distortions of the prototype as the most typical member of a category, a difference which cuts across sets in which the natural prototypes were and were not actually central.

The results presented so far have rested on data combined across the three form categories. Was the same direction of results characteristic of all three of the forms? Table 2, lines 2–4 and 6–8, shows, separated into form category, mean errors and mean rank as best example for each figure. The same methods of statistical analysis, one-way analysis of variance and t tests between all pairs of figures, that had been applied to the combined data were applied to the data of each separate form category. For circle and square, the results were essentially identical to those already reported for the combined data; the one difference was that, for both circle and square, errors for the irregular variant did not differ from errors for the freehand variant. However, the triangle category showed a somewhat different pattern. Neither in errors nor in mean rank as best example was there a significant difference between the basic (equilateral) triangle, gap, one-line-extended, two-lines-extended or the irregular figure. All five of those figures were learned with fewer errors than the line-to-curve and the freehand figure. Thus, for the triangle, it appeared that any three-sided, straight-line figure was an equally good "triangle prototype," and that all such figures were superior to the curved and freehand figures.

Statistics combined across sets fail to represent with full force the effects obtained for basic circle and square in the sets in which they were peripheral. It was not simply that, on the average, the basic figures were more easily learned and ranked higher as best example than the other figures. In five of the sets (1, 2, 4, 5, and 7), the basic circle actually received a higher mean best-example rank than any of the other figures in those sets, although the basic circle was not the actual prototype in four of the sets. Basic square received the highest mean best-example rank in four sets (1, 2, 5, and 7). Basic circle was actually learned with fewest errors of any figure in the set in four sets (1, 4, 5, and 7), although it was the actual prototype only in Set 1; basic square was learned with fewest errors in two sets (1 and 5).

The fact that there was a strong and consistent effect in errors to criterion and rank as best example associated with whether stimuli were natural prototypes or not, and that this effect cut across whether they were the central or peripheral members of sets, does not rule out the possibility that there was also an effect of centrality. That is, for all stimuli combined, the central figure (actual prototype) of a set might tend to be learned more rapidly and ranked higher as best example than peripheral members. The mean errors per subject for the actual (central) prototype figures for all stimuli and sets combined was 3.36; the mean errors for peripheral figures 4.95, a difference which was statistically significant, $t(12) = 3.61, p < .01$. Similarly the mean best-example rank of the actual prototypes for all stimuli and sets combined was 3.12; the mean rank for those same figures when they occurred as peripheral members of categories was 4.90, a difference which was also statistically significant, $t(12) = 2.83, p < .02$. Such a finding is consistent with the effects of centrality in the learning of artificial categories (Reed, 1970). However, the effects of the natural prototype on learning and definition of best example of categories is one which could not have been discovered except with the use of natural categories.

The present research was designed to measure the effect of category structure on learning *within* the modalities of color and form and was not designed to compare color-category with form-category learning. However, one difference between Dani response to colors and forms requires discussion. In Dani form-category learning, subjects could easily make the judgment of the most typical member of the category, a judgment which Dani subjects had been incapable of making for the color categories. In addition, centrality in the form categories appeared to affect errors and best-example rank, an effect not found for the color categories. It is not clear why such differences should have occurred between categories in the two domains. The fact that the color categories were composed of only three stimuli per category may have been a contributing factor. An additional intriguing, but purely hypothetical, possibility is that for Dani, hue and brightness may be even less "analyzable" into separately processed dimensions than they are for Americans (Garner, 1970; Shepard, 1964). That is, the Dani may not have perceived the three hue-varying or brightness-varying chips in a category as three related chips varying on one dimension. Dani may not have "perceived" that the three chips had a physically central member.

One final finding, which should by now be quite apparent from the data, is that the three basic measures—ease of learning sets of form categories when a particular type of figure was the prototype, ease of learning individual types of figures within sets, and rank order of judgment of types as best example of categories—were highly correlated. Almost identical orders have emerged from analysis of each of the three variables. Such a correlation invites the speculation that it is generally true that categories whose central members are, in their own right, easy to learn stimuli will be easier to learn than categories whose central members are more difficult to learn. Such a general hypothesis can be tested with artificial stimuli and artificial categories.

Implications of the Research on Perceptual Categories

The utility of the concept of internal structure has been demonstrated for color and for form categories. The findings for these perceptual categories appear to have three types of more general implications. In the first place, colors and forms are a case in which the natural structure of "real" categories made the learning of those categories unlike, in some respects, the learning of artificial categories (even the relatively "naturalistic" artificial categories of Posner, 1969). In the second place, the findings suggest that natural categories may represent a domain in which a direct relation between physiology on the level of single cells (De Valois & Jacobs, 1968) and behavior may be demonstrated. (Research better suited to a precise demonstration of such relations is planned.) In the third place, the general concept of internal structure of categories (a focal center and nonfocal surround) may be applicable both to other perceptual domains and to "nonperceptual" semantic categories. Examination of the latter possibility is the topic of the second part of the paper.

PART II: SEMANTIC CATEGORIES

Not all categories have an obvious perceptual basis, and many categories may be culturally relative. For colors and forms, internal structure of categories and the concept of focal and nonfocal category members had a relatively concrete meaning. Are such concepts more generally applicable to noun categories of other types? "Applicability" actually refers to two issues: can subjects make meaningful judgments about internal structure—that is, about the degree to which instances are "focal" members of categories; and can a reasonable case be made that internal structure affects cognitive processing of the categories? The experiments to be reported represent only preliminary attempts to define these problems.

Judgments of Internal Structure

When speakers of a language which has hue terms are asked to point to the best example of a basic color name, they (a) find it a meaningful question to which they can respond, and (b) agree with each other in their choices. Neither the ability to make such judgments nor agreement between subjects in making them has been previously demonstrated for semantic categories. It seemed initially quite possible that the extent to which an instance was a good example of a semantic category would prove a meaningless concept to subjects—that subjects would protest the possibility of the judgment task, refuse to complete test items, or fall back on judging some other quality, such as how much they liked the instance. It also was entirely possible that, even if subjects could make the judgment, there would be little agreement in how instances were judged; for example, the subject whose family dog had been a collie might judge collie to be the most "doglike" dog, whereas another subject who had grown up with a dachshund might consider dachshund a "focal" dog and rate the "doglikeness" of other dogs according to how similar they were to dachshunds. The following experiment was a first approach to answering these questions.

Experiment 3

METHODS

Subjects.   One hundred and thirteen summer school students in an introductory psychology class at the University of California, Berkeley filled out the test forms.

Stimuli.   In order to test the experimental hypothesis, groups of category instances were needed which might reasonably be expected to range from very good to very peripheral members of their categories. It seemed also desirable to have some external basis for choosing category instances and for matching instances across categories. Eight categories (six instances of each) were chosen from the Battig and Montague (1969) norms. The instances were chosen both to match across categories in the frequency with which they were produced in response to the category name by the Battig and Montague subjects and to represent what the author subjectively judged to be a wide spread in how focal the instances were to the category. The categories were: fruit, science, sport, bird, vehicle, crime, disease, and vegetable. The six instances from each category were chosen to approximate the following frequencies in Battig and Montague: 400, 150, 100, 50, 15, and under 5. The specific instances and their Battig and Montague frequencies are shown in Table 3.

Procedures.   Instructions were as follows:

> This study has to do with what we have in mind when we use words which refer to categories. Let's take the word "red" as an example. Close your eyes and imagine a true red. Now imagine an orangish red ... imagine a purple red. Although you might still name the orange-red or the purple-red with the term "red," they are not as good examples of red (as clear cases of what "red" refers to) as the clear "true" red. In short, some reds are redder than others. The same is true for other kinds of categories. Think of dogs. You all have some notion of what a "real dog," a "doggy dog" is. To me a retriever or a German shephard is a very doggy dog while a Pekinese is a less doggy dog. Notice that this kind of judgment has nothing to do with how

well you like the thing; you can like a purple red better than a true red but still recognize that the color you like is not a true red. You may prefer to own a Pekinese without thinking that it is the breed that best represents what people mean by dogginess. On this form you are asked to judge how good an example of a category various instances of the category are. The first category is "fruit." On the left side of the page are six different kinds of fruit; the first is "apple." To the right of apple are seven blanks; the blank closest to apple is to be checked if an apple is a good example of your idea or image of what a fruit is; the blank to the extreme right is to be checked if apple fits very poorly with your idea or image of a fruit. The other blanks represent the range in between a very good and very poor fit—for example, the middle blank represents a moderate fit. Mark one and only one blank for "apple," one and only one blank for "fig," one and only one for "strawberry," etc. Don't worry about *why* you feel that something is or isn't a good example of the category (and don't worry about whether it's just you or people in general who feel that way)—just mark it the way you see it. Okay? You can go ahead and finish the form.

Both the order of categories and order of instances within categories were different for each group of five forms.

RESULTS AND DISCUSSION

Subjects found the task readily understandable. None questioned or protested the task. The form (which had been allotted 15 min of class time) was completed by all subjects by the end of 5 min. Roughly estimated, most subjects appeared to be devoting little more than three seconds to each choice.

Agreement between subjects was high, especially in ranking the "best examples" of categories. Table 3 shows the mean ranks of all instances. Notice that all 113 subjects agreed perfectly in giving a rank of one (best example) to chemistry as a science, murder as a crime, and car as a vehicle. Were there no agreement betweeen subjects in ranking a given instance, that instance should have received an equal number of ratings in all seven places on the scale. The extent to which the actual distribution of ratings departed from that expected distribution, represented the degree of nonrandomness (agreement) in ratings. (In fact, a correction was used for subjects' tendency not to use the lower end of the scale.) A χ^2 test of the fit of expected and actual distributions of ratings was performed separately for each of the 48 items. Of the 48 items, the ratings for 46 departed significantly from a chance distribution (the 2 items on which there failed to be significant agreement were rheumatism as a disease and wrestling as a sport).

A third obvious, but perhaps spurious, result was that the mean rank of goodness of example in the present task and the item's Battig and Montague frequency were highly correlated (compare ranks and frequencies in Table 3). However, the category instances used were not a random sample from the Battig and Montague lists—items were specifically chosen, on the basis of

Table 3 Judgments of "Goodness of Category Membership"

Category	Member	B & M[a] frequency	"Exemplariness" rank	Category	Member	B & M[a] frequency	"Exemplariness" rank
Fruit	Apple	429	1.3	Vehicle	Car	407	1.0
	Plum	167	2.3		Boat	145	2.7
	Pineapple	98	2.3		Scooter	99	2.5
	Strawberry	58	2.3		Tricycle	43	3.5
	Fig	16	4.7		Horse	14	5.9
	Olive	3	6.2		Skis	3	5.7
Science	Chemistry	367	1.0	Crime	Murder	387	1.0
	Botany	242	1.7		Assault	132	1.4
	Geology	76	2.6		Stealing	95	1.3
	Sociology	46	4.6		Embezzling	40	1.8
	Anatomy	19	1.7		Blackmail	16	1.7
	History	3	5.9		Vagrancy	3	5.3
Sport	Football	396	1.2	Disease	Cancer	316	1.2
	Hockey	130	1.8		Measles	168	2.8
	Wrestling	87	3.0		Cold	90	4.7
	Archery	49	3.9		Malaria	54	1.4
	Gymnastics	16	2.6		Muscular dystrophy	15	1.9
	Weight lifting	3	4.7		Rheumatism	3	3.5
Bird	Robin	377	1.1	Vegetable	Carrot	316	1.1
	Eagle	161	1.2		Asparagus	138	1.3
	Wren	83	1.4		Celery	96	1.7
	Chicken	40	3.8		Onion	47	2.7
	Ostrich	17	3.3		Parsley	15	3.8
	Bat	3	5.8		Pickle	2	4.4

[a]Frequency with which the member was listed in response to the category name from Battig and Montague (1969).

the author's "intuitions," to be likely to show a spread in rank. Clearly the relationship of focalness of category membership and the frequency with which words are listed in response to the category name is of interest and should be systematically investigated.

An objection which might be raised to the present findings is that subjects could have ranked the items, not on the basis of how well instances fit their ideas about the meaning of the category, but on the basis of a simpler judgment, their preference for the items. To test this possibility, a second study was performed. An additional 32 subjects were given the same forms but now asked simply to rank how much they liked or disliked each instance. The results were quite different from those of the initial study. Most mean ratings were around 2.5, and this represented general disagreement between subjects. Only two categories (disease and crime) had more than one instance whose distribution departed significantly from the flat distribution (corrected for tendency not to use the extreme lower end of the scale) that would be expected on the basis of total disagreement. Only in the case of "crime" was the order of preference related to the original judgment of "focalness" of instances— that is, the more negatively evaluated a particular crime, the better it represented the meaning of "crime" to most people. Such a relationship is part of the meaning of "crime" in English and not a sign that subjects cannot distinguish between their own preferences and the "core meanings" of category terms.

At the very least, this study has shown that questions about centrality or peripherality of category membership are meaningful to subjects; such questions can be answered quickly, and subjects agree with each other in their ratings of instances.

Internal Structure and Reaction Time[2]

A number of recent studies of retrieval from semantic memory have used tasks which required subjects to respond "true" or "false" to statements of the form: "A (member) is a (category)," where the dependent variable of interest was reaction time. The independent variables whose effects on reaction time have been investigated—such as levels of superordination (Collins & Quillian, 1969) and category size (Landauer & Freedman, 1968; Meyer, 1970)—have been variables which characterize categories (classes) as a whole. In such studies, all instances of a category at a given level of abstraction are typically considered equivalent.

[2]Performed with Dr. Richard Millward and supported in part by Grant MH-11255 from the National Institute of Mental Health.

The present paper has argued that instances of categories are not equivalent. The extent to which a category member represents the core meaning of the category (is a good member of the category) might well be expected to affect the time needed for subjects to judge that the member belongs to the category. Our first hypothesis was, thus, that reaction times would be faster when subjects respond "true" to true statements of the form "An x is a y" when x is a central member (a good example) of y than when x is a peripheral (not a very good example) of y.

A second hypothesis was developmental. In Part I, evidence was presented that focal colors and forms were learned before nonfocal. A reasonable hypothesis is that the best examples of semantic categories are learned as category members before the less good examples. (Such a hypothesis does not imply a direction of causality.) We predicted that children would not only show the same differential reaction time as adults when judging category membership of central and peripheral instances, but that, in addition, children would make more errors in judging peripheral members.

Experiment 4

METHODS

Subjects. Adult subjects were 24 undergraduates at Brown University. All were paid volunteers. Children, also paid volunteers, were 20, 9- to 11-year-old boys attending a private school in Providence, Rhode Island. One additional subject was eliminated because his reading ability was not adequate to the requirements of the experimental task.

Stimuli. Out of a pool of words rated by 27 undergraduates for goodness of membership in their superordinate categories according to the format previously described, 24 pairs of words were selected which had the following characteristics: (*a*) The pair consisted of two instances of the same category, one word rated a good example of the category (mean rank higher than 2.00) and one word rated not as good an example (mean rank lower than 2.00). (*b*) The two instances were matched in word frequency according to the Thordike and Lorge (1944) count. (*c*) All of the 27 judges agreed that the peripheral instance was, in fact, a member of the category. (*d*) There were at least two such pairs for a given category. The 12 categories, and the two central and two peripheral instances of each category, which met these requirements are shown in Table 4.

Each word (category member) appeared once in a true sentence (e.g., "A pear is a fruit.") and once in a false sentence (e.g., "A pear is a metal.") The block of 96 sentences so constructed consisted of an equal number of true and false statements. Ten additional practice sentences contained instances and categories not included in the test set.

Table 4   *Categories and Members Used in Reaction Time Experiment*

	Member	
Category	Central	Peripheral
Toy	Doll	Skates
	Ball	Swing
Bird	Robin	Chicken
	Sparrow	Duck
Fruit	Pear	Strawberry
	Banana	Prune
Sickness	Cancer	Rheumatism
	Measles	Rickets
Relative	Aunt	Wife
	Uncle	Daughter
Metal	Copper	Magnesium
	Aluminum	Platinum
Crime	Rape	Treason
	Robbery	Fraud
Sport	Baseball	Fishing
	Basketball	Diving
Vehicle	Car	Tank
	Bus	Carriage
Science	Chemistry	Medicine
	Physics	Engineering
Vegetable	Carrot	Onion
	Spinach	Mushroom
Part of the	Arm	Lips
body	Leg	Skin

Procedure.   Sentences were displayed on the scope of a PDP/8 computer. A trial consisted of the following events: the subject, sitting in front of a keyboard, pressed the space bar to signal that he was ready; after a random variable interval of 100 msec–4 sec, one of the 96 sentences appeared on the screen; the subject pressed one of two keys to indicate "true" or "false." Subjects were instructed to respond as quickly as possible without making errors. The 96 sentences were presented in random order. Ten practice trials preceded the start of testing. Adult subjects received four runs (four blocks of the entire set of 96 sentences). Children received two runs. The sentences were shown in a different random order on each run. Both the response and the reaction time were recorded by the computer.

RESULTS

Table 5 shows reaction times and errors for each type of sentence: true central, true peripheral, false central, and false peripheral. We predicted

Table 5 *Response Times and Error Proportions for Central and Peripheral Category Members*

| | Response | | | |
| | True sentences | | False sentences | |
Category member	Reaction time (msec)[a]	Error proportion	Reaction time (msec)[a]	Error proportion
	Adults			
Central	1011.67	.028	1089.84	.024
Peripheral	1071.45	.071	1115.52	.032
	Children			
Central	2426.45	.056	2692.40	.038
Peripheral	2703.45	.228	2799.30	.029

[a] Reaction times shown in milliseconds but analyses performed on $\log_{10}$ of time in milliseconds.

differences in reaction time and errors for central and peripheral words, but this prediction applied only to the true sentences. That is, instances were "central" or "peripheral" only within their true superordinate category. We matched word frequency of central and peripheral pairs in order to exclude variables that would make the peripheral words more difficult to process as words, apart from their category membership. However, we were unable to match word length completely. The false sentences offered an opportunity to check whether our control was effective; if central and peripheral false sentences did not differ, it was evidence that peripheral words were not intrinsically more difficult to read or understand than central words. In fact, none of the differences between central and peripheral false statements were significant: adult reaction times t (23) = 1.21; child reaction times, t (19) = 1.69; adult error proportion, χ^2 (1) = 1.93; child error proportion, χ^2 (1) = 2.08.

Figure 3 shows mean reaction times for true central and true peripheral sentences for the adult and the child subjects. Because adults had received twice as many runs as the children, and because the child reaction times were more variable than the adult, the two groups of subjects were analyzed separately. Central true sentences took significantly less time to answer correctly than peripheral true sentences, both for the adult subjects, t (23) = 6.54, p < .001; and for the child subjects, t (19) = 2.63, p < .01. These results confirmed our first hypothesis; that it required less time to judge that a good example of a category belonged to that category than to decide that a peripheral example of the category belonged.

Our second hypothesis was that central members of categories are learned

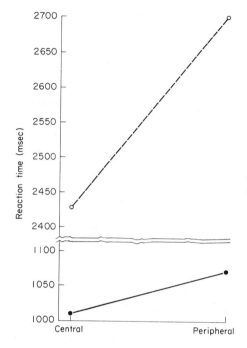

FIG. 3. Reaction times for correctly answered true central and true peripheral sentences. (---): Children; (—): Adults.

as category members earlier than peripheral members. Figure 4 shows adult and child error proportions for central and peripheral sentences. Differences were analyzed by χ^2. Adult error proportions for all sentences were low, and central and peripheral sentences did not differ significantly from each other. Children, however, made more errors for true peripheral than for true central sentences, χ^2 (1) = 16.59, p < .001.

DISCUSSION

Both of the specific predictions of the study were confirmed: true central sentences were responded to more rapidly than peripheral both by adults and children, and children made more errors in judging true peripheral than true central sentences.

In fact, variables related to internal structure are already known in verbal learning research. Clustering by category in free recall is known to be affected by "item dominance," that is, the frequency with which words are listed as responses to the category name (determined by normative studies such as Battig & Montague, 1969, and Cohen, Bousefield, & Whitmarsh, 1957). Item dominance has recently been shown to correlate with reaction time for judgments of category memberships (Wilkins, 1971).

"Category dominance," the frequency with which superordinates are listed as responses to subordinates (Loftus & Scheff, 1971a), is also correlated with reaction time in judgments of category membership (Loftus & Scheff, 1971b). We have already pointed out that ratings of exemplariness in our task appear correlated with Battig and Montague frequency. In an additional study, using the methods employed by Loftus and Scheff (1971a), we found that our central words, as a group, were more likely to elicit the superordinate with which we had paired them in the experiment than were the peripheral words, suggesting that judgments of exemplariness are also correlated with category dominance.

It would be surprising if the best examples of categories were not highly associated with the category name, and it is not surprising that best examples of categories elicit the category name as a superordinate more frequently than do peripheral examples. At present, it is not clear what additional predictions are implied by each of these variables. What is needed is an understanding of categories which will allow us to sort out the full meaning of the variables and a theory which will allow us to explain how and why they are related.

Internal Structure and Memory Search

When a subject's task is to decide whether a given instance is a member of a small, newly learned, "artificial" category, such as a list of digits which the experimenter has just enumerated, response time is typically a direct

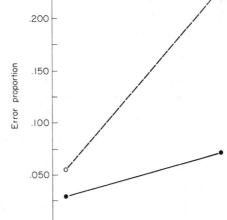

FIG. 4. Error proportions for true central and true peripheral sentences. (---); Children; (—): Adults

function of the size of the category (cf. Sternberg, 1969). Such findings have been interpreted as evidence that items are retrieved from short-term memory by successive scanning of the memory contents. Attempts to find evidence for a similar scanning process in retrieval from natural language categories in long-term memory have produced controversial results. Landauer and Freedman (1968), Collins and Quillian (1969), and Meyer (1970) found small increases in reaction time to negative instances with increased category size but no effect of category size on the time of retrieval of positive instances. Using a somewhat different task and systematically varying several different aspects of category size, Freedman and Loftus (1971) found no effect of category size. In the Freedman and Loftus technique, the subject is given the name of two intersecting categories and asked to produce the name of an instance that belongs to both categories; for example, a noun category such as animal and a letter of the alphabet such as *z*. Freedman and Loftus interpreted their failure to find an effect of category size as evidence for parallel rather than serial scanning of category members in long term memory.

However, in a production task such as Freedman's and Loftus's, category size would be directly related to retrieval time only if search were exhaustive and/or if subjects entered and scanned the category at random. An alternative hypothesis is that natural language categories are entered at their "core meaning"; searched in a relatively fixed order (from best examples of the category to the least exemplary category members); and that the search is terminated when the instance is located. If such were the case, the variable affecting reaction time would not be total size of category but the distance of the target item (or most dominant target item) from the focal category meaning; that is, reaction time should be a function of the number of items which are better examples of the category than the target. In fact, Freedman and Loftus present evidence which suggests that that is the case. Although reaction time was unrelated to category size, it was highly correlated with target frequency in the Battig and Montague norms. (Our last comments in regard to the relation between item dominance, category dominance, and item exemplariness are also applicable to this discussion.)

GENERAL DISCUSSION

The argument has been made that psychological categories have internal structure. By structure it is meant that categories possess a core meaning (or focal examples) and that instances of categories differ in the degree to which they fit the core meaning or are like the focal examples. For perceptual categories, such structure can be specified in relatively concrete terms; Part I attempted to demonstrate that color and form categories develop around perceptually salient "natural prototypes." In support of this hypothesis, it was shown (a) that subjects from a culture which did not initially possess hue or form concepts could learn names for the presumed natural prototypes faster than for other stimuli even when the natural prototypes were not the central members of categories; (b) that members of that culture could more easily learn hue and form concepts when the presumed natural prototypes were the central members of categories than when the categories were organized in other ways; and (c) that, at least for the forms, subjects tended to "distort" their definition of the category toward the natural prototype; that is, they tended to choose the natural prototype as the most typical member of the category even when it was actually peripheral.

Is a similar concept of internal structure applicable to nonperceptual semantic categories? The research described in Part II demonstrated that American subjects could easily rate how exemplary they felt instances to be of categories; that subjects agreed with each other in these ratings; and that exemplariness of instances was related to adult and child speed of judging category membership and to child errors in judging category membership. On the basis of previous research (Freedman & Loftus, 1971), it was also argued that retrieval of category instances from long-term memory may be performed by means of a serial, fixed-order, self-terminating search which begins with the best examples of the category. It may be concluded that internal structure is an introspectively meaningful variable which may be relevant to the cognitive processing of semantic categories; such relevance is not conclusively demonstrated because the reaction time data of the present studies are also predictable on the basis of "item dominance" and "category dominance." Associative strength (both forward and backward) to a category name is itself a concept of internal category structure. The relation between these different structural variables needs to be more fully explored.

The psychological reality of internal structure implies that the abstract, "formal" definition of categories (in terms of genus and differentia, or in terms of an intersection of criterial attributes) does not fully correspond to the category as a psychological "unit." In the first place, the attributes which define an instance as a category member and the attributes which define it as a good or less good member may be different. Attributes which are "noisy" with respect to category membership (such as size or color), may contribute to the exemplariness of an instance. Subcategories which are identical with respect to criterial attributes may differ in the extent to which they represent the core meaning of the category—for example, the distinction between wild and domestic is irrelevant to the formal definition of "bird" since both birds and nonbirds may be either wild or domestic; however, wild birds are judged more central to the bird category than domestic ones. Where criterial attributes can vary in "amount," good examples of the category may require a particular amount, much narrower in its extent, than the amount acceptable for general category membership.

Formal and psychological aspects of categories are also separable to the extent that, in many cognitive tasks, categories may be processed in terms of their internal structure rather than in terms of the attributes of their formal definitions. We have already argued that speed of judgment of category membership and order of search through category instances in long term memory are functions of internal structure. It is quite likely that mental images of categories are predictable on the basis of internal structure, and an investigation of imagery using the technique of "priming" is in progress. In some tasks, of course, formal attributes may be explicitly processed—for example in "figuring out" whether a newly encountered and doubtful item should be classified as a category member or not. However, no one type of task can ever be considered representative of all tasks.

The concept of internal structure has implications for several areas of research, among them child development. Studies of the development of word meaning have tended to focus on the child's understanding of criterial attributes and hierarchies of superordination; such studies have found consistent evidence that children do not categorize or define words by the same principles of abstraction used by adults (Anglin, 1970; Bruner, Olver, & Greenfield, 1966). In the present research, we found evidence that category membership of central instances was learned before membership of peripheral instances. It is possible that children initially define a category by means of its concrete "clear cases" rather than in terms of abstract criterial attributes. In a pilot study for Experiment 4, we found that 5-year-olds knew that an apple was a fruit and that an apple was not a sickness although they did not know (in the sense of the logic of class inclusion) what superordination and subordination were. Such a speculation leads to the prediction that children will be similar to adults in tasks where adults use internal structure as the basis for processing (we have argued that speed of judgment of category membership and order of memory search are such tasks), but different from adults in tasks for which adults use abstract criterial attributes (deciding whether a doubtful instance is a member of a category).

Internal structure also has implications for cross-cultural research. For most domains, we have little information about how the domain is categorized in different cultures, how much agreement in categories exists between cultures, nor why cultures should cut up the domain in the way that they do. The present trend in anthropology to study "folk" classification has tended to emphasize methods, such as "componential analysis," which seek to find the minimum basic criterial attributes by which folk use of the terms of a domain can be formally ordered (cf. Tyler, 1969). We would argue that, at present, too little is known about the laws of classification to justify ignoring the less elegant information about internal structure of folk categories. It may be recalled that a very misleading view of the color space was obtained from research which dealt only with the boundaries of color terms.

What factors determine the internal structure of categories—how does such structure come into being? Part I of the present paper argued that, in the domains of color and form, perceptually salient "best examples" were "prior" to the categories, and themselves determined the nature of the categories. Although perceptual factors may play a role in the formation of many other categories, it is doubtful that all categories evolve in this manner.

In the learning of artificial categories composed of distributions of attributes, central tendency appeared to be a very influential factor in the formation of "prototypes" (Reed, 1970). However, to form a concept of the central tendency of a category, one must already know something about the category members and boundaries. It is unreasonable to suppose that the extension of natural language categories evolves completely prior to the concept of best example of the category. Probably, centrality acts interactively with extension, and is only one factor among many which influence definitions of exemplariness. It is often suggested to the author that it is the most common (frequent) members of a category which become the best examples of the category. For the particular artificial categories used in the Reed (1970) study, frequency was less effective than centrality in determining the prototype. However, frequency may make some items salient in a not-yet-organized domain and may influence how that domain comes to be divided. (In regard to frequency, it should also be realized that we have data only about word frequency, not object frequency, and do not know to what extent the two are related.) Another intriguing possibility is that cultures come to define as best examples of categories those members which are maximally different from other categories on the same level of linguistic contrast. Such a principle would render categories maximally discriminable, and suggests a specific cognitive mechanism underlying the evolution of internal structure. Maximum discriminability would also result if best examples of categories were those instances which were not also salient members in other categories—which was, in fact, generally the case for the central and peripheral items in our study (e.g., relevant to "category dominance," a sparrow is a central bird and little else; a chicken is a salient food and a peripheral bird). All such mechanisms remain speculative at present.

Summary.   It has been argued that psychological categories have internal structure (that is, instances of categories differ in the degree to which they are like the "focal examples" of the category); that the nature of the structure of the perceptual categories of color and form is determined by perceptually salient "natural prototypes"; and that nonperceptual semantic categories also have internal structure which affects the way they are processed.

DEVELOPMENTAL CHANGES
IN MEMORY AND THE
ACQUISITION OF LANGUAGE

GARY M. OLSON
Michigan State University

We are coming to realize that although purely syntactic considerations in language acquisition are of great intrinsic interest, changes in the semantic structure of language and in many underlying cognitive processes are necessarily related to syntactic development. One important mental ability needed by the competent language performer would have been taxed if I had read the previous sentence aloud to you. That sentence, both because of its length and its structural complexity, would have required that you store large segments of information in immediate memory in order for you to come up with its meaning—if in fact you could. Adult memory performance has been studied very extensively in the experimental laboratory, leading to a small but significant set of theoretical insights into the nature of remembering. If I were going to discuss how the adult's language ability interacts with the nature of the adult's memory abilities there would be much more substance to this chapter than there in fact will be. Instead, I will consider the relationship between the development of memory abilities in the child and the acquisition of language. Regardless of what we might know about language acquisition, we just do not know very much about the developmental aspects of remembering. But in recent years increasing attention has been given to memory development, so that it should be possible to reach a few conclusions about language development from the point of view of the developmental psychology of memory.

This chapter will concentrate on the relationship between short-term or immediate memory and language acquisition, but toward the end some brief remarks will be made on issues involving longer-term memory as well. The discussion of short-term memory cannot be totally divorced from that of long-term memory anyway, since many general considerations are relevant to both. The term immediate or short-term memory (these two expressions will be used interchangeably) has had several uses. For some it has had a purely temporal definition, referring to any remembering that occurs within some specific short temporal interval of the original experience, say 15 to 30 sec. For others it has referred to a very short-term iconic or echoic trace, for which the term "echo box" has been used. In this paper short-term memory will be given a functional interpretation, and will refer to the limited capacity store within which the initial or terminal computations of reception or of production are performed. It represents, for example, the first stage of processing between perception and subsequent higher order processing, and is largely oriented toward preserving transient features of the environment long enough so that relatively slow mental processes have a chance to operate upon environmental input. Its contents are themselves relatively transient but are not raw or uninterpreted. They are, in a sense, already one large step removed from the environment. Given a functional characterization of short-term memory it becomes an open question as to the ontogenetic status of characteristics like the limits of its capacity, its primary mode of representation, the reasons for the transience of its contents, the role of rehearsal or recycling processes, and the like, all of which have been important in the study of adult short-term memory.

The topic of short-term memory is certainly not new in discussions of language acquisition, especially those relating to the very early stages of development. In particular, much attention has been given to the potential role of developmental changes in immediate-memory span for language acquisition (e.g., Bloom, 1970; Brown & Bellugi, 1964; Brown & Fraser, 1963; Ervin-Tripp, 1971; Slobin, 1970, in press). There are obvious ways in which the ability to produce or to understand sentences depends upon the ability to remember temporarily certain constituents while processing others. In fact, without temporary storage there would seem to be no way we could speak or understand the speech of others. There are two parameters of sentences that critically involve immediate memory. One is sentence length. In general longer sentences are more difficult than shorter sentences, other things being roughly equal, since we have to remember more or larger constituents before attaining some kind of closure on the semantic message of the sentence. One of the most obvious changes in the language of very young children is the systematic growth in the average length of utterance that a child will produce or will give in imitation of an adult sentence, and it has been tempting to implicate immediate-memory span in these changes. The classical empirical news on this matter has been that the child's immediate-memory span does in fact increase throughout early childhood, so there has been at least a correlational basis for the assertion that span changes are implicated in mean utterance-length growth. This question will be examined in detail in a moment.

The other obvious parameter that involves immediate memory is structural complexity. Most of us find that a sentence with self-embedding like *The ball player whom the boy admired hit a home run* is comprehensible, but a sentence like *The playwright whom the editor whom the novelist whom the poet advises summons bothers feared the audience*[1] is usually judged to be incomprehensible or ungrammatical even though it is in principle accounted for by the same transformational grammar of English as that which generated the previous embedded sentence. Our problem with such sentences is obviously mnemonic, since by the time we reach the long lineup of verbs at the end we have forgotten what goes with what. Yngve (1960) constructed a model of language which explicitly related structural complexity to considerations of immediate memory; and regardless of how we might judge the usefulness of his efforts, at least an attempt to relate these two factors has great psychological plausibility.

Let us now consider in greater detail the ostensive relationship between memory span and utterance length, looking both at some regularities of language development and some facts and points of view about developmental changes in remembering. It will be my contention here—and it is by no means original with me—that the correspondence between changes in mean utterance length in early stages of language acquisition and the reputed increases in immediate-memory span in childhood does not mean that some memory structure like a short-term memory buffer is changing size or capacity. I hope to show that the ostensive change in memory span is indicative of something more complex and interesting than a simple change in the capacity of a static mental object, and that the complex changes that underlie the classical data on memory span are related to the kinds of mental activities responsible for changes in the average length of the child's utterances or imitations.

---

[1] The example is from Freedle and Craun (1970), who also summarize data relevant to the general conclusion made here.

The relevant facts on language acquisition are well-known and require little elaboration. Once the child begins to put words together into multiple-word strings or simple sentences, there is a systematic increase in the average length of utterance the child produces (McCarthy, 1954). A graph of mean utterance length versus chronological age for Adam, Eve, and Sarah has appeared in several of Roger Brown's papers (e.g., Brown, Cazden, & Bellugi-Klima, 1969; Brown, 1970) and is now quite familiar. Along with this we find that when children imitate sentences produced by adults they usually produce something that is considerably reduced in length and complexity, and in fact the average length of such imitations corresponds fairly closely to the average length of the child's spontaneous utterances at the earliest stages (Brown & Bellugi, 1964; Ervin, 1964; Ervin-Tripp, 1971).

The facts about measured memory span are equally straightforward. Simple digit-span memory and both chronological age and IQ are so systematically related that digit span is one of the basic indices on children's intelligence tests like the Stanford-Binet or the Wechsler (see summary in Woodworth & Schlosberg, 1954, Ch. 23). Brown and Fraser (1963) observed that on the Stanford–Binet scales the normative digit span at 30 months of chronological age is two digits, at 36 months three digits, and at 54 months four digits. This progressive increase in digit span continues to adulthood, at a steadily decreasing rate, eventually stabilizing at something like five to seven digits, the exact number still being controversial.

So much for the data. I think the neat correlation can be seen between these two sets of facts which has led to the implicating of changes in memory span with changes in mean utterance length. In order to assess the meaning of the developmental changes in memory we have just discussed, it will be necessary to consider some things we know about the ways in which adults remember. Miller (1956), in a classic paper on immediate memory, called attention to some basic characteristics of immediate memory which now seem to be relatively uncontroversial. First, there is some upper bound on the number of information units we can retain in our immediate memory, and this upper bound is relatively small as the range of numbers that have been mentioned would indicate. One of the advantages of even a simple mechanical desk calculator, not to mention an electronic computer, is that its immediate-memory span is not so severely restricted. Most of us find it impossible to multiply two six-digit numbers in our heads while such feats are routine for desk calculators (see discussion by Hunter, 1968). However, a second point made by Miller was that there is flexibility as to what the five to seven information units in immediate memory can be. If we encode our information cleverly we can store five to seven units of incredible richness while still constrained by the same overall restrictions on capacity. This means that the practical effect of a severely limited immediate-memory span can be alleviated if we can recode the material into informationally richer units. Instead of storing elementary units of information we can store the components of an organized retrieval scheme. Such retrieval schemes are used to regenerate or reconstruct the elementary units of information originally studied by using knowledge we have in our permanent memory store. Thus, in a well-worn example, we can describe increases in the speed of translating Morse code into ordinary English as arising from successively more efficient encodings. The beginner memorizes dot and dash equivalents for individual letters but as he gains experience he is able to decode directly larger and larger units, learning to decode letter sequences, words, and phrases without having to decode their individual letter constituents. Although the potential gains via such recodings are not infinite, they are important enough so that the study of the diversity and complexity of possible encodings in adult short-term memory is clearly more significant than the study of the quantitative parameters of the limits.

Bower and Winzenz (1969; Winzenz & Bower, 1970) have shown how important such recoding schemes are even for the immediate recall of materials as simple as strings of digits, the same kinds of materials used in the classical assessments of immediate-memory span. Their research has shown that the internal representation of such digit strings seems to be organized into subgroups of digits, so that a subject who was presented the string

$$4 \quad 1 \quad 6 \quad 7 \quad 3 \quad 9 \quad 2 \quad 5$$

might encode it in immediate memory as "forty-one, sixty-seven, thirty-nine, twenty-five" or as "four hundred and sixteen, seventy-three, nine hundred and twenty-five" or some such grouping. These kinds of encodings are so dominant, in fact, that experimentally forcing a subject to encode the same nominal digit string in a different grouping prevents the subject from benefitting from repetitions of the string (Bower & Winzenz, 1969). That is, encoding the same string differently is the same as encoding a totally different string. An older study by Martin and Fernberger (1929) showed that improvement in digit-string recall over many days of practice was due to increased proficiency in grouping the digits into unitized subgroups. Improvement in performance as a result of prolonged, intensive training appeared to be due to increased facility at higher-order organizational strategies.

What about the child? The assessment of his ability to remember is complicated by the fact that so many aspects of his mental life are changing at the same time, and the interdependencies among the various abilities make the interpretation of any one of them very difficult. Let us look at one such interdependency which eliminates any simple interpretation of the classical memory span data. We have just seen that with adults the whole question of the capacity of immediate memory can be reduced to the question of how the information is to be represented internally, since it is what is represented, not what is presented, that is subject to the restrictions on information processing that Miller (1956) spoke of. My hypothesis is that these limits on information processing are ontogenetically invariant, that nominal quantitative changes in the amount of externally defined information that can be handled have to do with the nature of the child's internal representations.

An experiment by Corsini (1969a) examined the implications for remembering of Bruner's (1964) proposal that the dominant form of internal representation in the child progresses from the enactive to the iconic to the symbolic, with, respectively, motor acts, visual imagery, and language being typical mediums of these modalities. Symbolic representation will dominate adult cognition, reflecting the important role of language in all of the adult's cognitive activities. But when the child is just beginning to use language, his representations of experience will tend to be iconic rather than symbolic, nonverbal rather than verbal. Why, then, should we suppose that a verbal measure of memory span, i.e., digit-span recall, is an adequate index of the child's mnemonic capacities? If we could assess his ability to remember by employing techniques or materials that were more consonant with the child's dominant or preferred modes of representation would we find that a different picture of developmental changes in memory span emerges?

Indeed we would. Corsini (1969a) found that for children in the age range of $3\frac{1}{2}$ to 7 years, the purely verbal assessment of memory yielded data which parallel the classical results on digit span, that is, that older children are able to remember more than younger children. But, if the children were tested in a manner which allowed them to employ nonverbal cues in retention, the younger children were able to remember just as much as the older children. Simple mnemonic capacity did not differ as a function of age within the range Corsini investigated when materials were appropriate to the children's predominantly nonverbal representational modes. What differs is the inability of the younger children to handle verbal information as well as older children. Data collected for 5-year-olds (Corsini, 1969b) and for 3-year-olds (Corsini, Jacobus, & Leonard, 1969) were also consistent with this interpretation.

Hoffman (1971) has reported a similar set of findings. The to-be-remembered materials in his experiment were color pictures taken from popular magazines, and after having been shown a series of such pictures the children were asked to pick out which one of a pair of test pictures was the one they had seen previously. Children from ages 3 to 9, and adults were tested in this fashion, and performance differences as a function of age were either greatly attenuated or absent. In fact, the only significant difference was that between the 3-year-olds and all the rest but even the absolute magnitude of this difference was quite small, especially when compared with traditional verbal recall measures. In a related experiment, Brown and Scott (1971) found that the performance of children in a continuous recognition task with pictorial materials did not differ significantly from that which has been reported for adults. As has been found with adults, the children showed an impressive ability to recognize pictures, indicating they had no overall deficit in the capacity of their memory.

Not all of these tasks explicitly involved immediate memory, but these results suggest that the classical findings on memory span reflect the development of the child's ability to handle verbal information rather than changes in memory or information processing capacity per se. Furthermore, we need not accept Bruner's characterization of development in order to accept the impact of these results. The point is that the child's internal representations, whatever they might be, are largely nonverbal when language development first begins. If this is true one impact is to decouple the neat correlation between mean utterance length and memory span. The classical memory span data are symptomatic of more fundamental changes that are taking place in the developing child and simple-minded extrapolations of these data to the explanation of the growth of average utterance length is unjustifiable. In fact the simple-minded explanation is reduced to circularity, the now vacuous explanation of mean utterance length being that the capacity to handle verbal information increases because the capacity to handle verbal information increases.

I am not the first to suggest that the developmental changes underlying the classical findings on digit span have little or nothing to do with simple capacity changes, that the digit span data are instead symptoms of more interesting underlying changes. However, I think we are now in a position to describe with greater confidence the nature of these underlying changes. Let us make the broadest characterization possible of the nature of memory development: The performance deficits we find in younger children's remembering are due to their failure to organize, plan, monitor, and integrate their information processing and remembering as effectively as older children or as adults (evidence to support this characterization has been summarized recently in sources like Belmont & Butterfield, in press; Corsini, 1971; Flavell, 1970; Hagen, 1971). As adults we usually remember the name of a class rather than each of its members, we remember rules rather than exemplars of the rules, or we use other strategies which enable us to let a small unit of information stand for a procedure that can be used to generate a set or subset of the materials that are to be remembered. Young children are not as likely to do these things. I have carefully avoided saying that young children are not *able* to use these mnemonic techniques, for evidence summarized recently by Flavell (1970) indicates that children as young as 3 or 4, if not younger, can employ many of the strategies they will later use routinely in remembering. But unless prompted they do not. What the child most needs to develop are higher-order integrating and monitoring abilities so he can use effectively many representational skills he already possesses.

A further word of caution is needed at this point. Explicit reference to specific chronological age ranges has been minimized in many of these most recent remarks because here we are in a bit of trouble when it comes to relating these findings to those most critical early stages of language acquisition. Most of the generalizations can be applied confidently to children from age $3\frac{1}{2}$ or 4 on, but in the range most critical for early language development, say roughly $1\frac{1}{2}$ to $3\frac{1}{2}$ or so, we have little or no direct evidence on these questions. Most of what I say is intended to apply to this age range by retrospective analogy, but I am well aware that such generalizations are not without many dangers. It is of course because language is so immature at this stage that it is so difficult to study the child's remembering, which only increases the frustration of those of us who seek more direct evidence on such questions.

Methodological consternation should not prevent our realizing that in addition to this age range being focal for early language development, it is also a most important period in the development of mnemonic abilities. All of the information-processing demands that are faced by the young child are difficult to identify, but of those that are obvious language presents the earliest and most acute challenge to the child's ability to handle information in real time. Miller and Chomsky (1963) speculated that it is just this need to handle speech in real time that means natural languages need to have as complex a basis as a transformational grammar. Since natural languages are transmitted via the transient auditory medium, special adjustments must be made to take into account the need to do rapid computation on the presented speech train before the trace of the sentences is lost; and they hypothesized that the output of immediate memory is a parsed surface structure which then goes into longer-term memory where transformations are applied to get to the logical, underlying meaning—the deep structure—of the utterance. The significance of this kind of speculation for memory development is that language is the first system the young child encounters that makes information-processing demands so severe as to require the construction of something as complex as a transformational grammar.

Memory capacity or memory span is an ambiguous concept. It may refer to what we measure, or it may refer to the mental structures we hypothesize, and there need be no simple or direct relationship between the two. A brief dramatization with two hypothetical subjects, Cain and Abel, will clarify this. Suppose I present random series of ones and zeros to these subjects for immediate ordered recall, and using the standard digit-span paradigm of having them recall successively longer and longer strings, I try to discover the longest series of digits the subject can recall consistently. Cain and Abel are run in such an experiment; and I find that Cain is able to recall sequences as long as six digits but no longer, whereas Abel can recall sequences as long as eighteen digits. I could go no further than this and conclude that Abel has a much longer digit span than Cain. This would be an example of immediate-memory span standing for what we measure in an appropriate kind of task. However, suppose I am not content with this analysis, and upon further inquiry find that Abel, but not Cain, recodes triplets of ones and zeros into the octal digits, zero through seven, and remembers the sequences of ones and zeros as sequences of octal digits. This might force me to hypothesize that in fact both Cain and Abel have immediate-memory spans of six, but that in terms of my nominal stimuli, strings of ones and zeros, Abel's ability to convert binary notation to octal reduces the practical effects of his limited memory span.

Whose memory span is greater? I think it is clear by now that this is the wrong comparison to be making, and this is also the conclusion that is emerging from the developmental data. Does the child's memory span increase with age? Theoretically this question is secondary, since quantitative changes are symptoms or by-products, not the process. Verbal measures like digit-span recall cannot adequately reflect the capabilities of a mind that is preverbal. The changes we find are associated with the child's ability to recode or encode, to plan and monitor, to integrate and unitize. Broad limits on information processing capacity, which may be biological in origin, are relatively constant, but how the child operates within these limits undergoes systematic and profound development.

These are not angels-on-the-heads-of-pins distinctions. What we have done is to reclaim an interesting problem from the grasp of a solution that looked too easy. Mean utterance length is not a performance restriction due to a simple memory-span limit. The correlation between the two is probably meaningful but it is the correlation of two symptoms of the same underlying affliction.

But what, then, is behind the growth of mean utterance length? I would like to outline three or four proposals which are united only in their speculativeness. The first of these is almost too easy, but leads to several important points. There simply must be, for logical reasons, a growth in the length of possible utterances as the child's language increases in the number and complexity of its syntatic and semantic rules. This pushes the question back one level, for now we ask why does the rule system increase in this way? Why does the child learn the grammar of his native language in increments instead of successively testing and rejecting relatively complete grammatical systems until he homes in on the adult grammar? This strategy is not implausible for an arbitrary computational device without specifically human characteristics or limitations. In a trivial sense this has to do with general questions of efficient learning strategies, of the development of supralinguistic communicative competence, and of the acquisition of general conceptual knowledge, but what we have learned about the development of memory abilities suggests yet another reason for this. In order for a child to generate and test full-blown grammars he would have to possess encoding, organizing, planning, and monitoring abilities which would allow him to represent a complicated rule system in his mind. But from what we know about the way the child's ability to remember develops, these are just the abilities the younger child most needs to learn. The child is limited in the complexity of the rule system he can store and use by the same cognitive processes which limit his ability to represent information effectively in immediate memory.

However, the real problem in looking at mean utterance length in terms of the development of rules is that, as Bloom's (1970) longitudinal data in particular have revealed, children do not produce utterances as long as their underlying grammar would allow. For example, the following sequence was produced by Kathryn, one of Bloom's longitudinal subjects, when she was almost 23 months old. Kathryn was looking at the picture of a mother cooking:

> *cereal. hmmmmm.*
> *raisin there.*
> *buy more grocery store.*
> *raisins.*
> *buy more grocery store.*
> *grocery store.*
> *raisins ə grocery store.*

The adult paraphrase of what Kathryn was trying to say probably includes something like *buy more raisins at the grocery store*, but although Kathryn's rule system enabled her to construct the underlying representation of this she could not produce it all in one utterance. Bloom proposed that surface structures systematically emerge from deep structures via reduction transformations which obligatorily delete various structures. So the grammar itself is only a loose limit, not a precise one, on mean utterance length.

A second source of explanations for the mean utterance-length increase is in the nature of language used for communication during these early stages. There is some evidence that the child's early single-word utterances are holophrastic, that is, that they stand for complex ideas rather than for the simple ideas associated with the adult meaning of the term (e.g., Bloom, in press; McNeill, 1970b). By associating speech with action or with the objects and persons in the setting, the child can apparently make a single word convey a meaning that an adult requires a sentence to paraphrase. If this is so, then as the child begins to produce multiple-word utterances he may still rely upon extralinguistic factors to facilitate his communication, so that in a sense he finds it unnecessary to use longer, more complete sentences to say what he is trying to say. Initially this is sufficient, for as Piaget has suggested, the child's mental life during these early stages is highly egocentric, his intellectual activities bound largely to the conditions of self or of self's immediate surroundings. Much of the later complexity of language will arise because the child's cognitions will need to cope with other times, other places, other points of view, other possible worlds, and the like, none of which can be conveyed via extralinguistic cues in the immediate situation.

A final set of factors underlying mean utterance length is directly related to what we have learned about the young child's memory. The changes in the child's ability to encode, plan, and monitor his information processing which affect the child's immediate-memory span as classically measured, also have something to do with the average length or complexity of the child's utterances. Let us look at one way in which such abilities could affect language performance. Most analyses of adult language performance have assumed a close isomorphism between the complexity of some aspect of linguistic descriptions like deep structures and the complexity of the mental processing underlying production or comprehension. However, I suspect that in many instances this isomorphism is quite loose, that in performance we are often able to reduce the effective complexity of utterances through the use of preprogrammed routines which represent components of the full description of a sentence as a single label or recoding. For instance, for academicians the subjunctive probably has less effective structural complexity than it does, say, for the hard-hat, since the academician uses it so routinely that it is represented internally as a unitized subroutine rather than as the full set of specific algorithms needed to do the appropriate computation from scratch. Similarly, the phrase *the old gray mare* is not as effectively complicated as *the old orange cat* because it has become unitized or, as Vendler (1968) would say, "petrified." These examples at the level of dialect are paralleled by similar unitizations at the level of idiolect. Each of us has characteristic turns of phrase, customary ways of talking about certain kinds of things, which achieve similar kinds of encoding economies within our idiolects. Out of the many possible ways in which we might say something we tend to use routinely only a small number of them. We encode various linguistic subunits into unitized subprograms for performance which allow us to produce utterances without having to do the complete set of computations warranted by the structural complexity described in the formal grammar.

The child does not have a repertoire of such prepackaged, efficiently encoded sentence-constituent routines and cannot achieve similar economies in the planning and production of his utterances. Thus, in addition to learning the system of rules or algorithms which will enable him to compute the structure of an utterance in order to be able to produce it at all, the child also learns ways to recode portions of these structures so as to reduce the computational weight associated with longer, more complex utterances. Interestingly enough, we often find in the corpuses of those children who have been studied longitudinally a small subset of utterances that seem to be out of character in both their length and complexity. For example, Eric, another one of Bloom's (1970) subjects, produced the complex negative, ə *don't want baby*, at a stage where independent evidence appeared to indicate that he did not compute the full internal structure of this utterance. Such utterances manifest structures that are nonproductive in the child's language at that particular stage, but the utterances are used as a unit for some specific semantic or pragmatic purpose without the child's knowing in some sense the internal structure of the string. These kinds of utterances may be precursers of the preprogrammed routines I am talking about, an example of how the child can produce longer or more complicated utterances by, in a sense, avoiding the computation of all the internal structure of the string.

In general those abilities the child fails to employ in remembering would seem to be important for language performance as well. From the constructing of an internal representation to the performing of some appropriate behavior which depends upon this internal representation, the young child apparently has difficulties at every stage. In addition to the use of encoding economies, adult performance will also require the ability to plan and organize an output, the ability to monitor or assess the state of this planning and the readiness to perform, and the ability to integrate in real time the flow of information through immediate memory and the retrieval of information from long-term or permanent memory. Evidence from recent developmental research on remembering has shown how important all these are for memory performance, and I hope the discussion of the example of encoding economies has suggested how this whole range of factors is also implicated in language performance.

I chose not to say much about longer-term, more permanent memory, and to emphasize immediate memory instead, because I think some of the things I have mentioned are less well-known than some of the relevant aspects of longer-term memory. Obviously issues like the modality of internal representations or the development of higher-order organizing and monitoring abilities are not specific to immediate memory and are evident in the longer-term memory involvements in language as well. As other papers in this volume suggest (E. Clark, H. Clark, Bowerman, Rosch), the underlying semantics of linguistic systems develops to mirror certain cognitive–perceptual facts about the internal representation of knowledge of the world. I would like to suggest that the nature of a cognitive system, like the ability to remember, may also influence the kinds of distinctions which must be made in vocabulary or in other aspects of semantics in order to meld the characteristics of the cognitive system with the requirements for language performance. Furthermore, differences in strategies for language acquisition may be related to characteristics of both short- and long-term memory organization (for some recent discussions of strategies in acquisition, see Bever, 1970; Bloom, 1970; Slobin, in press).

I think it can be seen from the quantity of speculation in this chapter that I have laid a host of blank checks and promissory notes on the table. As I said at the beginning, I think we are now beginning to learn enough about both language performance and memory abilities in the child so that we can draw some general conclusions about their interrelationships. Obviously the hard work of filling in the details remains. I hope I have shown that the simple-minded correlation of utterance length with memory span does not buy us much theoretical insight, that there are profound changes taking place which have something to do with both of these covarying variables. One thing this analysis does, however, is to make even more puzzling the apparent quantitative strictness of utterance lengths during early stages of acquisition. At a stage when the child apparently can construct the underlying representation SVO he seems unable to produce this intact, producing instead SV, SO, or VO (Bloom, 1970). More detailed analyses of the kinds of mechanisms I have been describing will be needed to account for the strictness of such production limitations, but I think it is clear that in the long run this route will lead to more insight into language acquisition than would stopping with an account based on simple memory span.

CODE SWITCHING IN CHILDREN'S LANGUAGE[1]

JEAN BERKO GLEASON
Boston University

Somewhere along the road to language acquisition children must gain control over not only a vast vocabulary and a complicated grammar, but a variety of styles of speaking to different people under differing circumstances. The code for addressing a policeman who has just stopped you for speeding is not the same as the code for addressing either little babies or old friends; and anyone studying adult language who restricts himself to one or another of these situations would obviously have only a part of the picture of the complexity and variety that exists in adult language. Paradoxically, until recent times, those of us who have studied child language have restricted ourselves to samples of the child's language to us, the interviewer, or to the child's mother or teacher, and we have assumed that that was it: child language. Whether children, like adults, have control of several codes, and vary their speech in accordance with the situation they are in or the person they are addressing has become an area of increasing interest to a number of researchers in the past few years. In order to investigate code switching in children's language, it is necessary to observe the same child in a number of different speech situations.

This chapter is a preliminary report on a study that Elliot Mishler and I conducted. The findings are observational, rather than quantitative; and

[1] This research was supported in part by Grant GS-3001 from the National Science Foundation to Elliot Mishler. The paper was written while I was a senior research associate in the Laboratory of Social Psychiatry at the Harvard Medical School. I am grateful to Dr. Mishler for many of the insights reported here.

it is my hope that experiments with hard data and statistically meaningful results will follow.

In order to investigate the child's emerging control of different styles or codes, we began with the study of the natural conversations that occur in families with several children; this enabled us to study the way that parents alter their style in speaking to children of different ages and sexes, and it put the children in a natural position to direct their language to a variety of addressees: their parents, ourselves, other children, and babies.

Our basic data were collected from five similarly constituted families who have children attending a private school in Cambridge, Massachusetts. Each of these families has at least three children: a first- or second-grader; a preschool child aged 4 or 5; and an even younger child under the age of 3. All of these families are well-educated and upper middle-class. Most of the data were taped in the families' homes in two 1-hour sessions by Sara Harkness, a doctoral candidate in social anthropology at Harvard, or by myself and Elliot Mishler, head of the Laboratory of Social psychiatry at the Harvard Medical School. In addition to these tapes we have recorded one other family whose children attend public school in another community. Finally, I made extensive recordings of the 4-year-old son of one of the five families in several different settings: in his own home with his parents; outdoors with his younger and older brothers; at my home talking to me and playing with my 8-year-old daughter, Cindy; and at his nursery school with his friends and teachers. For this one 4-year-old, at least, I have captured a broad variety of speech situations and the stylistic variations that attend them.

ADULT LANGUAGE TO CHILDREN

Since we were observing families, it was inevitable that our sample contain a great deal of language to children from adults, and we examined this adult language for evidence of stylistic variation. Since this adult language is the basic input to the child, some understanding of it is prerequisite to understanding the full significance of the children's productions. It is important to know, for instance, which codes are the children's own, passed on by the peer group, and which codes are passed to the child by adults. Therefore, before discussing the children's language some description of the salient features of the adult codes is in order.

The adults use baby-talk style in talking to the babies. The features of this style have been well reported by others but, briefly, we can say they raised the fundamental frequency of their voices, used simple short sentences with concrete nouns, diminutives, and terms of endearment, expanded the children's utterances, and in general performed the linguistic operations that constitute baby-talk style. There was a lot of individual variation in the extent to which all of these features might be employed. One mother, for instance, spoke in a normal voice to her husband, a high voice to her 4-year-old, a slightly raised voice to her 8-year-old, and when she talked to her baby she fairly squeaked. Fathers and mothers did not talk in exactly the same way to the babies, and there seemed to be some sex differences, as well, in how the babies were addressed. Some of the boy babies were addressed, especially by their fathers, in a sort or hail-baby-well-met style: While turning them upside down or engaged in similar play, the fathers said things like "Come here, you little nut!" or "Hey fruitcake!" Baby girls were dealt with more gently, both physically and verbally.

Adults used a quite different style to the children who were no longer babies, although there were some common features—the use of endearments, for instance. Both children and babies might be called "sweetie" or have their names played with—one baby was called "funny bunny," for instance, and in a different family a 5-year-old girl was called "Huffy Muffy," so this kind of rhyming play is not uncommon. Otherwise, once the little children's language was comprehensible, expansion and similar devices dropped out while other features assumed salience. Several of these features might be sketched here.

The language addressed to the children we saw who were between the ages of 4 and 8 was basically a language of socialization, and it was a very controlling language in so far as it told the child what to do, what to think, and how to feel.

Although the language was not rich in actual imperatives, the implied imperatives abounded; a mother might say to a child: "Do you want to take your own plate off the table, sweetie?" when the child really had no options in the matter. We saw a lot of dinner-table interaction because we were hoping to get samples of the father's speech as well, and this talk contained many instructions on sitting up, not throwing forks, and generally, how to behave.

The parents typically spelled out explicitly the dangers of situations: a mother might place the food in front of a child while saying, "hot, hot!" One does not give boiling hot food to a little baby, and hostesses do not say, "hot, hot!" as they serve their dinner guests, so this is a special situation. A hostess might, of course, say, "Watch out for this dish—it's just out of the oven."

In their conversations with the children of this age, parents typically supplied the entire context. If they asked a question, they included with it the answer. We have, for instance, the following: a father comes to pick up his son at nursery school and says: "Where's your lunchbox? I bet it's inside." or the following conversation between a mother and her 5-year-old son:

MOTHER: *How was school today? Did you go to assembly?*
SON: *Yes.*
MOTHER: *Did the preschoolers go to assembly?*
SON: *Yes.*
MOTHER: *Did you stay for the whole assembly or just part of it?*

The child really does not have to do anything but say yes or no—the mother is providing the whole conversation herself, and, undoubtedly, in the process, teaching him how to make a conversation and what kind of responses are expected of him.

Another feature of this adult to child language was that the adults frequently exaggerated their responses, almost beyond reason, or reacted in the way they thought the child ought to feel. For instance, the following:

A child in nursery school fills a bucket with a hose. The teacher says: "Hey, wow, that's almost full to the *top*!"

A child shows his mother some old toys that he has just been given by another child. The mother whoops with joy.

A child shows his father a simple model he has made. The father says: "Hey, that's *really* something, isn't it?"

A child tells a neighbor he has been to the circus. The neighbor says: "Boy! That must have been fun."

Since full buckets, old toys, simple models, and even the circus do not really impress adults that much, they must be telling the child how *he* ought to feel.

These are only a few of the special features of the language of socialization.

The transition from this directive socializing language to the colloquial style used by adult familiars is not easily accomplished. Quite to the contrary, parents often persist in addressing their 8-year-olds as if they were 4, much to the dismay of the children. From what we have seen, it is actually because of signals from the child, often very explicit and angry signals, that the adult ceases to address him as if he were very little. Mothers, for instance, typically spell out all the dangers of the situation to young children, as I have said. At some point the child begins to act quite disgusted with what the parents say. When the mother tells him to be careful crossing the street, he says something like, "O.K., O.K., I *know* how to cross the street." This angry negative feedback to her utterances in the language of socialization eventually teaches her to address him in a different style, and perhaps only mention that traffic is very heavy that day. Of course some parents never do seem to understand the angry signals and continue telling their children to wear their rubbers until they are 35.

THE CHILDREN'S LANGUAGE

The children in our sample ranged in age from infancy to 8 years. By and large we were not primarily looking for evidence of code switching or stylistic variation in the children under 4. These children were included in the sample because we wanted to get examples of the adults and older children talking to them for evidence of baby-talk style. Some things did seem readily evident from observing the very young children and talking to their parents, however. The first is that even the tiniest children make some distinctions. The basic, earliest variation is simply between talking and not talking. Very small children will frequently talk or jabber nonsense to their own parents or siblings, but fall silent in the presence of strangers. When the parent tries to get the baby to say, "Hi," or "Bye-bye," to the interviewer, the baby stares blankly; and the mother says, "I don't know what's wrong. He really can talk. He says bye-bye all the time." The baby remains silent. After the interviewer leaves, surrounded once more by familiar faces, the baby suddenly springs to life and says a resounding "Bye-bye!" So the first variation is between speech and silence.

Another, more obviously stylistic variation we have seen in the language of the children under 4 as well as those over 4, has been the selective use of whining, by which I mean a repetitive, insistent, singsong demand or complaint, and not crying, which is very difficult for little children to inhibit. The whining basically occurs to parents and parent figures, and a child may abruptly switch to a whine at the sight of his parent, when he has previously been talking to someone else in a quite normal tone. In the nursery school I visited, for instance, one child was talking with his friends when his father arrived. At the sight of his father, he abruptly altered his tone and began to whine, "Pick me up" at him.

In listening to the tapes of the children's speech, we had in mind the generally recognized kinds of language style that linguists talk about. Baby-talk style, peer-group colloquial style, and a more formal style for talking to older people and strangers seemed to be three kinds of codes that all adults have and that we might expect to see emerging in the children as they grow older. We thought that the interviewers or other strange adults would bring out the formal style; that the other children of about the same age—close siblings and the many friends who appeared— would bring out the colloquial style; and that baby-talk style would begin to emerge in the language of these children when they talked to the babies in their families.

We did not originally count on the presence of the language of socialization, but it soon became evident that it was there in many cases where children were talking to somewhat younger children. Part of a conversation between my 8-year-old daughter, Cindy, and the 4-year-old I was studying went as follows. She wanted to give him some of her toys, and she said, "Would you like to have some for you at your house?" When he agreed, she said, "Now you just carry them home, and don't run." She then helped him across the street to his house, and when they got there said, "Ricky, you want to show your mother? You want to show your mother that you got these?"

He said, "Yeah. For me." And she replied, "You share them." We have many other instances of older children talking to younger children this way.

We have no real instances of these children using typical adult formal style, probably in part at least because we, as interviewers, were familiar to them and part of their own community. We failed to be formidable strangers, and the parents addressed us in familiar ways as well, so there was very little in the way of formal greetings and farewells, or politeness formulas. Only in one family did we get anything like formal language, and this was the one family outside our Cambridge private school sample that Elliot Mishler and I visited together. In this family, our language and the language of the family proved far more formal. The mother, for example, said to us after we had come in "Have a seat. It's the best one in the house." We had brought some small toys for the children in the family, and the first-grade boy approached Dr. Mishler somewhat later and said, "Thank you for bringing the presents" in a very formal way, with pauses between the words, careful enunciation, and a flat, affectless tone. The other families treated us in a far more colloquial way.

While it was not marked by adult formal features, the children's language to us had its own characteristics. Ricky, the 4-year-old, who said to his father things like "I wanna be up on your shoulder" *fourteen times* in a row, gave me the following explanation of the tooth fairy:

> *Uh, well, you see, if your teeth come out, the teeth come back and by, uh, a fairy. And, you see, the teeth that came out you have to put under your pillow, and then the fairy comes and takes 'em, you see, and he leaves a little money or a little candy.*

This language is far more narrative and far more didactic than anything he directed at either his parents or other children. This is clearly different speech.

The style the children employed in talking to one another was markedly different from their style to adults or to babies, especially in those cases where they were playing together. This peer-group style included a very rich use of expressive words like "yukk" and "blech," and of sound effects. Our tapes are full of bangs, sirens, airplane noises, animal sounds, and explosions. There are some sex differences, since the boys played more violent games and accompanied them with appropriate sounds, but the girls made a lot of noises as well.

The children playing together often launched into chants, rhymes, television commercials, theme songs of favorite shows, and animal acts. They frequently took off from what they were saying into dramatic play involving changing their voices and pretending they were other people or other creatures. This peer-group language was very different from the language directed at adults. Other features of this child-to-child language that might be mentioned are the very frequent use of first names, as in adult–child language, but no endearments, even in those cases where a somewhat older child was speaking to a somewhat younger one as if she were a parent, as I mentioned before. Finally, there was a striking amount of copying behavior in the children's utterances; many instance of one child saying just what another child has said, without any change in emphasis or structure. For instance, the following example from the nursery school:

SUE: *Well, don't you want to see the raspberries?*
MALCOLM: *How 'bout you pick some for me and I'll eat them?*
ERIC: *Yeah, and how 'bout pick some for me and I'll eat them?*

The third child adds *yeah, and* to the second child's statement and then repeats it. An adult would not have repeated *and I'll eat them* under the same circumstances, although he might have said, "How 'bout picking some for *me*?" Eric's repetition is quite flat—the intonation contours are the same as Malcolm's, and there is no shift of emphasis. He is really not varying the statement so much as echoing it. Where an adult says just what another adult has said, his intention is usually mockery, but for the children, imitation of this sort is very common, and passes unremarked.

The children's language to the babies in the families was also examined for evidence of baby-talk style. While most of the features of peer group code appeared in the language of the entire 4- to 8-year-old sample, there were age differences in the ability to use baby-talk style. The older children were in control of the basic features of baby-talk style—their sentences to the babies were short and repetitive, and uttered in a kind of singing style. In one family I asked an 8-year-old to ask his 2-year-old brother to take a glass to the kitchen. He said: ·

"Here, Joey, take this to the kitchen. Take it to the kitchen." (Baby-talk intonation, high voice.)

A little while later, I asked him to ask his 4-year-old brother to take a glass to the kitchen. This time he said:

"Hey, Rick, take this to the kitchen, please." (Normal intonation.) This is clear evidence of code switching in the language of this 8-year-old child.

On the other end of the spectrum, the 4-year-old, Ricky, whom I followed about, did not use baby-talk style to his 2-year-old brother. He typically did not use either a special intonation or repetition. He said to the baby: "Do you know what color your shoes are?" in just the same way he said: "What's the name of the book, Anthony?" to his brother; and "I don't think he know how to climb up" to his father.

Somewhere in between no baby-talk style and full baby-talk style lies slightly inappropriate baby-talk style, which we saw particularly in some 5- and 6-year-old girls. Unlike the 4-year-olds, 5- and 6-year-old children made clear efforts to adjust their language to suit the babies they addressed. We have the following conversation:

2-YEAR-OLD: *Dead bug!*
6-YEAR-OLD: *That ant!*
2-YEAR-OLD: *That bug!*
6-YEAR-OLD: *Hey, Susie, that's ant; that's not bug, that ant!*

The 6-year-old is here obviously trying to accommodate the baby sister by talking in what she regards as "her language," but she misses the cues when she says "That's ant." Good baby sentences would be either "That ant," as the child says, or "That a ant," but a copula without an article in "That's ant" doesn't ring true.

Listening to these children begin to use baby-talk style and then use it fluently by the time they are 7 or 8 makes it clear that knowing how to talk to babies is not something you keep with you from having been a baby; you have to learn it again. The young children in the sample who were still completing their knowledge of regular English syntax were in no position to play with it. They made their sentences the only way they knew how, grinding them out with laborious intensity at times, looking neither to the baby left nor formal right.

The observations we have made thus far are in their preliminary stages, based on only five families, all from the same socioeconomic background and geographical region. The similarities among these families were, however, so great as to make us feel confident that they are generally occurring features, at least in upper middle-class homes. From what we have seen, it seems clear that children are not faced with a vast undifferentiated body of English from which they must make some order as best they can. The parents in these families talked in a very consistent and predictable style to their babies, a style which other researchers have described; and we have found that parents and other adults use a separate style for talking to growing children. This style is different from the informal or colloquial style that teenagers or old friends use to one another, and serves special functions: It is the language of socialization. While baby-talk style is concerned with learning the language, with establishing communication, the language of socialization is filled with social rules. The mother's questions contain answers and in this way show how to make a conversation. The adult emphasizes and exaggerates his own reactions, points up relationships, names feelings, controls and directs the child, and in many ways makes explicit his own world view. The language directed at young children is a teaching language. It tells about the world, and must, because of its special features, be recognized as a separate code.

The original aim of this study was to see if, indeed, children talk in different ways to different people. The answer is yes; infants are selective about whom they talk to at all. Four-year-olds may whine at their mothers, engage in intricate verbal play with their peers, and reserve their narrative, discursive tales for their grown-up friends. By the time they are 8, children have added to the foregoing some of the politeness routines of formal adult speech, baby-talk style, and the ability to talk to younger children in the language of socialization. The details of the emergence of these codes are yet to be elaborated.

THE GENESIS OF COMPLEX SENTENCES[1]

JOHN LIMBER

University of New Hampshire

One of the most interesting and important aspects of language acquisition is the child's development of an ability to produce and understand complex sentences of various kinds. Lees (1960) puts his finger on perhaps the most important issue, one distinguishing human language from many other symbolic systems.

> Even if we disregard all those nominal expressions employed with purely connotative meaning, that is, those which do not refer to any object, and confine our attention to nouns which are names of things, it is clear that no extant lexicon contains anywhere near enough expressions of this kind to suffice even for ordinary daily life. We cannot get along with any single common noun to refer to a familiar object, but must have at every moment modifiers with which to construct new, more complex names to use for all the specific instances of that object which we encounter and talk about [p. xvii].

From many reports on early syntactic development, it would seem that most children display the ability to construct various complex nominal constructions—syntactically generated names—as well as other complex constructions out of simpler components well before their third birthday

[1] This research was done at the Department of Psychology, M.I.T., where the author is a research associate. It was supported by a grant to Dr. J. A. Fodor from the National Institute of Child Health and Human Development (HD 05168). I take this opportunity to thank Dr. J. A. Fodor, Dr. M. F. Garrett, and especially my research assistant, Rhoda Goodwin for their contributions to this work.

(3;0). Leopold (1949b), for example, in his classic study, remarks about his daughter of 2 years, 11 months (2;11) that: ". . . with the mastery of complex sentences, the linguistic development has reached the last stage. In the future only refinements can be expected. In general, it is astonishing how little her language differs from recognized usage [Vol. 4, p. 37]."

This chapter concerns the development of complex sentences in a number of English-speaking children before their third birthday. In large part, I believe, Leopold's remarks are borne out by our research. Needless to say, the extent to which anyone will subscribe to this proposition will depend on a number of things including (1) what aspects of linguistic behavior or knowledge one wants to count as syntactic; (2) how finely one discriminates among various constructions; (3) what one will accept as evidence that a child has or has not productively acquired a given construction; and (4) perhaps the most important, which particular children one happens to observe. I do not think, however, that I want to directly take up any of these notorious issues save the last at this time; instead I prefer to simply report and discuss some of the implications of our observations of the spontaneous production of complex sentences by children under 3.

These sentences I am about to consider come from the records of a number of children in the Boston area between the ages of 1;6 and 3;0 who for the past year and a half have participated in a longitudinal developmental study of early language acquisition whose focus is on early segmentation, morpheme structure, and phonological development (cf. Kornfeld, 1971; Limber, 1970b). The relevant details of this study are, in brief, as follows. The child and parent—generally the mother—visit our laboratory monthly for a recording session in which we obtain up to 30 minutes of spontaneous speech between parent and child alone, and up to 30 minutes of experimenter-elicited speech, generally naming objects, describing pictures or toy situations. In addition to the speech samples, we have administered the Bayley Scales of Infant Development (Bayley, 1969) to each child on approximately his second birthday (2;0). Also at this time the parent is interviewed in depth concerning the child's home environment, behavior patterns, etc. Currently there are twelve children in our study. They range between 1;11 and 3;0. Most of my remarks here are based upon the records of three of these children—two girls and a boy. These children had no siblings for at least their first two years, have no health problems, and all have above average scores on the Bayley mental scales. Their parents have attended or were graduated from college.

We have gone to considerable effort to obtain a variety of nonlinguistic behavioral and environmental information on each child. We have done this following the hypothesis that much of the often-lamented individual differences known to exist in the course of early development are not due to vagaries in the child's language learning processes but rather to systematic variation in other aspects of development and environment. To point out one obvious factor, it is striking to what extent studies of phonological development have been carried out on children raised in multilingual environments. No one would be surprised if such children differed characteristically in some developmental respect from the children of monolingual homes in our study. It is our hope that by being able to compare our children on the various factors likely to affect development, we will be able to reduce the environmental noise and thereby permit the basic acquisition processes to be observed more clearly. Although it is premature to draw any conclusions as to the effectiveness of this research strategy, already it appears possible that we will be able to partition children into two groups. One group is characterized by relatively high intelligibility in one word utterances and very predictable developmental sequences in morphology, phonology and syntax, and in general, a relatively small amount of individual variation within children. The other group is essentially the converse of the former group—unpredictable with a relatively large amount of individual variation, and relatively slower development. The sentences discussed in this paper are exclusively from the former group; the others (two in number of age 3;0) being nowhere near this level of productive development.

Before going on, I might point out that the design of this research is not optimal for the study of syntax. Our data are quite fragmentary. Although in a one-hour session a good sample of output bearing on phonological issues is readily obtained through elicitation, we have to make do with whatever sentences are spontaneously produced. Because of the fragmentary nature of my data, I am only able to report on the development of production and not that of comprehension. Therefore, all references to development are to be taken as referring to spontaneous production, i.e., anything but obvious imitation.

A CHRONOLOGY OF THE DEVELOPMENT OF COMPLEX SENTENCES

Various aspects of syntactic development are displayed in Fig. 1. Only some of these will be discussed here although the others may help in conveying a more complete picture of overall development. The complex constructions include verb object complements, *wh*-adverbials, question-word (Q) clauses, relative clauses, and a variety of coordinate and subordinate conjuctions. As a rule of thumb, I will consider any sentence with more than one verb (V) as complex; auxiliaries and possessives are perhaps arbitrarily excluded. It is important to understand that I do not intend the above gram-

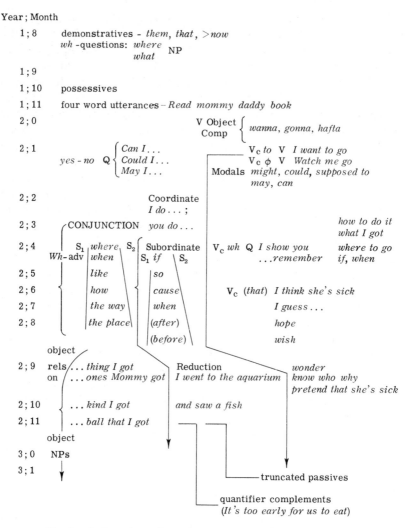

Year; Month

1;8	demonstratives - *them, that,* >*now* *wh* -questions: *where* NP *what*
1;9	
1;10	possessives
1;11	four word utterances – *Read mommy daddy book*

FIG. 1.   A chronology of complex constructions for three children.

matical descriptions to be mutually exclusive or imply an independent genetic or linguistic analysis. I believe quite the contrary to be true and hope that a careful study of development will shed light not only on the acquisition processes but also on the linguistic mechanisms of the mature speaker–hearer. Indeed the structural schemata of 2-year-old speech discussed in (2) and (5) following are remarkably similar to those reflected in the speech of the mature English speaker (cf. Limber, 1970a). The major discrepancies generally seem to arise from a proliferation of exceptions rather than the introduction of wholly new structures.

Precomplex Constructions

The earlier stages of language development are relatively well studied—if not understood (e.g., Bloom, 1970; Braine, 1963a; Brown, in press; McNeil, 1970b). Here it may be useful to very briefly review some commonplace aspects of precomplex development—in particular, simple names and predicates, pronouns, wh-question, and possessives.

Simple Names and Predicates

The earliest intelligible words for most children appear to be lexically simple names or predicates, e.g., *mamma* [mama], *milk* [mīy], *bottle* [ba], *shoe* [šu]. As I have suggested elsewhere (Limber 1970b; 1971), many children appear to follow a nearly optimal segmentation strategy for isolating their early word forms from utterances in English directed to them—take the last relatively stressed syllable in the utterance as a word form. Not only does this generally get the form for a predicate or name; it gets one of immediate semantic salience, e.g., *Where's Mommy? Do you want some milk? That's a shoe!* It also avoids having to look at reduced syllables as targets for learning the English vowel system and takes advantage of recency effects in short-term acoustic memory. Until the child develops the ability to syntactically generate names by using combinations of words, he must make do with using single words when referring to objects in his perceptual field, his wants, various actions, etc.

Referential Pronouns

One way to make reference or individuate things is by using pronouns of various sorts—*that, there, it, now*. Of course, this avoids the problem of selecting names altogether and is quite satisfactory when objects are immediately present and in some sense perceptually salient. It is not so satisfactory when the object is not close at hand or is abstract, e.g., an action, want, or proposition. For a considerable time after 1;6, however, children make frequent use of such referential pronouns. To look ahead a bit, the emergence of complex constructions—nominalizations or complements in particular—enables the child to describe and individuate for others instances of those concepts such as object, action, event, place, time, and manner which at first he can only refer to by using a pronoun or simple lexical predicate—if at all.[2]

---

[2]Of course I am talking about the ability to individuate entities linguistically, I have absolutely nothing to say about the conceptual bases for those distinctions.

Wh-*questions*

Questions such as *What's that? Where's Mamma?* and *What doing?* are among the earliest multiword constructions, appearing before 2;0 in many cases. Questions involving *how, when, who,* and *why* appear somewhat later throughout the third year. There can be little doubt of the importance of the patterning of questions between parent and child for both syntactic and cognitive development (cf. Ervin-Tripp, 1970a). As Fig. 1 suggests, there seems to be a developmental relationship between indirect questions, *wh*-adverbials, and relative clauses.

The Possessive

Typically the earliest departure from the two- or three-word utterances generally interpreted by the listener as somehow fitting the schema (*Agent*) (*Action*) (*Patient*) (*Object*) is the modification or syntactic individuation of the object noun phrase (NP) by a possessive, for example, from *want hat* to *want daddy hat*. This construction foreshadows several aspects of both complement and relative constructions. It is an NP expansion expressing a relationship among its constituents that is itself subordinate to the main clause. It is perhaps the child's first attempt to individuate entities syntactically by combining lexical items rather than using a pronoun or simple lexical item. Furthermore, this NP expansion typically occurs on the object NP, or in an alternate description, the utterance-final NP. The relationship of these features of the possessive to aspects of various complex constructions will be seen in the discussion of relatives and complements.

The Complex Constructions

Complements

The first complex constructions to appear in the children's speech are object complements or what Lees (1960) in his *Grammar of English Nominalizations* calls complex nominals. These are, on his account, nounlike versions of sentences, functioning as nominals within another sentence. Some ideas of the variety of constructions in English falling under this description are as follows:

(1)　　　　　a. *I* **want** *Bill to go*
　　　　　　　b. *That I left* **surprised** *Mary*
　　　　　　　c. *I* **heard** *him leave*
　　　　　　　d. *I* **compelled** *Bill to leave*
　　　　　　　e. *I* **like** *playing cards*
　　　　　　　f. *I* **like** *to play cards*

> g. *I* **promise** *that I will clean up my room*
> h. **Watch** *the girl feed the ducks*
> i. *Did you* **ask** *Mary to put her toys away?*
> j. *I'll* **show** *how to do it*
> k. *I don't* **remember** *if I was there*

What is characteristic of all these examples, is of course, that they are composed of two elements—the main clause or matrix sentence (verb **boldface**) and a more-or-less sentence-like element containing the verb and perhaps other residue of the complement or constituent clause now embedded in the main clause.

The development of complements can be summarized in the following generalizations (or hypotheses—to put it more conservatively).

G1. Invariably the first complements are object nominals.

G2. Complements with a given complement-taking verb will appear within a month after the first use of that verb in any construction *unless* the child has not produced any four-word utterances. This last qualification is necessary as children may use *want juice*, etc., as early as 1;6.[3]

G3. Verbs from various complement-taking verb classes have a characteristic order of appearance across children.

The first generalization (G1) simply follows the pattern set out by the possessives—expand the object NP first. There is no question as to its validity; no subject complements appear in the speech of any child up to 3.

The second and third generalizations, G2 and G3, are most interesting, and somewhat less firm. Consequently, they demand further scrutiny in light of the fragmentary data upon which they are based. I can perhaps put the issue of verbs and their complements in some perspective by noting that there are over 200 verbs in English which may take complements; verbs familiar to most adults (cf. Rosenbaum, 1967). Looking over the records of the children in our study, I have found that about 30 of these verbs appear in their spontaneous speech. These are listed in Table 1. Of these only three did not appear in a complement construction—*find*, *miss*, and *help*.

The fact that children use these various verbs in object-complement (G1) constructions almost immediately upon using them in any construction (G2)

---

[3] In the talk upon which this paper is based I mentioned that I had not observed *make* and *help* with complements. Afterward several people informed me that they had in fact observed the use of *make* with complements shortly after 2. In a check of my records I have found I was in error about *make*—it does follow G2 and there are isolated instances of *help* with complement; not enough however to let me conclude *help* does follow G2.

Table 1 *Complement Verbs Used during Third Year*

Age 1;11–2;5[a]	Age 2;5–3;0
want	think
need	told
like	guess
watch	know
see	hope
lookit	show
let	remember
ask (tell)	finish
say[b]	wonder
go[b]	wish
make	help
	said
	pretend
	decided
	forgot

[a]Auxiliaries excluded, e.g., *going to*, *'posed to*, *have to*, and some modals.
[b]*Say* and *go* are used to express direct speech and noises, e.g., *Cows go "moo."*

should not, upon reflection, be very surprising. For many of them like *guess*, *wish*, *think*, and *pretend* there is scarcely any way to refer to their objects other than by using a nominal complement of some type. Where simple NP objects do appear in adult speech, those NPs must be interpreted as elliptical,[4] e.g., *I guess a goat, I suggest a goose, I think a martini*. Even *I want a martini* might be argued to imply some implicit verb whose object is *a martini*, e.g., *to drink* or *have*.

Some investigators may be reluctant to consider utterances such as *I wanna go* or even *I want to go home* as evidence for embedding processes in the child unless he also produces contrastive examples with an overt subject of the embedded constituent sentence present, for example, *I want mommy do it*. Several recent grammars describing early sentences in children (Bloom, 1970; Brown, in press) have characterized the verbs, *wanna*, *want to*, and *gonna*, *going to* as a special distributional class of catenative verbs, perhaps on analogy to English auxiliary verbs. There seems to be no objection to such a descriptive analysis permitting $NP–V_{cat}–V$ strings as long as no suggestion is intended that catenative verb constructions are somehow simpler than com-

[4]I have discussed these and similar examples in Limber (1969; 1970a).

plement constructions—or auxiliaries for that matter.[5] However, with the uncertainty attendant upon any classification of lexical items into grammatical categories in children's speech, I would be chary of assuming that an utterance such as *I want car* differs syntactically from *I want see* or even *I want up* as far as the child's language processes are concerned. For all anyone can tell, it might be that in such examples, the word following *want* is not selected on any intrinsic syntactic basis at all. Instead it may be that the child simply selects any lexical item which strikes him as an effective description of whatever it is he wants. Thus *car*, *see*, and *up* in the previous examples may all serve the same semantic-syntactic function, namely, to refer to the object of the verb *want*. The child is temporarily in a dilemma implicitly raised by Lees's passage quoted above. He does not have enough names (predicates) in his lexicon to adequately individuate those objects of which he is capable of conceiving and would like to talk about. Not enough that is, until he catches on to the English rules for syntactically generating complex names, i.e., the various nominalizations.[6]

The claim that many children at 2 produce complex sentences does not solely depend on instances of *want* utterances. Not only are such sentences as *I don't want you read that book* common; but also complements with *watch*, *see* and *lookit*, for example: *Watch me draw circles, I see you sit down,* and *lookit a boy play ball*. There are, thus, two classes of verbs—the *wants: want*, *need*, and *like*; and the *watches: watch*, *see*, and *lookit*—taking complements at the very beginning of the third year. Of the former class, only *want* appeared with a noncoreferential infinitival complement subject, though all three appear with a wide range of embedded verbs and occasionally without the infinitive mark *to*. *Want* would appear to provide an important model for the child in his attempts at formulating rules for production and perception of a wide variety of infinitival constructions. *Watch*, *see*, and *lookit* provide

---

[5] It is perhaps of some interest to note at this point that most auxiliary verbs appear several months after instances of the complement verbs. The obvious exceptions are the early use of modals such as *can*, *could*, *may* in *yes-no* questions, e.g., *Can I knock it over?* One might consider the possibility that inductions made by the child on the modals in questions is related to their later appearance as auxiliaries. As Ross (1967) points out, auxiliaries are not your randomly selected verbs. A detailed longitudinal study of the development of the auxiliary system would be of great interest.

[6] The practice of assigning morphemes used by the child to the most appropriate adult grammatical categories raises many questions. As early as 2;6 I have observed several instances of apparent generalization from noun to verb form, i.e., using established noun forms as verbs, e.g., *Is he typewritering? Can I fire the candle?* These seem to be novel creations on the part of the child. As an alternative to crediting the child with plausible but incorrect generalizations in such cases, it is worth considering that perhaps he never made a syntactic distinction between nouns and verbs in the first place.

a somewhat different model in that all complement subjects must be overtly indicated. The fact that the children use verbs from both classes, generally all the *wants* and one or two of the *watches*, suggests that the productivity of object complement constructions is firmly established.

Unfortunately, my data are too fragmentary to make a fine-grained analysis of the order of appearance of individual verbs profitable. However, the order of the following groups of verbs appears reliable across a number of children (cf. Fig. 1). First, at about 2 come the *want* and *watch* groups with complements; both, especially *want*, may have been used previously without full complements. About the same time, most auxiliaries, *is*, *will*, *may*, *can*, *could*, appear initially in *yes-no* questions. A month or two later (2;2) all the auxiliaries appear in declarative sentences, *I can go*. This is followed (before 2;6) by several verbs taking *wh*-clause objects, e.g., *I show you how to do it*, and the first verb—generally *think*—taking propositional objects. Finally, throughout the last half of the third year come a variety of verbs also taking propositional objects; these are without a *that* complementizer until close to 3.

Examining the right-hand side of Fig. 1, it is apparent that most of the major object-complement structure types in English are represented: unmarked infinitive—*Watch me go*; marked infinitive—*I want to go*; full sentence and *wh*-clause—*I guess she's sick* and *I show you how to do it*. Missing are a variety of *-ing* complements; for example, *I like eating lollipops* in contrast to the very common *I like to eat lollipops*. A few instances of the *-ing* form were found with *finish* or *all done*, e.g., *I all done eating*.

It is of some interest, I believe, to notice that the child's inferences about English complement structures are based on a very small sample of all English verbs. In particular, those inferences are based exclusively on a subset of true object-complement-taking verbs in contrast to other complement —taking verbs, such as *defy* or *force* (Rosenbaum's oblique-object verbs). One feature of the true object verbs not shared by the oblique-object verbs is that while both appear in surface structures of the form *I V-ed Bill to leave*, only the true object verbs have corresponding questions of the form *What did I V?*, i.e., *What did I want?* but not *What did I force?* (in the analogous sense). Thus in the true object-complement verbs, *want*, *think*, *wish*, etc., the entire complement structure is a constituent. Thus on the basis of a very small set of verbs, the child learns structures that are shared by verbs he has not yet encountered.

From one point of view this would seem to be merely a reflection of a general feature of English; namely, that relatively few syntactic formats serve to carry a much larger variety of syntactic–semantic relationships—a fact often causing linguists headaches and perhaps microcomplexities in the everyday sentence processing of fluent English speakers as they work, for example, to interpret appropriately a string containing . . . *to V* . . . .

From the child's point of view, however, things are not so chaotic. Since he only uses true object-complement verbs, he can count on the syntactic structure to give him the unique and correct semantic relationship of the word or words following the main verb. For the child at this stage, English verbs take the object structures schematized in (2).

(2)

	Subject	Main verb	Object
a.	(NP)	V	(NP)
b.	(NP)	V	(NP)-V-(NP)

Elements in parentheses are optional in certain constructions. Thus the child, who does not use such verbs as *force*, *defy*, or *promise* has no problem interpreting the superficially similar sentences in (3)

(3)
$$I \left\{ \begin{array}{l} \textit{defied} \\ \textit{forced} \\ \textit{wanted} \\ \textit{guessed} \\ \textit{remembered} \\ \textit{promised} \end{array} \right\} \textit{Bill to be quiet.}$$

according to schema (2b). When he does begin to use those verbs[7] which do not have the same underlying structures as the other verbs sharing a surface structure in the adult language, it would seem that he incorporates or assimilates the new verbs into the old surface forms. *Force*, for example, fits either into the (2b) structure or that of an oblique form NP-V-NP-P-NP, i.e., *I forced Bill into eating lollipops* on the model *I put baby into her carriage.*

Surely a basic process or strategy in language development is using previously acquired decoding devices in order to interpret or produce new ones. From the primitive initial segmentation strategy for isolating word forms up through the use (Limber, 1970a) of such schemata described above, to the mature speaker–hearer trying to infer the meaning of an unfamiliar word from its sentence, that process is operative. One consequence of such a developmental process would be that surface form of an utterance becomes progressively less valuable as an indicant of the basic semantic-syntactic structural relationships as more alternative underlying structures share a given surface form. Correspondingly more attention must be given to idiosyncratic properties of the lexical items involved in order to interpret such structures appropriately.

Several such constructions involving verbs having particularly idio-

---

[7] I believe the verbs *force* and *promise* do not appear in the speech of most children before age 6.

syncratic syntactic properties have been recently studied by C. Chomsky (1969). She reports that several constructions involving the verbs *ask* and *promise* indeed are not correctly interpreted by many children between 6 and 9 years. C. Chomsky (1969, p. 121) claims that this indicates many children have not acquired all the syntactic rules of their native language as late as 9 years. Another way of putting these same facts, however, is to say simply that the child's previously developed normal interpretation devices—involving assignment of coreference in this case—do not work when those particular verbs take infinitival complements. It cannot be a surprise that a generalization made by the child between 2 and 3 and found valid for a number of years should give rise to problems when exceptions are encountered. To suggest that the child has not learned certain syntactic rules seems misleading in this case; what the child must learn is to give up certain effective structural generalizations, i.e., syntactic rules, when confronted by specific lexical items, e.g., *ask*, *promise*. One wonders to what extent such syntactic irregularities hinder the child's acquisition of the appropriate semantic concepts corresponding to those words. It appears fair to conclude that the child at 3 has acquired in some sense the syntactic structures for most object complements except the various *-ing* forms. What remains for him to learn is how to handle the various exceptions associated with certain verb classes and individual verbs that he encounters after 3.

Wh-*Clause Constructions*

A number of more or less related constructions come under this heading including *wh*-adverbials, question-word clauses, and relatives. Their chronological development is outlined in Fig. 1. The *wh*-clause is essentially a grammatical device like the complement clause for syntactic generation of individuating expressions. Whereas complements are typically generated names for abstract entities such as proposition, facts, events, actions, the *wh*-clauses in general individuate or describe concrete and abstract objects, and the adverbial notions of place, time and manner.[8]

Referring back to Fig. 1, one can see that around 2;6 or before that, the *wh*-adverb sentences such as *Do it how I do it, Can I do it when we go home?* appear at the same time that those same adverbial forms appear in question-word complements to verbs, e.g., *show, remember*, as in *I show you how to do it, I remember where is it*. Other *wh*-clauses also appear in such constructions;

---

[8]The syntax of relatives and complements is similar in several respects, converging in the ambiguous *The fact that Otto knew was surprising*. The semantic differences between relatives and complements is more interesting and elusive. One difference seems to be that relatives may be used to make indirect reference, picking out an entity by its stated relationship to some other entity presumed known by the listener. Complements are more like proper names, making direct reference.

e.g., *I show you what I got, I don't know who is it.* The precise onset of relative clauses will depend on one's view of the relationship of relatives to *wh*-adverbs and question clauses. Although it has on occasion been proposed that the adverbs *when*, *where* and *how* be derived from the corresponding abstract NPs, time, place, and manner, Fig. 1 indicates that the corresponding *wh*-adverbial precedes the use of the abstract noun plus relative by more than a month, e.g., *I show you where we went*, then *I show you the place we went.* It is of some interest that generally if two constructions have been derived from a common base form within a transformational analysis, it is a good bet that the construction furthest from the base will be produced earlier. The effect of the additional transformational rules is typically to further reduce the construction in contrast to its counterpart.

The general trend in the development of the clear relatives seems to be as follows: first on the abstract adverbial nouns, *place* and *way* (but not *time*); next on various empty noun heads, e.g., *thing, one, kind*; and finally on common nouns like *ball* or *cheese*. These latter forms in fact are quite rare up to 3. Compared with complement constructions, use of relative clauses is very infrequent. Furthermore there is a curious gap in the relative clause distribution: There are no subject relatives or any relative clauses attached to subject NPs. I will come back to this point during my concluding remarks. One more thing deserves mention. Although I have referred to relative clauses as *wh*-constructions, in fact no *wh*-morphemes were observed up to 3. The order of embedding morphemes is ∅, then *that*.

Conjunctions

The third group of complex sentences in Fig. 1 includes various coordinate and subordinate conjunctions (C). Representative examples taken from the records of one child are found in (4).

(4) a. *You lookit that book; I lookit this book.* (2;0)
   b. *I do pull it the way he hafta do that so he doesn't—so the big boy doesn't come out.* (2;6)
   c. *And that mouse is not scary; it's a library friend.* (2;8)
   d. *You play with this one and I play with this.* (2;8)
   e. *He was stuck and I got him out.* (2;8)
   f. *I can't put it on—too little.* (2;8)
   g. *He still has milk and spaghetti.* (2;8)
   h. *Here's a seat. It must be mine if it's a little one.* (2;10)
   i. *I went to the aquarium and saw the fish.* (2;10)
   j. *I want this doll because she's big.* (2;10)
   k. *When I was a little girl I could go "geek-geek" like that; but now I can go "this is a chair."* (2;10)

The earliest suggestion of conjunction is the grouping of two sentences (S) together without a distinguishable conjoining morpheme. Very often in listening to tapes made between 2;0 and 2;4, one is apt to perceive a *so*, *and*, or *if*, when in fact, upon replay there is not any direct basis for this percept.

Throughout the second half of the third year a variety of adverbial conjunctions come into frequent use. Many are of the form S_1-C-S_2 or the preposed version C-S_2-S_1 where C includes *so*, *if*, *because*, *when*. There are also sporadic appearances of *before* and *after*.

SUMMARY AND CONCLUDING REMARKS

Having surveyed various aspects of syntactic development taking place in the third year, we are now in a somewhat better position to evaluate the issue raised at the beginning of this paper—how does the syntactic structure of these 3-year-olds compare with that of a mature English speaker? Among the many points to consider are the following:

(1) By 3 these children have unmistakably acquired the ability to generate syntactically complex names and descriptions—complements and relatives. Thus they are able to individuate linguistically a wide variety of abstract and concrete entities, e.g., desires, actions, foods for which syntactically simple expressions may be inadequate.

(2) Their utterances display the basic structural features of English. The major exceptions to this, that is those aspects of English syntax not present in the child's production during this period, include subject complements and subject relatives, relatives attached to subject NPs, *-ing* complements, ordering of elements in the auxiliary system, full passives, and a number of lexical–specific morphological features, e.g., tense marking, choice of preposition.

(3) The major developments involving complex sentences during the third year are informally summarized in (5).

(5) a. An N-V-N sequence is the common simple sentence.
    b. Form complements: expand (or substitute) an N-V-N sequence for certain noun phrases.
    c. Conjoin two sentences as S_1-C-S_2.
       1. conjunction: C = ∅, *and*, . . .
       2. *wh*-adverbial: C = *where*, *how*, *when*
       3. relative: C = ∅, *that*
    d. Do not explicitly express an N in a lower clause (4b, 4c) if that N is coreferent with the last (i.e., rightmost) N in the main clause.
    e. Do not apply syntactic operations to any subject NPs.

It goes without saying, of course, that there are a number of alternative observationally equivalent descriptions or analyses of these utterances which may turn out to be preferable for one reason or another. Time does not permit consideration of the many alternatives; however one interesting case in point involves (5e), which serves to rule out production of subject complements and subject relatives, along with object relatives attached to subject NPs. While this restriction accurately excludes the appropriate constructions, it does not as it stands explain why such constructions are not observed.

Several possibilities suggest themselves, of course. One might interpret (5e) as reflecting the current state of the child's grammar, perhaps as a function of some universal heuristic concerning the acquisition of grammatical rules, e.g., generalize from object NPs to the others. On the other hand one might appeal to certain performance factors, or simply to various pragmatic aspects of the child's language behavior. Notice, for example, that (5e) has the effect of maintaining the contiguity of all elements within each clause, i.e., it precludes nested clauses. Since nesting is a recognized factor complicating production and perception even for the fluent speaker, it is not surprising that children refrain from using nested constructions.[9] We cannot however simply rewrite (5e) as (5e′); it would not explain the lack of subject relatives on object NPs.

(5e′)   MAINTAIN THE CONTINUITY OF ALL ELEMENTS IN A SINGLE CLAUSE.

As an alternative to a structural or performance oriented explanation, we might look into the possibility that the observed distribution results from what children of that age talk about, i.e., general exigencies of communication rather than as a gap in their knowledge of English syntax or whatever. Consider the distribution of relative clauses in mature English. A (restrictive) relative, with few exceptions, can be attached to any NP in a clause other than a proper name or pronoun. Thus the distribution of relative clauses is dependent on that of names and pronouns—an extensive use of names and pronouns in an environment precludes or reduces the observation of relatives in that environment. One must therefore consider the possibility that the observed patterning of relatives is not a consequence of the familiar competence or performance factors, but simply of the extensive use by these children of names and pronouns in subject NP position.

---

[9]Complete and grammatical utterances containing nested clauses are much less frequent than one might suppose even in adult speech. Very often there is some kind of breakdown in structure—anacoluthon, recapitulation, insertion of pronoun into the relative clause coreferent with the deleted NP (cf. Quirk, 1957). Remarkably similar phenomena are frequently seen in the writing of early Anglo-Saxon writers (Mitchell, 1968). Of course today we edit out such things when writing.

A preliminary evaluation of this hypothesis was made by examining the simple declarative sentences (156 sentences in this sample) produced by one child between 1;11 and 2;11. Looking only at subject and object NP positions in sentences of the form NP-V-(NP)-NP, the following pattern emerges. Nearly all subject NPs are animate; the few exceptions are demonstratives, e.g., *that's mine*. Furthermore, the vast majority of these animate NPs are in fact personal pronouns or names. Less than one in 30 are animate phrases like *the baby*.

Object NPs, in contrast, are typically inanimate although they display the entire range of the child's vocabulary and simple syntactic combinations; 43% inanimate nouns including body parts; 29% inanimate pronouns; 12% animate pronouns or names including indirect objects; 11% animals; and 5% humans, including dolls. To put it another way, the object NP position carries more information, that is, is less predictable, than the constrained and quite predictable subject NP position.

These observations, taken together with the assumption that complex sentences will be formed from the child's repertoire of simple sentences, clearly suggest that pragmatic factors alone may suffice to explain the lack of relatives involving subject NPs. There is simply no opportunity for a relative clause in environments where the NP is typically a name or pronoun —hence no relatives on subject NPs. Similarly one does not expect to see many subject relatives on object NPs when relative clause formation requires that the matrix and constituent NP be coreferential but not a name or pronoun. Even for the few animate objects which could take relative clauses there is a greater chance of finding an appropriate coreferential NP in another object NP than among the predominately name and pronoun subject NPs.

It is likely that these same distributional differences between subject and object NPs can explain the fact that the possessive and complement constructions, like the relative, appear in object position when first acquired.

I should perhaps add here that I certainly do not want to discount the importance of other factors, especially the performance one noted earlier, in children's production. Indeed the first subject relative observed in the speech of this one child (at 3) was *I think that the girl ... that's here ... doesn't ... she doesn't want me to open it*; i.e., a subject relative on the subject NP in an object NP complement. A clearly interpretable yet ungrammatical utterance of this sort would hardly be unexpected in the speech of a mature speaker of English (see footnote 9) and certainly suggests that this child does have productive control of subject relatives by this time even though they may be very infrequent.

(4) There are several lacunae in the children's productive syntax that seem to be inextricably related to the development of certain semantic

notions. Carol Chomsky's verb-complement examples can be thought of in this way. Time-related constructions, e.g., coordination between tense and temporal adverbs, may not be used properly until the child's conception of time reaches a certain level. In such cases I have no reason to believe that it is the syntax per se that has not been learned rather than the semantic notions involved. Nor do I want to claim that use of a certain construction necessarily implies that the child has developed the appropriate, i.e., adult, semantic concepts corresponding to a certain word or construction.

As an example, all these children use *think* with increasing frequency after about 2;6; typically in sentences like *I think I want grape juice, Do you think he wants some?* In such sentences my guess is that the *NP think* is used parenthetically, especially in the first person, *I*, with the sense of *perhaps* or *maybe* (Urmson, 1963). A bit later some children seem to associate *think* with some kind of activity or at least believe that thinking requires a characteristic posture or facial expression. Perhaps due to their egocentric nature, or whatever, it is likely that children at this age have no (tacit) knowledge of the many complexities attending the use of cognitive verbs and opaque contexts in adult speech at the time when they first begin to use such verbs.

In conclusion, I believe my observations both confirm and extend those made by Leopold over 30 years ago. What I have not been able to do, unfortunately, is to alleviate by explanation any of the astonishment Leopold —or anyone else—is compelled to express upon consideration of the linguistic achievements of these 2-year-old children.

CONNECTING CHILDREN'S
LANGUAGE AND LINGUISTIC THEORY[1]

THOMAS ROEPER

University of Chicago

The problem of origins is old: Shakespeare scholars have, when baffled, looked back to Plutarch to find the roots of Elizabethan dramas. They find, not surprisingly, that the mundane origins of Shakespeare's plots provide little with which to fathom his genius. In similar fashion scientists have sought the origin of speech in crying behavior. While crying, if arduous, may exercise those muscles that need exercise to prepare for the speech process, it possesses nothing that resembles sentence structure. Consequently, though crying could be a necessary preliminary to speech, it is categorically not the origin of speech structures.

The problem recurs in later stages of acquisition: suppose we discover that mothers (but not others) speak in clearly simplified structures to their children, and that children acquire just those simplified structures (Bowerman, this volume). We would still not know how a child knows what role those structures play in a complex grammar. We need not conclude, therefore, that knowledge of the context of language learning is useless knowl-

[1] Revised version of a paper presented at the Buffalo Conference on Psycholinguistics. I am indebted to members of the conference for a number of pertinent criticisms, some of which have led to alterations in the paper. Further theoretical discussion can be found in Roeper (1972).

edge. On the contrary, it may be vital for us to know the original context in which language is learned in order to know the terms in which a child frames hypotheses about language. For instance, does a child limit the corpus of utterances he analyzes by focusing upon a certain person as a model, or does he treat all examples of speech as equivalent? If he does focus upon one person—presumably the mother—then the specific character of the mother's simplified speech may prove to be of special importance. He might then use a procedure of this kind: Identify the structure of the mother's most frequent utterances. Form an hypothesis: Some features of deep structure—such as the position of the subject and main verb—are revealed in her structures. For reasons discussed below, some but not all features of deep structure could be inferred in this manner. Other algorithms are also quite plausible. A child might, for instance, limit his corpus by eliminating all utterances spoken with an intonation of hysteria because those utterances are likely to be grammatically deviant or incomplete. In any case at some point—not necessarily at the outset—a child must adopt the hypothesis that a structure known to him can serve as deep structure.

Nonetheless, it is the child's hypothesis about his context—not the context itself—that must be the origin of much of his language. We might, in that vein, keep separate two research areas: *exposure* and *recognition*. (1) In what manner is a child exposed to language? (2) How does he use this exposure to recognize language structure? It is possible, through exposure, that a child might acquire certain grammatical forms before he recognizes their role in a grammatical system. In particular, he might acquire a surface structure form (such as indirect object precedes direct object) before he recognizes that it is a reflection of deep structure.

In what follows I shall consider the problem of a child's recognition of nonuniversal aspects of deep structure. In particular, how does a child know the positions in deep structure of subject, verb, object, indirect object, negatives, and adverbials? There has been some confusion among a few researchers on several related points. (1) It is *not* the case that deep structure is the same for all languages. Grammatical relations are, by hypothesis, universal, but the order of elements is not. Noam Chomsky (1965) comments: "the system of base rules . . . carry out two quite separate functions: they define the system of grammatical relations *and* they determine the ordering of elements in deep structure [p. 123]." (2) It is *not* the case that simple, active, declarative sentences always reflect deep structure order directly. German, as discussed below, is a counterexample. (3) It is *not* the case that the most frequent forms in surface structure reflect deep structure. (It could be the case, however, that a mother's speech may be altered to highlight deep structure features.) German again is a counterexample.

How then does a child learn what the correct deep structure for his language must be? Fodor (1966) comments: "The problem of characterizing a device that, given as input a sample of the utterances drawn from a natural language, supplies as output a system of rules that correctly assigns base structures to the sentences of the language is considerably beyond the capacities of current psycholinguistic theory [p. 113]."

Traditionally the determination of base word order depends upon analysis of the transformational component. The linguist seeks an order which will make the distance between deep structure and surface structure as short as possible in terms of the number of transformations that are necessary. If the language is highly inflected, the problem is more difficult because the inflections permit greater variation in word order.

A child faces the same task. Two frequent observations become, in that light, astonishing: (a) Children often seem to be able to control the sentence types of an inflected language before they have mastered the inflections. (b) Children seem to comprehend deep-structure order before they have learned any transformations.[2] It looks, therefore, as if some other means must exist for the determination of deep-structure order.

Let us, for illustration, consider some of the sentence types a child faces:

(1)   SVO: *He has a yo-yo.*
(2)   VSO: *Has he a yo-yo?*
(3)   OVS: *A yo-yo has he.*
(4)   OSV: *A yo-yo he has.*

Within this simplified scheme where adverbs, negatives, etc. have been excluded, there are still four possible orders. The child must solve a real conundrum: any of these sentences could provide him with a base order; all of these sentences could be transformed into each other. He cannot know, it seems, the base structure until he knows what transformations have applied, and he cannot know what transformations have applied until he knows the base structure to which they apply. In particular, if we take VSO as base order, then the declarative *He has a truck* would be generated by subject-preposing and no transformation would be necessary for questions. German, as we discuss below, uses a verb-second transformation to produce declaratives. If we take SVO as the base, then we have the familiar subject–verb inversion transformation and no transformation for declaratives is necessary. Use of a simplicity metric would, then, choose between possible base orders. But this calculus requires the evaluation of too many alternatives to be plausible. There must be some direct clues to deep struc-

---

[2]Although young children may clearly lack adult transformations, it is possible that they have prototype transformations at a very early age.

ture elsewhere. We shall discuss one kind of clue that emerges from recent work in linguistic theory, but the problem, nonetheless, persists.

The deep structure of German contrasts with English and provides a better basis for the discussion of these issues. It happens to be the case that in English simple, declarative sentences often do mirror base structure. German, like English, has SVO order in present tense declarative sentences: *Hanns schreibt einen Brief* (Hanns writes a letter), and subject–auxiliary–object–verb order in past and modal sentences. By several accounts, however, it has verb-final order in base structure. This is the order we find in German subordinate clauses. The claim that German is verb-final not only agrees with the intuition of native speakers, but it has been used in the most comprehensive description of German transformational grammar by Manfred Bierwisch (1963) and it has been independently supported in recent work by Bresnan (1971), Emonds (1970), and Maling (1972).

Let us consider Bierwisch's model:

Dependent clauses: *Ich weiss dass Hanns im Hause seinem Bruder den Brief nicht gegeben haben soll.*

$$S \longrightarrow NP + VP$$
$$VP \longrightarrow MV + Aux$$
$$MV \longrightarrow (VE)\ (Pv)\ V$$
$$VE \longrightarrow (adv)\ (Obj_2)\ (Obj_i)$$
$$Pv \longrightarrow (+ \text{ or } - Adv),\ \text{e.g., Neg}$$
$$V \longrightarrow Verb\ (Tense)$$

(a) Four primary and permutable sentence parts are: NP. VE, Verb, Aux.
(b) VE includes: sentential adverb, indirect object IO, direct object DO, in that order.
(c) Pv refers to negation or affirmation.

Notice that the subordinate clause order places Aux (*haben soll*) next to the main verb on one side, and Neg on the other (see Fig. 1). The direct object is closer to the verb than the indirect object. There may be some sense in which it is more natural for Aux, Neg, and DO to have positions close to the verb.

Digression: It is interesting to note that English, which once had verb-final structure, may still be in the process of shifting to a verb-medial structure. J. Maling (1970) has pointed out that the present order in English IO–DO puts the verb further from the direct object. If English were still verb-final, however, the order S–IO–DO–V would put the verb next to the direct object as it is in German. To correct this situation there has been a gradual shift, still incomplete, toward putting the indirect object in a final prepositional phrase. This restores the direct object to a position next to a medial verb. If children's grammars are one vehicle for linguistic change, then we may expect to see a gradual preference for prepositional indirect

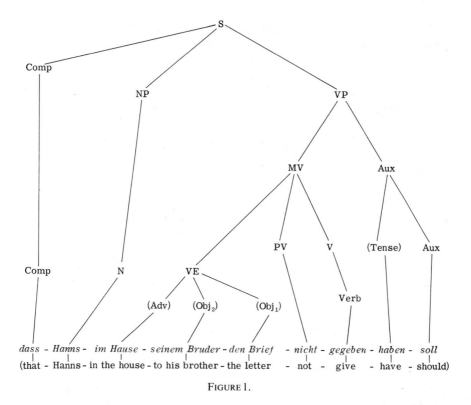

FIGURE 1.

objects (McNeill, Yukawa, & McNeill, 1971). This brief digression illustrates one ramification of a child's decision to consider his language verb-final or verb-medial.

The most important transformation in German is the Verb-second transformation which transfers an element from final position to second position in the creation of declarative sentences. It is the broad applicability of this transformation which makes elegantly simple a description of German that uses a verb-final base structure. If there is a modal, then the modal is put in second position; if there is no modal, then the same transformation puts the main verb in second position:

(5) a. *Hanns das Madel lieben kann* ⟶*Hanns kann das Madel lieben*
     b. *Hanns das Madel liebt* ⟶*Hanns liebt das Madel*

I did a small experiment to illustrate the psychological reality of the verb-second transformation with older children. Menyuk (1969) reports that children often fail to perform subject–verb inversion for questions in English.

They produce, for example: *Why he can go outside?* If the structure of German were like English, then both would use subject–verb inversion, and one would predict that German and English children would make the same mistake. However we found that with two or three exceptions, from 75 children 4 to 6 years old, German children never failed to put the verb after the question word: *Warum spielt er Fussball* (why plays he football) and never *warum er spielt Fussball* or *warum er Fussball spielt.* The explanation is that Germans must create declaratives and questions with the same verb-second transformation. It has, therefore, much broader scope than the subject verb inversion transformation in English; hence it is acquired earlier. Use of the verb-second transformation presupposes that the verb does not originate in second position. The experiment provides therefore indirect support for the claim that German is verb-final.

Let us return to the larger question: How and when does a German child learn that his language has verb-final structure and not some other structure? T. Z. Park (1971) has recently gathered evidence from three German children at the two- and three-word stage. He found that over 80% of the utterances of the three children at the two-word stage place the object before the verb. English children, by contrast, consistently place the verb before the object. Following are some examples.

Two-word
Bleistift holen
(pencil get);
Kaffee trinken
(coffee drink)
Auto fahre
(car drive)

Turm gehen
(tower go)
dies haben
(this have)
Noppa haben
(Noppa have)

Three-word
Puppi Strumpfe anziehen
(doll socks put on);
Ulrike wieder suchen
(Ulrike again look for)
Ulrike Roller fahre
(Ulrike skates rides)
Ich Schiff mache
(I ship make)
Nikolaus immer Brot machte
(Nicholas always bread made)
Ich Pullover zeige
(I pullover show)

das auch nicht malt
(that also not paint)
Ich nicht spiele
(I not play)
ande Auto suchen
(another car look for)
Mama Schüchen anziehen
(Mother shoes put on)
Papi Wäsche runter
(Papi laundry down)
Keller Wäsche runter
(Cellar laundry down).

Statistics:

	Ulrike		Angela		Georg	
	N–V	V–N	N–V	V–N	N–V	V–N
agent–action	16	1	16	1	39	4
action–object	16	13	35	3	42	14
SVO (agent–action–object)	3		6		13	
SOV (agent–object–action)	4		4		15	

Notice that the verb in the two-word sentences is in the infinitive form. This suggests that they might be the latter portion of sentences that have a modal in second position, for instance, *Er kann Wasser trinken* (he can drink water).[3] Since modal sentences are frequent in adult speech, a child might learn them first simply because of their frequency. If they are a kind of repetition of form, then the child may not realize that object–main-verb order reflects deep structure. They would be instances of child language that had no connection to linguistic theory (which, in a crude sense, he is said to have somewhere in his head). On the other hand, the child might possess an algorithm which says that the object–verb positions—but not the modal position—reflect deep structure. The evidence at the two-word stage seems insufficient for any conclusion.

When we look to the three-word utterances, however, we find sentences for which there is absolutely no adult model, but which are direct reflections of German deep structure. Park (1971) comments:

> Indeed, these ungrammatical sequences turn out to be grammatical if they occur in subordinate clauses, but construction of complex sentences lies beyond the capacity of children. Moreover, there were exceptionally few complex sentences spoken by the mothers to their children. Ulrike's mother constructed no complex sentences. Imitation or linguistic environment fails to provide any reliable explanation of the occurrence of the ungrammatical sequences [p. 13].

The sentence *Ich Pullover zeige* does not have an infinitival verb; as a declarative sentence, which it is, it would be decidedly ungrammatical for an adult. The child seems to have insight into deep structure, but there is no apparent clue. Some higher order analysis must be available to him.

The matter is complicated however; the children use an almost equal number of sentences at this stage that have the SVO structure that adults use in declarative sentences. One might think that this is a free word-order

---

[3] I am indebted to Hermine Sinclair-de Zwart for this observation.

phenomenon (although German has free word order only with nouns). However Park points out that a Korean subject, whose language has freer word order than German, used a verb-final sentence on only one occasion. Otherwise the Korean child used the SVO deep structure of Korean. It seems unlikely that these sentences are a sudden exhibition of free word order. Instead it seems that their grammar is in a state of flux between structures, rather than without structures (Menyuk, 1970). It is difficult to develop a comprehensive hypothesis to account for their inconsistency. Let us, for now, pursue a method whereby, possibly, children could discern base structure order before they acquire a full system of transformations.

J. Emonds (1970) has developed an hypothesis about language structure which, though still controversial, is the kind of hypothesis that has the power to explain how a child could acquire deep structure quickly. It is at least valuable as a model, if not a solution. The principle applies to complex sentences and might be, consequently, the kind of principle that a child connects with the structures he uses during a latter phase of acquisition.

Emonds claims that all cyclical transformations—those that apply to embedded sentences (subordinate clauses)—preserve structure, although lexical items are moved from one position to another. For instance, the passive moves an object into subject position, but it does not move the subject position. On the other hand, a transformation like subject-verb inversion *does* move the positions themselves: subject and auxiliary change places. This means that embedded sentences, but not declaratives, will reflect deep structure order directly. Notice that English as well as German allows indirect questions in subordinate clauses, but they do not permit subject-verb inversion:

(6)   a. *He knows why the man can sing.*
                       b. **He knows why can the man sing.*

The passive transformation, though it is intrinsically more complex than subject–verb inversion, does not shift positions and is therefore permitted in subordinate clauses.[4] Topicalization, adverb-preposing, tag questions, etc. are all prohibited.

In other words, a universal constraint limits transformations that apply to embedded sentences to those that do not shift positions. This rule is not without exceptions; in particular, direct quotations and embedded sentences that are not marked by a complementizer—usually *that*—may not adhere to this principle.

---

[4] I am grateful to Dan Slobin for pointing out that sentences like *I wonder did he come?* are acceptable in Black English. Such examples may require revision or abandonment of the theory. However, in this instance, one might examine the intonation pattern to discover whether the subordinate clause might not be uttered as direct discourse, which is not true subordination.

If it is a universal constraint, then it might form part of a child's perceptual strategy. A child—or any person—might find that his system is rapidly overloaded by structure-altering transformations upon embedded sentences, just as the human system is overloaded by self-embedded sentences such as *the rat the cat my mother bought bit died.* In some sense they are related phenomena; both show that embedded sentences place a special tax upon perception. Self-embedded sentences are limited to one embedding; normal embedded sentences are limited to transformations which preserve structure.

If Emond's principle is upheld as linguistic theory grows, then it is difficult to imagine that it would not form part of an acquisition strategy in some phase. It might not be the mechanism that reveals the locus of subject, verb, and object, but rather the deep structure locus of adverb, negative, and indirect object. The latter constituents are particularly subject to movement in declarative sentences through stylistic transformation, etc.

How could a child identify the subordinate clause? The key may be the presence of the complementizer *that.* In Bever's (1970) recent work on perceptual strategies, the recognition of subordinate clauses figures prominently. The role of *that* as a perceptual cue is also made very clear. Edmonds shows that where the complementizer morpheme Comp is not present, the universal constraint is liable to permit exceptions. Bresnan (1970) and N. Chomsky (1971) have adopted the notion that the complementizer morpheme must be present in deep structure. Edmonds theory works with:

(7)   Comp-Subj-Aux-Verb-IO-DO

The presence of Comp in deep structure allows embedded sentences such as *whom I saw* to be structure-preserving. The object in this case has been moved into the Comp position with the marking *wh-.* Emonds offers a more precise definition of "root" clauses which permit structure-altering transformations.

Could a child be sensitive to subordinate clauses when he himself is capable of only three-word utterances? It is true that the word *that* is one of the first pivots he learns.[5] Nevertheless such a claim would require that a child's comprehension be far in advance of his production. Available evidence, which is small, suggests that parents say few complex sentences to their children. They would have to encounter subordinate clauses through listening to conversations between adults. There is some evidence that children do learn from listening to adults. Children who are spoken to in one

---

[5] We intend to perform the following experiment, suggested by Christine Tanz, to see if and when children perceive the difference between quotation and subordination. Give a child two instructions: "Ask him what you like," and "Ask him 'what do you like?'" If the child perceives the difference in reference for the word *you,* then he must perceive subordination. See Tanz (in prep.) for a study of the acquisition of personal pronouns and shifters.

language, but hear another language as well, often learn parts of the other language (especially the phonology).

On the whole, these reflections about linguistic environment seem more suited to older, less egocentric children. But if we reject the notion that the very young child can recognize the subordinate clause, we are still left with a problem: how does a child learn the deep-structure position of the main verb at the three-word stage?

Let us assume that the child has some unknown means of knowing that German is verb-final.[6] Why, then, does he use SVO structures in nearly half of his utterances? This is just the structure that is produced by the verb-second transformation. It seems plausible to me that a child might acquire deep structure and a first major transformation concurrently. His use of a transformation at an early stage may reflect the fact that the verb-second transformation plays a more central role in German than any transformation does in English. He might also learn each structure separately and discover their transformational relation at a later point. It seems difficult to choose between such alternatives. Neither disturbs the claim that these children have some insight into deep structure.

In sum, the subordinate-clause strategy is a powerful mechanism for the discovery of deep structure. If it is not invoked by the very young child, it might be used by older children to ascertain the permissible positions in deep structure of the adverbial and negative elements as well as the indirect object. That is, a child's awareness that a sentence was embedded, and therefore had to be processed with cyclical transformation, would entail an awareness that positions of (almost) all elements were fixed, and therefore reflected deep structure. Further research with this hypothesis in mind could shed more light on the matter.[7]

One further comment. There has been a good deal of attention given recently to correspondences between semantic concepts and grammatical relations in deep structure. It has provided a rich new dimension of grammatical study, but it has also overshadowed the purely syntactic aspects of deep structure. It is difficult to see how any kind of semantic knowledge could reveal base order. A purely syntactic strategy, of the kind outlined in the preceding, seems unavoidable. A separate, but possibly concurrent, semantic strategy could then map semantic structure onto syntactic structure.

[6]Other kinds of clues are imaginable. For instance, the position of the verbal negative *nicht* in final position in declarative sentences (as in *Er nimmt das Auto nicht*), or the position of adverbs, might suggest verb-final structure to the child. It is also possible that the stress upon sentence-final verb particles might contribute to a child's perception of deep structure. (see Bierwisch, 1968; Bresnan, 1971).

[7]There is some evidence that children are aware of subtle movement restrictions that depend upon the choice of the complementizer *that* or *to*. Cf. Roeper (1972).

STRUCTURAL RELATIONSHIPS IN CHILDREN'S UTTERANCES: SYNTACTIC OR SEMANTIC?[1]

MELISSA BOWERMAN[2]
University of Kansas

Until recently, the investigation of children's knowledge of linguistic structure was based primarily upon analyses of the superficial form and arrangement of the words in their spontaneous utterances. In the last few years, however, there has been an increasing realization that we can discover much more about children's early linguistic competence if we take apparent meanings into account as well. It has been convincingly argued, especially by Bloom (1970), that children's utterances express a variety of structural relationships. Some of these relationships are not distinguishable purely on the basis of formal differences, however. As in the case of adult language, this gap between meaning and form can best be accounted for by postulating a distinction between deep and surface structure. The information which is necessary for assigning meanings to utterances is provided by the deep structure representations specified for them.

What is the nature of the deep structures of children's utterances? How should we characterize the structural relationships which children apparently intend? Attempting to answer these questions involves making judgments about what kinds of concepts and categories are functional in

[1]Portions of this paper appear in expanded form in Chapter 6 of the author's work *Early syntactic development: A cross-linguistic study with special reference to Finnish*, Cambridge University Press, 1973. They are used here by permission of the publisher.

[2]This research was supported in part by PHS Training Grant NS05362-10 from the National Institute of Neurological Diseases and Stroke to the Bureau of Child Research, University of Kansas.

children's early linguistic competence, and perhaps also about what linguistic knowledge is innate as opposed to what must be learned.

The following discussion is divided into three parts. First some proposals which have been made concerning the structural relations of children's utterances are outlined. This is followed by an evaluation of certain aspects of these proposals, based primarily on data I have collected from two Finnish children, Seppo and Rina, and an American child, Kendall (Bowerman, 1973). Finally, I offer some suggestions and supporting evidence for a plausible interpretation of the kinds of concepts underlying children's earliest constructions.

SOME EXISTING PROPOSALS ABOUT THE
UNDERLYING NATURE OF CHILDREN'S UTTERANCES

One important issue on which researchers differ is whether the underlying structural relationships of children's utterances should be given a syntactic or a semantic characterization. McNeill (1966a, b, 1970a, b, 1971) has used transformational generative grammar as outlined by N. Chomsky (1965) to describe child speech. This entails postulating deep structures which are basically syntactic. The syntactic description of a sentence serves as input to the semantic interpretation of the sentence. The syntactic deep structures of a transformational grammar provide information about both the hierarchical organization of sentence constituents, or constituent structure, and the grammatical relations which hold between these constituents. Many linguists (e.g., N. Chomsky, 1965, pp. 71–72; Katz & Postal, 1964, p. 159) believe that certain grammatical relations are fundamental to the structure of sentences in all languages. These include the functions *subject of the sentence, predicate of the sentence, verb of the verb phrase*, and *direct object of the verb phrase*. McNeill proposes that the existence of language universals results from the inherent characteristics of the child's capacity to acquire language. He suggests, therefore, that knowledge of the basic grammatical relations is innate, and guides the child's understanding and production of utterances from the beginning of language development.

In a contrasting view of children's initial linguistic knowledge, Schlesinger (1971) has proposed that the components of the structural relationships expressed by children's utterances are semantic concepts like *agent, action, object*, and *location* rather than syntactic notions like *subject* and *predicate*. He notes that these concepts do not reflect specifically linguistic knowledge, but, rather, are determined by the more general innate cognitive capacity of the child. Children acquire language by learning realization rules which map underlying semantic intentions directly onto surface structures. Schlesinger's model of language acquisition, while explicitly a production model rather than a grammar, shares with the generative semantics accounts of grammar proposed by linguists such as Fillmore (1968) and McCawley (1968) the idea that semantic concepts are the primitive structural components of sentences. These are thought to be encoded by syntactic devices, rather than being themselves derived from the interpretation of more basic syntactic information.

In writing grammars for three American children early in their syntactic development, Bloom (1970) specified deep structures with the formal configurational properties which define the basic grammatical relations in a transformational grammar. Unlike McNeill, Bloom (1970, pp. 227–228) did not feel that knowledge of these relations is innate, but only that her subjects had learned some or all of the relations by the developmental points at which she placed her grammars. Elsewhere, Bloom (in press) has suggested that there is perhaps no important distinction between syntactic functions like subject of the predicate and object of the verb and semantic concepts like agent of the action and object of the action, since both are "necessarily linguistic categories, determined by formal criteria of arrangement and relationship." She adds that the important distinction to be made is not among "domains of linguistic categories," but "between *linguistic* categories —categories that are dependent on formal specification of relationship—. . . and *cognitive* categories which may be experientially defined in quite another way."

The debate about the underlying structures of children's early utterances may be more than terminological, however. There may in fact be an important difference between interpreting a child's construction such as *man drive car* as *subject-verb-direct object* and as *agent-action-object acted upon*. Determining whether or not children's early linguistic competence includes a knowledge of syntactic relationships and the constituent structure they entail has some important consequences for a theory of language acquisition.

Before examining these consequences, let us consider briefly the difference between syntactic and semantic concepts. Syntactic concepts are more abstract than semantic ones. A verb may take several noun arguments, each performing a different semantic function such as *agent, object acted upon, location, instrument,* and so on. Deep structure syntactic functions are not always associated with particular semantic roles. Fillmore (1968), for example, has shown that the deep structure subjects of English sentences play such diverse semantic roles as agent (as in **John** *opened the door*), object involved (**the door** *opened*), instrument (**the key** *opened the door*), person affected (**John** *wants milk*), and location (**Chicago** *is windy*). Direct objects likewise do not have a constant semantic function. The subject and direct object for any particular verb, however, identify noun phrases in particular semantic roles. For example, the subject of the verb *eat* identifies the agent, while that of *want* identifies the person affected. Being able to implicitly identify the deep structure subject and direct object of a given sentence involves knowing which semantic roles function in these syntactic capacities for the particular verb involved. (See Brown, in press, for a further discussion of the differences between semantic and syntactic relationships.) What it means to understand an abstract syntactic function like *subject* is taken up in a later section.

Now let us return to the question of whether there is any essential difference between describing children's utterances in terms of syntactic relationships and in terms of semantic concepts. If we assume, with N. Chomsky, McNeill, Bloom, and many others, that adult competence includes knowledge of the basic grammatical relations, we must determine where this knowledge comes from. If we should find that knowledge of the basic grammatical relations is reflected in children's earliest utterances, it would at least be plausible to argue that this knowledge is not learned at all but rather constitutes part of children's basic capacity to acquire language. But if, in contrast, it turns out that these utterances are produced without a specific understanding of syntactic relationships but only with rules based upon semantic notions, we must then account for how the more abstract knowledge embodied in the basic grammatical relations is eventually attained. It is possible that achieving an understanding of the abstract, specifically linguistic relationships which hold between parts of sentences is an important part of the language acquisition process. If syntactic and semantic terms are not carefully distinguished and structural specifications like *subject-predicate* and *agent-action* are regarded as equivalent, we have no motivation to look for such a learning process.

EVALUATING PROPOSALS ABOUT CHILDREN'S DEEP STRUCTURES

How can we determine which interpretation of children's deep structures— the syntactic or the semantic—provides a closer approximation to the form of children's linguistic knowledge? Only by examining the data closely without preconceptions. A great advance in the study of child language was made in the early 1960s when several researchers (Braine, 1963; Brown & Fraser, 1963; Miller & Ervin, 1964) realized that children's word classes might not be the same as those of the adult language, and began to do distributional analyses of the words in children's constructions to see what classes in fact were functional. The same unbiased approach is needed now that we are looking at children's deep structures. We need to guard against assuming that children's deep structures have a certain form simply because an adequate description of the adult language must specify such a form for equivalent adult utterances. We may find that those structural phenomena of adult speech which motivate the postulation of syntactic concepts like subject and predicate are absent in child speech. In my view, the evidence available so far does not appear to be strong enough to justify crediting children in the initial stages of syntactic development with knowledge either of the basic grammatical relations or of the constituent structure upon which these depend.

Constituent Structure

Let us first examine constituent structure. In representing children's early utterances, McNeill, Bloom, and Schlesinger all provide an account of constituent structure in which three-term strings like *man drive car* and *mommy go store* are hierarchically organized along the traditional lines. The initial noun (N) constitutes one constituent, while the verb (V) plus the direct object or locative element constitute another. McNeill and Bloom, but not Schlesinger, consider the former the subject and the latter the predicate. According to McNeill (1971), this hierarchical organization results automatically from the child's application to sentences of his knowledge of the basic grammatical relations.

What is the justification for this analysis of the constituent structure of children's early three-term constructions? N. Chomsky (1965) notes that there are various ways to justify assigning constituent structure. One must show, for example, that "there are perceptual grounds for the analysis," or that the postulated intermediate phrases "must receive a semantic interpretation," or "are required for some grammatical rule," or "define a phonetic contour [p. 197, fn. 7]."

The few attempts to use strictly linguistic criteria to determine the constituent structure of children's early utterances have had inconclusive results. For example, Brown (unpublished materials) asked whether Adam, Eve, and Sarah, his three English-speaking subjects, regularly used the predicate verb phrase as an answer to *what are you doing?* or *what is it doing?* questions, as adult speakers do. He found that the children often did not respond to these questions at all and almost never answered them appropriately. The same is true of Kendall and of my two Finnish subjects. Brown also tried to determine whether in Adam's speech the privileges of occurrence of V + N were the same as those of V alone, which might have suggested that V + N should be considered as a single constituent. He found that the privileges of occurrence were the same, since both V and V + N could occur after initial nouns or pronouns. This finding does not constitute sound evidence for a verb phrase (VP) however, since N + V, or the subject plus the verb, also had the same privileges of occurrence as V alone: both could precede nouns or pro-locatives. Thus, on the basis of this test, either V + N *or* N + V could be considered a constituent substitutable for V alone. This was true not only in Adam's speech but also in that of my three subjects.

Other linguistic grounds which might be used to justify postulating a VP constituent in children's early utterances are also lacking. For example, children do not initially use phrases like "do (so)" which make reference to a preceding VP. In samples of speech from the earliest stages of word combining, one does not find sentences like *Daddy like cake. Mommy does too*, or *Johnny went home (and) so did Jimmy*.

In sum, no one has yet to my knowledge succeeded in demonstrating on purely linguistic grounds that the verb "belongs with" the direct object or the locative in child speech rather than, for example, with the subject—in other words, that verb plus direct object or locative is a constituent in a way in which subject plus verb is not. Arguments for a verb phrase constituent in children's utterances have been based on a weaker sort of evidence, evidence which bears only on the question of whether the verb plus the direct object or the locative element has a psychological unity for the child which the subject plus the verb lacks.

One such argument draws on the observation that verb–object strings are more frequent in early speech than subject–verb strings. This was true of Brown's subjects Adam, Eve, and Sarah and of Bloom's three subjects. McNeill (1970b) notes that the predominance of predicates without subjects over predicates with subjects in Adam's speech "would result if the sentences without subjects had existed in Adam's repertoire for some time [p. 1090]." McNeill (1966b, pp. 44–45) also suggests that children may initially practice subject noun phrases in isolation and only later realize that subjects and predicates can be brought together into one sentence.

According to this line of reasoning, which is based on the relative frequency of verb–object, subject–verb, and subject–verb–object strings in a speech sample, if some children from an early stage of development produced more subject–verb than verb–object strings, we might argue that for them, subject–verb had a psychological unity which verb–object lacked. Similarly, if even full subject–verb–object strings were more frequent than verb–object strings, perhaps subject–verb should be considered an initial unit to which object is added only later, just as McNeill suggests that verb–object is a unit to which subject is added later. These were, in fact, the distributional facts of the speech of my two Finnish subjects and my American subject. All of these children produced far more subject–verb than verb–object strings, and they produced either about equal numbers of verb–object and subject–verb–object strings, or more of the latter. Table 1 presents the relevant figures from samples of their spontaneous speech.

Table 1 *Frequency of Production as a Clue to Constituent Structure: Number of Utterance Types of Subject–Verb, Verb–Object, and Subject–Verb–Object Strings in Samples of Spontaneous Speech*[a]

	Kendall (English) MLU[b] 1.10	Kendall (English) MLU 1.48	Seppo (Finnish) MLU 1.42	Seppo (Finnish) MLU 1.81	Rina (Finnish) MLU 1.83
Subject–verb	19	31	25	64	21
Verb–object	5	12	4	9	4
Subject–verb–object	—	7	7	8	19

[a]All samples contained a total of 713 utterance tokens (both constructions and single words) from consecutive tapes, except for the first from Kendall, which consisted of 136 construction tokens (102 types) noted by hand over a period of almost two full days.

[b]MLU: mean length of utterance (counted in morphemes), a measure of linguistic maturity.

If we followed to its logical end the argument that constituent structure is revealed in the relative frequency with which these various strings are produced, we would have to conclude that for these children the hierarchical organization of sentence elements was not

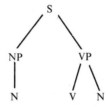

but rather

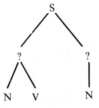

—in other words, that the subject plus the verb constituted one constituent and the direct object another. Such an organization would be a false step toward the adult understanding of constituent structure which we assume they will ultimately attain.

Another sort of argument that predicates have psychological unity is presented by Braine (1971b). Like McNeill, Braine has suggested that the first English sentences consist of a predicate with an optional subject. He finds evidence for this in children's "replacement sequences," a term he uses to describe sequences of utterances in which a short utterance is followed or preceded by a longer string which incorporates it and suggests what grammatical relations are intended by it. Braine found that these sequences tend to consist of an utterance without a subject followed by the same utterance with a subject. For example:

    chair . . . pussy cat chair
    want that . . . Andrew want that
    off . . . radio off
    fall . . . stick fall
    go nursery . . . Lucy go nursery
    build house . . . Cathy build house

Replacement sequences also occurred, although relatively infrequently, in the speech of the two Finnish children and of my American subject Kendall. Some of these did involve producing a predicate and then adding a subject. But many involved instead the operation of producing a subject first and then adding the predicate, or, even more interestingly, of producing the subject and the verb and then adding a direct object or a locative. The following are some examples:

    Seppo (translated):
        horsie . . . horsie . . . horsie sleeps
        chick . . . chick sings
        mother . . . mother opens
        daddy . . . daddy wash . . .
            daddy . . . daddy already wash train
        this belongs . . . this belongs there
        Immi draws . . . Immi draws there
        man captain . . . comes . . . (to) take-care-of . . . man
            captain comes . . . (to) take-care-of . . . bird . . . man captain
            takes-care-of-bird.

    Kendall:
        'lissa . . . 'lissa . . . 'lissa . . . 'lissa write
        Kendall . . . Kendall gone
        Kristin . . . Kristin sit chair
        Kendall innere . . . Kendall innere bed
        Kendall pick up (O + V) . . . Daddy pick up (S + V) . . . Kendall (O) . . .
            Mommy pick up Kendall (S + V + O)

To summarize, arguments about constituent structure which are based upon the relative frequency of production of different types of strings or upon the characteristics of replacement sequences are not conclusive.

Using these criteria on data from certain children leads to an analysis of constituent structure which specifies subject plus verb as one constituent and direct object or locative as another. It appears that frequency of production and the characteristics of replacement sequences may not be reliable clues to hierarchical organization. In short, we still do not know whether children produce their early subject–verb–object and subject–verb–locative constructions with the particular understanding of constituent structure which has been ascribed to them, or even with any concept of hierarchical organization at all.

The Grammatical Relation "Subject of"

What evidence is there that an understanding of the concept *subject of* is part of children's early competence? In transformational theory, the deep structure subject of a sentence is defined as the noun phrase immediately dominated by *S*. We have just seen that the analysis of constituent structure upon which this definition depends may not be applicable to children's utterances. If this is the case, then justification for crediting children with the concept *subject of* must come from elsewhere.

Why do we need the concept of deep structure subject for an adequate analysis of adult language? This is a difficult question. In my understanding, the answer might go something like this: In linguistic theory, the relationships which hold between underlying meanings and actual sentences are indicated by transformations. According to N. Chomsky's outline of grammar, the operations involved in transformations cannot be specified simply by reference to the semantic functions of words in sentences. For example, a rule for deriving passive sentences which specified that the word functioning as agent of the verb should become the object of the preposition *by* would be inadequate. Passives can also be created out of sentences in which there is no agent, like *your mother wants you* or *John sees Mary*. The constituent which becomes the object of *by* in passive sentences can only be defined in an abstract way, as a noun phrase with a certain syntactic function which we call *subject*. The semantic function of this noun phrase is different for different subclasses of verbs. The need for the concept *deep structure subject* arises because there are transformations—including the one which derives passive sentences—which treat certain noun phrases as though they were identical for the purposes of a particular operation, even though they do not necessarily have identical semantic functions in their respective sentences. Such transformations can cause deep structure subjects to appear in a number of different positions and different syntactic roles in surface structure. But if a person's competence is such that he knows what the deep structure subject of a sentence is regardless of its position and syntactic function in surface structure, and if he knows what semantic role is associated with the grammatical function of subject for the particular verb involved, he will understand the sentence.

Fillmore (1968, p. 58) notes that some languages have been described as not having passives and others as able to express transitive sentences only passively. He argues that since these languages offer no choice of surface structure subject, the concept of subject is not applicable to them. To pursue this argument further, if a particular language lacked syntactic operations which treat a particular noun argument for each verb in the same way across a number of different verbs, and which could cause deep and surface structure subjects to differ, why would there be any need for the syntactic abstraction of *subject*?

The language of children appears initially to lack such operations. It has often been noted that children's early utterances can be generated almost entirely by the base component of a transformational grammar (Bowerman, 1973; Brown, Cazden, Bellugi, 1968, p. 40; McNeill, 1966b, p. 51). Virtually all constructions follow the simple active declarative pattern, although certain elements obligatory in adult speech are absent. Thus, no transformations need to be specified which require reference to a sentence constituent with the abstract syntactic function which defines subjects in adult speech. Deep structure and surface structure subjects are therefore always identical.

On what grounds can the abstraction of *subject* be made in the case of a language which lacks transformations requiring it? In simple active declarative sentences of adult English and Finnish, the particular noun argument of a verb which functions as deep structure subject (and therefore also as surface structure subject) governs person and number concord in the verb, is in the nominative case (pronouns only in English, nouns and pronouns both in Finnish), and has a characteristic position. In early child speech, subjects cannot be identified on the basis of either verbal concord or case, since verbs initially have an invariant form, personal pronouns are rare or absent, and (relevant only for the Finnish children) nouns in *all* syntactic roles are in the nominative, not just subjects.

This leaves only position as a basis for the abstraction of *subject*. The particular noun argument of the verb which functions as deep and surface structure subject in simple active declarative sentences typically occurs in preverbal position in both English and Finnish (other orders are possible as well in Finnish). This ordering is generally observed in children's early constructions. In studies of child speech, the noun which occurs in preverbal position is identified as the subject—provided that it would be considered the subject in adult speech too. But when the child produces constructions like *ball hit* and *apple eat*, we simply conclude that he has reversed the normal verb–object order. We do not consider the possibility that he might have mistakenly identified the wrong noun argument of a particular verb as subject, perhaps by analogy with sentences like *the toy broke*, *the door opened*, *the page ripped*, or *the ball dropped*. All of these sentences involve verbs which can take a noun which functions semantically as *object acted upon* as either subject or direct object, depending upon whether or not an agent is also expressed. The verbs *hit*, *eat*, and many others do not have this flexibility. It is conceivable that a child might at first not recognize this distinction between verb classes, and so would assume that all objects acted upon can be subjects in agentless sentences. In summary, then, we do not even make consistent use of position to help us identify subjects in children's utterances, even though it is the only criterion we have available. Instead, we simply rely on our knowledge of what the subject would be in equivalent adult utterances.

Occupation of identical position is in any event not a sufficient reason to assume identical syntactic function. For example, in the sentences *John eats cake* and *John goes home*, the nouns *cake* and *home* occur in the same position, but they do not perform the same syntactic function. Similarly, why should the first words in typical child utterances such as *John eat cake* and *John want cake* be considered to perform the same syntactic function when their semantic functions are different?

To summarize, the structural phenomena which require the concept of subject in adult speech are evidently missing in early child speech. To credit children with an understanding of the concept is an act of faith based only on our knowledge of the characteristics of adult language.

A SEMANTIC INTERPRETATION OF
CHILDREN'S DEEP STRUCTURES

The purpose of the foregoing discussion has not been to demonstrate that children initially lack knowledge of the basic grammatical relations and of the constituent structure which they entail, but only to show that there is as yet no evidence in their spontaneous constructions that they have it. It is possible that children use this knowledge in their comprehension of adult sentences before their own productions begin to reflect it, but this has not been demonstrated.

Finding compelling support for either a syntactic or a semantic interpretation of the structural relations expressed in children's early utterances will probably require experimental study. Of particular interest will be information about the levels of abstraction at which children make generalizations to form novel constructions. However, nonsystematic evidence which suggests one interpretation or the other for particular children may be obtainable from samples of spontaneous speech. For example, if a child initially began to observe inflections or verbal concord only for agentive subjects, this would suggest that *agent* rather than *subject* was a functional concept for him. One bit of evidence of this sort comes from a Russian child, Zhenya (Gvozdev, 1961). Initially, Zhenya did not formally mark direct objects, but rather used the nominative form of the noun in all syntactic functions. When he began to acquire the accusative case, he used it only to mark those direct objects which designated the objects of action, particularly those occurring with verbs referring to the transfer or relocation of objects, such as *give, carry, put,* and *throw.* At this time, Zhenya rarely marked the direct objects of verbs like *read, draw,* and *make,* in which the relations between action and object are more complex. This pattern of marking indicates that at first Zhenya did not regard all direct objects as functionally equivalent, but only that subset of them which referred to objects acted upon in certain rather direct ways.[3]

Cross-linguistic comparisons of children's speech may also yield information about the concepts which are functional early in linguistic development. Striking similarities in the constructions of children learning unrelated languages provide some support for a semantic rather than a syntactic interpretation of the deep structures of early word combinations. The most common productive construction patterns across languages involve a fairly small set of relationships, which have been described in the literature in semantic terms such as *agent–action, action–object acted upon, object located–location, possessor–possessed,* and *demonstrator–demonstrated* (see Bowerman, 1973; Brown, in press; Slobin, 1970, for further discussion).

While these relationships can be given syntactic interpretations as well as semantic ones, the semantic descriptions often provide a more exact characterization than their syntactic counterparts. For example, the words in children's earliest utterances which appear to function syntactically as subjects or direct objects initially play a more restricted number of semantic roles than they do slightly later in development and in adulthood. Table 2 illustrates this observation. It lists the frequencies with which two- and three-term constructions expressing subject–verb–object relations in various semantic roles were produced in samples from my two Finnish subjects and one American subject, and from two Samoan children (Kernan, 1969). The samples are arranged by increasing MLU (mean length of utterance counted in morphemes, a measure of linguistic maturity). At the lower MLUs, there is a very strong tendency for sentence subjects to have an agentive relationship to the verb. Expressed in a different way, the verbs children initially use in subject–verb combinations are those which take agentive subjects—for

---

[3] I am grateful to Dan I. Slobin for bringing this example to my attention.

Table 2 *A Cross-Linguistic Comparison of the Syntactic and Semantic Relationships Expressed in Early Subject–Verb–Object Constructions*[a]

Syntactic relations	Semantic relations	Kendall (English) MLU 1.10	Seppo (Finnish) KLU 1.42	Kendall (English) MLU 1.48	Sipili (Samoan) MLU 1.52	Tofi (Samoan) MLU 1.60	Seppo (Finnish) MLU 1.81	Rina (Finnish) MLU 1.83
Subject–verb	agent–action	19	25	28	3	10	60	19
	person affected[b]–state	—	—	1	—	—	2	1
	object involved[c]–action	—	—	2	—	6	2	1
Verb–object	action–object acted upon	2	3	6	6	16	8	3
	action–object created[d]	—	1	1	—	—	1	1
	state–object[e]	1	—	1	—	—	—	—
	action–object	2	—	4	—	1	—	—
Subject–object	agent–object acted upon	1	3	—	—	—	2	3
	agent–object created	1	—	2	—	—	1	—
	agent–object	3	—	—	—	—	—	—
	noun–(has)–noun	2	—	2	—	—	—	—
Subject–verb–object	agent–action–object acted upon	—	7	7	—	1	8	9
	agent–action–object created	—	—	—	—	—	—	4
	agent–action–object	—	—	—	—	—	—	1
	person affected–action–object	—	—	—	—	—	—	4
	person affected–state–object	—	—	—	—	1	—	1

[a] Utterance types only (not tokens). All word orders of a given construction pattern are counted.

[b] Fillmore's Dative case, with verbs like *want*, *see*, *receive*, *be afraid*.

[c] Fillmore's Objective case, with verbs like *fall*, *break* (intransitive).

[d] Fillmore's Factitive case, with verbs like *make*, *draw*.

[e] *Object* has been used as a neutral term to designate the direct objects of verbs like *want*, *look at*, *see*, *leave*, *find*, *read*, and *receive*, which are difficult to characterize semantically.

example, *sleep, drive, eat, sit, sing, ride, go*, and *open*. Children's lexicons at first include only a handful of verbs which take persons affected or objects involved as subjects (e.g., *want, see, fall*), and these are often used without explicit subjects. In particular, states like *want* are rarely predicated of persons other than the child himself, so these verbs usually appear without subjects or at best are paired only with the child's name.

This suggests that children are initially not seeking the means of expressing the grammatical relation between subject and predicate but rather, more concretely, of expressing the interaction between an agent and the action he initiates. As MLU increases, more verbs which take nonagentive subjects come into use, and are increasingly frequently paired with noun or pronoun subjects referring to inanimate objects or to beings other than the child himself. Examples of such sentences are Seppo's *tower falls-over* and *mouse is–afraid*, Rina's *Rina receives cake*, and Tofi's *baby wants clothes*. It is difficult to decide whether the number of different semantic notions the child is working with has simply increased at this point or whether the more abstract and inclusive concept of *subject* has now become functional.

The case for a semantic interpretation of direct objects is less strong. In adult English and Finnish—I don't know about Samoan—direct objects can designate an object receiving the force of an action (*John hit* **the ball**), a person affected (*John murdered* **George**), or an object created (*John built* **a table**; *Rina draws* **a horse**). Direct objects play other semantic roles as well which are more difficult to characterize. I have grouped the direct objects of verbs like *want, look at, see, leave*, and *receive* together simply as *object* for lack of a better way to describe them. There is a tendency throughout the samples for direct objects to designate objects physically acted upon, but this is not so strong as the initial tendency for subjects to designate agents, nor is there the same sort of developmental trend towards diversification as there is for subjects.

These comparative data suggest that *subject* and possibly *direct object* are more powerful and abstract than the concepts which children use early in their linguistic development. The linguistic knowledge which underlies the earliest two- and three-word constructions may be no more complex than simple rules to order words which are understood as performing various semantic functions. In some constructions, a semantic relationship may be expressed simply by words occurring together without a characteristic ordering.

According to this view of language acquisition, children's initial efforts at word combination result from their discovery of ways to express various semantic relationships in the language they are learning. These semantic relationships are similar across languages because, as Schlesinger has proposed, they originate in the way human cognitive abilities process nonlinguistic experiences common to children everywhere. Children may be able to grasp the concept *initiator of an action* before the concept *person affected by a state or stimulus* becomes available to them. This would account for their early preference for verbs which name actions and require agents in the role of subject.

Of course, the semantic categories I have mentioned are not necessarily the particular ones children use. They are abstractions, although not at such a high level as syntactic concepts like *subject*, and perhaps children do not even make these abstractions. Possibly, for example, an individual rule is made for each verb specifying that the name for the one who initiates the particular action of the verb, such as eating or driving, precedes the name for the action. An abstraction could also be made at some intermediate level between the initiators of particular actions and the concept of agent.

When the deep structure relations expressed in children's early constructions are given a semantic interpretation, the question arises of how N. Chomsky's level of syntactic deep structure is acquired, if, in fact, it is acquired at all. Several investigators have argued that learning theories cannot account for the acquisition of information represented only in deep structure, since this is abstract and never directly exhibited in the speech to which the child is exposed (e.g., Bever, Fodor, & Weksel, 1965; McNeill, 1971). In particular, McNeill (1971) has argued that because the basic grammatical relations "can be consistently defined only in the deep structure of sentences, they are beyond the reach of any linguistic experiences a child may have [p. 23]."

Some researchers who advocate a semantic interpretation of children's early utterances, such as Schlesinger (1971) and Kernan (1970), resolve the problem of how children can learn something which is never directly represented in speech by arguing that they do not have to—that an abstract syntactic level of deep structure does not exist. Acquiring a language simply involves learning how to translate semantic intentions directly into surface structures.

Doing away entirely with syntactic deep structures need not be the inevitable outcome of a theory of language acquisition which holds that most aspects of linguistic structure are learned rather than innate. As Ervin-Tripp (1971) observes, "the weakest argument of all is the notion that if we cannot think of a way to teach something, it must not be learned or learnable [p. 190]." It seems plausible, both intuitively and on the basis of a certain amount of experimental evidence, that certain abstract representations of linguistic structure are included in a speaker's knowledge of his language, even though these may not correspond exactly to those outlined by Chomsky and may be at an intermediate level between a semantically described deep structure and the surface realization of sentences.

The argument that the basic grammatical relations are unlearnable simply because they are definable only in the abstract underlying representation of sentences is not very convincing. If we accept this, we must agree that all aspects of deep structure are unlearnable for the same reason. But many aspects of deep structure, as specified in transformational generative theory, are language-specific, such as the underlying order of constituents. If the deep structure representation of sentences is to be considered part of adult competence, we can only assume that these language-specific aspects of deep structure are learnable. To argue otherwise would be to support the untenable position that children are born with a bias toward acquiring the particular language they in fact learn. And if children command some process of learning powerful enough to make these abstractions purely on the basis of linguistic experience, why should the same process not also be able to deal with abstract concepts which are believed by some to be universal, such as the basic grammatical relations?

There is, in any event, some evidence that the basic grammatical relations themselves are not universal. As we noted, Fillmore (1968) observed that certain languages do not offer a choice of subjects and therefore appear to lack the process of subjectivalization. If, in fact, the subject–predicate division is language-specific, we must rule out the possibility that it constitutes part of children's innate knowledge.

It is possible that children can acquire an understanding of the basic grammatical relations through an increasing comprehension of the way various semantic relationships are formally dealt with in their language. The concept of *subject*, for example, might develop in the following way: the child initially formulates rules specifying that words designating initiators of actions precede words designating actions (or, alternatively, that the name of the one who initiates a particular action precedes the name of the action). As the child acquires verbs which take nonagentive noun arguments as subjects, he learns additional rules for the placement with respect to the verb of words performing such semantic functions as *person affected* and *instrument*. The concept of *subject* emerges when the child eventually realizes that nouns in various semantic roles are treated identically for different subclasses of verbs not only with respect to position but also with respect to transformational possibilities, and thus have an equivalence of function at a higher level of abstraction than the particular semantic functions they perform.

Parental speech may play an important role in the child's acquisition of abstract syntactic concepts. A study by Drach (1969) indicates that the sentences mothers direct to their children may be shorter, more grammatical, and syntactically simpler than those they address to other adults. Ervin-Tripp (1971) speculates that these speech modifications could make apparent "the phrases which comprise the basic units of language" and aid the child in recognizing constituent structure. A study by Pfuderer (1969) suggests that the syntactic complexity of mothers' utterances increases as their children mature. Such an increase in complexity could provide a sort of programmed text for introducing the child gradually to progressively more abstract and difficult syntactic relationships.

A mother may even unconsciously modify her speech in a way which facilitates the child's initial search for consistencies in the expression of semantic concepts and which perhaps even suggests to him which semantic concepts he should consider important. An analysis of a sample of 1000 utterances addressed to Seppo by his mother, taken from consecutive tapes, revealed that verbs which take agents in the role of subject occurred five and one half times as frequently as all verbs which take other semantic concepts as subjects combined (Bowerman, 1973). Unfortunately, control data are not available to indicate whether this emphasis was stronger in the mother's speech to Seppo than in her speech to adults. If it was, then it would seem that the agent–action relationship was especially heavily modeled in the input to Seppo, and other semantic versions of the subject–verb relationship which might initially have confused him were kept to a minimum.

SUMMARY

According to the view of language acquisition I have sketched, the linguistic knowledge which lies behind children's initial attempts at word combining may not and need not include information about the basic grammatical relations or the constituent structure they entail. There is, in any event, no compelling evidence as yet that it does. The characteristics of cross-linguistic data suggest the alternative view that children launch their syntactic careers by learning simple order rules for combining words which in their understanding perform semantic functions such as *agent*, *action*, and *object acted upon*, or perhaps other even less abstract semantic functions. Through additional linguistic experience a child may begin to recognize similarities in the way different semantic concepts are formally dealt with and to gradually reorganize his knowledge according to the more abstract grammatical relationships which are functional in the particular language he is learning.

THE DEVELOPMENT OF
PHONEMIC SPEECH PERCEPTION[1]

OLGA K. GARNICA
Stanford University

INTRODUCTION

Roman Jakobson in his classic work *Child Language, Aphasia, and Phonological Universals* (1941), hypothesized that the child follows a relatively invariant order of phonological development and that this order is universally valid. This hypothesis applies to phonemic acquisition, the functional use of sounds by the young child, which in his later work with Halle (Jakobson & Halle, 1956), he claimed could be explained by a hierarchy of binary feature distinctions. Certain distinctions in the child's speech appear before others and later distinctions are not produced unless the earlier ones have already been acquired.

In 1948, working independently of Jakobson, a Russian psychologist, Kh. Shvachkin, reported in an experimental study that Russian children between the ages of 10–21 months developed the ability to perceive all the vocalic and consonantal distinctions in their language and that the order in which they acquired these distinctions was strikingly similar to that

[1] I am indebted to Dr. Charles A. Ferguson and Dr. Eve V. Clark for reading the manuscript at various stages of preparation and for the many helpful suggestions they offered during the duration of the project. I acknowledge with thanks the assistance of Marcy Macken and Carolyn Johnson who worked with the subjects and participated in solving the problems that arose during testing. This research was supported by NSF Grant GS-2329 to the English Phonology Project, Stanford University.

proposed by Jakobson and Halle for production. Since an English translation of Shvachkin's article is not widely available, and the experiment which
is the subject of this paper is an attempt to replicate some of his results, a
brief summary of his experiment is in order.

Shvachkin hypothesized from the results of exploratory observations that
phonemic speech perception develops concomitantly with semantic development during the second year of life, and that this development follows
an ontogenetic sequence.[2] In the experimental portion of his work, Shvachkin presented each child he tested ($N = 18$) with various objects which he
designated by nonsense monosyllables. The child's task was to choose one of
the three objects placed before him on the basis of a nonsense syllable
associated with it. Two of these objects had nonsense syllables associated
with them that were identical except for the initial phoneme. The child was
considered to have mastered a particular distinction if he correctly completed every task within a given set. The details of what constituted a set,
however, were not made explicit. The results of the study indicated an ontogenetic sequence of development which Shvachkin divided into twelve
stages. These stages are shown in Table 1. Each child he tested acquired the
distinctions in this order with very little variation.

Serious objections can be raised as to the validity of Shvachkin's results.
He does not report how often the children were tested, how many choices
the child was asked to make during a testing session, what criterion (i.e.,
percentage of correct choices) was used to decide that a child could perceive
a particular opposition, and what controls were employed to eliminate the
use of situational cues as a basis for choice between the objects. However,
his hypothesis is an interesting one because it makes a very strong claim and
has been referred to in a number of discussions in the literature (Kaplan &
Kaplan, 1970; McNeill, 1970). The remainder of this paper is a preliminary
report of an experiment designed to test this hypothesis for consonant oppositions in initial position with English-speaking children.

PILOT STUDY

A pilot study (Garnica, 1971) was conducted (*a*) to develop a controlled
method for testing oppositions, (*b*) to obtain a preliminary ordering of the
various consonantal oppositions, and (*c*) to determine the age at which to

---

[2] In the sense that Shvachkin used the term, phonemic speech perception differs from the
phenomenon that has been discussed by Moffitt (1968) and Eimas, Siqueland, Juscyk, and
Vigorito (1971) in that the child is asked to make a distinction between two objects or referents
on the basis of the sound difference of the syllables associated with the objects. Meaning
plays an important role. To make such a choice, the child must perceive the difference
between, for example, /p/ and /b/, and not just between *p* and *non-p*.

Table 1   *Stages in the Development of Phonemic Speech Perception (Shvachkin, 1948)*

Stage	Phonemic distinction
1.	Vowels
	a. *a* versus other vowels
	b. front versus back: i–u, e–o, i–o, e–u
	c. high versus low: i–e, u–o
2.	presence versus absence of consonant: CVC–VC
3.	sonorant versus articulated obstruent: m–b, r–d, n–g, y–v
4.	palatalized versus nonpalatalized: n'–n, m'–m, b'–b, v'–v, z'–z, l'–l, r'–r
5.	sonorants
	a. nasal versus liquid or glide: m–l, m–r, n–l, n–r, n–y, m–y
	b. nasal versus nasal: m–n
	c. liquid versus liquid: l–r
6.	sonorant versus nonarticulated obstruent: m–z, l–x, n–ž
7.	labial versus nonlabial: b–d, b–g, v–z, f–x
8.	stop versus fricative: b–v, d–z, k–x, d–ž
9.	velar versus dental or palatal: g–d, x–s, x–š
10.	voiced versus voiceless: b–p, d–t, g–k, v–f, z–s, ž–š
11.	"hushing" versus "hissing" sibilants: ž–z, š–s
12.	liquid versus glide: r–y, l–y

begin testing. Since it was not possible to test all the oppositions because of the large number of combinations, certain sets of oppositions, such as voiced versus voiceless and stop versus fricative, were selected. The oppositions which constituted each set were established on an a priori basis using Shvachkin's sets as a guide and then verified by data from the pilot study. A listing of these sets appears in Table 2. In an attempt to keep all but one variable constant, in general, for each set of oppositions only voiced consonants were used; and, when the opposition being tested involved a difference in manner (such as stop versus fricative), the place of articulation was held constant and vice versa. The set CVC–VC was added because Shvachkin's results indicated that this stage of development marked the onset of the perception of initial consonant oppositions.

Twelve children ranging in age from 1;2–2;5 were tested on several oppositions within each set over a 6-week period. The testing procedure varied only in minor respects from that used in the main experiment and will be discussed in detail presently. After having established that a child could perceive a particular opposition by this procedure, the method for determining a preliminary ordering was as follows. First, we found an opposition which one child could distinguish and another could not (*yes–no* opposition). Then for the same two children we found an opposition which both could distinguish (*yes–yes* opposition) and one which both could not (*no–no* opposition). The set which contained the *yes–no* opposition was ordered after the one containing the *yes–yes* opposition and before the one containing the

Table 2 *Preliminary Ordering of Sets of Oppositions from Pilot Study (Garnica, 1971)*

Group A
 1. CVC versus VC: b–∅, m–∅, v–∅, z–∅, g–∅, l–∅
 2. sonorant versus stop: m–b, w–b, n–d, r–d, l–d, n–g
    sonorant versus fricative: m–v, n–ð, w–v, l–z, r–z, n–z
    sonorant versus affricate: n–J̌, l–J̌, r–J̌
 3. nasal versus liquid: m–r, m–l, n–r, n–l
    nasal versus glide: m–w, m–y, n–w, n–y
    nasal versus nasal: m–n

Group B
 4. labial versus nonlabial: b–d, b–g, v–z, v–ð, f–š, f–θ
    stop versus fricative: b–v, d–z, g–z, k–š
 5. glide versus glide: w–y
 6. liquid versus liquid: l–r
 7. affricate versus fricative: č–š, J̌–z
    alveolar versus palatal: s–š

Group C
 8. stop versus affricate: d–J̌, g–J̌, t–č
 9. velar versus dental or palatal: g–d, g–š, g–z, k–š
10. liquid versus glide: l–w, l–y, r–w, r–y
11. interdental versus alveolar: ð–d, θ–t, ð–z, θ–s
12. interdental versus palatal: θ–š
13. voiced versus voiceless: b–p, d–t, g–k, J̌–č, v–f, ð–θ, z–s

no–no opposition. By combining all such comparisons for all children, we arrived at the preliminary ordering of all sets as listed in Table 2. Where several sets of oppositions are listed together, such as affricate versus fricative and alveolar versus palatal, insufficient data was available to determine how these should be order with respect to each other.

EXPERIMENT

Subjects

Sixteen children ranging in age from 1;5–1;10 served as subjects. The pilot study had shown that children older than this could already perceive most of the oppositions. The following criteria were used in the selection of subjects: (1) age: 1;5–1;10; (2) both parents native speakers of American English; (3) no foreign language spoken in the home; (4) no serious speech defects in parents or siblings; (5) normal hearing, as determined by a test administered by a licensed clinician; (6) availability for duration of testing period. One subject was excluded from the data analysis due to the child's uncooperative behavior during a majority of the testing sessions.

Procedure and Scoring

Each child was tested three times a week for a period of approximately 4 months which included a period of training sessions. Two female experimenters conducted the testing sessions. They alternated as experimenter and observer; however, the same experimenter tested any given subject in all testing sessions.

At each testing session, the child was presented with two objects. The objects were painted wooden blocks which varied on three dimensions: shape, color, size. The two objects presented together at any given session differed on at least two of these dimensions. Eyes, mouth, nose, and hair made out of colored paper and/or felt were affixed to each block to give it a face. This provided the opportunity to introduce the blocks as personalities to the children. The nonsense syllables associated with each block were introduced to the child as the block's "name."

For each opposition tested, the nonsense syllables were CVCs which differed only in the initial consonant sound. The sounds /ŋ/ and /ž/ were excluded because they do not occur initially in English. The vowels in the CVCs were the lax vowels /I/ (high, front), /ʌ/ (mid, central), and /U/ (high, back). To minimize the focus of attention on the final portion of the syllable, the final consonant in the CVC was a voiceless stop. All the CVCs obeyed the sequential constraint rules of English and in no cases were the initial and final consonants in a given syllable the same sound.

On each trial, the two objects were placed directly in front of the child at an equal distance from him. The experimenter produced each CVC in turn, pointing to the appropriate block as she said the CVC associated with it. Then the experimenter repeated one of the CVCs and requested the child to perform some activity involving that object, thus forcing the child to choose one of the objects.

Activities which could be performed with the objects were devised. They included giving the block a ride in a toy car, putting a doll-size hat on the block, and hiding the object under a doll blanket. The activities were varied during a testing session to keep the child's interest and attention.

Over all trials in a testing session, whether a given object was on the right or the left was randomly varied, as was whether the experimenter asked the child to choose the first or second block named on that trial. During each testing session the child was asked to choose each CVC an equal number of trials in random order. All this information was printed on cue cards in advance which were manipulated by the observer who also recorded the subject's responses and made written comments regarding any other behavior on the part of the child.

The testing sessions lasted 20–25 min each with a minimum of ten completed trials. At the completion of the session, the number of trials on which the child made a correct choice was tabulated. The criterion used to determine whether the child was regarded as perceiving the difference between two consonants was established by using the binominal probabilities distribution.

If the child could not distinguish the initial consonants of the CVCs presented, the hypothesis was that his responses would be random and by chance a correct choice would be made on half of the trials. If the observed number of correct choices is much greater than $.5x$ (x standing for the number of trials) and, therefore, the probability of obtaining that frequency of correct responses by chance low, then there is a basis for rejecting the hypothesis of random choice. Since the subjects during the training period made one or two incorrect choices per ten trials when the CVCs associated with the objects were maximally different (i.e., the first consonant, vowel, and second consonant were all different sounds for the two CVCs), and the probability that by random choice two or less errors will occur is slightly less than .05, that was the criterion adopted.

Training sessions during which maximally different CVCs were used were instituted to teach the child the experimental task, e.g., the necessity of making a choice on the basis of the "name" of the object, of choosing only one object, etc. When the child performed to criterion on two successive sessions, in the next session CVCs differing on the initial consonant only were introduced. The number of training trials varied, the average being six and the range being four to nine, with the older children requiring fewer training sessions.

The order of testing was determined in the following manner. The sets of oppositions were divided into three groups (A, B, and C) indicated in Table 2. These groupings were based on the pilot study results. For each child it was determined whether he was less advanced or more advanced on the basis of (i) age, and (ii) a general ranking of production abilities as indicated by language behavior in a free play situation. The less advanced children were tested on oppositions from two sets in both Group A and Group B; the more advanced children were tested on oppositions from two sets in Group B and Group C. From the results of these testing sessions it was possible to determine which sets of oppositions within A, B, and C should be tested further.

During the first half of the testing sessions (Time period I), oppositions from each set in the groups in which the child was placed were tested. Then, testing of oppositions from other groups proceeded according to the listing in the preliminary ordering. During the second half of the testing sessions (Time period II), oppositions not heretofore examined were tested. Those oppositions which gave negative results in the first testing period were retested to check for possible acquisitions.

Preliminary Results and Discussion

A preliminary analysis of the data ($N = 15$) shows that those oppositions listed in the earlier part of Table 2 are more likely to have been acquired than the ones at the end of the list, even during Time period II (cf. Table 3). However, there is considerably more variation in terms of which oppositions are acquired and in which order than was reported in Shvachkin's original study.

In considering the data for the subjects individually, the same variation is evident (see Table 4). For example, two subjects (4 and 5) who had acquired almost all the sets of oppositions in Group B and Group C did not yet perceive the nasal–liquid opposition; whereas, two subjects (1 and 2) who had failed to acquire some of the sets of oppositions in Group B and all the oppositions in Group C, on which they were tested, had acquired it.

These results, although highly preliminary, cast some doubt on Shvachkin's hypothesis that there is a universal ontogenetic order of acquisition in phonemic speech perception. Nevertheless, some general trends are visible in the data, which suggest that the order of acquisition is simply more variable than Shvachkin's data indicate. One possible explanation for such variability would be the choice of different strategies in approaching the task of acquiring phonology. Perhaps a distinctive feature analysis which is planned would provide some explanation of the apparent discrepancies between the present data and the data collected by Shvachkin.

Table 3 *Percentage of Subjects Having Acquired Opposition Sets by Time Period*

Sets of oppositions	Time period I	Time period II
CVC versus VC	67	87
sonorant versus stop	64	87
sonorant versus fricative	83	100
sonorant versus affricate	92	100
nasal versus liquid	50	79
nasal versus glide	86	100
nasal versus nasal	50	91
labial versus nonlabial	80	79
stop versus fricative	50	75
glide versus glide	75	100
liquid versus liquid	25	91
affricate versus fricative	20	75
alveolar versus palatal	38	75
stop versus affricate	28	71
velar versus dental or palatal	28	80
liquid versus glide	30	79
interdental versus alveolar	40	75
interdental versus palatal	28	70
voiced versus voiceless	20	63

Table 4 Sets of Oppositions Acquired during Time Periods I and II by Each Subject (N = 15)

Subject number:	#1		#2		#3		#4		#5		#6		#7		#8		#9		#10		#11		#12		#13		#14		#15	
Time period:	I	II	I	II	I	II	I	II	I	II	I	II	I	II	I	II	I	II	I	II	I	II	I	II	I	II	I	II	I	II
Group A																														
CVC versus VC	+	+	+	+	–	–		+		+		+	–			+	+	+	–	+	+	+	–	+	+	+	+	+		+
sonorant versus stop	+	+	+	+	+	+	+	+	+	+	–	+	+	+	+	+	+	–	+	+	+	+	–	–	–	+	–	+	+	+
sonorant versus fricative	+	+	+	+	+	+	+	+	+	+	–	+	+	+	+	+		+	+	+	+	+		+	+	+	+	+	–	+
sonorant versus affricate	+	+	+	+	+	+	+	+		+	+	+	+	+	+	+		+	+	+	+	+	–	+	+	–	+	+	+	+
nasal versus liquid	–	+	–	+	–	+	–	–	–	–	+	+	–	+	+	+		+	+	+	+	+	+			+		+		+
nasal versus glide	+	+	+	+		+	+	+	+	+	+	+	+	+	+	+	+		+	+	–	+			+	+		+		+
nasal versus nasal	+	+	–	+	+		+	+	+	+	+	+	–	+	–	+	+		+	+	–	–			+	+		+	+	+
Group B																														
labial versus nonlabial	+	+	–	–	–	–	+		+	+	+	+	+	+	+		+				+		+		+	+	+	+	+	–
stop versus fricative	–		–	–	–	–	+	+	+	+	+	+	+	+	–	+	+				+	+				+		+		+
glide versus glide	–	+	+	+	+	+	+	+	+	+	+	+	+	+	+	+	+								+		+		+
liquid versus liquid	–	–			+	+	+	+	–	+	+	+	–	+	+	+	–	+	+	+	+	+	+		+		+		+
affricate versus fricative					–	–	+		–	–	+	+	–	+	–	+	+	+	+	+	–	–			+	+	+	+		+
alveolar versus palatal					–	–	+		–	+	–		–	+	–	+	+	+	+	+	+	+			+	+	–		–	–
Group C																														
stop versus affricate	–	–	–	–	+		+		+	+	–		+		+		+		+		+		+		–	+	+	+	–	
velar versus dental or palatal			–	–																	+	–								
liquid versus glide	–	–			+		+		–	+	–		–		–	+	+	+	+	+		–	+		+		+	+		+
interdental versus alveolar					–	–	+		+	+			–	+	+		+		+				+		+	+			–	
interdental versus palatal					–	–	+		+	+			–	+	–	+	+	+	+	+			–		–	–			+	+
voiced versus voiceless							–	–	–		–		–	+	–	+	+	+	+	+	–	–			–	–			+	+

Note. + indicates *S* has acquired set of oppositions
– indicates *S* has not acquired set of oppositions
blanks indicate set not tested.

ON THE STATUS OF
VOWEL SHIFT IN ENGLISH

BREYNE ARLENE MOSKOWITZ
University of California, Los Angeles.

INTRODUCTION

Language is a function of the human brain. A description of language ought to reflect that function. It is assumed at the outset of this chapter that any linguistic theory is required to be sensitive to a large range of evidence—from the millennia of language change to the minutiae of language acquisition—bearing on the facts which are to be described. It is also noted that this requirement is met in many covert ways by the theory of English phonology which will be under discussion: that proposed by Chomsky and Halle (1968) in their important and elegant contribution to phonological theory, *The Sound Pattern of English* (SPE).[1]

It is further assumed, in accordance with scientific tradition, that a theory must not only be testable, it must also be tested.

THE GREAT VOWEL SHIFT

The Great Vowel Shift (GVS) which occurred several centuries ago substantially changed the qualities of long, tense vowels in English. The particu-

---

[1]Whether or not "psychological reality" is a concept to which the authors of SPE have committed themselves has been a subject of considerable discussion. Without reiterating endlessly the arguments, I will cite only the notion that each morpheme has only one underlying form in the speaker's mental lexicon as evidence of that commitment.

$$ai \leftarrow i\cdot \qquad u\cdot \rightarrow au$$
$$\uparrow \qquad\quad \uparrow$$
$$e\cdot \qquad\quad o\cdot$$
$$\uparrow \qquad\quad \uparrow$$
$$\varepsilon\cdot \qquad\quad \mathfrak{o}\cdot$$
$$\uparrow$$
$$a\cdot$$

DIAGRAM 1.   The Great Vowel Shift.

lar changes which occurred have been outlined by Jespersen as in Diagram 1. The shift was quite general, affecting a massive portion of the native vocabulary. Diachronic accounts list hundreds of Germanic words whose unique pronunciations changed over the course of the GVS. Some typical examples offered by Jespersen are given in Table 1.

Spelling substantially stabilized long before the completion of the GVS, permanently leaving behind information about former pronunciations in thousands of words which do not have—and never have had—synchronic alternate pronunciations in different environments. Thus the major mark that the GVS has left on English is the nonphonetic spelling of vowels.

The Great Vowel Shift has left another mark on English in the form of vowel alternations which occur in the pronunciation of a portion of the Romance vocabulary. Among these words, a single morpheme in isolation may have undergone vowel shift while an allomorph of it which occurred with a derivational morpheme and therefore had a lax vowel of the same quality was ineligible for the shift. Thus today a single morpheme may have two pronunciations, differing with respect to the vowel,[2] usually the stressed vowel, depending on whether it occurs in isolation or with one of several

Table 1   *Typical Examples of the Effect of the Great Vowel Shift*[a]

Middle English		Modern English	
bite	/bi·tə/	bite	[bait]
bete	/be·tə/	beet	[bi·t, bijt]
bete	/bɛ·tə/	beat	[bi·t, bijt]
abate	/aba·tə/	abate	[əbeit]
foul	/fu·l/	foul	[faul]
fol	/fo·l/	fool	[fu·l, fuwl]
fole	/fɔ·lə/	foal	[foul]

[a]This table was taken from Jespersen (1909, p. 232).

[2]Other differences, such as consonant alternation, are ignored for the purpose of this paper.

inflectional suffixes. For example, the morpheme *divine* in isolation historically underwent vowel shift (parallel to *bite* above) while in *divinity* it did not,
resulting in different vowels synchronically. As a result of the regularity of
the diachronic process, there are certain internal and environmental regularities in the behavior of the alternating vowels which can be noted in a
synchronic description of English phonology.

Phonetically, the internal regularities are not precisely parallel among
the affected vowels (see footnote 3 and *Underlying Back Vowels*). Those environments which are involved in word pairs which exhibit alternations are
also involved in word pairs which do not (see *Predominant Pattern*). The derivational suffixes which make up this list of morphological environments
largely are dead (unproductive) at the present time; those suffixes which
remain productive, such as *-ness*, do not trigger shift.

Those word pairs which exhibit alternating vowels constitute a small percentage of the total English vocabulary.[3] The individual words are among the
most literary in the lexicon, and, with a few exceptions, occur with low
frequency in speech. They are learned late by children, probably because of
not only their low frequency but also their relative semantic abstractness.

In comparison to productive inflections such as *-ness*, the inflections
which largely make up the environment for vowel shift, such as *-ity*, are not
nearly so parallel semantically as they are phonologically, principally because there have been many abstract semantic changes subsequent to the
demise of the productivity of the morphological patterns. Thus information
about the identity of a single morpheme in two different environments is no
longer as accessible to the naive native speaker as it once was, and it is not
a priori obvious that historically related words are also synchronically
related. For example, we can compare such pairs as *rape–rapture, regulation
–regularity, weal–wealthy,* and *cave–cavity,* with *aware–awareness, fat–fatness,* and *red–redness.*[4] The matter is no doubt further complicated by the
existence of semantically and historically unrelated pairs which follow the
same phonological pattern, e.g., *dime–dimity, comply–complicity, admire–
admiral, mate–mattress.*

This second mark left on English by the GVS, then, is not as clear-cut as the
first. The remainder of this section will briefly review the facts of the synchronic residue of the Great Vowel Shift.

---

[3]I know of no study which indicates an approximate percentage or numerical figure,
although one such study would be an important contribution to the resolution of these issues.

[4]For other examples of etymologically related words for which a synchronic morphological relation on semantic grounds is not necessarily justifiable, as well as discussion of
related issues, see Bolinger (1948).

The Predominant Pattern

Table 2a lists some sample word pairs exhibiting a regular alternation which occurs in parallel fashion for three pairs of front vowels, /ăy/[5] ~ /ĭ/, /ēy/ ~ /ǎ/,[5]/īy/ ~ /ĕ/. In all of these words, a stressed tense diphthongized vowel appears in the isolated morpheme and a stressed lax vowel in the derived word. A variety of derivational processes is exhibited among the word pairs in this group.

There are also a number of morphemes which occur in environments similar to those exemplified in Table 2a, but which do not involve alternating full vowels. Some examples are listed in Table 2b. A lax vowel occurs in the stressed position of most of the underived morphemes in this group, although there are a few pairs which occur with tense vowels in both members.

A few words also involve front vowel alternations different from those in Table 2a, e.g., *clear–clarity*, or tense–lax pairs of unshifted vowels, e.g., *detain–detention, chlorine–chlorinate*.

Secondary Patterns

In another set of morphemes, a non-low vowel occurring in one word alternates with a reduced vowel in another. Examples are in Table 3. Among these word pairs—with exceptions such as *Canadian*—the member with a reduced vowel is typically a high-frequency word while the member with a full-value, stressed vowel is part of the marginalia of educated speech. These word pairs differ further from those of Table 2a in that the alternations noted in the predominant class involve a consistently stressed vowel while these involve shifting stress patterns.

This alternation does not seem to occur with the low vowel /āy/. Instead, an alternation of /āy/ and /īy/ occurs in a few words, such as those in Table 4. These words are affected by a surface structure constraint of English which requires a stressed vowel to be tense before another vowel.

Back Vowels

Three sets of back vowel alternations occur in an extremely limited set of words, as exemplified in Table 5. These alternations, namely /ə/ ~ /ōw/,/ōw/

---

[5]Although ă is actually a back vowel, I will follow the practice of SPE in ignoring the difference between α and æ in establishing the framework of front vowel alternation. (In SPE a later rule readjusts the value of the feature [back] for ă. It should be noted, however, that this choice is one which further ignores the reality of the surface phonetics of English and the contribution they make towards a characterization of English.) To this end, the symbol a will be used throughout the remainder of this chapter to signify both of the vowels as they participate in the front vowel shift. The symbols α and æ will continue to be used for them as they participate in back vowel shift.

Table 2a   *Derived Morphemes with Front Vowel Alternations*

āy ~ ĭ	ēy ~ ă	īy ~ ĕ
divine – divinity	profane – profanity	serene – serenity
line – linear	explain – explanatory	obscene – obscenity
derive – derivative	grateful – gratitude	meter – metric
collide – collision	opaque – opacity	receive – reception

Table 2b   *Derived Morphemes without Alternations of Full Vowels*

stupid – stupidity	total – totality	base – basic
rustic – rusticity	mental – mentality	scene – scenic
valid – validity	simple – simplicity	obese – obesity
liquid – liquidity	lax – laxity	phoneme – phonemic

~ /ā/, /ʌ/ ~ /ǣw/, are not phonetically parallel to any of the front vowel alternations heretofore discussed, although the diachronic process of vowel shift did involve the front and back vowels in an almost completely parallel fashion.

THE VOWEL SHIFT RULES

Recently, in the framework of generative phonology, Chomsky and Halle (1968) have attempted to incorporate all these facts of synchronic vowel shift into a phonological description of English. To do so, they found it necessary

Table 3

īy ~ ə
funereal – funeral
managerial – manager

ēy ~ ə
Canadian – Canada
marginalia – marginal
algebraic – algebra

Table 4

various – variety
impious – pious

Table 5

ə ~ ōw
Newton – Newtonian
custody – custodian

ā ~ ōw
verbosity – verbose
conic – cone

ʌ ~ ǣw
profundity – profound
abundant – abound

to construct four rules which are separately integrated into the larger set of rules which constitute the phonological component. (Several other rules relevant to the process—but not central—will be ignored for convenience.) These four rules are *vowel shift, tensing, laxing*, and *diphthongization.*

Briefly, the vowel shift rule changes the quality of a vowel under specified conditions, the most important of which is that the vowel is both [+ tense] and [+ stress]. The specific quality changes are those in Diagram 2. In the SPE formulation, these quality changes are accomplished in two steps, one or the other of which is vacuous in some cases. Alternative formulations by Wang (1968) and Ladefoged (1971) have proposed one-step formulations of the rule.

$$
\begin{array}{cccccc}
i & u & e & o & a & ɔ \\
\downarrow & \downarrow & \downarrow & \downarrow & \downarrow & \downarrow \\
a & ɔ & i & u & e & o
\end{array}
$$

DIAGRAM 2.   The vowel shift rule.

The SPE rule is actually a rule schema, a consolidation of a large number of elementary rules which are considered to be of sufficient similarity that their consolidation "captures a generalization" about the language. Whether in fact the rule does serve to capture a significant generalization more than to obscure valid information is a question still open to linguistic investigation, and will be examined at several points in the course of this paper.

As the input to the vowel shift rule is a tense vowel, one of the functions of the tensing rule is to change a vowel from [− tense] to [+ tense] in appropriate environments, thus making it eligible for the operation of vowel shift. The laxing rule changes a [+ tense] vowel to [−tense], thereby making it ineligible for vowel shift.

This set of four rules will be referred to as the vowel shift rule*s* when reference to their combined operation is necessary.

They are considered in SPE to provide an adequate account of the facts which have been described in a preceding section (*Great Vowel Shift*). The sections following will describe the manner in which they do so.

The Underlying Front Vowels

The morphemes of Table 2 are the most numerous by far and therefore have served as the base for a synchronic description of vowel shift facts. Considering only these words, an adequate account of the facts could be derived from the assumption that the tense, monophthongal vowel of the isolated form is the underlying vowel. Such a solution would enable us to derive the form *line* simply by applying the diphthongization rule, while vowel shift and laxing would be required for the derivation of *linear*. The relevant vowel shift rule would be of the form ā → ī, ē → ā, ī → ē. One appealing facet of this solution is that it retains as the underlying vowel that which occurs in the shorter—and usually more common—form.

Chomsky and Halle, however, have chosen to remove the underlying form still one more step from the surface phonetics. Their underlying vowels for these forms are ī, ā, and ē, and the proposed rule is ī → ā, ā → ē, ē→ī. The motivation of this choice is the incorporation of forms such as those of Tables 3 and 4 into the domain of the rule.

The eligibility of the forms in Tables 3 and 4 for appropriate stress rules and vowel reduction is dependent on the assumption that they contain appropriate underlying lax vowels. A shifting rule designed to account only for these forms would be the opposite of one required solely for the first set of words. The compromise choice of SPE serves to consolidate into one rule —namely that of vowel shift—precisely that which is considered to be common to these two processes. What differs between them is taken care of by the other three rules.

One might wonder why forms such as those of Table 3 could not be accounted for by having a vowel which would not be eligible for vowel shift at all. In such a view, the final lax vowel of *algebra* would be reduced, and the lax ĕ of *algebraic* would undergo the rules of tensing and diphthongization. Vowel reduction is extremely widespread in English and is accounted for in SPE by a rule of wide applicability in addition to this particular set of words. Note, e.g., some words of Table 2b.

The SPE rejection of this possibility is due to a requirement that any word must undergo every rule of the phonological component unless it is specifically marked as an exception. To mark as exceptions all words except those in the category of Table 2a would be highly uneconomical. It is not only Table 3 type words that must be listed in the lexicon as having underlying vowels different in quality from any of those which occur in surface forms, but also the entire set of nonalternating words which contain tense vowels, such as those which formed the original scope of the diachronic process of vowel shift. Thus, e.g., *pool* and *loud* are required to have the underlying vowels /ō/ and /ū/.

Economy

In terms of the evaluation metric employed in SPE, this choice results in greater economy in the grammar. Beyond the evaluation metric, however, it is obvious that the choice involves considerable cost. While the total vocabulary motivating the rules is a small percentage of the English lexicon on which to base such structure, examples of the types listed in Tables 3 and 4 are still significantly less numerous than those in Table 2a. And yet their inclusion

into the motivational base for the rules significantly complicates the underlying structure of the larger group of morphemes in Table 2a. In addition, the
considerable discrepancy in the surface phonetic facts of these three sets of
words has been completely hidden by the grammar which has unified these
sets by means of a "significant generalization." The proposed solution is
elegant and pleasing, but the price paid is the obscuration of the unbeautiful
but inescapably real sound pattern of English.

Underlying Back Vowels

To achieve greater generalization and to allow the diphthongization rule
to operate on them, back vowels were included in the vowel shift rule schema
although the particular shifts imposed by that schema never occur in surface
alternations. Because the surface back vowel alternations are not parallel to
the front ones, the costs of this added generalization are the inclusion of
further rules to fix up the output for the few relevant words and the postulation of unmotivated vowels in the underlying forms of a large number of irrelevant words. With the exception of *profound–profundity* and *verbose–
verbosity*, the remainder of the back-vowel vocabulary which is inflectionally
parallel to the words in Table 2a exhibits no surface alternation, e.g., *absurd–
absurdity, crude–crudity, nude–nudity, odd–oddity, false–falsity, prior–priority*.
Presumably, these regular forms must be lexically marked as exceptions.

The Importance of Vowel Shift

Vowel shift, according to SPE, is "without doubt the pivotal process of
Modern English phonology."

There is no doubt that there are some important—regular and consistent—
facts about English synchrony which remain as the legacy of the Great Vowel
Shift. Whether the vowel shift is the pivotal process of the phonology of the
English language is a question whose answer is in large part affected by the
confirmatory or disconfirmatory evidence of experimental investigation.
Chomsky and Halle have made vowel shift without doubt the pivotal process
of their particular grammar of English phonology. Behavioral evidence
about the "psychological reality" of this pivotal rule therefore may offer
insight into the usefulness of their formulation as a model of English phonology.

The experiments discussed in the next section suggest (1) that in fact the
theory has, through ingenious manipulations, captured generalizations
which remain uncaptured by speakers of English, and (2) that there are some
lesser generalizations about vowel shift not captured by SPE which are indeed real for speakers, and which, when viewed by themselves, can be
explained in a way which offers a more useful insight into the nature of
English phonology.

AN EXPERIMENT WITH VOWEL SHIFT

Because the SPE formulation of English phonology is a preliminary—perhaps even tentative—proposal, it is especially important that some aspects of it be tested, and that the results of such testing be considered in future revisions of the theory. Vowel shift, the pivotal process of the theory, is an optimal area on which to concentrate initial testing. Any indication that this formulation captures important features of native speakers' knowledge of vowel shift would strengthen the theory. On the other hand, evidence that it does not represent speakers' knowledge would undermine the entire theory that incorporates such a version of vowel shift.

It has been shown that there are some purely linguistic grounds on which to doubt the centrality of vowel shift in a phonological theory which is designed to reflect the knowledge of a speaker of English. It would be nice to test directly the reality of underlying forms; it is not obvious precisely how that would be done. As an alternative, testing of the rules of the phonological component can be used as a direct form of evidence for their own existence and as an indirect form of evidence for the existence of underlying forms. Assuming that there is some level of representation approximately of the order of systematic phonetics,[6] if the existence of rules can be shown, then it can be inferred that there is an additional level of systematic representation which those rules connect to the systematic phonetics.

Pretest with Adults

Appendix A describes in detail an experiment that was run with adult subjects. The test was designed to explore the nature of adults' knowledge of vowel shift and not to test explicit hypotheses. A large number of linguistic variables were included in the design in order to determine which ones could feasibly be included in an experiment with children. Each subject heard a list of English nouns and was asked to respond to each with a related adjective. Real and nonsense words were used; some involved vowel shift and others did not.

Some features of the test proved to be extremely difficult for adults, and were therefore not included in the subsequent test. One such was the variability of the suffix. Thus the experiment with children utilized only one suffix, -ity. The length of this experiment also proved unmanageable, and so

---

[6]Although the level of systematic phonetics is not rigorously defined in SPE, it is a level of description relatively acceptable to almost all linguists. In a separate paper it is shown that the major processes of phonology acquisition lead the child to a representation which is probably almost identical to that of systematic phonetics (see Moskowitz, 1971).

the section which included elicitation of speaker judgments about the grammaticality of words was completely eliminated.

Other problematic features, whose inclusion seemed necessary, were simplified in the subsequent experiment. For example, the adults heard a number of different patterns with respect to vowel alternations, randomly presented. Each child heard only one pattern, but three different patterns were included by assigning the children to one of three groups. Thus it was possible to retain this feature in the design.

Both real and nonsense words were used with adults; although this presented no real problems, a number of considerations indicated that it would be more feasible to use only nonsense words with children. Among these considerations were (1) some of the adults indicated that they did not know many of the real words in the experiment; (2) some of the extremely common real words, such as *marine*, were not recognized by the adults as real words when paired with nonsense words; (3) in general, pre-junior-high-school children do not use a large part of the Romance vocabulary in their free speech, but have certainly heard many of these words—therefore their degree of familiarity with the vocabulary cannot easily be controlled for, and the use of real words would introduce another confounding variable.

The Experiment with Children

It was decided to carry out an experiment with children to determine: (1) whether they do have knowledge of vowel shift; (2) if so, at what age they acquire such knowledge; (3) what the source of the knowledge is; and (4) what form the knowledge takes.

Design

Diagram 3 should clarify the interrelation of several variables in the experiment and can be referred to throughout the next several sections.

The experiment was carried out in three parts (A, B, and C). Prior to part A, each subject was instructed that he would hear a word and should respond with another, similar word. He was specifically told that the difference between the two words was that his should end with *-ity*. In fact the words also differed with respect to the stressed vowel, the stimulus word always having a tense vowel and the correct response always having a lax vowel. The instructions, however, included no mention of the vocalic difference. The four sample word pairs in the instructions, of course, exhibited the vowel alternations. Two examples of each of two front vowel pairs were given. The first goal of the experiment, therefore, was to determine the number of trials it would take the child to notice and correctly manipulate the vowel alternations. (Complete instructions are given in Table 6.)

Part A included 72 word pairs, 36 for each of the two front vowel alternations. The experimenter read the stimulus (underived) words one at a time. After each, the child responded with another word. If the response was correct—exhibited the expected lax vowel—the child was told, "Yes, that's right," or "That's exactly right." After an incorrect response the subject was told, "No, the correct answer would be ____," or, if possible, "No, that's close, but the right answer is ____." Ten correct responses in a row were considered to indicate that the child had learned to criterion adequately. In the event that the child did not learn to criterion, part A terminated after all 72 trials were completed.

Whether termination resulted from completion of 72 items or criterial performance, it was immediately followed by Part B, which involved six

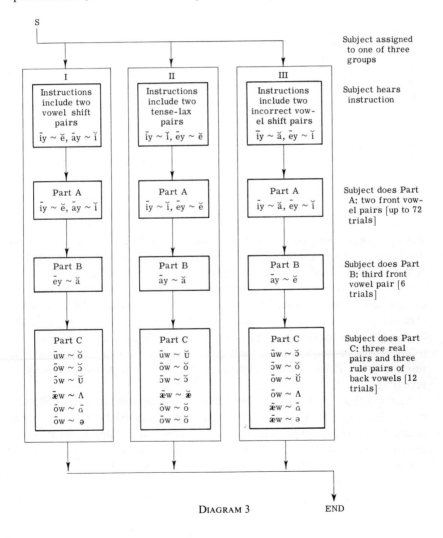

DIAGRAM 3   END

Table 6 *Instructions*

Basic instructions, Condition I

I am writing a paper for school and I want you to help me. We're going to play a word game together, and this will be an important part of my paper. I am going to say a word to you and I want you to answer with another word. Your word will be very similar to mine, but not exactly the same.

My word will be shorter than yours: I want you to say a word that is almost the same as mine but has the sounds *-ity* on the end. So if I say *sīyp*, you should say *sĕpity*. If I say *pāyp*, you should say *pĭpity*. Or, if I say *indīyk*, you would say *indĕkity*. And if I say *ənvāyn*, you would say *ənvĭnity*. So your word is almost like mine, but it has *-ity* on the end.

[If subject looks totally confused, offer to repeat last paragraph of instructions.

O.K. Now I'm going to start saying my words. After each one, you tell me your word. If you want me to repeat my word before you say yours, just ask me. O.K.? The first word is . . .

Alternate instructions, Condition II
[Substitute the following for the middle paragraph above.]

My word will be shorter than yours: I want you to say a word that is almost the same as mine but has the sounds *-ity* on the end. So if I say *sĕyp*, you should say *sĕpity*. If I say *pĭyp*, you should say *pĭpity*. Or, if I say *indĕyk*, you would say *indĕkity*. And if I say *ənvīyn*, you would say *ənvĭnity*. So your word is almost like mine, but it has *-ity* on the end.

Alternate instructions, Condition III
[Substitute the following for the middle paragraph above.]

My word will be shorter than yours: I want you to say a word that is almost the same as mine but has the sounds *-ity* on the end. So if I say *sĕyp*, you should say *sĭpity*. If I say *pĭyp*, you should say *păpity*. Or, if I say *indĕyk*, you would say *indĭkity*. And if I say *ənvīyn*, you would say *ənvănity*. So your word is almost like mine, but it has *-ity* on the end.

---

word pairs exhibiting the third front vowel alternation. No new instructions were given. The first item of Part B simply followed the last item of Part A. It was hypothesized that correct production on B would indicate that criterial performance on A resulted from prior knowledge which encompassed the three vowel pairs, while incorrect production on B following criterial performance on A would indicate that A had involved only the learning of two specific vowel alternations. For Part B the subject was also told whether her response was right or wrong, and if wrong what the correct response was. Therefore the response to the first item would be especially revealing.

Again without pause or new instructions, the last item of B was followed by the first of C. Part C included 12 pairs of words exhibiting back-vowel alternations. Six of the pairs included back-vowel alternations which follow the pattern of English surface forms and the other six included back vowels which follow the pattern of the vowel-shift rule. Thus there were two examples of each of six alternations. (The three alternations which follow the vowel-shift rule, of course, involved vowels which are technically unpronounceable. The experimenter pronounced them by giving the corresponding phonetic value, e.g., ɔ̄ was produced as [ɔ:] and ɔ was produced as [ɔ].) It was hypothesized that a comparison of the two different kinds of alternations would shed some light on whether the subject's strategy actually involved knowledge of surface alternations or of underlying rule-governed relationships—if performance on A and B indicated that prior knowledge was indeed involved. Further, it was assumed that general performance on C would indicate whether in fact back vowels should truly be included along with the front vowels in any account of the vowel shift.

Since C included only 12 examples—two for each of six alternations—which were randomized, it was felt that feedback about correct (expected) responses could potentially be more confusing than helpful to the subjects. Also, as this part tested generalization rather than learning, feedback was nonessential. Therefore all answers were accepted without comment, and only a nod of the head acknowledged that they had been heard and accepted.

Experimental and Control Conditions

The subjects were randomly assigned to three groups, an experimental (I) and two control (II and III) conditions. Instructions differed for the three groups only in that the vowels in the sample words were different; parallel differences occurred in the test stimuli and responses. Otherwise, the experimental situation was identical for all three groups.

Group I utilized vowel pairs which occur in English words such as those of Table 1a. Thus they heard pairs like *sīyp–sĕpity* and *pāyp–pĭpity*. As these vowel alternations do occur in a number of morphologically-related words, learning them in an experiment of this type ought to be "natural." This naturalness can be explained in at least two ways.

(i) They are phonetically paired as alternate surface pronunciations, e.g., āy and ĭ simply alternate under specified surface conditions, as do īy and ĕ.

(ii) There is a single underlying representation for a given morpheme, and a particular subset of the rules of the phonological component are utilized in arriving at appropriate surface forms. In other words, the child must hypothesize an underlying vowel, such as ī, and employ the rules of laxing, diphthongization, and vowel shift to derive from ī the surface forms āy and ĭ under specific conditions stated in the rules. Schematically this process can be seen as:

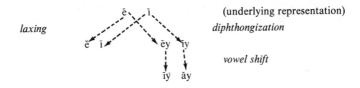

As has been mentioned before, the SPE formulation of the relevant rules requires that diphthongization be ordered earlier in the phonological component than vowel shift so that the glide inserted by the rule will be appropriately marked for the feature of backness; a later adjustment rule changes the backness feature of some vowels (e.g., ā) to differ from that of the associated glide.

Therefore the vowel alternations designed for Condition II employed a smaller subset of rules, omitting the vowel shift rule, which is ordered last. These vowel pairs differed only in tensing and diphtongization, and can be represented as:

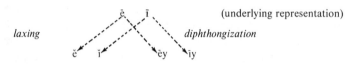

It was hypothesized that if children really do know the vowel shift rules as a natural part of English phonology, i.e., adopt strategy (ii) above, for Condition I, then Condition II might be slightly simpler than I, for it involves fewer rules. In other words, a comparison of I and II minimally tests the separability of diphthongization and vowel shift as phonological processes.

The counterargument that II involves only a subset of rules is made irrelevant by noticing that I also involves only a subset of the rules of the phonological component. Further, it should be noted that the subset employed by II results in fully pronounceable forms which as individual items conform strictly to the constraints of English phonology. In fact, there are even some morphologically related words which conform to this surface pattern, e.g., *detain–detention, retain–retention*. In a study of the invented spellings of preliterate children, Read (1971) found evidence for a number of ways that children group the diverse vowel phonemes of English into five vowel letters. Many of these children did in fact pair vowels precisely as in Condition II although none ever did as in Condition I.

Condition III vowel pairs (īy-ă, ēy-ĭ) can also be seen as employing the rules of laxing and diphthongization. In addition, as compared with I, they necessitate postulating a new vowel shift rule which is "incorrect" for English: ī → ē → ā → ī.

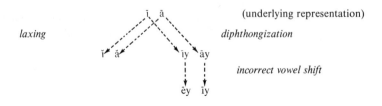

Returning again to strategy (i), neither Read's study nor any other suggests that children naturally pair vowels in this way. In the context of strategy (ii), correct performance on III would involve the use of a non-English rule. Therefore it was hypothesized that III ought to be the most difficult to learn.

Summary of Design

To summarize, then, several kinds of controls were built into the experiment to test aspects of the SPE formulation of the facts of vowel shift in English. All subjects were required to learn two front vowel alternations and then were tested for generalization to a third from vowel alternation as well as two kinds of back vowel alternations, the surface ones and the rule-predicted ones. (Surface and rule-predicted forms, of course, are collapsed for front vowels.)

This process was undertaken for each subject with one of three sets of vowels. These sets of vowels were: (I) those which conform to the predominant pattern of English surface alternations, the vowel shift; (II) those which differ by tenseness and diphthongization but involve no quality shift; and (III) those which undergo an incorrect quality shift. For all three parts of an individual experimental session (A, B, and C) a single one of these patterns was utilized throughout.[7]

Stimuli

To develop stimuli for the experiment, a list of 25 nonsense words with the internal vowel ĕ and the suffix -ity was constructed. Each was paired with another word which differed by having the vowel īy and no suffix. The "underived" words were either one or two syllables long and conformed to the shapes of possible monosyllables and disyllables in English.

---

[7]For simplicity of exposition one additional feature of the design has not been included in this description. It was originally planned that half of the subjects on each condition would be given the test as it has been outlined, while for the other half of the subjects the stimuli and responses would be reversed. The experiment was in fact conducted in this way for the first 12 subjects (four on each condition) in the 9–12 age group. A two-way analysis of variance was then used to ascertain that there was no significant difference in the results related to which of the words in a pair was used as stimulus. Those subjects who heard the "underived" word as stimulus did very slightly better, and had a shorter response latency—both probably due to the slightly greater simplicity involved in adding rather than removing a part of a word. Since shorter latency was desirable in order to avoid the boredom (for subject and experimenter) that resulted from long test sessions, all further subjects (the remainder of the 9–12 groups as well as all younger ones) were given the shorter word as stimulus. Subjects 2-3, 1-6, 1-3, 2-2, 1-8, and 1-4 are those who differed from the rest in this facet of the design. This difference is relevant only to the error analysis as these six subjects are among the 12 examined there.

Then a second list was constructed, identical to the first except that the vowels ï and ãy were used. Whenever either member of a pair in the second list happened to be an English word, both members of that pair were changed by one consonant to produce nonsense words.

The 50 word pairs were then randomized by means of a random number table. The randomized list was then repeated, to produce a list of 100 pairs, of which only the first 72 were used.

Similar words were then constructed for Conditions II and III by repeating the identical lists and changing the relevant vowels appropriately.

Subjects

Twenty-five children between the ages of 9 and 12 served as subjects.[8] The results indicated that further study with younger children would be interesting, so nine children aged 7 years and four children aged 5 years were added to the sample. All were from middle-class homes in the San Francisco (East) Bay Area, and were native speakers of Standard English.[9] Half of the subjects were from two Girl Scout troups in Berkeley. The remainder were students at the Anna Head School in Oakland.

As primary-language acquisition is generally thought to end by the early teens, it was assumed that if children do acquire information about vowel shift as part of their primary-language acquisition, it should be apparent in the 9–12 age group. Since almost all other phonological acquisition concludes considerably earlier,[10] phonological information about vowel shift which is unavailable to this age group must be considered to be acquired by a different process entirely.

Procedure

The test was conducted in a room with only one subject present at a time. Each session was tape recorded. Subjects were randomly assigned to the experimental and control groups: the first was assigned to Condition I, the next to II, etc.

The subject was asked about previous language experience and instruction, and about previous residences. Instructions were then read to her. After the child indicated that she understood the instructions, the stimulus words were read to her one at a time. Correct and incorrect responses were re-

---

[8]One pilot subject, who is not included in the results, and 24 experimental subjects. The pilot results were the same as those for the subsequent subjects also tested on condition I.

[9]All subjects were questioned about previous language training, exposure to other languages, and places of residence. One child (# 1-2) reported being bilingual in English and Hungarian.

[10]For further discussion of this point, see Moskowitz (1971).

corded as "c" or "i" on the answer sheet. The test proceeded through Parts A, B, and C.

Subjects involved in Condition II were ascertained to speak a dialect of English which did not involve neutralization of ǐ and ě before nasals.

Table 7 *Stimulus List[a]*

Condition I	Condition II	Condition III
Part A		
māyš – mǐšity	mīyš – mǐšity	mēyš – mǐšity
klīyǰ – klěǰity	klēyǰ – klěǰity	klīyǰ – klǎǰity
fāyp – fīpity	fīyp – fīpity	fēyp – fīpity
kǐyč–kěčity	kēyč – kěčity	kīyč – kǎčity
lāyp – lǐpity	līyp – lǐpity	lēyp – lǐpity
spāyb – spǐbity	spīyb – spǐbity	spēyb – spǐbity
impīyg – impěgity	impēyg – impěgity	impīyg – impǎgity
tāyb – tǐbity	tīyb – tǐbity	tēyb – tǐbity
vīyv – věvity	vēyv – věvity	vīyv – vǎvity
nīyf – něfity	nēyf – něfity	nīyf – nǎfity
vāyv – vǐvity	vīyv – vǐvity	vēyv – vǐvity
intīyp – intěpity	intēyp – intěpity	intīyp – intǎpity
wǐym – wěmity	wēym – wěmity	wǐym – wǎmity
nāyb – nǐbity	nīyb – nǐbity	nēyb – nǐbity
əlīyr – əlěrity	əlēyr – əlěrity	əlīyr – əlǎrity
ispāys – ispǐsity	ispīys – ispǐsity	ispēys – ispǐsity
dīyl – dělity	dēyl – dělity	dīyl – dǎlity
fǐyp – fěpity	fēyp – fěpity	fīyp – fǎpity
ispīys – ispěsity	ispēys – ispěsity	ispīys – ispǎsity
tīyd – tědity	tēyd – tědity	tīyd – tǎdity
wāyn – wǐnity	wīyn – wǐnity	wēyn – wǐnity
tāys – tǐsity	tīys – tǐsity	tēys – tǐsity
bāys – bǐsity	bīys – bǐsity	dēys – dǐsity
nīyg – něgity	nēyg – něgity	nīyg – nǎgity
nīyb – něbity	nēyb – něbity	nīyb – nǎbity
rǐys – rěsity	rēyf – rěfity	rǐys – rǎsity
wǐyb – wěbity	wēyb – wěbity	wǐyb – wǎbity
nāyk – nǐkity	nīyk – nǐkity	nēyk – nǐkity
nāyg – nǐgity	nīyg – nǐgity	nēyg – nǐgity
nīyk – někity	nēyg – někity	nīyk – nǎkity
bǐys – běsity	bēyv – běvity	bǐys – bǎsity
skāyg – skǐgity	skīyg – skǐgity	skēyg – skǐgity
nīyš – něšity	nēyš – něšity	nīyš – nǎšity
spīyb – spěbity	spēyb – spěbity	spīyb – spǎbity
rāyš – rǐšity	rīyš – rǐšity	rēyš – rǐšity
nāyz – nǐzity	nīyz – nǐzity	nēyz – nǐzity
klāyǰ – klīǰity	klīyǰ – klīǰity	klēyǰ – klīǰity

[a]Note.—The vowels written as āy and ǎ were pronounced ɑ̄y and ǽ.

Table 7—(*Continued*)

Condition I	Condition II	Condition III
skīyg – skĕgity	skēyg – skĕgity	skīyg–skăgity
kāyč – kĭčity	kīyč – kĭčity	kēyč – kĭčity
nīym – nĕmity	pēym – pĕmity	nīym – nămity
nāym – nĭmity	nīym – nĭmity	bēym – bĭmity
wāyb – wībity	wīyb – wībity	wēyb – wībity
grīyč – grĕčity	grēyč – grĕčity	grīyč – grăčity
dāyg – dĭgity	dīyg – dĭgity	dēyg – dĭgity
grāyč – grĭčity	grīyč – grĭčity	grēyč – grĭčity
impāyg – impĭgity	impīyg – impĭgity	impēyg – impĭgity
līym – lĕmity	rēym – rĕmity	līym – lămity
tīyn – tĕnity	tēyn – tĕnity	tīyn – tănity
intāyp – intĭpity	intīyp – intĭpity	intēyp – intĭpity
əlāyl – əlĭlity	əlīyl – əlĭlity	əlēyl – əlĭlity
[repeat first 22 items if necessary]		

Part B

zèyg – zăgity	zăyg – zăgity	zăyg – zĕgity
iygrèyp – iygrăpity	iygrâyp – iygrăpity	iygrâyp – iygrĕpity
wèys – wăsity	wâys – wăsity	wâys – wĕsity
lèyʃ – lăʃity	lâyʃ – lăʃity	lâyʃ – lĕʃity
nèyn – nănity	nâym – nămity	nâym – nĕmity
fèyb – făbity	fâyb – făbity	fâyb – fĕbity

Part C

spōwb–spɔ̆bity	spōwb – spɔ̆bity	spɔwb – spŏbity
tǣwd – tʌdity	tǣwd – tædity	tōwd – tʌdity
mǣwš – mʌšity	mǣwš – mǣšity	mōwš – mʌšity
kɔ̄wč–kūčity	kɔ̄wč – kɔ̆čity	kōwč–kŭčity
bōws–băsity	bōws – bŏsity	bǣws–băsity
lōwm – lɔ̆mity	lōwm – lŏmity	lɔwm – lŏmity
nōwf–năfity	nōwf – nŏfity	nǣwf–năfity
nūwk – nɔ̆kity	nūwk–nŭkity	nūwk – nɔ̆kity
wōwb – wəbity	wōwb – wŏbity	wǣwb – wəbity
tūwp – tŏpity	tūwp–tŭpity	tūwp – tŏpity
rōws – rəsity	rōws – rŏsity	rǣws – rəsity
fɔwp – fŭpity	fɔwp – fɔ̆pity	fōwp–fŭpity

Results

The overall results of the study were quite different from those that had been anticipated.

Age Group 9–12: Part A

The results of part A for the oldest age-group are presented in Table 8. Three measures were used to describe performance: whether or not the subject learned to criterion, the number of trials completed before the ten criterion trials, and the number of errors made.

It is apparent from the table that Condition I was considerably easier than either II or III.[11] There also seems to be a tendency for III to be easier than II on all three measures. The standard deviation is greater for III, however, reflecting the greater range of performance.

Condition I, involving correctly shifted front vowel pairs, seems indeed to be easy for children of this age group. All subjects learned to criterion. Three subjects made no errors at all. The others, once they began to produce correct responses, in general did not regress to incorrect patterns. The small discrepancies between the number of errors and the number of trials before criterion was usually due to the occurrence of a two-syllable stimulus word, i.e., following some number of correct trials the subject would respond to a two-syllable stimulus by incorrectly shifting the wrong vowel. (This phenomenon will be discussed further under *Additional Results.*) For subsequent single-syllable stimuli, correct responses were resumed.

Correct responses on Condition II show a large range of variation. A subject such as 5-2 had frequent opportunity to be told that the answer she offered was correct; despite this, she was unable to perform consistently. Utilizing the rules of laxing and diphthongization without vowel shift seems to be extremely difficult if not impossible.

The results on Condition III are even stranger. Incorrect vowel shift is not impossible, as two subjects were able to learn to criterion, one of them rapidly. Even if subject 5-6 were disregarded, the mean number of errors on III would be 46.8, which remains lower than the mean of 49.5 for II.

It may be that the knowledge of children in this age group is such that the vowel alternations on I are completely natural and those of II are completely unnatural. For a small percentage of individuals those of III are possible while for the rest they are in the same category as II. Thus children in this age group can be divided into two groups.

Age Group 9–12: Parts B and C

Two measures were used to analyze the results on B. As an important aspect of B was to test transfer from A, whether the first item was responded to correctly is reported in Table 9. Also reported there are the total number of correct responses out of six.

First of all, the aim of testing transfer was not relevant anymore under the unfortunate result that the majority of subjects did not learn to criterion

---

[11]An analysis of variance and a Mann-Whitney U test were performed on the data for errors and trials. Both indicated that the data exhibited a difference significant at $p < .001$. As neither test is absolutely appropriate to these data, the procedures are not reported.

Table 8 *Results on Part A, Age Group 9–12*

	Learned to criterion?	Number of errors	Number of trials before criterion	Percentage of total trials correct
Condition I				
2-3	yes	16	25	54
1-6	yes	3	3	77
1-2	yes	15	27	59
3-3	yes	0	0	100
4-6	yes	11	16	58
5-1	yes	0	0	100
5-4	yes	5	14	79
6-8	yes	0	0	100
Mean		6.25	10.63	
Standard deviation		6.80	11.41	
Condition II				
1-3	no	57	72	21
2-2	no	48	72	33
1-5	no	38	72	47
3-1	no	44	72	39
4-7	no	60	72	16
5-2	no	31	72	57
5-5	no	52	72	28
5-9	no	66	72	8
Mean		49.50	72.00	
Standard deviation		11.66	0.00	
Condition III				
1-8	no	61	72	15
1-4	no	59	72	18
2-1	no	50	72	31
2-4	yes	36	61	49
4-8	no	60	72	16
5-3	no	37	72	49
5-6	yes	1	1	91
5-10	no	25	72	65
Mean		41.12	61.75	
Standard deviation		20.92	24.85	

on A. Correct performance on B is highest for Group I but this may be due only to the fact that these subjects actually did learn to criterion. In particular, the performance of subject 5-10 suggests that had all subjects learned to criterion on A there might have been equivalent transfer to B. Although

Table 9 *Results on Part B, Age Group 9–12[a]*

	A: learned to criterion?	B: first correct?	B: total correct
Condition I			
2-3	yes	yes	5
1-6	yes	yes	6
1-2	yes	yes	1
3-3	yes	no	3
4-6	yes	yes	6
5-1	yes	yes	6
5-4	yes	yes	4
5-8	yes	yes	6
Condition II			
1-3	no	no	0
2-2	no	no	0
1-5	no	no	1
3-1	no	no	0
4-7	no	no	0
5-2	no	no	0
5-5	no	no	0
5-9	no	yes	1
Condition III			
1-8	no	no	2
1-4	no	yes	3
2-1	no	no	0
2-4	yes	no	1
4-8	no	no	1
5-3	no	no	2
5-6	yes	no	0
5-10	no	yes	6

[a]Dotted lines indicate anomalous correlations.

5-10 did not learn to criterion, she produced 47 correct responses and only 25 errors on A, and was successful on all 6 trials of B.

The results of B are far from clear-cut. At least two Condition I subjects produced strange results. Subject 1-2, after correctly responding to the first item, missed the remaining five; and subject 3-3, who made no errors on A, did far less well on B. Two additional subjects who had learned to criterion on A made at least one error on B.

Group III subjects performed uniformly poorly, although it is anomalous that the one correct answer given by 5-9 was the first.

A larger amount of transfer was shown by III than by II. Interestingly, the two subjects who learned to criterion on A did quite poorly on B, while two

244   *Breyne Arlene Moskowitz*

who did not learn to criterion on A did well on B. As was the case with the
results on A, B also indicates the strange status of III being apparently
easier than II.

On the other hand, the results for C were equally bad for all three groups.
Some subjects gave only front vowel responses. Others responded consistently with a stressed schwa. A few subjects therefore accidentally responded
with a correct schwa. One Condition I subject once responded correctly for
an /ǎ/ ~ /ōw/ alternation. No subject correctly responded to any of the
stimuli which matched the precise output of the vowel-shift rule.

Ages 5 and 7

The 7-year-old subjects were asked only to do Part A. Among the five
who did not learn to criterion, only one completed all 72 trials; the session
was terminated for each of the others when the subject was obviously unable or unwilling to proceed further.

Two out of three subjects on Condition I and also on III learned to criterion; none did on II. The two who learned to criterion on III did so more
rapidly than the two on I. (The results are given in Table 10.) In terms of the
error measure also, Condition III seems to be easier for this age-group.

The 5-year-old subjects also were asked to do only Part A. The attention

Table 10   *Results, Age Group 7*

	Learned to criterion?	Number of errors	Total number of trials	Percentage of total trials correct
Condition I				
1-7	yes	8	27	70%
2-7	no	25	40	38%
4-1	yes	23	63	63%
Mean		18.67		
Condition II				
2-8	no	41	65	37%
4-2	no	38	72	47%
4-4	no	24	50	52%
Mean		34.33		
Condition III				
3-5	yes	2	17	90%
4-3	no	36	50	28%
4-5	yes	1	15	93%
Mean		13.00		

span of the 5-year-olds was limited, and they only completed the first 22 items. As can be seen from Table 11, they understood the task well enough to produce correct answers sporadically. They were all able to add the appropriate suffix. It seemed, however, that the control of vowel alternations was beyond their knowledge.

Error Analysis

An analysis of the error patterns was carried out for the data from the first 12 subjects from among the 9–12 age-group on Part A. (Methodological considerations explained in footnote 7 are relevant to these subjects and will be apparent in the error analysis.)

In order to simplify the presentation, responses were coded into five categories. These categories were chosen to reveal major patterns among the error types for the different test situations because these patterns are less accessible from the raw data. The categories are as follows:

(1) correct response for condition being taught;
(2) repetition of stimulus vowel;
(3) response which would be correct for other vowel alternation included in part A;
(4) response predicted by vowel shift facts;
(5) other.

Category (1) is self-explanatory. Errors of type (2) might indicate that the subject has not yet inferred that he must change the vowel in some way. Those of type (3) might signify that a paired-associate learning paradigm is being used by the subject, while those of type (4) indicate interference from previous knowledge. [(4), of course, is not relevant to Condition I.] Errors coded as (5) included primarily those instances when a subject offered more

Table 11   *Results, Age Group 5*

	Number of trials	Number correct	Number of errors	Percentage of total trials correct
Condition I				
3-2	22	0	22	0%
3-4	22	4	18	18%
Condition II				
2-5	22	6	16	27%
Condition III				
2-6	22	2	20	9%

than one response, although there were also some errors which did not fall into one of the other four categories.

The categories were chosen so as to be mutually exclusive so far as possible. However, there is one ambiguous aspect of this error analysis. For II and III a particular response to one of the two-vowel stimuli can be coded as either (3) or (4). This can be seen in Diagram 4.

	Condition II				Condition III			
stimulus vowel	ĭy	ĕy	ĭ	ĕ	ĭy	ĕy	ă	ĭ
correct response (1)	ĭ	ĕ	ĭy	ĕy	ă	ĭ	ĭy	ĕy
error response (3)	ĕ	ĭ	ĕy	īy	ĭ	ă	ēy	īy
error response (4)	ĕ	ă	āy	īy	ĕ	ă	ēy	āy

DIAGRAM 4.   Coding difficulties.

To clarify the interpretation of these ambiguous errors, they were first compared to the unambiguous responses of types (3) and (4) which occurred for the other vowel pair in each situation. Table 12 presents a breakdown of error types for each of the three conditions.

Table 12   *Error Types*

Response types:	1	2	3	3-4	4	5
Condition I						
2-3	19	7	9	—	—	—
1-6	10	2	1	—	—	—
1-2	22	3	10	—	—	2
3-3	10	—	—	—	—	—
Total	61	12	20	—	—	2
Condition II						
1-3	15	21	1	8	16	11
2-2	24	6	1	22	9	10
1-5	34	7	7	23	—	1
3-1	28	17	—	26	—	1
Total	101	51	9	79	25	23
Condition III						
1-8	11	9	2	9	—	41
1-4	13	—	8	20	21	10
2-1	22	2	4	23	7	14
2-4	35	—	7	17	9	3
Total	81	11	21	69	37	68

There are few unambiguous responses of either type (3) or (4) while there are many ambiguous ones. For some individual subjects it seems possible to attribute the ambiguous responses to one category or the other, on the basis of adjacent responses, but overall it is more reasonable to conclude that this large number of ambiguous responses occurred precisely because they were ambiguous, i.e., these responses may in fact truly represent a neutralization of (3) and (4) type errors, occurring when both factors contribute to their plausibility. Prior knowledge of the facts of vowel shift does not seem to be an overriding factor in the errors, and there is relatively little difference in its contribution to the errors of Conditions II and III.

The error patterns for these two control conditions are in fact quite similar. The only obvious difference is the greater number of type (2) errors for II. It is possible that this could be due to difficulty in hearing the difference between the stimulus and response vowels. If this is true, it would indicate that tensing and diphthongization are quite inseparable.

Graphs of the response patterns for individual subjects can be found in Appendix B. Ambiguous (3)–(4) errors are all coded as (4) in the graphs. The graphs are supplemented by explanations of the type (5) errors and by discussion of the strategies adopted by each subject wherever it was possible to identify those strategies.

Additional Results

A few other factors ought to be noted with respect to errors and strategies.

(1) It was my impression that there was a large difference in the latencies of response time, that for Condition I subjects being considerably shorter than that for II or III.

(2) Condition I subjects typically responded using a declarative intonation, and II and III subjects, using an interrogative one.

(3) Subjects often responded to two-syllable stimuli by altering the wrong vowel, even when that vowel was ə. This difficulty was more frequent for Condition I subjects.

(4) Several subjects on Condition I asked questions which related the task of the experiment to their knowledge of spelling rules, typically: "Oh, you just want me to make a long 'i' into a short 'i', right?" This question was asked during the first several trials. No response was given by the Experimenter.

Preliminary Conclusions

Recall that the experiment was designed to answer four questions: (1) whether children do have knowledge of vowel shift; (2) if so, at what age they acquire such knowledge; (3) what the source of the knowledge is; and (4) what form the knowledge takes.

There is no doubt that these children have knowledge of vowel shift, since the data are almost overwhelming. The differences among the results for the three age-groups indicates that the acquisition of this information takes place gradually. Seven-year-olds and some 9–12-year-olds seem to tolerate any kind of alternation of vowel quality while other 9–12-year-olds tolerate only the major alternation pattern of English.

This age of acquisition pattern is fundamentally tied to the answers to the other two questions posed. It seems at first mysterious that at an age when children are relatively unfamiliar with much of the relevant vocabulary, they not only are able to manipulate vowel-shift patterns well but also are *strongly* resistant to other patterns in such an easy task. Likewise it seems mysterious that an incorrect vowel-shift pattern is easier than a phonetically simpler pattern involving no shift. These facts are less mysterious when it is considered that a substantial amount of time is spent on spelling during the early years of education. Children who have no occasion to hear *opaque* and *opacity* learn that in hundreds of monosyllabic words the letter *a* is used to spell the sounds ēy and ǽ. Many children are explicitly told about "long" and "short" varieties of the same vowel letter, others may only be told about the relationship between a "silent" *e* and the preceding vowel, as well as other spelling patterns which relate vowels, and still others may have to infer the pattern for themselves from the many pairs like *fat–fate, cat–Kate, fit–fight, kit–kite, pet–Pete, Ned–need*, etc. Whatever way they arrive at a conclusion about alternate vowel pronunciations, the knowledge is essential to success in reading and spelling.

Read (1971) found that in the invented spellings of preschool children, vowel letters were used to spell their "own" names as well as the related lax vowel. Thus *e* spelled īy and ǐ, *a* spelled ēy and ě, *i* spelled āy, ǽ, and ɑ. (E.g., *lade* "lady," *lik* "like," *fes* "fish," *fall* "fell," *git* "got.") The letter *i* was also used for ʌ, indicating its relationship to other back unrounded vowels, while *ow* was used for both ōw and ūw and *o* for ɔ. At the same stage other peculiarities of their spelling, such as the elimination of nasals before homorganic consonants (e.g., *agre* "angry") also indicate a spelling based exclusively on phonetic perception. Thus, prior to indoctrination into the written form of English, children find tense–lax pairing of vowels natural and offer no evidence of knowledge of vowel-shift alternations.

Read's data also indicate that upon being taught the correct spellings *i, e, a* for the lax vowels ǐ, ě, ǽ, the children again extend the spellings to phonetically related tense vowels. Thus there is a second stage of vowel spelling which again does not reflect vowel shift. In this stage, *i* spelled īy and ǐ, *e* spelled ēy and ě, *a* spelled āy, ǽ, and *a*. It is not until the third stage that vowel shift alternations are reflected in learned spellings.

The 7-year-olds of the vowel-shift experiment have been exposed to one year of reading and spelling education. They have enough information about the standard system to have abandoned the previous strategy of phonetic spelling, and they have learned that vowels are paired in spelling in ways which must seem odd to first graders. Accurate performance on both I and III probably reflects a lack of certainty about the precise nature of that odd pairing. By two years later, the exact details of the system have been assimilated.

The source of these children's knowledge of vowel shift, then is the spelling system of English. And it is likely that the form it remains in psychologically is a reflection of that source.

The data provide strong indication that the SPE proposal about vowel shift bears no resemblance to the functional grammar of native speakers. *The vowel-shift rule is not separable from the rules of tensing and diphthongization* as indicated by the extremely poor results for condition II. As mentioned earlier, tensing and diphthongization also may be inseparable for speakers of English. On what basis, then can such a formulation of the vowel shift facts be justified as a part of the grammar of English phonology? Wang (1968) has stated that:

> The synchronic description of a language is part of an explanatory theory of man's faculty of language. As such, the theory must not make use of information about his language that cannot be directly or indirectly attributable to him in a general and systematic way. . . . It is by no means easy, of course, to establish what types of technical linguistic information can be attributed to the speaker. Some of the statements a linguist makes in a phonological description may be justifiable on the basis of the synchronic pattern, but may not have any productive use for the speaker. There is a whole class of fascinating questions to be asked concerning how we can determine the psychological reality of the various components of a phonological description. When we say, somewhat metaphorically, that a speaker "knows" the phonology of his language, we are in fact using the verb "know" to cover many types of awareness [p. 706].

I believe that the SPE statements about vowel shift are not justifiable on the basis of the synchronic pattern. To so attribute them is to overlook the important participation of the writing system in the structure of a language. In order to examine this participation, several related issues must first be introduced.

ACQUISITION OF RULES

The knowledge of a speaker of English includes at least three kinds of rules which can fundamentally differ in the manner of acquisition and incorporation into the grammar:

Allophonic rules, which encompass the predictable phonetic variations utilized in the actual production of the sound segments included in phonetic representation. These rules include not only the obvious, conditioned phonetic differences in the language—such as the difference in voice onset time between initial and medial consonants—but also those which are not usually recorded by linguists, such as the distinction between the exact physical manifestation of [a] after [p] versus after [b] or [m] or [t]. Certain of these allophonic variations, such as the front-to-back variation of [k], which is dependent on the following vowel, may be universal, i.e., may be predictable from the configuration of the human vocal tract, and do not need to be learned by children. Others, such as the front-to-back variation of [s] in English, which is also predicted by the following vowel, must be learned. All of this allophonic information, from the minuscule details of vowel differences to the complex rules of positional variation within syllables and words, are natural by-products of the processes of syllable, segment, and distinctive-feature learning which every child normally undergoes. (Complete details of the processes of phonology acquisition on which this and subsequent claims about children's knowledge are based can be found in Moskowitz, 1971.)

Evidence of the acquisition of allophonic rules in English is plentiful, as is that of the temporary use of incorrect rules by some children. For example, one subject (Erica, reported in Moskowitz, 1970) substituted an unaspirated dental stop for the cluster /st/ almost everywhere. She also had an incorrect rule limiting the occurrence of the voiced interdental fricative to the position immediately after a nasal segment (both at age 2;0).

Phonotactic rules, which delineate that which is a possible morpheme in English by indicating structural limitations on words. Where such rules are of a very general nature, they frequently occur in the grammar of English as morpheme structure conditions or redundancy rules. Some of the more limited ones are omitted entirely from the grammar. We can recognize at least three types of phonotactic rules of decreasing importance. First, there are general rules describing predictability of occurrence: e.g., in a three-consonant sequence the first must be /s/. Second, there are rules delimiting the positional occurrence of phonemes: e.g., limiting the occurrence of /ž/ and /ŋ/. Third, there are rules for which the evidence is explicit but extremely infrequent, such as the nonoccurrence of labial and velar consonants after /aw/. There may well be different degrees of knowledge that speakers have of these three types of rules, and in fact a breakdown on the basis of such knowledge could well lead to a finer grid than has been presented. Brière (1968) has shown that speakers of English are much more adept at pronouncing /ž/ in word-initial position than /ŋ/. It may be that the low frequency of the fricative plus the high frequency of the velar nasal with respect to the morphological processes to which it it psychologically connected, cause this result: namely, that the phonotactic restrictions on the fricative can be violated with greater ease. It is doubtful that any speaker of English, despite an ability to produce world-initial /ž/, is not aware of its non-English sound. It is likely that, even though speakers of English never produce English words with labials or velars following /aw/, not all of them would be aware of the non-English sound of such words when asked to judge them. And it is even more likely that all speakers of English could produce such sequences when called upon to do so.

Morphophonemic rules, which describe the systematic alternations of phonemes. It is possible to distinguish two types of morphological rules in English which involve morphophonemic patterns. These two types correspond roughly to inflectional and derivational morphophonemics. The data on morphophonemics which are relevant to this discussion are the derivational alternations which are word-internal and the inflectional alternations which are suffixes. Tentatively I will adopt the terms "internal" and "external" for these two distinct types of morphonemics. The regular inflections of English all have a high frequency of occurrence; those which involve morphophonemics, such as the plural inflection, have a small number of alternants, governed by rules which are quite similar to rules of the phonotactics in general. The internal morphophonemes of English, on the other hand, are far more numerous, have a much lower token/type ratio, occur with a more limited vocabulary, and involve more alternants. The latter, in any formulation, involve rules which are much more complex; the relevant vocabulary is less likely to be heard by preschool children, and is not in general a part of their productive speech.

Braine (1971b) proposed a distinction between high-level and low-level morphophonemic rules. His distinction is roughly equivalent to that between internal and external morphophonemics.

Reviewing several examples of acquisition of low-level rules, Braine concluded that these are learned in general in the same manner as phonotactic rules. One of his examples is from the speech of a boy at 2;2, whose word-final stop consonants were voiceless, but who could phonetically produce both voiced and voiceless consonants medially. Thus Steven, who had learned a general diminutive suffix -*iy*, produced such alternations as [dak] ~ [dagiy] "dog," [pik] ~ [pigiy] "pig," and [buk] ~ [bukiy] "book."

Such examples are frequent in the literature on children's speech. This example, and the others like it, can be explained very simply as a by-product of syllable learning and the resultant segmental and distinctive feature analyses. Because CV is acquired earlier than CVC, distinctions develop more rapidly in syllable-initial than syllable-final position. Thus there is a voicing distinction only syllable-initially. Rules of this type, despite the linguistic convenience of categorizing them logically as morphophonemic, are learned in the same manner as allophonic and phonotactic rules and are therefore not necessarily distinct from them psychologically.

As an example of a high-level rule, Braine cites an example from Bar-Adon, who studied Hebrew verb morphology among Israeli children.

> Hebrew lexical roots usually consist of three consonants; vowels intercalated between the consonants belong to formative morphemes distinct from the lexical root. Because they have more than one phonemic realization, several of these consonants have to be considered as morphophonemes, and their varying phonemic shapes are determined in a complex way by the position of the consonant in the root (i.e., whether first, second, or third consonant), the "conjugation" in which the root appears, and the tense form. Note the alternations . . . in the following examples . . .: /hu šofex/ "he is spilling it", /al tišpox/ "don't spill [it]"; /liftoax/ "to open", /ptax/ "open!"; /lixtov/ "to write", /hu kotev/ "he is writing"; /levaker/ "to visit", /hu biker/ "he visited"; /yivke/ "he will weep", /hu baxa/ "he wept". These and similar morphophonemic alternations are not found regularly in children's speech; instead, one shape of the consonant tends at first to be used in all forms of a particular verb, so that /šopex/, /ftax/, /xotev/, /viker/ tend to replace /šofex/, /ptax/, /kotev/, /biker/ in the above examples. Regularizations of this sort may be found as late as adolescence, and suggest that to a substantial degree the two realizations of a consonant are learned separately in each verb. In short, where the standard language contains a high-level morphophoneme, children's speech tends to contain a single phoneme. These phenomena indicate that children have difficulty learning phonological entities at this level of abstraction, under some conditions, and point to the desirability of further study of such learning (including the contribution of the learning of standard spellings) [p. 28–29].

The acquisition of morphophonemic information has been discussed for several languages. [See, for example, Berko (1958), Ervin (1964), Slobin (1966), Guillaume (1927a).] First the child produces a few "irregular" forms, e.g., the present tense forms of a few high-frequency irregular verbs in French. These forms have a high token/type ratio in surrounding speech. These forms, if they do occur, are literally memorized items with no internal analysis. Next the child selects a single representative of a given morpheme, such as the first conjugation morphemes for French verbs, rather than second, third, or irregular. The representative morpheme is selected usually because there are more different types which represent it, irrespective of the number of tokens for each individual type. These may actually occur as regularized endings for irregular verbs before they occur with first conjugation verbs. One of the most important aspects of this process is that, as is true of phonology acquisition in general, the child is able to utilize a form which he knows is incorrect. Considerably later, the child will begin again to correctly use the irregular forms. All documented cases of acquisition of morphophonemics have this common property: They document this regular process of overgeneralization which is impervious to feedback, indicating that supposedly incorrect decisions have been made.

Abstraction and Representation

The job of the naive infant in learning a language is to develop a representation of language in his head. He must arrive at a representation by means of processes of abstraction. Available to him is only the raw acoustic data. On the basis of it he must make judgments about a representation of the essential information. The processes of abstraction available for making such judgments are used by humans in many other activities as well.

Induction involves the derivation of a general principle on the basis of several observed instances. For example, after repeated exposure to examples of 2 oranges and 2 oranges equal 4 oranges, 2 apples and 2 apples equal 4 apples, 3 bananas and 3 bananas equal 6 bananas, a child can eventually conclude that 2 + 2 always equals 4 and that 3 + 3 always equals 6. Deductive abstraction does not need to be confined to only those examples on which the abstraction was based, and the child who has undergone the the above process could just as easily add mangoes as apples. This kind of abstraction is dependent on the consistency of the data presented. From 18 examples of 2 + 2 = 4 and 19 examples of 2 + 2 = 5, without a prior representation of the number system to indicate that some of the examples should be disregarded, a human child could abstract no information at all, and would just be confused. Finally, the form of representation derived from this type of generalization is not essentially different in form from the original data.

Abduction [see, for example, Knight (1965)] is not a process of conclusion from examples but instead one of hypothesis from examples, and this includes the possibility of examples which are already represented. In other words, unlike the previous type, this form of abstraction can lead to a series of progressively more sophisticated representations. Once a representation is formed, the resultant generalizations can be put to use in furthering the process. Seemingly contradictory examples can be ignored, for generalizations can be made on fewer examples, and others can be taken care of at a later time. This type of abstraction is exhibited in the problem-solving behavior of humans. Eliminating the need for trial and error approaches to a solution—and the surprise which results from the accidental occurrences of a nonerror trial—humans are able to abstractly represent a problem and derive a solution. Extending one's reach by tying together two sticks and using the elongated one, using the wheel to increase one's working capacity, building a vehicle for transportation to places which are inaccessible by foot—all of these are tasks utilizing abstract representation. Since such abstraction can include a representation of a solution as well as of a problem, it is not largely dependent on feedback. A good example of abstraction representation of potential outcomes is offered by the atomic weapons industry, which does not need to drop a new bomb on a city in order to determine how many people it can kill.

This second type of abstraction is the major process of phonology acquisition. On the basis of the output of other people's grammar the child must construct an internal grammar. In other words, the child does not strive to match his output to the model output, as is amply shown by the phenomena of phonological idioms, productions involving phonetic complexity considerably beyond that displayed in the child's phonologically regular output. He rather strives to construct a grammar which will account for what he hears—i.e., match the grammar which produces what he hears—and which will eventually enable him to produce a similar output. Thus, if an adult grammar includes a representation X, and a rule $X \rightarrow A$, all that is available to the child is A. He must, by abduction, hypothesize both that X exists and that $X \rightarrow A$ is appropriate. Of course, he might first hypothesize Y and $Y \rightarrow A$ and much later revise this. This is the case, roughly, in the morphological acquisition discussed earlier.

Biological Considerations

The capacity for this second type of abstraction may be present to some small extent in a few animals besides man. But man is the only animal who has used it to any great extent. Biologically, this means that the human being does not have to be instinctively adapted to his environment. Unlike other animals, he does not have to be preprogrammed with innate knowledge of what kinds of natural environments can be selected as shelter. All he needs is a preprogrammed ability to abstract by abduction, to represent a problem so that it can be solved. Thus language learning does not need to assume any other innate features in addition to the ability to abstract a representation of language from the data of speech. And that representation, being of the second type, does not suffer from a small number of negative instances; thus the child can ignore erroneous examples which he hears, provided that they are relatively small in number, so that they do not counterindicate an entire complex structure. Linguistic abstractions are made on the basis of a large number of previous instances—not necessarily all—and are confirmed by being tested out against new, future instances. Because they are not disconfirmed by a minority of counterexamples, they are in fact overgeneralized. Notice that *it is the rules of external morphophonemics, and not internal, which exhibit this important aspect of overgeneralization.*

Symbolic Systems

An important extension of abstract representation has been the development of symbolic systems to record that which is represented. Such systems extend the powers of the human brain by allowing the manipulation of such representations. An ideal symbolic system represents all and only that which is inherent in the system, and adds no additional structure. But human symbolic systems are not always ideal, and writing systems, being conventional, may be highly deviant.

English orthography no longer represents the phonological system of the language in an absolutely appropriate way. The standardization of spelling has resulted in the incorporation into the symbolic system of some aspects which are not facts of the nonwritten system, such as the results of the Great Vowel Shift in English monosyllables.

Just how extensive this deviation is is a matter of dispute at the moment. It is relevant to that dispute to consider the possibility that an inaccurate representation is capable of imposing additional structure that was not present before, so that English orthography would have imposed some "facts" onto the phonological representation of English which might not have been there at all given a different system of orthography. This possibility is seriously strengthened by the reality that many of these facts of underlying phonology are known only to the highly educated segments of our population, and not to the entire number of literate English-speaking people who do not spell properly and are not able to guess at the appropriate pronunciation of words they have seen spelled only and have never heard.

Knowledge of a symbolic system is capable of extending the process of abstraction one step farther to include the additional structure imposed by the symbolic system itself, and this may be precisely the source of knowledge of vowel shift, etc., among speakers of English.

A clear way in which spelling has overextended vowel shift in English is in the alternate pronunciations which currently exist for several lexical items. Both alternates are often possible for a single individual. For example,

āy~ĭ: ideology, Italian, italic, sycophant, sinecure, divisive;
ēy~ă: data, various, forbad(e), Sather, ration, radiator, radio;
īy~ĕ: economics, leisure, genic.

Many other examples can be found. To account for such pronunciations in the SPE framework would mean the supposition of two competing underlying forms. Recognition of the contribution of spelling to speakers' knowledge of English phonology places these competing pronunciations in a more reasonable perspective.

CONCLUSION

External morphophonemic, allophonic, and phonotactic rules are learned by children as a part of the early phonology acquisition process. Internal morphophonemic rules, particularly vowel shift, are learned considerably later and by means of a different process, that of deductive abstraction based on the written representational system of the language. Negative feedback or negative instances strongly interfere with this overlaid function. The result in actual language use is that it is more difficult for English speakers to learn contradictory spellings than complex phonological information. The result in the experiment which has been reported here is that subjects were unable to learn contradictory alternation patterns.

This distinction is an important aspect of a speaker's knowledge of English. An adequate grammar of English phonology must recognize and incorporate such information.

APPENDIX A: PILOT STUDY

A short pilot test was done with adult native speakers of English in order to determine the necessary constraints on a test with children. The test included from six to nine word pairs in each of seven categories, the total list being randomized by means of a random number table. The categories were as follows:

1. Six pairs of real words; front vowel shift; postulated underlying tense vowel. E.g., austerity–austere, gratitude–grateful, salinity–saline.
2. Nine pairs of real words; no vowel shift; postulated underlying lax vowel. E.g., scarcity–scarce, rusticity–rustic, grandity–grand.
3. Six pairs of real words; no vowel shift; postulated underlying tense vowel. E.g., obesity–obese, vagary–vague, cycle–cyclic, scene–scenic.
4. Nine pairs of real words; vowel reduction and postulated vowel shift; postulated underlying lax vowels. E.g., manager–managerial, algebra–algebraic, impious–impiety.
5. Seven pairs of words: unreal noun with lax vowel, expected response real adjective with tense vowel. E.g., muscatinity–muscatine, marenity–marine, arcanity–arcane.
6. Seven pairs of unreal words, expected to follow vowel shift. E.g. salkïrity–salkãyr, mətǽnity–mətēyn, inðěnity–inðīyn.
7. Six pairs of common words. no vowel shift. E.g. height–high, fatness–fat, wealth–wealthy.

Subjects received a brief explanation of the fact that English includes pairs of words which share something of the same meaning, and they were given three example pairs, one of which exhibited vowels which followed the vowel shift pattern. They were told that I would read to them a noun and they would have to respond with a related adjective. They were further cautioned that some of the words to be used were quite rare in English, and that if they had never heard them they were to guess. Three practice items were included to be sure that they understood the instructions. After the entire set of words on the list was completed, the subject was further instructed that he would hear the taped session repeated, and after each word on the tape—both the stimulus nouns and the response adjectives— he was to judge which of four categories the word belonged to:

(1) word known and used in speaking;
(2) word known—understood and read—but not used;
(3) word unknown;
(4) not an English word.

Whenever the subject's response adjective differed from the expected response, the tape was interrupted and the subject was asked to judge the expected response adjective also.

It was found that the first task was too difficult, and the experiment was modified to include information about the suffix which was to be included in the response form. For example, the subject would hear "algebra—suffix *ic*" or "austerity—no suffix" as stimulus.

Of primary interest was performance on words of categories1, 5, and 6. One subject correctly produced almost all of these forms. The other five subjects had considerably more difficulty with words of 5 and 6 than of 1; one of the five produced no forms correctly. With the exception of those words in categories 2, 3, and 7, most stimulus words met with complaining responses, and long silences preceded the response decision. The five unsuccessful subjects considered the task extremely difficult, and in general found manipulating inflections to be frustrating. No subject rated any item as (4) not an English word, although (3) was a very frequent rating— even for category (1) words and the real words of category (5).

The conclusion from this pilot test, then, was that the place of the vowel shift rules in the competence of speakers of English is uncertain. The test used, however, would be impossible to use with children and several major modifications would have to be made before a reasonable task could be presented to younger subjects.

APPENDIX B: ANALYSIS OF ERRORS

The following comments refer to noncriterion trials for the 12 subjects whose results are in the following graphs.

Subject 2–3.   Fifteen of 25 precriterion trials were āy responses (6 correct, 9 incorrect), indicating that this was the strategy she adopted.

Subject 1–2.   Type (5) errors: one was an incorrectly-selected vowel on a multisyllabic word, the other was the sequence ĭ–ĭy–ĭ (3–2–3). Strategy was to respond with ĭ usually.

Subject 1–3.   Initial strategy seemed to be repetition of stimulus vowel. The strategy then switched as the vast majority of answers were v̄y, some of which (randomly) were correct. On the last third the answers were almost all āy, which was not one of the two correct responses. Answers coded (5) are: ĕ for ĭ → ĭy on   28, 37, 46; āy for ĕ → ēy on 33, 60, 63, 65, 67, 68, 69; ĕ–āy–ĕ for ĕ → ēy on 60.

Subject 2–2.   No obvious strategy. For 4 multisyllabic stimuli, no response attempted [coded (5)]. Other (5) responses were: āy for ĕ → ēy on 30, 57, 62; ʌ or ĕ for ĭ → ĭy, ĭ for ĕ → ēy.

Subject 1–5.   This subject showed a strong tendency to answer ĕ to anything. Response # 14, coded as (5) was ēy for ĭ → ĭy.

Subject 3–1.   The tendency to respond frequently with ĕ also occurred for this subject. One type (5): ĭy, ĕ for īy → ĭ. (# 8).

Subject 1–8.   Until close to the end (approximately at # 54) this subject's strategy was to respond with lax vowels rather than tense ones.

Subject 1–4.   This subject did not ever develop an appropriate, non-random strategy for pairing vowels. With 2 exceptions, all answers were tense vowels.

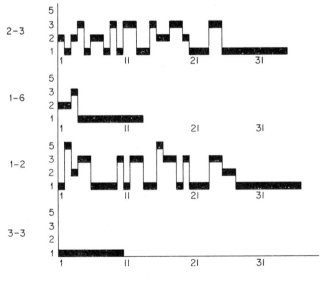

Condition I errors

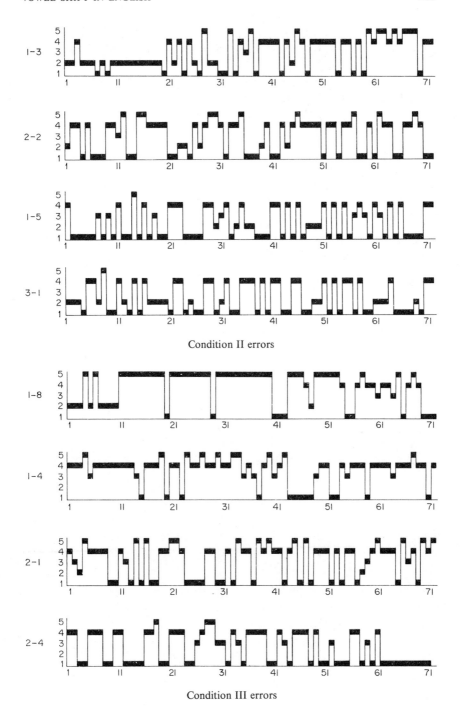

Condition II errors

Condition III errors

Subject 2–1. Also never adopted a consistent strategy. Type (5) errors were random: For īy → ă, there were 3 ēy responses (4, 38, 40), 3 ĕ responses (21, 45, 61) and 3 ēy, ă responses (14, 16, 22).

Subject 2–4. Type (5) errors were ĕ for ēy → ĭ (# 28, 29) and ĭ, ĕ for īy → ă (# 18). Strategies before criterion were not apparent.

ACKNOWLEDGMENTS

I am grateful to John Ohala, Charles A. Ferguson, Victoria A. Fromkin, Robert H. Whitman, William S-Y. Wang, and Susan Ervin-Tripp for their helpful comments on earlier versions of this paper, and to the Anna Head School of Oakland and the Girl Scouts of Berkeley for their cooperation in the experiments described here. Carol Ann Moore, Robert Krones, and Gus Haggstrom were very helpful with the statistical analysis. I also want to thank the members of the Phonology Laboratory of the University of California, Berkeley for their support and encouragement. The work was supported by the National Science Foundation.

SOME STRATEGIES FOR THE FIRST TWO YEARS[1]

SUSAN ERVIN-TRIPP
University of California, Berkeley

Studies of children's texts and of such other performances as comprehension and imitation have given some basis for testing plausible generalizations about what is necessary for language processing in its early stages. In this chapter, the prerequisites to language will be considered in the form of environmental circumstances, cognitive development, and children's information storage. On the basis of these considerations, we will examine the basic acquisition of regularities of order and inflection, the fundamental grammatical features found in the early performances of children.

PREREQUISITES TO LANGUAGE LEARNING

Languages consist of patterned surface signals which are correlated, under particular circumstances, with extralinguistic events. In the adult language learner, who hears talk about abstract ideas and about events at a distance in time and space, the meanings of utterances may appear to bear little relation to external events, except when he goes shopping. Yet, *the learner must know the referent for learning of language to occur.*

We shall consider here three categories of prerequisites to language learn-

---

[1] An earlier version of this paper appears as "The onset of grammar" in a memorial volume for Ruth Hirsch Weir edited by M. J. Hardman-de Bautista and V. Honsa. This version has been considerably enriched by the papers and the discussion at the Buffalo conference, as it was scheduled for the final day.

ing. The first consists of what the environment must provide, the others the knowledge which language refers to, and the processing skills which the child brings to the learning task. Where evidence is lacking, we hope in this way to draw attention to the need.

Environmental Input

Since children learn to speak except under conditions of radical isolation, we assume that the input conditions necessary are relatively simple:

Orientation toward the Signals

If acoustic input is relatively random in relation to events of importance to the child, as is the case if it consists entirely of radio or TV broadcasts, the child may be unable to discover its structure. We have observed hearing children of deaf parents who had learned no speech from such input. The recurrence of signals at times of significance to the child, such as feeding, being changed, being held, being stimulated visually, may single out that channel, be it sound or gesture, for special attention.

Co-occurrence of Speech with Referential Events

Let us suppose that parents held philosophical discourse in the presence of a baby, but never talked about the here and now. A child might in these conditions parrot gross features of their behavior, but the imitations would contain as many fortuitous as linguistically important features of speech. A significant portion of speech must refer to those relations, concrete objects, and events which are already attended to by the child.

Linguists argue that it is contrast of meaning which identifies which features of the sounds or of the grammatical patterns are significant; without such a criterion, the child would have no clue, except recurrence, to indicate which features must be stored as critical in absolute identification of items.

Is this to argue that nothing at all is learned from input devoid of meaning? Experiments with adults (see description in Ervin-Tripp, 1970b, p. 340, 341, 348) suggest that meaningless material, even presented systematically so as to contrast acceptable and extraneous sounds, is destructive to language acquisition, possibly because the adults assign invented meanings to the forms. But these were adults. We do not know the extent to which hearing sentences without any referent can be in any way instructive about the structure of the sound system. The Hayes and Clark (1970) experiment with artificial sounds suggests that recurrent sequences may become salient and be stored even without the help of meaning, but their material lacked the phonetic diversity of actual speech since it was artificially produced.

It is certainly the case, however, that reference must be present for the new learner to acquire syntax. We do not always know, of course, what the content of the recurrent reference is for the child, what features of the environment, of his own states, or of the consequences of his speech he observes in storing words like *want*, *all-gone*, and *more*. Reference is not meant here in the simple sense of observable objects, since it is clear that, from the beginning, children's interpretations are more complex.

If stability of interpretation is required, then a considerable amount of the speech environment of children may be irrelevant to the learning of grammar, because the interpretation of none of the utterance is clear to him.

It may not be necessary that repetitive exposure occur, if conditions are optimal. Asher (1965) has experimented with brief learning trials in which second language input cooccurred with actions by the learner to which the sentences or words referred. There was a dramatic effectiveness in making the cooccurrence of signal and referent optimal in time, in salience, and in sensory richness. The rapid fading of the acoustic signal may make simultaneity important.

Recurrence of Vocabulary in Diverse Environments;
Moderate Vocabulary Diversity

In order to identify the more abstract units, starting with form classes, children must hear component units in the diverse positions possible. Not all lexicon, obviously, needs to meet this condition; once classes, or phrase markers for lexicon are acquired, a single encounter can mark new vocabulary appropriately. Conversely, varied entries in a fixed environment may be needed to teach formal features. This is less clear, since if entries share semantic features, they may be spontaneously grouped as a class, without this requirement.

The issue of formal class learning is obviously central. Some characteristics of the input may affect efficiency of learning. It could be argued that the existing properties of languages have arisen because they create input distributions which accelerate acquisition, a point which will be expanded later in this chapter.

In addition, observations of input in this country have shown that special conditions of parent and sibling style to infants may contribute to the type of diversity experienced by the child. One feature is simplicity of structure, in the sense of brevity, few subordinations, few passives, lack of false starts and intercalated material. The result is a surface that maximizes the frequency of simple declaratives and of the constituent phrases that occur in answers.

The argument that input is degenerate, confusing, that the surface orders in English are displayed in so many permutations that simple order heuristics relating surface orders to meanings would be impossible must be produced from observations of speech styles at conferences, not in family kitchens. Input simplicity and grammaticality do not remove the problem of later learning of complex orders, but they do make the discovery of the first structures much less a problem.

Further, input to children is characterized by repetitiveness. Contrary to linguists' belief that phrases are not repeated, in speech to children they are repeated ad nauseam. Kobashigawa (1968) found that it was common in speech to children to maintain the same message across several sentences, varying minor features which do not alter meaning, such as intonation, rate, word order where noncritical, or optional deletions and contractions. In input to Finnish children, elements such as subject–verb–object are permuted in such repetitions (Bowerman, 1970). In these circumstances, the semantic equivalence of formal alternatives, given maintenance of the external situation across the sentences, would be apparent.

Several special styles which occur in some cultures as inputs have theoretically possible accelerating effects. One is discourse modeling, in which questions and answers are both supplied by the interlocutor. Examples are given by Jean Berko-Gleason in this volume. The *Where's the doggy, There's the doggy* types of sentences found in early child texts may reflect such input, in which replacement or discourse agreement is instructed.

In expansions, the child phrases his intention as an utterance, and the interlocutor alters the utterance in the direction of the presumed adult model. The child who has simply made an omission at that point is likely to imitate the expansion correctly, with no effect on his basic system of comprehension or production (though he learns what adults attend to). If the child uses the information in the missing morphemes already, as shown by comprehension tests, but makes uniform or linguistically conditioned omissions, he may not even recognize any difference in surface structure between his own output and the expansion because the omission arises from a low-level production rule, like certain articulatory neutralizations. The effectiveness of expansions in changing basic language structure probably is increased when (a) the interlocutor's interpretation matches the child's intention; and (b) the child's deletions arise because he has not attended to the missing elements, which are just "noisy" to him (Shipley, Smith, & Gleitman, 1969). Under these conditions, when the child has already produced part of the sentence, his storage capacities may be freed for attention to and storage of additional components.

In Cazden's (1963) experiment comparing expansions with modeling (supplying relevant comments in reply whenever the child spoke), the expansions were not controlled for either of these features, yet some gain in output mastery over controls occurred. The increment in output length or output developmental measures was greatest for the modeling condition. It seems likely that the experimenters unwittingly supplied some structural repetition of the child's speech with added vocabulary diversity.

Prerequisite Knowledge

In discovering the relation between utterance and meaning, the child must bring his knowledge of possible meanings to the analysis of input. Thus, a major issue for the study of the development of grammar is the assessment of knowledge through nonlinguistic means. In the case of the child's communicative acts, the problem includes the study of intentions.

It is a striking finding of observers in a wide variety of languages around the world that the meanings in the early sentences of children seem to be confined to a relatively restricted and shared set. While it is true that some samples have not included all of this set, the omissions are slight, and could easily reflect sampling deficiencies or cultural and situational biases which affect the child's intentions while being taped.

Here are two sample lists:

List A	*List B*
Cigarette down.	Girl rides.
Give me candy.	Bring candy.
Candy mine.	Baby's eyes.
Hit you.	Baby fell.
Give me banana.	Put down.
You eat?	Baby walks.
I want water.	Wants sleep.
Ball there.	Keith there.
Go home.	Go there.
This visitor.	Your baby.

It is not obvious that List A was collected in Kenya from Luo children (Blount, 1969), and List B in Samoa (Kernan, 1969).

Establishing early knowledge from a list of sentence meanings is obviously not the best route. It is too limited. As Bloom (in press) points out some utterances (her examples were *away*, *there*, and *more*) are not in fact semantically richer when the noun is produced. The child's early one-word utterances in these cases may arise from a poverty of naming lexicon. It is common, also, in the case of possessives to find the named possessor used alone in the same contexts as the later construction. There is no reason to assume any enrichment of the child's intentions or knowledge at this point, though linguistic skill has increased.

On the other hand, while many meanings in common early sentences may antedate sentence output considerably, sentences may deceive us. We do not know whether the production of actor-action sentences implies any abstraction of a concept of actor. Therefore, the following collection of examples is given to suggest that we need much richer studies of the intentional evidence concerning these relations using techniques which are not linguistic.

(*a*) *Modality* refers to the contrast between asking, demanding, and commenting. This difference may be signaled by gesture and paralinguistic features before identifiable words begin. Gruber (1967) has claimed that one child whom he studied intensively with particularly rich extralinguistic filmed information, did not make any comments in the earlier stages of multimorphemic utterances. She always made demands, either that the listener look at or hand over.

Early sentences often contain explicit lexicon referring to questions (*Where shoe?*), or to demands (*I want dolly.*), but where a single noun occurs, it may not be obvious whether the utterance functions as a demand or as an identification or existence predication.

(*b*) *Vocatives* occur early, but are not, strictly speaking, relations. In many early texts we have examples of attention-getters, whether gestural—by tugging on an arm—or vocal—by calling a name. The name of the addressee, or a vocative, is often included in sentences having other functions and is typically not integrated grammatically.

(*c*) *Identification* and *Existence*. Statements naming referents may be one-term nominatives, like *dolly*, or they may contain more elements like *see dolly, this dolly*. There is no evidence that these differences in surface representation represent semantic contrasts. This category is of course rich in cognitive antecedents since it requires isolation of objects and categories. Proper and common names appear undifferentiated at first, in the sense that in both cases the child supplies a generalization range.

Existence or notice utterances are situationally marked by a kind of discovery, but they do not appear to be marked by enough structural contrast to allow easy separation from demonstratives.

(*d*) *Nonexistence* and *negation*. *No page, no rabbit, all gone puzzle, car away*, are examples, and of course single negators in isolation precede. In the text of a deaf child's early two-component sign utterances, Geballe (1969) found an absence of negators, but this may be idiosyncratic, or due to small sample size. In Park's text of a Korean child, there were substantial numbers of negatives, both of the refusal and nonexistence type. *Train there-is-not, no eat* (imp.).

(*e*) *Recurrence* of objects or events appears in *more apple, another toy, more throw*. These can be either descriptions or demands, and may occur without specification of object.

(*f*) *Location*. Locational notions are among the earliest acquisitions of the child, and in the course of language development locational questions and adverbs precede temporal expressions of analogous structural difficulty by years. The questioned location, as in *Where shoe*, to which the answer is pointing, is produced and understood from the beginning of questions. Early locational statements like *dolly car*, or *go car* refer to places, on, or in which another thing or action is, or to destinations. Prolocatives like *here*, or *there*, appear in a variety of languages, but it is not evident that they are differentiated.

Many forms used in English as verbs contain locational contrasts: *baby up* means to lift the baby up, *sweater off* to change the location of a sweater. *Fall down* is an early English term requiring locational change in a specific direction. Given the presence of locations in identification and action sentences at Stage I, it is not surprising that at the next stage, when the surface structure is longer, locational information often is added to otherwise long strings, and that in the development of prepositions, differentiation of location occurs relatively early.

(*g*) *Possession*. In early sentences it is common to find utterances like *candy mine*, *your baby*, and *baby's eyes*, which are very stable in the order of elements or locus of suffix. The constituents are a possessor, which usually is + animate, allowing for metaphorical extension to dolls and stuffed animals, and an object consisting of a part of the body, clothing, or a concrete object not inherently possessed. In the ontogeny of these representations, we may find *Mommy* when pointing to Mommy's shoe, suggesting a loose associational relation.

But if all that the possessive relation involved for a child was a loose association of possessor often seen with possessed, the order stability in the surface representations would be impossible, since there would be no designation of an asymmetry in the relation to identify an order.

In one sense, the relation of possession is the first in English in which the components do not themselves specify the structural meaning, with the exception of possessive pronouns. Lois Bloom (in press), has pointed out that "certain conceptions of experience are coded by particular word forms, function forms, which however, make reference only by virtue of their contextual relations to other features of experience. . . . Certain conceptions of experience are coded by the interrelations among different categories of substantive word forms. Such categories are linguistic, and defined on the basis of relative occurrence of words in structural relationships that have distinctive meanings. Such structural meanings are independent of the lexical meanings of the forms within categories."

If the possessive construction, such as *Mommy glove* meets this criterion, it does not preclude the existence of what appear to be possessive assertions prior to two-word utterances. As Bloom points out, the conception of experience is separable from the form of codification, and could well much antedate overt realization in language. Because of its structural interest, the contrast between acquisition of pronoun and nominal constructions of the possessive (using order, not inflection) provides a nice contrast for study of Bloom's ideas of alternative strategies for the acquisition of grammatical structures.

(*h*) *Conjunction.* Pairing, usually of nominals without a marker. I do not know of any cases of pairing of other forms in hearing children. Possibly, sensory adjacence, even visual, is the only source at first, for pairing. It may be that even a slight time delay on input, as in the case of successive acts, may impede coding at first, except in separate utterances. It certainly is the case that children can perceive and store successions of acts, since they can even perform integrated imitated sequences by the end of the second year.

(*i*) *Attribution.* The ability to discern attributes obviously must be a fairly early feature of child cognition, but the eventual coexistence of attribute and head term in linguistic codification implies a further distinction, between the term which functions as head and a subordinated feature which is considered secondary to a primary class membership. It is not clear what the cognitive implications of the difference may be. In some cases, where there is feature intersection, the distinction would appear to be somewhat arbitrary or conventional, but in English at least, head terms tend to refer to the function class of an object rather than to its size, shape, color, or material, or to temporary conditions. The fact that changes of focus can lead to the shift of the head must make the surface difference somewhat opaque semantically, to children, in instances where the shift is common. In some of my early texts, such descriptive terms as *broken* had distributions identical to nouns, e.g., *see the broken.*

Attributes are not among the most frequently coded aspects of child experience, except for possession and quantification, and one would guess that the differences which appear in the texts so far may reflect some differences in input to children. The common adjectives used in English are such terms as *big, little, pretty, poor* (in the sense of injured), and *broken.* Most commonly, these occur in prenominal rather than predicate position, suggesting that they are usually used either as identifiers or conventional parts of names, rather than as foregrounded predications by those who speak to children. In some cases, adjective–noun, or noun–noun sequences appear from the phonological forms to be unsegmented, as in the case of *mommycar* and *daddycar* in some texts of mine, the basis being a possessive noun used in the family as a conventional identifier and thus always present as part of the object name. In the case of Kathryn II, cited by Bloom (1970), the terms *bear book, puppy book,* and *tiger book* are quite possibly not invented by the child, since there is a series of books so titled.

(*j*) *Action–agent–object.* Words describing actions occur early, though it is common to specify only one or two of the components of a three- or four-part predicate like *put* or *give*, which have three nominal complements. Normally, the agent is animate and the majority of objects, but not all, are inanimate. Bowerman found that subjects of action verbs might be vehicles. When expansion of noun phrases occurs, it is either in identification sentences or in objects. Perhaps inanimates more often have attributes as identifiers.

(*k*) *States.* Stative verbs like *want, like, see, have,* appear in the earliest sentences. It is not always obvious, of course, that they are semantically clearly distinguished from active counterparts (*see the book, look at the book*). Nor do all children have such forms in the texts we have seen. Both the Luo and Samoan, but not the Finnish texts had *want,* the most common of these.

(*l*) *Recipients.* Datives or indirect objects can be found in early texts, though like attributives and states they may be sparse. Parisi and Antinucci (1970), have pointed out a parallel between the complement structure of verbs like *give* which require recipients, and *put* which requires a locative complement. In these cases, languages impose obligatory components which are already well within the cognitive capacity of children.

However, the complexity of codification is increased by these linguistic rules, and it is in the coding task that the children have trouble. Parisi's and Antinucci's system permits comparison between development of coding in different languages or in different types of sentences within a language, with the complexity of formal structure controlled.

It is obvious that semantic development precedes its verbal expression and continues to grow independently, as manifested, for instance, in temporal categories. Slobin (in press) has asserted that these cognitive relations are not affected by the learning of language, which merely provides representations for them. This may well be the case with universal categories, in which common conditions of life, or, at least, of the interaction of child and milieu, have been such as to guarantee development; in these cases it must be true that language is merely a manifestation. On the other hand, in cases where particular languages have categories that are idiosyncratic, the presence of the contrast might accelerate observation of a cognitive category or relation. An example is the study by Carroll and Casagrande (1958) of the shape categories codified by Navaho verb stems of handling and placement. These are high frequency forms in child speech, and strikingly correlated with concrete categories of shape like long rigid, flat flexible, and so on. Navaho-speaking children choose shape over color earlier than non-Navaho-speaking children from the same milieu. Nursery school training in Boston had the same impact in creating form preference in English-speaking children, so there are other ways besides language to create dimensional saliency.

The requirement that the child be able to identify sames in the signal is simply one other aspect of isolating recurrences with many transformations in the environment, but the fact that these events are auditory, and involve changes related to features of the adjacent sounds rather than spatial and light transformations, may alter what properties of perception and storage are required. Bever's (1971a) observation that long jargon utterances of a baby may be consistent situationally suggests that the first units may be fairly large. Since we are concerned here with grammatical acquisition, we will simply have to assume the child's ability to process speech sounds in such a way as to identify and store recurrent patterns.

Storage Factors

If simultaneity of referential event and speech is a precondition of learning to understand speech, then it is necessary that one, or both, be stored for comparison. Young children's own speech tends to refer to ongoing events like naming of time or locations, or to immediately past events, as in *dolly fall down*. When adults speak of distant events, they may overtax the child's ability to match meaning and utterance.

But even when utterances refer to the present, the rapid fading of the acoustic signal may require a short-term storage of acoustic information to allow work by the hearer in comparing the input with his referential knowledge. Given the small capacity in the immediate-memory span, the selectivity of such storage is important in child language learning. Studies of imitation and of detection thresholds suggest the following generalizations about material with the highest probability of retention in short-term storage:

(*a*) *The most recent material.* On the whole, spontaneous imitations draw selectively on the end of input material. Theories of memory would predict the strongest control of the most recent input, given the fluctuating attention of spontaneous imitations.

(*b*) *Initial words.* There may be some slight advantage of onset material over what is in the middle, for unanalyzed new input, providing the child is already attending.

(*c*) *Vowel quality of stressed syllables.*

(*d*) *Intonational contour*, level of pitch, and other gross paralinguistic features.

(*e*) *Friction and nasality.*

(*f*) *Order* properties of sequential auditory material as discribed above.

Since short-term storage is a prerequisite to building up long-term information about language, there will be prior acquisition of contrasts of the following types:

(*i*) *Prosodic contrasts and terminal juncture contrasts should be acquired early.*

In languages where modality contrasts can be signaled by prosodic cues, these occur before segmental contrasts like question words or inversions are used. In Japanese, Miyakara (1971) found that prosodic cues were used before the postpositional -ka.

(ii) *Particles, enclitics and items which are sentence final should be learned early, before prefixes and other material earlier in utterances.*

In Japanese, *yo* and *ne*, which are clause-final, are the first functors (Miyakara, 1971).

(iii) *Suffixes should be learned more easily than prefixes, and postpositions more easily than prepositions.*

The most striking support comes from the Mikeš and Vlahović (1966) study, in which bilinguals learned locatives in Hungarian before they used comparable prepositions making similar semantic contrasts in Serbo-Croatian, Slobin quotes Pačesová (1968) on Czech evidence that recency is stronger than stress as a determinant, since initial stressed syllables are often omitted in Czech child speech.

A beautiful example of the intersection of the two systems in the long-term storage of a child is provided by Malmberg's 1945 account of the acquisition of Swedish by a Finnish-speaking child. In this case, of course, we are examining the cumulative effects of varying short-term storage experiences, in which the child was able to juxtapose presumed meaning with whatever surface she stored. Saliency of meaning obviously led to the retention of the noun stem, but the rest of the material gives a good comparison between prestem and poststem order. The initial pattern of the child of course had a Finnish noun stem followed by Finnish morphological material. The replacement as she began to change her speech was in the following order:

(1) Replacement of noun stem by Swedish noun.
(2) The Swedish noun stem receives a Swedish suffix, followed still by the Finnish postpositional as before.
(3) The Finnish postposition is replaced by a Swedish preposition used *following* the noun and its suffix.
(4) The preposition is correctly placed.

It can be seen here that the general order of putting in information in produced sentences is the hardest to change. The first shift is in the lexical material, as we would expect, rather than in inflections. The Swedish suffix, rather than the preposition, is the next most noticeable element, and is readily produced because it can replace a Finnish suffix in the same position. The preposition was the last feature, and curiously enough, though it was learned correctly, at first it was produced in the position of the semantically corresponding form in Finnish. The formal skeleton for the production of semantic information still retained a Finnish syntactic programming, though the morphophonemic content was Swedish. In terms of the order of intro- duction of morphological elements, the order noun stem, then suffix, and preposition last to be learned, is what we would expect on the basis of semantic and perceptual salience.

(*iv*) *Sentence-initial fixed-position forms should be learned more easily than material in the middle of utterances.*

In English, question words are learned very easily, as well as the demon- stratives and pro-locatives which often initiate descriptions. According to my evidence, English-speaking children learning French systematically omit preverbal pronouns in both imitation and production unless they are sentence-initial—even when there is no difference in the sentence length or the specific pronoun involved.

(*v*) *Morphemes which are syllabic should be learned more easily than con- sonantal morphemes.*

In the Mikeš and Vlahović (1966) study, the suffix-*u* rather than-*t* was used in both languages, then -*ut*.

(*vi*) *Friction and nasal morphemes should be understood sooner than stop or glide forms*, though there could be articulatory problems in their production by the child.

(*vii*) *Relative order of stem and affix should not be altered.* There is no case in the child-language data in which this has occurred, to my knowledge.

(*viii*) *Relative order of high-frequency morpheme sequences should not be altered.*

(*ix*) *Where there is dominant order for classes having structural meaning, when that construction is acquired, it will reflect input order.*

(*x*) *Unstressed syllables may be lost in storage of words.* The Czech case cited earlier indicates that recency may be a stronger factor than stress.

LONG-TERM LEARNING

Braine (1971a) has proposed that recurrence prevents the decay of stored information, and that certain properties of the stored surface string, when repeatedly processed through short-term storage, will be preserved as the normal form of strings. Presumably, according to his model, this will happen whether or not the sentences have meaning, and his experimental work shows that adults can recognize novel but meaningless utterances conforming to a recurrent simple set of morphological rules.

Acquisition of Affixes and Function Words

Like lexicon in particular sentences, functors differ in saliency. The factors which are likely to influence the frequency with which functors are kept in short-term storage and become candidates for the discovery of relations to extralinguistic conditions have been discussed earlier.

We can expect that if the semantic motivation for inflectional variation is not apparent, (e.g., in the gender variation instance) the child may store the most frequent lexical form. He may learn *shoes* before *shoe*, but *dog* before *dogs*. In Finnish, verbs are first represented in the third singular form, and locatives in the allative or directional case, in Bowerman's sample. Park, on the other hand, found action verbs more often in the Korean imperative. It seems obvious that the milieu of use will influence the most frequent form of an inflected item, and this milieu probably varies with the semantic content of the item, as well as with such factors as whether the form is explicitly taught to the child in a citation form. Even siblings learning French under very similar social conditions have been observed to differ in the preferred form of some items (e.g., *pris* for one child, *prends* for the other, for the French *prendre*) before inflection or conjugation occurs. At any rate, we probably cannot make the assumption that conditions are the same for all items in a form class or for all children. We know, for example, that some children select *foot* and some *feet* as the basic form, and can only guess that input frequency is the determinant.

The first appearance of contrastive inflections seems to depend on the obviousness of the semantic contrast as well as the salience of the morpheme. It seems plausible that as early as a child could semantically contrast subject and object orders productively in English, he might be able to use inflections for the same purpose, say in Garo (Burling, 1959), and we do learn that Burling's child used inflections simultaneously with syntactic contrast, and that inflectional contrasts appear very early in Finnish (Argoff).

The importance of the semantic function of the morpheme rather than its frequency is brought out by the example of *wa* and *ga* in Japanese. *Wa* occurs more frequently, yet it is *ga* that appears earlier in children's usage. Two differences in semantic function seem to account for the preference for *ga*. *Wa* can mark either the subject, the object, or any phrase to which attention is drawn. It is often translated as "as for *x*," so one can say "as for the table, we ate on it," or "as for John, he left," or "as for Mother's, it was lost." *Ga*, on the other hand, only can mark a subject, so that it differs in marking a class with a unique grammatical function. Further, rather than reforegrounding understood, often antecedent information, *ga* typically identifies new information, and in that sense is likely to be more focal and more important: "As for the glass, it was the boy who broke it." In this sentence, it is the boy, rather than the glass, which is new information to the hearer, and we have glass-*wa*, boy-*ga*. The glass has been mentioned before, is presumably implicit, or was an implied contrast to some anteced- ent. The phrase could in fact be omitted if the presumption is clear. Thus, both clarity of grammatical function, and novelty and focus would give preference to *ga*. With *ga*, there need be no ambiguity of subject and object; with only *wa*, there would be.

If the clarity of the correlation between the surface form and the meaning is obscured by the intersection of factors like gender which produce noise, or by allomorphs related to phonological conditioning, then we would expect the most information-bearing minimal features for the contrast.

For example, in Serbo-Croatian, the contrast between locative and direc- tional suffixes is complicated by gender, so we have -*a*, -*i*, and -*u* as feminine case contrasts, and for the same three cases ∅, -*u*, and -*a* or ∅ as masculine suffixes. Only the feminine locative -*i* is unambiguous, and other things being equal, we would expect it to be preferred as a locative suffix over -*u* when case distinctions begin. Thus we argue that clarity of contrast is more im- portant than frequency, since -*u* as accusative must be very frequent. In this argument we follow Slobin's similar notion, in his analysis of Russian affix acquisition.

By the same token, we would expect clear contrasts, like French *les* (plural object pronoun) to be acquired before *le* versus *la* for object pronouns even where gender is obvious for animate objects, because of the noisy presence of *le* and *la* for inanimate objects. This priority can be seen in second- language learning of French.

Most thinking about long-term storage of children has been focused on grammatical rather than phonological issues. We know now that infants can make fine phonetic distinctions, and recognize change between adjacent inputs, but we do not know from this finding how selection is made for the long-term storage which makes absolute judgments possible. How the critical distinctive information could be selected in the absence of experience with meaning contrasts remains puzzling unless holistic, long-term auditory "eidetic imagery" is possible.

Analysis of children's speech confuses the articulatory regularities of the child's system with the perception and storage issue, though it certainly provides some minimal basis for judging what must be a core system. In Braine's characterization of Joan Velten's development, for example, it is clear that lexical storage must at least provide for the fully controlled, nonredundant features, such as syllabic and coronal, and for some of the partially controlled features such as continuant and strident, since Joan could recognize words contrasted in these features and reproduce them at a later time. The notion that lexical storage is efficiently nonredundant does not necessarily correspond to the psychological facts.

Joan Velten clearly had some articulatory problems, since Velten reports that she produced /baza'/ as an output for /bada'/, and shortly after produced /bada'/ and contrasted the two. His description gives the impression that the problem was one of production. The phonotactic rules which affected her production could quite easily not have affected her discrimination. For example, she had considerable consistency in producing final consonants, even nasals, without voicing, but if such a feature affected her receptive processing she should have displayed recognition difficulties where voicing was an issue.

Messer (1967) and Menyuk (1968) have tried to find methods which locate phonotactic features of discrimination and recognition in children, and showed that children did react to violations of regular English phonotactic features. Children can also recognize accents. The extent to which this kind of learning could occur, apart from the acquisition of meaning, is not known. In addition, Menyuk and Messer did not provide the kind of stimuli which would allow the analysis of the order of acquisition of specific phonotactic rules, for comparison with the Braine characterization for instance.

While it is common for linguists to deplore the separation of the analysis of heard from spoken material because they do not want to think there are multiple grammars, there is no reason to assume that processing strategies for heard material would be identical with the organization required for production. This contrast is most striking, of course, in phonotactics.

LEARNING ORDER REGULARITIES

Potential Strategies

Grammar-recognition learning involves recognizing relations between order or function patterns and properties of meaning. Braine's (1971a) work has focused on the recognition of order regularities and the conditions for such learning without concern for the bearing that semantic correlates may have on facilitation of such learning. Semantic contrasts, of course, are only part of what is learned; it is a dramatic feature of both first and second language that they go further than intelligibility requires in the direction of learning of formal and stylistic correctness. In the case of children, meaning contrasts do seem important in relation to determinants of order of acquisition.

The logical possibilities for a child faced with a signal which cooccurs with understood meanings are that the child simply ignore order features in the signal, that she store order in terms of invariant positions, and that she store the relative orders in terms of probabilities when they are variable. These possibilities, and the relevant evidence, are considered below. A good deal of the evidence comes from sentence output by children, which, of course, has special characteristics relative to issues of recognition and storage.

Random Order

It used to be thought (see Burling, 1959, for example) that children's first sentences were somewhat randomly ordered in terms of syntax. Suppose that the child discerns the relation between words and their meanings, but does not store any information about the orders of words, erasing what is in short-term memory about word order, but retaining order information as it affects morphemes within words. In the texts, we have, we do not find random order. It seems unlikely that words are sufficiently distinct as units to children, especially in the typical repetitive input, to allow such a radical contrast between the type of information stored in the lexicon and in the rest of the storage device.

Preserve Features of Invariant Positions

If a fixed morpheme like a question particle occurs sentence-finally, the modality contrast it signals may be recognized early. In the case of English question words, a group of words have nearly invariant position; in child speech, question words are always sentence-initial, reflecting adult usage. We do not know whether relocating question words would interfere with their comprehension. In my work on answering questions, (Ervin-Tripp, 1970a) the question word seemed rather like a dummy item with a fixed position for 2-year-olds, in that children recognized that a question had been asked, but might answer as though a different question word had been used, the determinants of the choice depending on features of the rest of the sentence, like transitivity of the verb. The shared phonological features of question words in many languages may help in identifying them as such, at first, without any additional semantic features.

A storage device which marks certain lexical items as initial or final, or a sentence-producing device that is position-specified has quite limited utility. Speakers cannot in fact easily recall specific positions other than initial and final, so that only these positions could be indexed. The rest of the indexing would have to be relative rather than in terms of absolute position.

Store Relative Order

In languages where order carries semantic information, as in the contrast subject–object in English, the child must store specific instances like *pet the kitty* in order to allow him eventually to recognize that the item acted on normally follows the action word, and to abstract the relation between action and object, and match it with an order. In German, following modals the normal order is object–verb, and so it is common for children to learn object-action rather than action-object. Sentences with modals are frequent input to children, if our texts in English are appropriate examples. In Roeper's (this volume) new data, the morphological evidence is clear, since in many cases the children preserve the infinitive suffix, as in examples: *Bleistift holen*, and *Mama Schühchen anziehen*.

The eventual result is the strategy which Bever has identified as a matching of an NVN surface with an agent–action–object interpretation, at a certain age. Sinclair (this volume) reported that 37% of the 6-year-olds in her study still interpreted *box-push-boy* as agent–action–object. This strategy is found even later as well. We find that English speakers who firmly control passive structures in English use the NVN comprehension strategy at first on foreign language utterances, according to my evidence from French. Is this a reflection more strongly of relative noun positions, or the relation of one or both nouns to the verb? Sinclair's important study of French allows us to find that this strategy is much more complex in development than would at first appear.

She presented *garçon pousser fille* in six permutations. The form of this verb permits interpretation as a past participle (i.e., passive), imperfect, or imperative. Because French employs order rather than stress for foregrounding and contrast, it is likely that NVN order may be less common in input to children than it is in English. For example, one could say, "*C'est la fille que le garçon a poussé*," "*il a poussé la fille, le garçon*," or "*poussez, garçons et filles!*"

There were the following major types of response:

(*a*) Some of the youngest children themselves always acted as agents, disregarding completely the order of the words as though they heard only an imperative.

(*b*) Most of the children under 4 interpreted the sentences in terms of the dolls as agents. In particular, the noun just preceding the verb was likely to be treated as an agent, whether or not there was a transitive complement. Thus the subject–verb relation appears primary.

(*c*) The relative order of the two nouns played some role relatively early, so that the first of the two nouns in NNV might be interpreted as subject even though it did not immediately precede the verb. This strategy grew and dominated the choices of the 6-year-olds.

(*d*) Eventually some children, began to attend to the action-patient relation. This strategy of attention to VO occurred at the same age as the reappearance of the child-as-agent but only for NNV. These children of five seemed to be interpreting the sentence as *fille garçon poussés*. We could call this descriptive or patient-focused strategy. Eventually, such sentences can lay the basis for passives.

One of the mysteries in Bever's studies of the development of the noun–verb–noun strategy was that he has reported that some very young children correctly gave passive interpretations. We might attribute such responses to patient focus or a descriptive orientation which sees the verb as a kind of participle or description. The most important finding in Sinclair's study is that the first order strategy is agent–action focus, and that action–patient focus is not as early in appearance. This directly goes counter to McNeill's view that the verb–object unit is elementary, because it comprises a fundamental sentence constituent, the verb phrase. It is probably necessary to distinguish verbs with highly selective contexts from those, like *pousser* selected because its object could in fact be animate or inanimate. Such sequences as *drink milk* might very well be primary units of comprehension well before action-patient focus in reversible sentences.

If agent–action supplies the first-order rule, the expectation is confirmed that highly frequent and adjacent orders in the surface structure will be learned quite easily, as we find in looking at possessor–possessed, agent–action, demonstrative–nominal in beginning grammars. Sentences which deviate from adult order, like *all gone toy* reflect semantic overgeneralization since the attribute- or quantifier-head sequence of the sentence is quite suitable to the majority of input cases.

Store Probabilities of Order

The surface order of units may not be consistent, either because it is affected by transforms unfamiliar to the child (e.g., the English passive), or because the language does not in fact employ a consistent syntactic order in signaling a semantic contrast, as in the case of Finnish agent–action–object. In such cases, the learner is evidently capable of storing a probability record. In the case of English, we find children who make occasional reversals of verb–object to object–verb, possibly reflecting passives or infinitive inputs, though passives are rare in input to most children in our samples, according to Drach (1969) and Pfuderer (1969). In Finnish, Bowerman (1970) reported a rough correspondence between the relative order for given structural types in the adult input and the child's order.

This table makes clear that Rina's mother's most frequent construction was prolocative–noun, and this dominated for the child also. Seppo's mother's dominant type was subject–verb, and this dominated for Seppo.

Table 1 *Structural Frequencies in Finnish Speech (Bowerman)*

	Seppo	Seppo's mother	Rina	Rina's mother
Subject–verb	81	47	36	14
Verb–subject	27	5	1	2
Verb–object	24	16	16	14
Object–verb	7	3	5	—
SVO	13	32	27	11
SOV	—	1	3	1
OVS	2	1	—	—
OSV	1	—	2	—
VSO	—	1	1	1
VOS	—	—	—	—
Noun–prolocative	13	14	16	15
Prolocative–noun	19	41	97	31

The lower frequency of Seppo's SVO relative to his mother's is due to the fact he was at an earlier stage of language development than Rina, and used more two-word than three-word utterances. In each set of alternative orders, the dominant order is the same for adults and children, but the alternative orders, if adults use them, appear in child speech. It would take fine-grained contingency analysis of the texts to find out if this order correspondence simply reflects some discourse echoing on a short-range basis, rather than any basic features of the child's grammar. In examining some order alternations in my own texts involving verb–object and object–verb changes, I found that what the adult said was often picked up by the child, and therefore produced the appearance of alternation. In this way, I might be able to alter the frequency of passive in the speech of an interlocutor by raising my own frequency in a conversation.

Adult Repetitions and Expansions Define Equivalence

Where adjacent synonymous repetitions in the input are order-preserving, whether the repetitions are of the speaker or are expansions of the child's speech, the child learns to preserve order in imitations, and to retain order specifications in determining structural meanings. Where the parental repetitions or expansions freely transform order, as has been observed in Turkish and Finnish, children freely vary order in imitations. Whether there is a direct relation between this particular form of input and the child's processing of order information, we do not know. Such an experiment would require control over these varying types of input, including stability of order in all utterances of a given type addressed to the child.

GRAMMATICAL STORAGE

Word-Matrix Storage

What is the nature of the storage device? What does it store? One possibility is that it stores a word matrix. We know that speakers have remarkably good knowledge of word frequencies in the language (Howes, 1957). On this basis, maybe higher order matrices are stored. The strongest argument against such a device is its weakness. Such a device is too weak to generate novel sequences like *all gone puzzle* which we know occur and have consistent grammatical properties.

If a word matrix existed, then the tallying of adjacent stressed words in texts of input to children would yield sentences like those found in children's speech. Here is a set of examples: *does go, color my, what hold, come eat, happened know, going open, diaper for, animal this, here big*. To anyone familiar with children's sentences these sound strange.

It seems clear that many prepackaged sequences must be stored by speakers, appearing as phrases, idioms, cliches, whose production and comprehension can partially bypass normal sentence processing routes.

Whatever storage device makes possible the retention of lexemes realized as words and phrases must also contain material which involves sequences heard more than once. In comprehension we have usually assumed that there is erasure or loss of surface information with retention only of semantic material. Sachs (1967) has shown that synonyms cannot be distinguished nor passives separated from actives after relatively small intervening material. But if it were the case that only semantic information is retained, language learning could not occur. There must be some storage of the phonological markers and semantic features inferred from the milieu of a new item for it to become part of the dictionary.[2] It is not obvious that the device which accomplishes such storage has a strict word boundary and would refuse to store frequent sequences longer than words. The nature of the abstracting process which allows some efficiency in this storage is unknown.[3]

---

[2] During acquisition, early lack of segmentation may give the illusion of correct selection because a phrase is stored as a unit. When the units are segmented, the selection must be rewritten. An example is from data on French acquisition by English-speaking children, who say *regarde moi* before they say *regarde à moi*, just as we find children who say "comed" after saying "came." "*Regarde à moi*" of course reflects a dictionary matching between French and English, word-for-word.

[3] The superb study by Shipley, Smith, and Gleitman (1969), among its other contributions, included the observation that children after a certain point imitated the nonsense portions of sentences, instead of merely being disrupted in comprehension by nonsense. They did not normally imitate what was said, so it could be that when the surface features of the material do not lead to immediate, familiar, easy interpretation the kind of erasure Sachs observed does not occur.

Semantic Feature Storage

In order to account for novel utterances, Schlesinger (1971) has proposed that the child stores the semantic features of utterances and abstracts structural rules from a series of instances. When he hears "Mommy's shoe," "Daddy's shoe," "Daddy's hat," "Bobby's coat," he already knows that Mommy, Daddy and Bobby are people, and that shoe, hat and coat are movable objects, and that in each case the specific object has a particular relation to the designated person. In this case, the child would learn the possessive relation → (+ human) and (+ concrete object). The order, in this case, would be a feature of the rule. According to Schlesinger's formulation, the intention (possessive relation) is realized by possessor plus possessed. If I interpret Schlesinger correctly, the components of structural rules are semantic features, and the categories are classes of items sharing these semantic features.

It is clearly the case that there are such semantic unities in the structural classes in early sentences. In one of Braine's (1963b) list of pivot classes, we find a grouping of many words which can follow *all: broke, buttoned, clean, done, dressed, dry, fix, gone, messy, shut, through, wet.* They all share a common aspectual feature, and it is quite clear that the list is not interchangeable with a list of words following another pivot, *more: car, cereal, cookie, fish, high, hot, juice, read, sing, toast, walk.*

Melissa Bowerman (1970) noted that all of the items with action verbs in her Finnish corpus were either (+ animate) or (+ vehicle).

In my opinion, the insight of Schlesinger's about the relatively large semantic homogeneity of early classes is very important, in suggesting a major basis for acquisition; none of the early grammars captured this property of child speech. McNeill's (1971) analysis of early form classes allowed him to move directly from formal classifications such as NVN to assumptions about semantic relations—though it is possible that NVN could represent location, not merely object, or a vocative rather than a subject.

There are several serious weaknesses in Schlesinger's account as far as it goes, which also affect the attempts of Hebb, Lambert, and Tucker (1971) to subsume the ontogenesis of language under traditional acquisition of conceptual categories.

From early on, there are classes which are not semantically homogenous, but which share considerable structural similarity. For example, we find both *I want ball,* and *Daddy throw ball.* It is clear that *throw* and *want* have very little, if anything, in common semantically, and Fillmore (1968) would argue that *I* and *Daddy* have quite a different role in the two sentences. Yet it would clearly be inefficient to write a grammar of English which did not subsume the two under the same major category in view of their common destiny in tense change, and under a variety of transformations.

There are complex patterns such as the auxiliary system in English which are acquired in a relatively short period of time, obviously on the basis of transfer of patterns between items which do not share semantic features. I think it would be very hard to find any semantic communality between *can, will* and *do*, which would be adequate to the rapid acquisition of the system by the 2-year-olds in Boston and Berkeley. Yet, Schlesinger's system, so far at least, would require that formal classes all be defined in semantic terms.

On the other hand, there are semantically related forms which do not have the same formal functions, such as *eat, eating* and *food.* It is hardly a surprise that we need some formal marker systems, such as affixes and functors, to identify form classes, and that semantic unity is not enough. It is true that there are children like Park's (1970) who in learning Korean occasionally employed words of appropriate semantic features in the wrong form-class position, such as *throw* for *ball* and *sit down* for *bench.* The fact that these formal errors occur makes us wonder why such substitutions are not much more common, especially in languages without class-marking affixes.

Acquiring Formal Features

What could be the conditions for development of an abstract formal marker for lexical members of form classes? Morphemes and words and phrases which occur in the same environment, whether defined by surface forms or classes of forms, acquire a common formal marker. It is the case that those items occurring in the same environment will often have some semantic features in common, by virtue of the semantic cooccurrence constraints of the rest of the sentence.

The point where grammatical features must have been acquired is at the time when productivity occurs, and there is generalization from a semantically different item sharing distributional properties. For example, a child may say, "I'm knowing his name," generalizing from action verbs to statives, because of common distributions. It is the case, of course, that in most of the early grammars it would be possible to characterize the form classes by semantic features rather than a formal term.

Once formal features are acquired, many consequences follow—for example, the kind of associative behavior that Brown and Berko (1960) attribute to formal similarity of paradigmatic items.

McNeill (1971) has argued that some formal classes are already present innately, like noun and verb. Since languages differ in the formal classes required for their use, I should suppose that we must find some means by which classes are discovered. It is, of course, not necessary that the user of language, in fact, have all the formal classes linguists think will simplify the grammar. For example, many speakers may correctly employ verbal complements by learning them as phrases, just as we used to learn the preposition that followed French verbs, *réussir à*, and so on, by rote. Unless there is a fairly rich set of syntactic consequences, if the only property shared by such covert classes is the particular structure or morpheme that complements them, there is, it seems to me, no need to abstract a grouping. I suspect that some adult speakers have never done so, and if asked to generate lists of paradigmatic items would follow semantic and larger form class constraints, and not use the subclass list.

The richer the variety of structures in which a group of items occupies the same slot, the greater the likelihood that some formal marker will be generated, which in turn marks the lexicon and allows the structures to be organized as abstract rules, not low-level sequences.

Why Functors?

It is a striking fact of spoken languages that there always are classes of affixes or function words which are relatively small in number and high in frequency. Frequently, these forms are not necessary for comprehension, as we find in listening to the telegraphic speech of children or of Japanese learning English. It seems to me that they have a function for comprehension, not for production, in marking form classes unambiguously, and it must be through these markers, whether or not the child at first reproduces them, that a considerable aid in generation of formal classes must come. The children in the Shipley, Smith and Gleitman (1969) experiment who spoke in telegraphic utterances but understood normal better than telegraphic sentences were beginning to make use of this information.

Pidgin languages provide a natural experiment in the creation and preservation of fundamental features of languages. Under the social conditions in which pidgins arise, formalisms which mark social status are of minimal importance; concrete substantive communication and ease of acquisition for adults are the primary factors. What we might call transitory pidgins arise in many contact situations between monolinguals. The pidgins which have become conventionalized tend to share certain features, such as morphological simplicity and use of optional syntactic devices relaying on order rather than inflection. But it is the more surprising that in such languages entirely new derivational affixes are sometimes created. In Neo-Melanesian, for example, the suffix *-felə* occurs for numerals, demonstratives, and one-syllable adjectives (Hall, 1966). Other affixes appear to have more obvious semantic functions. For example, the transitive verb suffix *-im* marks transitive verbs. *Mi rid* = "I read," *mi ridim bUk* = "I'm reading a book," and *mi ridim* = "I'm reading something." The third person prefix provides a common surface marker for singular and plural third person, which standard English lacks. *All i-krosim* = "they are angry at him," *ɛm i-faytim jufelɔ* = "he fights you-all."

The implication is that oral languages must have surface bench markers to make complex sequences easy to process for the hearer. But we know that speakers are not, in fact adept at making their output pedagogically best. The assumption that hearer needs affect the structure of output by the speaker requires that one find some mechanism by which the speaker learns better those strategies and those features which maximize comprehension. We know from the Brown and Hanlon (1970) study that children, at least, are not, as speakers, very sensitive to reinforcement contingencies, and we know from Postovsky (1971), that one does not even have to speak to learn fine features of language.

Every speaker's primary role has been first as an understander. He has had to make sense out of what he hears, and he has only been able to interpret and store part of what he hears. If the suffixes are simple structurally, providing a one-to-one match between surface and a conspicuous meaning, if they elucidate units for comprehension, they are likely to enter storage as components of simple processing rules, early on.

Rather than a rule NVN = agent–action–object, which requires some kind of check to determine if a lexical item is marked as V, the hearer can use *-im* as input to a simpler rule. That is, the processing rule can short-cut the lexical check to the formal marker. In storing new lexicon, the surface form may facilitate correct marking of the transitive verbs too.

The morphological examples bear on the low-level marking of form classes unambiguously, but it is also the case that functors may allow surface marking of more complex units. Bever (1970), for example, as well as Shipley and Catlin (1967) working with children, have shown the importance of surface relative pronouns in facilitating comprehension of relative clauses, in contrast to deleted pronouns.

Explanations that languages have the best of all structures tend to be tautological. If certain functors have facilitative effects in simple comprehension, then there probably are others which do not. It may not be necessary, for example, to have functors to identify semantically clear classes like the class of names of all concrete objects. Indeed, pidgins tend not to have such functors. At the other extreme, if the functors are structurally complex, as in the case of Russian inflection, the time required for acquisition might make them unavailable for the conditions of brief acquisition required of pidgins.

It is clear that at the onset of grammar in children, while surface markers of simple structure may facilitate the discovery of processing heuristics they are not absolutely necessary. The abstracting process which allows children to discover formal similarities, presumably from distributional features, is at least as early in development as the appearance of the auxiliary system in English.

LANGUAGE ACQUISITION SYSTEM (LAS)

A human Language Acquisition System must be one that will develop typical ways of understanding and producing situated sentences. Such a system must include ways of changing stored knowledge and developed skills, on the basis of the types of input which are characteristic of human societies. We have discussed some of the properties of devices that at a minimum would need to be components of such a system:

(a) Selective retention of features in short-term memory, particularly order of acoustic input.
(b) Phonological and semantic selection and reorganization for retention in long-term memory.
(c) Interpretation templates, providing interpretations of structures according to the formal and semantic properties of sequences.
(d) Successive processing by alternative heuristics, allowing shortcuts for frequent phrases, instances where nonlinguistic determinants are strong, and so on.
(e) Formal feature generation, identifying abstract classes and providng marking of the lexicon.

These devices or processes need not be language-specific, though it appears at the moment that order retention may be stronger for acoustic than for visual signals. They may not be age-specific.

We can expect that age changes in acquisition will occur for three reasons, none of which affect the basic features in LAS. Input conditions are quite different for adults and children, because the external semantic reference of discourse may be reduced with age, and the linguistic complexity of input tends to be greater with age. Knowledge and availability of memory heuristics increases with age, making it easier to retain longer input and discover meanings. Often this knowledge is fairly specific; the knowledge of a larger vocabulary in one language may increase the probability of encountering cognates in the second language. The system in flux for the learner changes with age. By five, there is little important phonological change occurring other than style and register enrichment. At six, attention to phonological units is temporarily enhanced analytically by the acquisition of reading, if the system of orthography represents some morphophonological units. By ten, attention has shifted almost wholly to semantic and lexical expansion. Except in bilinguals, attention to phonetic nuances other than to those carrying social meaning will have been sharply reduced. We might expect that the processes which led to learning a phonological reorganization system suitable to the mother tongue, which must have required considerably more detailed and redundant retention of phonological information than is used later, would have long since been unused in most monolinguals.

REFERENCES

Ament, W. *Die Entwicklung von Sprechen und Denken beim Kinde.* Leipzig; Barth, 1899.
Anderson, J. M. *The grammar of case: Towards a localistic theory.* London and New York: Cambridge Univ. Press, 1971.
Anglin, J. M. *The growth of word meaning.* Cambridge, Massachusetts: MIT Press, 1970.
Argoff, H. D. The acquisition of Finnish. Forthcoming Ph.D. dissertation, University of California, Berkeley, in preparation.
Asher, J. J. The strategy of total response: An application to learning Russian. *International Review of Applied Linguistics,* 1965, Vol. **III**, 291–300.
Battig, W. F., & Montague, W. E. Category norms for verbal items in 56 categories: A replication and extension of the Connecticut category norms. *Journal of Experimental Psychology,* 1969, **80** (Monogr. Suppl. 3, Part 2).
Bayley, N. *Bayley scales of infant development: Birth to two years.* New York: Psychological Corp., 1969.
Belmont, J. M., & Butterfield, E. C. What the development of short-term memory is. *Human Development,* in press.
Bem, S. L. The role of comprehension in children's problem solving. *Developmental Psychology,* 1970, **2**, 351–358.
Berko-Gleason, J. The child's learning of English morphology. *Word,* 1958, **14**, 150–177.
Berlin, B., & Kay, P. *Basic color terms: Their universality and evolution.* Berkeley: Univ. of California Press, 1969.
Bever, T. G. Associations to stimulus—response theories of language. In T. Dixon & D. Horton (Eds.), *Verbal behavior and general behavior theory.* Englewood Cliffs, New Jersey: Prentice-Hall, 1968.
Bever, T. G. The cognitive basis for linguistic structures. In J. R. Hayes (Ed.), *Cognition and the development of language.* New York: Wiley, 1970. Pp. 279–362.
Bever, T. Discussion. In R. Huxley & E. Ingram (Eds.), *Language acquisition: Models and methods.* London and New York: Academic Press, 1971. (a)
Bever, T. G. The nature of cerebral dominance in speech behavior of the child and adult. In R. Huxley & E. Ingram (Eds.), *Language acquisition: Models and methods.* London and New York: Academic Press, 1971. (b)
Bever, T. G., Fodor, J. A., & Garrett, M. A formal limitation of associationism. In T. Dixon & D. Horton (Eds.), *Verbal behavior and general behavior theory.* Englewood Cliffs, New Jersey: Prentice-Hall, 1968.

Bever, T. G., Fodor, J. A., & Weksel, W. On the acquisition of syntax: A critique of "contextual generalization." *Psychological Review*, 1965, **72**, 467–482.

Bierwisch, M. *Grammatik des deutschen verbs*. Studia Grammatica II. Berlin: Akademie-Verlag, 1963.

Bierwisch, M. Some semantic universals of German adjectivals. *Foundations of Language*, 1967, **3**, 1–36.

Bierwisch, M. Two critical problems in accent rules. *Journal of Linguistics*, 1968, **4**, 173–178.

Bierwisch, M. On certain problems of semantic representations. *Foundations of Language*, 1969, **5**, 153–184.

Bierwisch, M. Semantics. In J. Lyons (Ed.), *New horizons in linguistics*. Penguin Books, 1970. (a)

Bierwisch, M. On classifying semantic features. In M. Bierwisch, & K. E. Heidolph (Eds.), *Progress in linguistics*. The Hague: Mouton, 1970. (b)

Bloch, O. Les premiers stades du langage de l'enfant. *Journal de Psychologie*, 1921, **18**, 693–712.

Bloch, O. La phrase dans le langage de l'enfant. *Journal de Psychologie Normale et Pathologique*, 1924, **XXI**.

Bloom, L. *Language development: Form and function in emerging grammars*. Cambridge, Massachusetts: MIT Press, 1970.

Bloom, L. One word at a time—the use of single-word utterances before syntax. The Hague: Mouton, in press.

Blount, B. G. *Acquisition of language by Luo children*. Working Paper No. 19, Language Behavior Research Laboratory, University of California, Berkeley, 1969.

Bolinger, D. L. On defining the morpheme. *Word*, 1948, **4**, 18–23.

Bourne, L. E. *Human conceptual behavior*. Rockleigh, New Jersey: Allyn & Bacon, 1968.

Bower, G. H., & Winzenz, D. Group structure, coding, and memory for digit series. *Journal of Experimental Psychology Monograph*, 1969, **80** (No. 2, Part 2).

Bowerman, M. F. Learning to talk: A cross-linguistic comparison of early syntactic development, with special reference to Finnish. Unpublished doctoral dissertation, Harvard University, 1970.

Bowerman, M. F. *Early syntactic development: A cross-linguistic study with special reference to Finnish*, Cambridge, England: Cambridge University Press, 1973.

Braine, M. D. S. On learning the grammatical order of words. *Psychological Review*, 1963, **70**, 323–348. (a)

Braine, M. D. S. The ontogeny of English phrase structure: The first phase. *Language*, 1963, **39**, 1–13. (b)

Braine, M. D. S. On two types of models of the internalization of grammars. In D. I. Slobin (Ed.), *The ontogenesis of grammar*. New York: Academic Press, 1971. Pp. 153–188. (a)

Braine, M. D. S. The acquisition of language in infant and child. In C. Reed (Ed.), *The learning of language*. New York: Appleton, 1971. (b)

Bresnan, J. On complementizers: Toward a syntactic theory of complement types. *Foundations of Language*, 1970, **6**.

Bresnan, J. Sentence stress and syntactic transformations. *Language*, 1971, **47**, 2.

Brière, E. *Psycholinguistic study of phonological interference*. The Hague: Humanities Press, 1968.

Brown, A. L., & Scott, M. S. Recognition memory for pictures in preschool children. *Journal of Experimental Child Psychology*, 1971, **11**, 401–412.

Brown, R. W. How shall a thing be called? *Psychological Review*, 1958, **65**, 14–21.

Brown, R. The first sentences of child and chimpanzee. In R. Brown, (Ed.), *Psycholinguistics: Selected papers*. New York: Free Press, 1970. Pp. 208–231.

Brown, R. *A first language*. Cambridge, Massachusetts: Harvard Univ. Press, in press.

Brown, R., & Bellugi, U. Three processes in the child's acquisition of syntax. *Harvard Educational Review*, 1964, **34**, 133–151.

Brown, R., & Berko, J. Word Association and the acquisition of grammar. *Child Development*, 1960, **31**, 1–15.

Brown, R., & Fraser, C. The acquisition of syntax. In C. N. Cofer & B. Musgrave (Eds.), *Verbal behavior and learning*. New York: McGraw-Hill, 1963. Pp. 158–197.

Brown, R., & Hanlon, C. Derivational complexity and order of acquisition in child speech. In J. R. Hayes (Ed.), *Cognition and the development of language*. New York: Wiley, 1970.

Brown, R., & Lenneberg, E. A study in language and cognition. *Journal of Abnormal and Social Psychology*, 1954, **49**, 454–462.

Brown, R., Cazden, C. B., & Bellugi-Klima, U. The child's grammar from 1 to 3. In J. P. Hill (Ed.), *Minnesota symposium on child psychology*, Vol. 2. Minneapolis: Univ. of Minnesota Press, 1969. Pp. 28–73.

Bruner, J. S. The course of cognitive growth. *American Psychologist*, 1964, **19**, 1–15.

Bruner, J. S., Olver, R. R., & Greenfield, P. M. *Studies in cognitive growth*. New York: Wiley, 1966.

Burling, R. Language development of a Garo and English speaking child. *Word*, 1959, **15**, 45–68.

Carroll, J. B., & Casagrande, J. B. The function of language classifications in behavior. In E. E. Maccoby, T. M. Newcomb & E. L. Hartley (Eds.), *Readings in social psychology*. New York: Holt, 1958.

Cazden, C. B. Social class differences and child language. Unpublished Ph.D. dissertation, Harvard Graduate School of Education, 1963.

Chamberlain, A. F. & Chamberlain, J. C. Studies of a child. *Pedagogical Seminary*, 1904, **11**, 264–291.

Chomsky, C. S. *The acquisition of syntax in children from 5 to 10*. Cambridge, Massachusetts: MIT Press, 1969.

Chomsky, N. *Syntactic structures*. The Hague: Mouton, 1957.

Chomsky, N. A review of B. F. Skinner's "verbal behavior." *Language*, 1959, **35**, 26–58.

Chomsky, N. Some methodological remarks on generative grammar. *Word*, 1961, **17**, 219–239.

Chomsky, N. Current issues in linguistic theory. In J. A. Fodor & J. J. Katz (Eds.), *The structure of language*. Englewood Cliffs, New Jersey: Prentice-Hall, 1964.

Chomsky, N. *Aspects of the theory of syntax*. Cambridge, Massachusetts: MIT Press, 1965.

Chomsky, N. The current scene in linguistics: Present directions. *College English*, 1966, **27**, 587–595.

Chomsky, N. *Language and mind*. New York: Harcourt, 1968.

Chomsky, N. Conditions on transformations. MIT, unpublished, 1971.

Chomsky, N., & Halle, M. *The sound pattern of English*. New York: Harper, 1968.

Clark, E. V. Language acquisition: The child's spontaneous description of events in time. Unpublished doctoral dissertation, Department of Linguistics, University of Edinburgh, 1969.

Clark, E. V. On the acquisition of the meaning of "before" and "after." *Journal of Verbal Learning and Verbal Behavior*, 1971, **10**, 266–275. (a)

Clark, E. V. Review of C. S. Chomsky: "The acquisition of syntax in children from 5 to 10." *Language*, 1971, **47**, 742–749. (b)

Clark, E. V. Semantic development in language acquisition. Paper presented at the Third Child Language Research Forum, Stanford University, March, 1971. (c)

Clark, E. V. On the child's acquisition of antonyms in two semantic fields. *Journal of Verbal Learning and Verbal Behavior*, 1972, **11**, 750–758.

Clark, H. H. Linguistic processes in deductive reasoning. *Psychological Review*, 1969, **76**, 387–404.

Clark, H. H. The primitive nature of children's relational concepts. In J. R. Hayes (Ed.), *Cognition and the development of language*. New York: Wiley, 1970. (a)

Clark, H. H. Word associations and linguistic theory. In J. Lyons (Ed.), *New horizons in linguistics*. London: Penguin Books, 1970. (b)

Clark, H. H. Semantics and comprehension. In T. A. Sebeok (Ed.), *Current trends in linguistics, Vol. 12: Linguistics and adjacent arts sciences*. The Hague: Mouton, in press.

Cohen, B. H., Bousefield, W. A., & Whitmarsh, G. A. *Cultural norms for verbal items in 43 categories*. Technical Report No. 22, University of Connecticut, Contract Nonr. 631 (00), Office of Naval Research, 1957.

Collins, A. M., & Quillian, M. R. Retrieval time from semantic memory. *Journal of Verbal Learning and Verbal Behavior*, 1969, **8**, 240–247.

Corsini, D. A. Developmental changes in the effect of non-verbal cues on retention. *Developmental Psychology*, 1969, **1**, 425–435. (a)

Corsini, D. A. The effect of nonverbal cues on the retention of kindergarten children. *Child Development*, 1969, **40**, 599–607. (b)

Corsini, D. A. Memory: Interaction of stimulus and organismic factors. Paper presented at the meeting of the Society for Research in Child Development, Minneapolis, April, 1971.

Corsini, D. A., Jacobus, K. A., & Leonard, S. D. Recognition memory of preschool children for pictures and words. *Psychonomic Science*, 1969, **16**, 192–193.

Danziger, K. The child's understanding of kinship terms: A study in the development of relational concepts. *Journal of Genetic Psychology*, 1957, **91**, 213–232.

Decroly, O. *Epreuves de comprehension, d'imitation et d'expression*. (Revu et complété par J. Jadot-Decroly & J.-E. Segers) Bruxelles: Collection Ivoire, Centre National d'Education, n.d,

De Valois, R. L., & Jacobs, G. H. Primate color vision. *Science*, 1968, **162**, 533–540.

Dewey, J. The psychology of infant language. *Psychological Review*, 1894, **1**, 63–66.

Donaldson, M., & Balfour, G. Less is more: A study of language comprehension in children. *British Journal of Psychology*, 1968, **59**, 461–472.

Donaldson, M., & Wales, R. J. On the acquisition of some relational terms. In J. R. Hayes (Ed.), *Cognition and the development of language*. New York: Wiley, 1970.

Drach, K. *The language of the parent: A pilot study*. In Working Paper No. 14: The structure of linguistic input to children. Language Behavior Research Laboratory, Univ. of California at Berkeley, 1969.

Eimas, P. D., Siqueland, E. R., Juscyk, P., & Vigorito, J. Speech perception in infants. *Science*, 1971, **171**, 303–306.

Elkind, D. Children's conceptions of brother and sister: Piaget replication study V. *Journal of Genetic Psychology*, 1962, **100**, 129–136.

Emonds, J. Root and structure-preserving transformations. MIT Thesis, 1970.

Ervin, S. M. Imitation and structural change in children's language. In E. H. Lenneberg (Ed.), *New directions in the study of language*. Cambridge, Massachusetts: MIT Press, 1964. Pp. 163–189.

Ervin-Tripp, S. Discourse agreement: How children answer questions. In J. R. Hayes (Ed.), *Cognition and the development of language*. New York: Wiley, 1970. Pp. 79–107. (a)

Ervin-Tripp, S. Structure and process in language acquisition. In J. E. Alatis (Ed.), *Bilingualism and language contact: Anthropological, psychological, and social aspects*. Monograph Series on Languages and Linguistics, No. 21. Washington, D.C.: Georgetown University, 1970. (b)

Ervin-Tripp, S. An overview of theories of grammatical development. In D. I. Slobin (Ed.), *The ontogenesis of grammar*. New York: Academic Press, 1971. Pp. 189–212.

Ferreiro, E. *Les relations temporelles dans le langage de l'enfant*. Geneva: Droz, 1971.

Fillmore, C. J. Deictic categories in the semantics of 'come.' *Foundations of Language*, 1967, **3**, 219–227.

Fillmore, C. J. The case for case. In E. Bach & R. T. Harms (Eds.), *Universals in linguistic theory*. New York: Holt, 1968.

Fillmore, C. J. Toward a theory of deixis. Paper presented at the Pacific Conference on Contrastive Linguistics and Language Universals, University of Hawaii, January, 1971.

Flavell, H. H. Developmental studies of mediated memory. In H. W. Reese & L. P. Lipsitt (Eds.), *Advances in child development and behavior*. Vol. 5. New York: Academic Press, 1970. Pp. 181–211.

Fodor, J. A. Could meaning be an r_m? *Journal of Verbal Learning and Verbal Behavior*, 1965, **4**, 73–81.

Fodor, J. How to learn to talk: Some simple ways. In F. Smith & G. Miller (Eds.), *The genesis of language*. Cambridge, Massachusetts: MIT Press, 1966.

Fodor, J. A., & Garrett, M. Some syntactic determinants of sentential complexity. *Perception and Psychophysics*, 1967, **2**, 289–296.

Freedle, R., & Craun, M. Observations with self-embedded sentences using written aids. *Perception and Psychophysics*, 1970, **7**, 247–249.

Freedman, J. L., & Loftus, E. F. Retrieval of words from long-term memory. *Journal of Verbal Learning and Verbal Behavior*, 1971, **10**, 107–115.

Garner, W. R. The stimulus in information processing. *American Psychologist*, 1970, **25**, 350–358.

Garnica, O. K. The development of the perception of phonemic differences in initial consonants by English-speaking children: A pilot study. NSF grant GS2329 study report. Multilith, 1971. (To appear in Papers and Reports in *Child language development*. Stanford University).

Garrett, M., & Fodor, J. A. Psychological theories and linguistic constructs. In T. Dixon & D. Horton (Eds.), *Verbal behavior and general behavior theory*. Englewood Cliffs, New Jersey: Prentice-Hall, 1968.

Geballe, C. Early sentences of a deaf speaker. Unpublished term paper, Rhetoric 156, University of California, Berkeley, 1969.

Geis, M. L. Time prepositions as underlying verbs. In *Papers from the Sixth Regional Meeting Chicago Linguistic Society*. Chicago: Chicago Linguistic Society, 1970.

Gibson, E. J. *Principles of perceptual learning and development*. New York: Appleton, 1969.

Greenberg, J. *Universals of language*. Cambridge, Massachusetts: MIT Press, 1961.

Greenberg, J. H. *Language universals*. The Hague: Mouton, 1966.

Gregoire, A. *L'apprentissage du langage*. Two Vols. Paris: Droz, 1937, 1949.

Gruber, J. S. Studies in lexical relations. Unpublished Ph.D. dissertation, MIT, 1965.

Gruber, J. S. Correlations between the syntactic constructions of the child and the adult. Paper presented at the Society for Research in Child Development, March 31, 1967.

Guillaume, P. Le développement des éléments formals dans le langage de l'enfant. *Journal de Psychologie*, 1927, **24**, 203–250. (a)

Guillaume, P. Les débuts de la phrase dans le langage de l'enfant. *Journal de Psychologie*, 1927, **24**, 1–25. (b)

Gvozdev, A. N. Voprozy izucheniia detskoi rechi. (Problems in the language development of the child.) Moscow: Academy of Pediatric Science, 1961.

Hagen, J. W. Some thoughts on how children learn to remember. Paper presented at the meeting of the Society for Research in Child Development, Minneapolis, April, 1971.

Hall, R. A. *Pidgin and creole languages*. Ithaca, New York: Cornell Univ. Press, 1966.

Hayes, J. R. *Cognition and the development of language*. New York, Wiley, 1970.

Hayes, J. R., & Clark, H. H. Experiments on the segmentation of an artificial speech analogue. In J. R. Hayes (Ed.), *Cognition and the development of language*. New York: Wiley, 1970. Pp. 221–234.

Hays, W. L. *Statistics.* New York: Holt, 1963.

Hebb, D. O., Lambert, W. E., & Tucker, G. R. Language, thought and experience. *Modern Language Journal,* 1971, **15**(4), 212–222.

Heider, E. R. "Focal" color areas and the development of color names. *Developmental Psychology,* 1971, **4**, 447–455.

Heider, E. R. Universals in color naming and memory. *Journal of Experimental Psychology,* 1972, **93**, 1, 10–21.

Heider, E. R., & Olivier, D. C. The structure of the color space in naming and memory for two languages. *Cognitive Psychology,* 1972, 3(2), 337–354.

Heider, K. G. *The Dugum Dani: A Papuan culture in the highlands of West New Guinea.* Chicago, Illinois: Aldine, 1970.

Heider, K. G. Development of kinship competency: The New Guinea Dani. Paper presented at a meeting of the American Anthropological Association, New York, November, 1971.

Hickerson, N. P. Review of "Basic color terms: Their universality and evolution." *International Journal of American Linguistics,* 1971, **37**, 257–270.

Hoffman, C. D. Recognition memory for pictures: A developmental study. Paper presented at the meeting of the Eastern Psychological Association, New York, April, 1971.

Howes, D. C. On the relation between the probability of a word as an association and in general linguistic usage. *Journal of Abnormal and Social Psychology,* 1957, **54**, 75–85.

Hunter, I. M. L. Mental calculation. In P. C. Wason & P. N. Johnson-Laird (Eds.), *Thinking and reasoning.* Baltimore, Maryland: Penguin Books, 1968. Pp. 341–351.

Idelberger, H. Hauptoproblemen der kindlichen Sprachentwicklung. *Zeitschrift fur padagogische Psychologie,* 1903, **5**, 241–297.

Imedadze, N. V. K psikhologicheskoy prirode rannego dvuyazychiya. *Voprosy Psikhologii,* 1960, **6**, 60–68.

Jakobson, R. Kindersprache, aphasie und allgemeine Lautgesetze, *Uppsala Universitets arsskrift,* [1941], 1–83. In Jakobson, R. Selected Writings I, The Hague: Monton, 1962.

Jakobson, R. Implications of language universals for linguistics. In J. Greenberg (Ed.), *Universals of language.* Cambridge, Massachusetts: MIT Press, 1961.

Jakobson, R. Why "mama" and "papa?" In *Roman Jakobson: Selected writings.* The Hague: Mouton, 1962.

Jakobson, R., & Halle, M. *Fundamentals of language.* The Hague: Mouton, 1956.

Jesperson, O. *A modern English grammar on historical principles. Part 1: Sounds and spellings* [1909]. London: Bradford and Dickens, 1954.

Kaplan, E. L., & Kaplan, G. A. Is there any such thing as a pre-linguistic child? In J. Eliot (Ed.), *Human development and cognitive process.* New York: Holt, 1970.

Katz, J. J. Mentalism in linguistics. *Language,* 1964, **40**, 124–137.

Katz, J. J., & Fodor, J. A. The structure of a semantic theory. *Language,* 1963, **39**, 170–211.

Katz, J. J., & Postal, P. M. *An integrated theory of linguistic descriptions.* Cambridge, Massachusetts: MIT Press, 1964.

Kenyeres, E. Les premiers mots de l'enfant. *Archives de Psychologie,* 1926, **20**, 191–218.

Kernan, K. T. The acquisition of language by Samoan children. Unpublished doctoral dissertation, University of California at Berkeley, 1969.

Kernan, K. T. Semantic relations and the child's acquisition of language. *Anthropological Linguistics, 1970,* **12**(5), 171–187.

Kessel, F. S. The role of syntax in children's comprehension from ages six to twelve. *Society for Research in Child Development Monographs,* 1970, **35**, (6).

Knight, T. S. *Charles Peirce.* New York, Washington Square Press, 1965.

Kobashigawa, B. Repetitions in a mother's speech to her child. In *Language, society and the child.* Working Paper No. 13. Language Behavior Research Laboratory, University of California, Berkeley, 1968.

Kornfeld, J. Spectographic analysis of liquids in young children. Quarterly Progress Report of the Research Laboratory of Electronics, No. 101, MIT, July 15, 1971.

Kuroda, S. Y. English relativization and certain related problems. *Language*, 1968, **44**, 244–266.

Ladefoged, P. An alternative set of vowel shift rules. Working Papers in phonetics, No. 17, UCLA, Los Angeles, Calif., 1971.

Lakoff, G. Global rules. *Language*, 1970, **46**, 627–639. (a)

Lakoff, G. Linguistics and natural logic. *Synthèse*, 1970, **22**, 151–272. (b)

Lakoff, G. On generative semantics. In D. D. Steinberg & L. S. Jakobovits (Eds.), *Semantics*. London: Cambridge Univ. Press, 1971.

Landauer, T. K., & Freedman, J. L. Information retrieval from long-term memory: Category size and recognition time. *Journal of Verbal Learning and Verbal Behavior*, 1968, **7**, 291–295.

Lantz, D., & Stefflre, V. Language and cognition revisited. *Journal of Abnormal and Social Psychology*, 1964, **69**, 472–481.

Leech, G. *Towards a semantic description of English*. Bloomington, Indiana: Indiana Univ. Press, 1970.

Lees, R. B. *Grammar of English nominalizations*. Bloomington, Indiana: University of Indiana Press, 1960.

Lenneberg, E. *Biological foundations of language*. New York: Wiley, 1967.

Leont'yev, A. A. Innerspeech and the processes of grammatical generation of utterances. *Soviet Psychology*, 1969, **7**(3), 11–16.

Leopold, W. F. Semantic learning in infant language. *Word*, 1948, **4**, 173–180.

Leopold, W. F. *Speech development of a bilingual child: A linguist's record*. Vol. 1. Vocabulary growth in the first two years. Vol. 2. Sound learning in the first two years. Vol. 3. Grammar and general problems in the first two years. Vol. 4. Diary from age two. Evanston, Illinois: Northwestern Univ. Press, 1939, 1947, 1949a, 1949b.

Lewis, M. M. *Infant speech*. London: Routledge & Kegan, 1951.

Lewis, M. M. *How children learn to speak*. London: Harrap, 1957.

Limber, J. Sentence interpretation and the meaning of adjectives. Unpublished paper, Department of Psychology, MIT, 1969.

Limber, J. Toward a theory of sentence interpretation. Quarterly Progress Report of the Research Laboratory of Electronics. MIT, January, 1970. No. 96. (a)

Limber, J. Some observations on language acquisition: The development of words. Quarterly Progress Report of the Research Laboratory of Electronics, MIT, July, 15, 1970. No. 98. (b)

Limber, J. Initial segmentation: A hypothesis. Unpublished paper, Department of Psychology, MIT. 1971.

Lindner, G. Beobachtungen und Bemerkungen uber die Entwicklung der Sprache des Kindes. *Kosmos*, 1882, **6**, 321–342, 430–441.

Lindquist, E. F. *Design and analysis of experiments in psychology and education*. Boston, Massachusetts: Houghton, 1953.

Loftus, E. F., & Scheff, R. W. Categorization norms for fifty representative instances. *Journal of Experimental Psychology*, 1971, **91**, 355–364. (a)

Loftus, E. F., & Scheff, R. W. Category norms. Paper presented at a meeting of the American Psychological Association, New York, September, 1971. (b)

Luria, A. R., & Yudovich, F. I. *Speech and the development of mental processes in the child*. New York: Humanities, 1959.

Lyons, J. *Introduction to theoretical linguistics*. London: Cambridge Univ. Press, 1968.

Maling, J. On "Gapping and the order of constituents." *Linguistic Inquiry*, 1972, **3**, 1.

Malmberg, B. Et barn bytar spark. *Nordisk Tidskrift*, 1945, **21**.

Martin, P. R., & Fernberger, S. W. Improvement in memory span. *American Journal of Psychology*, 1929, **41**, 91–94.

McCawley, J. D. The role of semantics in grammar. In E. Bach & R. T. Harms (Eds.), *Universals in linguistic theory*. New York: Holt, 1968.

McCarthy, D. Language development in children. In L. Carmichael (Ed.) *Manual of Child Psychology*. New York, Wiley, 1954, 492–630.

McKay, J. C. Some generative rules for German time adverbials. *Language*, 1968, **44**, 25–50.

McNeill, D. The creation of language by children. In J. Lyons & R. J. Wales (Eds.), *Psycholinguistic papers*. Edinburgh: Univ. of Edinburgh Press, 1966. (a)

McNeill, D. Developmental psycholinguistics. In F. Smith and G. A. Miller (Eds.), *The genesis of language: A psycholinguistic approach*. Cambridge, Massachusetts: MIT Press, 1966. (b)

McNeill, D. On theories of language acquisition. In T. R. Dixon & D. L. Horton (Eds.), *Verbal behavior and general behavior theory*. Englewood Cliffs, New Jersey: Prentice-Hall, 1968.

McNeill, D. Language before symbols: Very early children's grammar. *Interchange*, 1970, **I** (No. 3). (a)

McNeill, D. *The acquisition of language*. New York: Harper, 1970. (b)

McNeill, D. The development of language. In P. A. Mussen (Ed.), *Carmichael's manual of child psychology*, 3rd ed., Vol. 1. New York: Wiley 1970. Pp. 1061–1161. (c)

McNeill, D. The capacity for the ontogenesis of grammar. In D. I. Slobin (Ed.) *The ontogenesis of grammar*. New York: Academic Press, 1971. Pp. 17–40.

McNeill, D., Yukawa, R., & McNeill, R. The acquisition of direct and indirect objects in Japanese. *Child Development*, 1971, **42**, 237–249.

Menyuk, P. Children's learning and reproduction of grammatical and non-grammatical phonological sequences. *Child Development*, 1968, **39**, 849–858.

Menyuk, P. *Sentences children use*. Cambridge, Massachusetts: MIT Press, 1969.

Menyuk, P. Alternation in children's grammars. In D. Reibel & S. Schane (Eds.), *Studies in modern English*. Englewood Cliffs, New Jersey: Prentice-Hall, 1970.

Messer, S. Implicit phonology in children. *Journal of Verbal Learning and Verbal Behavior*, 1967, **16** (4), 609–613.

Meyer, D. E. On the representation and retrieval of stored semantic information. *Cognitive Psychology*, 1970, **1**, 242–300.

Mikeš, M. Acquisition des catégories grammaticales dans le langage de l'enfant. *Enfance*, 1967, **20**, 289–298.

Mikeš, M., & Vlahović, P. Razvoy grammatic kategorija u dečjem govuru. *Prilozi, proučavanju jezika, II*. Yugoslavia: Nova Sad, 1966.

Miller, G. A. The magical number seven, plus or minus two: Some limits on your capacity for processing information. *Psychological Review*, 1956, **63**, 81–97.

Miller, G. A. Some psychological studies of grammar. *American Psychologist*, 1962, **17**, 748–762.

Miller, G. A., & Chomsky, N. Finitary models of language users. In R. D. Luce, R. R. Bush & E. Galanter (Eds.), *Handbook of mathematical psychology*, Vol. 2. New York: Wiley, 1963. Pp. 419–491.

Miller, G. A., & McKean, K. A chronometric study of some relations between sentences. *Quarterly Journal of Experimental Psychology*, 1964, 16, 297–308.

Miller, W. R., & Ervin, S. M. The development of grammar in child language. In U. Bellugi & R. Brown (Eds.), the acquisition of language. *Monographs of the Society for Research and in Child Development*, 1964, **29**, 9–33.

Mitchell, B. *A guide to Old English*. Oxford: Blackwell, 1968.

Miyahara, K. *Language development in a Japanese child*. Japan: Hakosaki, 1971.

Moffitt, A. R. Speech perception in infants. Unpublished Ph.D. Thesis, University of Minnesota, 1968.

Moore, K. C. The mental development of a child. *Psychological Review, Monograph Supplements*, 1896, **1** (3).

Moskowitz, A. I. The two-year-old stage in the acquisition of English phonology. *Language*, 1970, **46**, 426–41.

Moskowitz, A. I. The acquisition of phonology. Unpublished dissertation, University of California, Berkeley, 1971. (To appear in *Project on linguistic analysis reports*).

Neisser, U. *Cognitive psychology*. New York: Appleton, 1967.

Nice, M. M. A child who would not speak. *Pedagogical Seminary*, 1925, **32**, 105–142.

Nickerson, D., Tomaszewski, J. J., & Boyd, T. F. Colorimetric specifications of Munsell repaints. *Journal of the Optical Society of America*, 1953, **43**, 163–171.

Öhman, S. Theories of the "linguistic field." *Word*, 1953, **9**, 123–134.

Pačesová, J. *The development of vocabulary in the child*. Brno: University J. E. Purkyn, 1968.

Park, T.-Z. Language acquisition in a Korean child. Unpublished manuscript. Berne, Switzerland, 1970.

Park, T.-Z. The acquisition of German syntax. Working paper, psychological institute, Univ. of Berne, Switzerland, 1971.

Pavlovitch, M. *Le langage enfantin: Acquisition du serbe et du francais par un enfant serbe*. Paris: Champion, 1920.

Perez, B. *Les trois premières années de l'enfant*. Paris: Alcan, 1892.

Pfuderer, C. Some suggestions for a syntactic characterization of baby talk style. In Working Paper No. 14, *The structure of linguistic input to children*. Language-Behavior Research Laboratory, University of California at Berkeley, 1969.

Piaget, J. *Judgment and reasoning in the child*. London: Routledge & Kegan, 1928.

Piaget, J. *La formation du symbole*. Neuchatel: Delachaux et Niestle, 1949.

Piaget, J. *La psychologie de l'intelligence*, 3rd ed. Paris: A. Colin, 1967.

Posner, M. I. Abstraction and the process of recognition. In G. H. Bower & J. T. Spence (Eds.), *The psychology of learning and motivation*. Vol. 3. New York: Academic Press, 1969.

Posner, M. I., & Keele, S. On the genesis of abstract ideas. *Journal of Experimental Psychology*, 1968, **77**, 353–363.

Postal, P. M. Review article: Andre Martinet, "Elements of general linguistics". *Foundations of Language*, 1966, **2**, 151–186.

Postal, P. M. The surface verb "remind". *Linguistic Inquiry*, 1970, **1**, 37–120.

Postovsky, V. Effects of delay in oral practice at the beginning of language learning. Dissertation, University of California, Berkeley, 1971.

Preyer, W. *The mind of the child*. New York: Appleton, 1889.

Quirk, R. Relative clauses in educated spoken English. *English Studies*, 1957, **38**, 97–109.

Rasmussen, V. *Et barns dagbog*. Kovenhavn: Gyldendal, 1922.

Read, C. Pre-school children's knowledge of English phonology. *Harvard Educational Review*, 1971, **41**, 1–34.

Reed, S. K. Decision processes in pattern classification. Technical Report 32, Perceptual Systems Laboratory, University of California at Los Angeles, 1970.

Reitman, W. R. *Cognition and thought*. New York: Wiley, 1965.

Ricciuti, H. N. Geometric form and detail as determinants of comparative similarity judgements in young children. In *A basic research program on reading*. Final Report, Cooperative Research Project N. 639, U.S. Office of Education, 1963. Pp. 1–48.

Roeper, T. Approaches to a theory of language acquisition, with examples from German. Unpublished doctoral dissertation. Harvard University, 1972.

Romanes, G. J. Mental evolution in men: origin of human faculty. New York: Appleton, 1888.

Rosenbaum, P. *Grammar of English complement constructions.* Cambridge, Massachusetts: MIT Press, 1967.

Ross, J. R. Auxiliary verbs as main verbs. Unpublished paper, Department of Linguistics, MIT, 1967.

Sachs, J. S. Recognition memory for syntactic and semantic aspects of connected discourse. *Perception and Psychophysics,* 1967, **2,** 437–442.

Savin, H., & Perchonock, E. Grammatical structure and the immediate recall of English sentences. *Journal of Verbal Learning and Verbal Behavior,* 1965, **4,** 348–353.

Schaeffer, B., & Wallace, R. The comparison of word meanings. *Journal of Experimental Psychology,* 1970, **86,** 144–152.

Schlesinger, I. M. Production of utterances and language acquisition. In D. Slobin (Ed.), *The ontogenesis of grammar.* New York: Academic Press, 1971.

Scupin, E., & Scupin, G. *Bubis erste Kindheit: Ein Tagebuch.* Leipzig: Grieben, 1907.

Segall, M. H., Campbell, D. T., & Herskovitz, M. J. *The influence of culture on visual perception.* New York: Bobbs-Merrill, 1966.

Shannon, C. E. A mathematical theory of communication. *Bell System Technical Journal,* 1948, **27,** 379–423 & 623–656.

Shepard, R. N. Attention and the metric structure of the stimulus space. *Journal of Mathematical Psychology.* 1964, **1,** 54–87.

Shipley, E., & Catlin, J. C. *Short term memory for sentences in children: An exploratory study of temporal aspects of imposing structure.* Technical Report V, Grant No MH 07990. Philadelphia, Pennsylvania: Eastern Psychiatric Institute, 1967.

Shipley, E. R., Smith, C. S., & Gleitman, L. R. A study in the acquisition of language: Free responses to commands. (Eastern Pennsylvania Psychiatric Institute: Technical Report N. VIII). *Language,* 1969, **45,** 322–342.

Shvachkin, N. Kh. "Razvitye fouematicheskogo vospriyatiya rechi v rannem vozraste" (Development of phonemic speech perception in early childhood). *Izv. Akad. Pedog. Nauk RSFSR,* [1948] **13,** 101–132. [English translation by Elena Dernbach in C. A. Ferguson & D. I. Slobin, *Child language acquisition: Readings.* New York: Holt, in press.

Sinclair, H. & Bronckart, J. P. SVO—A linguistic universal. *Journal of Experimental Child Psychology,* 1972, 14, 329–348.

Sinclair-de Zwart, H. *Acquisition du language et développement de la pensée, sous-systèmes linguistiques et opérations concrètes.* Paris: Dunod, 1967.

Skinner, B. F. *Verbal behavior.* New York, Appleton, 1957.

Slobin, D. I. The acquisition of Russian as a native language. In F. Smith & G. Miller (Eds.), *The genesis of language.* Cambridge, Massachusetts: MIT Press, 1966.

Slobin, D. I. *Universals of grammatical development in children.* Working Paper No. 22, Language-Behavior Research Laboratory, University of California at Berkeley, 1969.

Slobin, D. I. Universals of grammatical development in children. In G. B. Flores d'Arcais & W. J. M. Levelt (Eds.), *Advances in psycholinguistics.* New York: American Elsevier, 1970. Pp. 174–184.

Slobin, D. Suggested universals in the ontogenesis of grammar. Paper presented at the Conference on Developmental Psycholinguistics, Buffalo, August, 1971.

Slobin, D. Cognitive prerequisites for the development of grammar. In W. O. Dingwall (Ed.), *A Survey of Linguistic Science.* Linguistic Research Inc., Edmonton, Alberta, in press.

Smoczynski, P. Przyswajanie przez dziecko podstaw systemu jezykowego. *Societas Scientiarum Lodziensis,* 1955, Section **1,** No. 19.

Stefflre, V., Castillo Vales, V., & Morley, L. Language and cognition in Yucatan: A cross cultural replication. *Journal of Personality and Social Psychology,* 1966, **4,** 112–115.

Stern, C., & Stern, W. *Die Kindersprache: Eine psychologische und sprachtheoretische Unter-suchung.* (4th ed.) Leipzig: Barth, 1928.

Sternberg, S. Memory-scanning: Mental processes revealed by reaction-time experiments. *American Scientist,* 1969, **57,** 421–457.

Sully, J. *Studies of childhood.* New York: Appleton, 1896.

Taine, H. Acquisition of language by children. *Mind,* 1877, **2,** 252–259.

Tanz, C. Study of the acquisition of personal pronouns and shifters. University of Chicago dissertation. In preparation.

Tashiro, L. On the acquisition of some non-comparative terms. Senior Honors Thesis, Stanford University, 1971.

Teller, P. Some discussion and extension of Manfred Bierwisch's work on German adjectivals. *Foundations of Language,* 1969, **5,** 185–217.

Thorndike, E. L., & Lorge, I. *The teacher's word book of 30,000 words.* New York: Teacher's College, 1944.

Troyer, K. The semantic contribution of perceputal terms in a reasoning task. Unpublished Masters' Thesis, Stanford University, 1971.

Tulving, E. Theoretical issues in free recall. In T. R. Dixon & D. L. Horton (Eds.), *Verbal behavior and general behavior theory.* Englewood Cliffs, New Jersey: Prentice-Hall, 1968.

Tyler, S. A. (Ed.) *Cognitive anthropology.* New York: Holt, 1969.

Urmson, J. O. "Parenthetical verb." In C. E. Caton (Ed.), *Philosophy and ordinary language.* Urbana: Univ. of Illinois Press, 1963. Pp. 226–240.

Velten, H. V. The growth of phonemic and lexical patterns in infant language. *Language,* 1943, **19,** 281–292.

Vendler, Z. *Adjectives and nominalizations.* The Hague: Mouton, 1968.

Vygotsky, L. S. *Thought and language.* Cambridge, Massachusetts: MIT Press, 1962.

Wales, R. J., & Campbell R. On the development of comparison and the comparison of development. In G. B. Flores d'Arcais & W. J. M. Levelt (Eds.), *Advances in psycholinguistics.* Amsterdam: North-Holland, 1970.

Wales, R. J., & Marshall, J. C. Linguistic performance. In J. Lyons & R. J. Wales (Eds.), *Psycholinguistics papers.* Edinburgh: Univ. of Edinburgh Press, 1966.

Wang, W. S-Y. Vowel features, paired variables, and the English vowel shift. *Language,* 1968, **44,** 695–708.

Watt, W. On two hypotheses concerning psycholinguistics. In J. R. Hayes (Ed.), *Cognition and the development of language.* New York: Wiley, 1970.

Wilkins, A. Conjoint frequency, category size, and categorization time. *Journal of Verbal Learning and Verbal Behavior,* 1971, **10,** 382–385.

Winzenz, D., & Bower, G. H. Subject-imposed coding and memory for digit series. *Journal of Experimental Psychology,* 1970, **83,** 52–56.

Woodworth, R. S., & Schlosberg, H. *Experimental psychology.* (Rev. ed.). New York: Holt, 1954.

Yngve, V. H. A model and a hypothesis for language structure. *Proceedings of the American Philosophical Society,* 1960, **104,** 444–466.

AUTHOR INDEX

Numbers in italics refer to the pages on which the complete references are listed.

SUBJECT INDEX

Cartesian coordinate system, 31–32
Categories
  psychological reality of, 140–144
  structure and cognitive processing,
    130–144
Catenative verbs, 176–177
Clustering in free recall, 112, 138
Chaining, 83
Chunking, 148–149
Code switching in children's language,
    159–167
Cognitive structures
  acquisition of, 24–25
  and language learning, 11–16
Color
  categories, learning of, 115–123
  focal points of, 114–115
  as perceptual category, 112–122
  as perceptual feature in overextension, 83
Comparatives, 58, 92
Complements
  of objects, 174–180
  of verbs, 96–102, 176
Complex constructions, 174–182, 193–194
  complements, 174–180
  conjunctions, 181–182
  nominals, 174–180
  nouns, overextension of, 96–102
  sentences, development of, 169–185
  wh-clause, 180–181
Complexity hypothesis, 29–30, 54–62
Comprehension hypothesis, 57–62
Concept formation, 111–113
Conjunctions, 94–96, 181–182, 268
Consonant oppositions, perception of by
    children, 216–222
Constituent structure in child speech,
    201–205
Contrast of meaning, 262–263, 266
Co-occurrence of speech with referent,
    262–263
Correlation hypothesis, 28–29, 53–54
Criterial features
  in overextensions, 79–88
  in semantic acquisition, 72, 77, 79–88
Cumulative complexity hypothesis, 29
Cyclical transformations, 194, 196

D

Datives, 269

Deaf, sign language of, 4, 266
Deductive abstraction and phonology
    acquisition, 256
Deep–shallow, 37, 39–40, 44, 49, 53–58
Deep structure, 1–3
  and base rules, 188–196
  in children's utterances, 197–213
  recognition of, by children, 188–196
  and semantic relations, 207–213
Deixis, 47–48
Deletions, in child speech, 59–60
Derived morphemes, 226–227
Diary studies, 77–84
Digit span, 148–149
Dipthongization and vowel shift rules,
    228–230
Directional prepositions, 40–43, 58
Discourse modeling, 264
Distinctive features
  in phoneme acquisition, 215–222
  in visual perception, 102–106
Distributional analysis of child speech,
    200–207

E

Early language learning, 4–6
  and grammatical storage, 280–285
  and LTM, 272–275
  and order regularities, 275–579
  prerequisite knowledge, 265–270
  strategies for, 261–286
Early–late, 51–52, 57, 61
Ego, as a reference point, 37, 44–48
Embeddings, 195
Empiricism, 1, 3
English phonology, 215–222, 223–260
Environmental input
  constants in perceptual space, 30
  as prerequisite for language learning,
    262–265
Errors of reference in child speech, 72–73
Evaluation of children's grammars,
    200–213
Exemplars of categories, 112–116
Explanatory adequacy of grammars, 10–11
Expansions and order information, 279
  of adult utterances, 160–161
  of children's utterances, 264
Experiments
  on category learning, 115–144